DATE DUE

Social Protest Literature

Social Protest Literature
An Encyclopedia of Works, Characters, Authors, and Themes

Patricia D. Netzley

ABC-CLIO

Santa Barbara, California
Denver, Colorado
Oxford, England

Cover illustration: Bastille Mob Mural (Morton Beebe–S.F./Corbis)

Library of Congress Cataloging-in-Publication Data
Netzley, Patricia D.
    Social protest literature: An encyclopedia of works, characters,
authors, and themes / Patricia D. Netzley.
    p.   cm.
    Includes bibliographical references and index.
    ISBN 0-87436-980-0
    1. Social problems in literature—Encyclopedias. 2. Protest
literature—Encyclopedias. I. Title.
PN56.S65N48   1999
809'.93355—dc21   98-43005
                                                   CIP

05 04 03 02 01 00 99   10 9 8 7 6 5 4 3 2 1

ABC-CLIO, Inc.
130 Cremona Drive, P.O. Box 1911
Santa Barbara, California 93116-1911

This book is printed on acid-free paper ∞ .

Manufactured in the United States of America

CONTENTS

SOCIAL PROTEST LITERATURE

ENTRIES BY CATEGORY

Authors

Abbey, Edward
Abrahams, Peter
Alcaeus
Alegría, Ciro
Aleramo, Sibilla
Allende, Isabel
Anand, Mulk Raj
Angelou, Maya
Aristophanes
Ariyoshi, Sawako
Atwood, Margaret
Baldwin, James
Balzac, Honoré de
Beauvoir, Simone de
Behn, Aphra
Bellamy, Edward
Berger, Thomas
Björnson, Björnstjerne
Boulle, Pierre
Bradbury, Ray
Breytenbach, Breyten
Brown, William Wells
Bryant, William Cullen
Burdick, Eugene
Burgess, Anthony
Burns, Robert
Camus, Albert
Clark, Walter Van Tilburg
Crabbe, George
Crabbe, Jack
Cullen, Countee
Davis, Rebecca Harding
Dickens, Charles
Dostoyevsky, Fyodor

Dreiser, Theodore
Dunbar-Nelson, Alice
Edgeworth, Maria
El Saadawi, Nawal
Ellison, Ralph
Endō, Shūsaku
Farah, Nuruddin
Ferlinghetti, Lawrence
France, Anatole
Franklin, Miles
Fuentes, Carlos
Gaines, Ernest J.
Galsworthy, John
Ginsberg, Allen
Gissing, George
Golding, William
Gorky, Maxim
Greene, Graham
Hansberry, Lorraine
Heller, Joseph
Hellman, Lillian
Hesse, Hermann
Hood, Thomas
Howe, Julia Ward
Hughes, Langston
Hugo, Victor
Hurston, Zora Neale
Huxley, Aldous
Ibsen, Henrik
Jackson, Helen Hunt
Jackson, Shirley
James, Henry
Johnson, James Weldon
Kafka, Franz
Kesey, Ken

Kundera, Milan
Larsen, Nella
Le Guin, Ursula
Lederer, William J.
Lee, Harper
Lessing, Doris
Lewis, Sinclair
London, Jack
Lowell, James Russell
Mann, Thomas
Markham, Edwin
Miller, Arthur
Miller, Henry
Morrison, Arthur
Morrison, Toni
Norris, Frank
northSun, nila
Olsen, Tillie
O'Neill, Eugene
Orwell, George
Paton, Alan
Plevier, Theodor
Rand, Ayn
Sartre, Jean-Paul
Schreiner, Olive
Shaw, George Bernard
Sinclair, Upton
Solzhenitsyn, Aleksandr
Steinbeck, John
Stowe, Harriet Beecher
Swift, Jonathan
Thompson, Eloise Bibb
Toer, Pramoedya Ananta
Tolstoi, Leo
Toomer, Jean

PREFACE

Literature can have a profound influence on human thought. In particular, by challenging old ideas and inspiring new ones, literature has the power to change people's opinions on important social issues and act as the catalyst for reform. For example, the 1852 novel *Uncle Tom's Cabin,* by Harriet Beecher Stowe, furthered the antislavery movement in the United States, and the 1885 novel *Ramona,* by Helen Hunt Jackson, brought about changes in laws regarding Native Americans. Similarly, Upton Sinclair's 1906 novel *The Jungle* helped create new laws related to public health and food handling, and Arthur Morrison's 1896 novel *A Child of the Jago* caused England to change its housing laws.

These works were effective in part because they were social protest novels rather than political documents. When political writers criticize government policies and regimes, readers are presented with arguments that encourage them to think logically, rather than emotionally, about society's problems. In contrast, social protest authors encourage readers to empathize with those who suffer from a particular social problem. For example, Charles Dickens did not rail against poverty. Instead, he encouraged the people of Victorian England to imagine what it would be like to be poor. This is a very effective way of changing the public's attitude toward a particular group of people.

In fact, personalized suffering is an important part of social protest literature, and many of its main characters are innocent victims of social problems. For instance, in the novel *The Twilight Years,* Sawako Ariyoshi protests Japan's nursing care system through the character of Akiko Tachibana, who struggles to care for her senile father-in-law with little help from Japanese society. Similarly, Ciro Alegría protested injustices against Peruvian Indians in the early 1920s by showing the unjust imprisonment of an Indian mayor, Rosendo Maqui.

Ariyoshi and Alegría address problems specific to a particular government and time period. However, in doing so, they deal with the broader issues of ageism and justice. They also concern themselves with universal truths about the human condition. This is another important aspect of social protest literature. As a result, social protest works continue to have meaning long after a particular political era has passed. This is especially true for social protest fiction and poetry, which are the focus of *The Encyclopedia of Social Protest Literature.*

Such literature has appeared in every country in the world from ancient times to the present. For example, Alcaeus protested poverty in ancient Greece, and George Gissing did so in Victorian England. Sibilla Aleramo wrote about injustices against Italian women in the early 1900s, and Nawal El Saadawi wrote about injustices against Egyptian women in the 1970s. Peter Abrahams protested racism in South Africa in the 1940s, and Richard Wright protested racism in the United States in the 1950s. Other broad social issues that have been addressed in social protest literature include anti-Semitism, labor conditions, peace, and individual freedom.

Social protest authors also work in a variety of forms. Native American authors primarily use poetry to address social ills, as did writers from the Beat generation. Memoirs, short stories, and novellas are also common, although they are not as popular as novels. Regarding the latter, authors have used all types of genres to comment on issues. For example, Charles Dickens's *Bleak House* is in essence a mystery, and his *Little Dorrit* is a romance. Theodore Dreiser's *An American Tragedy* is a crime novel. George Orwell's *Animal Farm* is a fantasy, and Kurt Vonnegut's *Player Piano* is science fiction.

But no matter what genre or form a social protest author chooses, his or her intent is to challenge the status quo. Sometimes this entails criticizing a government system or policy. For example, to improve working conditions, writers in capitalist countries have suggested replacing capitalism with socialism. To end racism, South African authors advocated the end of apartheid. As a result of such criticism, many social protest authors have been perse-

cuted for their work, or they have endured government censorship and/or exile from their native countries. For example, Aleksandr Solzhenitzyn and Milan Kundera were expelled from the Soviet Union and Czechoslovakia, respectively, and Pramoedya Ananta Toer has been forbidden to leave his home in Indonesia. American author Tillie Olsen was denied employment during the McCarthy era.

Nonetheless, social protest authors continue to criticize societies and offer solutions to long-standing social problems. *The Encyclopedia of Social Protest Literature* offers entries for recent works that address contemporary concerns such as environmentalism, job satisfaction, and the rights of gays and lesbians and Native Americans in the modern United States. Through extensive cross-referencing, the encyclopedia relates these works to earlier writings on similar issues as well as to other social protest themes.

Exploring *The Encyclopedia of Social Protest Literature* will reveal much about the way authors typically approach important social problems. It will also provide new insights into the human experience. For although writers in North and South America, Africa, Europe, Asia, and other parts of the world, from ancient times to the present, have had different visions of how to solve social problems, they have all wanted the same basic things for humanity: freedom, justice, equality, dignity, and a social system that supports them.

A

Abbey, Edward

Environmental activist Edward Abbey is the author of more than a dozen fiction and nonfiction books, but he is best known for his novel *The Monkey Wrench Gang.* Published in 1975, this book protested the destruction of wilderness areas by road builders and developers. Its main characters, activists who practice a form of environmental sabotage, or ecotage, called "monkeywrenching," eventually inspired real-life environmentalists to create a similar group called Earth First! As Philip Shabecoff (1993, 123) explains in his book *A Fierce Green Fire: The American Environmental Movement:*

> These radicals . . . choose instead to defend the natural world by direct action, civil disobedience, and the kind of eco-sabotage romanticized by the novelist Edward Abbey as "monkeywrenching." Earth First!ers, some of them remnants of the back-to-the-land movement of the 1960s, have thrown themselves in front of logging trucks, pulled up survey stakes for an oil exploration project, chained themselves to the upper branches of centuries-old trees marked for the chain saw by timber companies, and driven iron spikes into trees to make it dangerous for loggers to cut into the wood.

Dave Foreman, one of the founders of Earth First!, convinced Abbey to join the group and to be present at its first major media event, the "cracking" of the Glen Canyon Dam in 1981. Abbey's *Monkey Wrench Gang* characters had advocated the dam's destruction; Earth First! accomplished it symbolically, unfurling a "crack" of black plastic over the face of the dam. According to Susan Zakin (1993, 150) in her book *Coyotes and Town Dogs,* Abbey watched the event from a nearby bridge, shouting, "Earth First!" and "Free the Colorado!"

For Abbey, radical politics was nothing new. Born on January 29, 1927, in Home, Pennsylvania, he was the son of an avowed anarchist, Paul Revere Abbey, and his wife, Mildred. At age seventeen Edward Abbey hitchhiked west and fell in love with the American desert. That same year he was drafted into the army, and after receiving an honorable discharge in 1946, he actively protested the draft. He also began attending the University of New Mexico, where he received his B.A. in 1951 and M.A. in philosophy in 1956. His thesis was entitled "Anarchism and the Morality of Violence."

While in college he wrote his first novel, the largely autobiographical *Jonathan Troy.* It was published in 1954 but soon went out of print, and Abbey considered it so bad that he refused to allow its republication years later.

Nonetheless, in 1957 Abbey received a writing fellowship to Stanford University in California. By this time he had married one woman, divorced her, and married another; he was to have five wives and several children in his lifetime.

From 1956 to 1971 Abbey spent his summers working for the U.S. National Parks Service, both as a park ranger and a fire watcher, at a succession of desert locations. He also continued to write. His second novel, *The Brave Cowboy*, was published in 1956 and later made into a movie. It focuses on two characters, a cowboy and an intellectual, both of whom are anarchists who suffer government persecution for their political views. According to Zakin, Abbey himself was investigated by the U.S. Federal Bureau of Investigation because of his draft protests. She (303) says:

> The McCarthyesque repression that hammered down on Abbey's fictional [characters] in *The Brave Cowboy* is more dramatic than what Abbey experienced—in Abbey's case, the FBI's busiest period was ten months of scrambling after him while he was working as a clerk-typist for the U.S. Geological Survey in 1952, supporting himself while he finished *Jonathan Troy*. The FBI kept trying to find out if he was a communist but failed to turn up enough evidence to get him fired. . . .The FBI says its investigation of Abbey ended in 1967, when Abbey was working in Death Valley as a school-bus driver.

Abbey's third novel, *Fire on the Mountain* (1962), has political elements, as does his nonfiction book *Desert Solitaire,* published in 1968. *Desert Solitaire* is a first-person account of Abbey's experiences as a ranger at Utah's Arches National Park, and in it he bemoans the negative effects of "industrial tourism" on desert land. He also criticizes the National Park Service. His next book, a novel entitled *Black Sun* (1971), is a love story between a young woman and a park ranger.

With the publication of *The Monkey Wrench Gang* in 1975, Abbey became a cult hero to environmentalists. He not only became involved in Earth First! but also increasingly spoke out against the ravages of technology. He continued to write essays, as well as newspaper columns and letters to the editor, expressing his views on a wide variety of subjects. He died on March 14, 1989, at his home in Tucson, Arizona. (Abbey 1975; McCann 1977; Shabecoff 1993; Zakin 1993)

See also Anarchism; Environmentalism; McCarthyism; *Monkey Wrench Gang, The*

Abolitionist Movement
See Slavery

Abrahams, Peter
Through poetry, short stories, and novels, Peter Henry Abrahams has protested official policies of segregation, or apartheid, in his native country of South Africa. Born on November 19, 1919, in the township of Vrededorp near Johannesburg, he had an Ethiopian father and a mother deemed "coloured," or mixed-race, by the white South African government. Abrahams was therefore also considered coloured, and as such he experienced racial prejudice from an early age.

He first expressed his struggles with racism and segregation in a poem entitled "A Blackman Speaks of Freedom," written in 1938. The following year he left South Africa for good, living first in Great Britain as a merchant seaman and later in Jamaica as a newspaper and radio journalist; however, he never forgot the apartheid of his native land. He used his experiences to write a collection of protest poems, published as *A Blackman Speaks of Freedom!: Poems* (1941); a collection of short stories entitled *Dark Testament* (1942); an autobiography called *Tell Freedom* (1954); and several novels set in South Africa.

His first novel, *Song of the City* (1945), addresses the conflict caused by Afrikaner nationalists who believed that South Africa should become independent from Great Britain and therefore should not enter World War II in England's defense. His second novel, *Mine Boy* (1946), inspired by a 1946 African mine workers' strike, concerns labor issues in a large South African city. His third novel, *The Path of Thunder* (1948), focuses on a coloured man's love for a white woman; it was banned for publication and distribution in South Africa because of that country's prohibitions against interracial marriage, which lasted from 1949 to 1991.

Subsequent novels by Abrahams, who sometimes wrote under the pseudonym Peter Graham, include *Wild Conquest* (1950), which concerns the Great Trek of the Boers in South Africa; *A Wreath for Udomo* (1956), which explores postwar liberalism in West Africa and the issue of independent black nations; and *A Night of Their Own* (1965), which concerns an underground resistance organization for South African Indians. Abrahams's later novels, *This Island Now* (1966) and *The View from Coyaba* (1985), are set in the Caribbean, where the author still lives.

In all of his novels, Abrahams exposes white injustice. However, he does not advocate black hatred for whites. In explaining the reason for this position, he (Ensor 1992, 112–113) says:

> In my fight against the system of South Africa, or against the South African whites, since the two are interlocked at times, I may so change myself that I, too, become diseased by the virus I fight against. That, I hold, is the horror that is active among many Negroes today. . . . In the struggle to be free, many Negroes have arrived at a position where they would counter the white bigot's race-hatred with race-hatred against whites: many who have been humiliated because of their colour, joy openly at the humiliation of a white person because he is white. So many have changed so much that they have lost the magic of the dream that carried them on the uphill journey till "they lifted themselves up by their own bootstrings." Large numbers of Negroes today counterpoise a black humanity against a white humanity.

Abrahams (1975, 113–114) believes that countering "bigotry with more bigotry, prejudice with more prejudice" might result in a disconnection with humanity that would mean "the battle will be lost, though won." (Abrahams 1975; Ensor 1992; Wade 1972)

See also Apartheid; Finkelberg, Isaac; Mako; *Path of Thunder, The*; Racism; Swartz, Lanny

Age of Innocence, The

The Age of Innocence, by Edith Wharton, won the Pulitzer Prize for fiction in 1921. It was first published in four installments in *The Pictorial Review* in 1920 and in book form later the same year. The novel criticizes upper-class social conventions in the United States during the 1870s, particularly in regard to the institution of marriage. Its main character, Newland Archer, is a member of New York high society. A successful attorney, he becomes engaged to May Welland, a socialite who conforms to rigid codes of etiquette. In this regard she is very unlike her cousin, the Countess Ellen Olenska. Ellen is an unconventional woman who does not pay attention to social codes. She wears the "wrong" kind of clothing, lives in the "wrong" neighborhood, and makes friends with the "wrong" people. The wife of a Polish nobleman, she arrives in New York intending to file for divorce. This scandalizes her relatives. They convince Newland to act as her attorney and talk her out of ending the marriage. In the course of doing so, he learns that Ellen's husband is an extremely cruel man. Nonetheless, Newland recommends against a divorce on the grounds that society's concerns are more important than any individual's. He explains, "The individual, in such cases, is nearly always sacrificed to what is supposed to be the collective interest; people cling to any convention that keeps the family together—protects the children, if there are any" (Wharton 1993, 111).

Later Newland regrets this advice, having realized that he has fallen in love with Ellen himself. He wants to ask her to divorce her husband and marry him, but all of his relatives expect him to marry May. He cannot bring himself to cancel his wedding. However,

The Age of Innocence *criticizes nineteenth century upper-class social conventions. This scene from the 1993 film depicts Newland Archer and the Countess Olenska. (Reuters/Archive Photos)*

after the ceremony he continues to long for Ellen. One day he asks her to run away with him as his mistress. She refuses and moves away. Newton is left behind to live out his life with May, conforming to society's expectations for him. Years later, after he is widowed, his son urges him to visit Ellen. The young man has difficulty understanding why his father refuses to do so. Newton reflects on the chasm between the generations, saying, "The difference is that these young people take it for granted that they're going to get whatever they want, and that we almost always took it for granted that we shouldn't" (353).

In discussing the novel in a 1968 introduction to the work, scholar R.W.B. Lewis (xi-xii) describes the theme of *The Age of Innocence* as "the losing struggle between individual aspiration and the silent, forbidding authority of the social tribe." He (xiii) compares this work by Wharton to the novels of Henry James because it shows "the expansive courtesies of the social ceremony which hide the carefully

executed act of destruction." (Howe 1962; Wharton 1993)

See also Class, Social; Feminism; Olenska, Countess Ellen; Wharton, Edith

Age of Reason, The

The Age of Reason was published in French as *L'Âge de raison* in 1945. It is the first and best-known volume in a trilogy of novels entitled *Les Chemins de la liberté* (The Roads to Freedom). The author, Jean-Paul Sartre, intended to write a fourth volume but never finished it, rejecting the novel form to concentrate on plays. The other volumes in the series are *The Reprieve* (Le Sursis), also published in 1945, and *Iron in the Soul* (La Mort dans l'âme; called *Troubled Sleep* in the United States), which was published in 1949.

The Age of Reason emphasizes Sartre's personal philosophy regarding the relationship between freedom and social responsibility. It is the story of Mathieu Delarue, whose mistress, Marcelle Duffet, has just discovered that she is pregnant. A professor of philosophy in Paris, Mathieu is opposed to marriage and speaks often of the importance of freedom. However, he refuses to join any political causes and lives a predictable, ordinary life. Not wanting his routine to change, he decides that Marcelle will have an abortion. For several days he tries to find someone who will loan him the money for the operation, but his friends are either poor or unwilling to help end the pregnancy. Finally Mathieu steals the money from a wealthy acquaintance. When he gives it to Marcelle, she throws him out, saying that she wants to have the child. Shortly thereafter she agrees to marry Mathieu's friend Daniel Sereno, a gay man who longs for the lifestyle that Mathieu has rejected.

The sequels to the novel, *The Reprieve* and *Troubled Sleep,* continue to express Sartre's views on freedom, but they focus more on politics than does *The Age of Reason.* They concern Adolf Hitler's activities in Europe and the fall of France in 1940. (Brustein 1964; Madsen 1977; Sartre 1947)

See also Delarue, Mathieu; Sartre, Jean-Paul; Sereno, Daniel

Ageism

The term *ageism* generally refers to discrimination against the elderly. In social protest literature the concept is most often presented as part of a discussion of poverty and/or working conditions in a particular time and place. For example, in John Steinbeck's *The Grapes of Wrath* the characters of Ma and Pa Joad demonstrate the plight of older migrant farmworkers during the Depression. Similarly, in Upton Sinclair's *The Jungle* the hardships experienced by Jurgis Rudkus's father illustrate the effects of poverty and discrimination on elderly slaughterhouse workers.

Authors use such characters, who are typically good-hearted mothers and fathers, to evoke sympathy from their readers. Their intent is to raise public awareness of problems that affect all age groups. However, a few authors have devoted entire works to the problems of the elderly. The most notable in this regard are French feminist Simone de Beau-

voir, who addressed the issue in both fiction and nonfiction, and Japanese author Sawako Ariyoshi, who made ageism the main theme of her 1972 novel *The Twilight Years.* (Barrow 1979; Copper 1988)

See also Beauvoir, Simone de; *Grapes of Wrath, The; Jungle, The;* Joad Family; Rudkus, Jurgis and Ona; Sinclair, Upton; Steinbeck, John; *Twilight Years, The*

Air-Conditioned Nightmare, The

The Air-Conditioned Nightmare, by Henry Miller, is a work of nonfiction that has fictional elements and includes poetry. Published in 1945, it documents a trip that Miller took through the United States a few years earlier and discusses America's social problems in terms of culture and history. For example, Miller (1970, 28–29) says:

I ought to have an American Indian by my side. . . . Imagine the two of us . . . standing in contemplation before the hideous grandeur of one of those steel mills which dot the railway line. I can almost hear him thinking—"So it was for this that you deprived us of our birthright, took away our slaves, burned our homes, massacred our women and children, poisoned our souls, broke every treaty which you made with us and left us to die." . . . Do you think it would be easy to get him to change places with one of our steady workers? What sort of persuasion would you use? What now could you promise him that would be truly seductive? A used car that he could drive to work in? A slap-board shack that he could, if he were ignorant enough, call a home? An education for his children which would lift them out of vice, ignorance and superstition but keep them in slavery? A clean, healthy life in the midst of poverty, crime, filth, disease and fear? Wages that barely keep your head above water and often not? Radio, telephone, cinema, newspaper, pulp magazine, fountain pen, wrist watch, vacuum cleaner or other gadgets ad infinitum? Are these the baubles that make life worthwhile?

Throughout *The Air-Conditioned Nightmare* Miller argues that the United States is flawed. His words are often harsh. For example, he (20) says:

> To call this a society of free peoples is blasphemous. What have we to offer the world beside the superabundant loot which we recklessly plunder from the earth under the maniacal delusion that this insane activity represents progress and enlightenment? The land of opportunity has become the land of senseless sweat and struggle. The goal of all our striving has long been forgotten. We no longer wish to succor the oppressed and homeless; there is no room in this great, empty land for those who, like our forefathers before us, now seek a place of refuge.

Miller continued his criticism in a sequel to *The Air-Conditioned Nightmare* called *Remember to Remember*, which was published in 1947. (Miller 1970; Widmer 1963)

See also Capitalism; Miller, Henry

Alcaeus

The Greek poet Alcaeus lived from approximately 620 B.C. to 580 B.C. in Mytilene on the island of Lesbos. He produced ten books of poetry, including hymns, drinking songs, love poetry, and social and political protest poetry. Only fragments of these works are known today, but the poet is mentioned in the writings of others from the period. For example, the Greek playwright Aristophanes refers to Alcaeus's political odes in his comedy *The Archanians*, which criticizes the circumstances surrounding the Peloponnesian War (431–404 B.C.). (Martin 1972)

See also *Archanians, The;* Aristophanes; "Poverty"; Poverty

Alegría, Ciro

Peruvian novelist Ciro Alegría dedicated his life to protesting the plight of Indians in his native country. Born on November 4, 1909, in Saltimbanca, Peru, he learned the craft of writing from his father, a noted Argentine novelist, and his teacher, a well-known Peruvian poet. Alegría's social protest inclinations came from his association with a militant pro-Indian organization, the APRA party, which he joined in 1930. Alegría was arrested in 1931 and 1933 for illegal political activities, and in 1934 the Peruvian government exiled him to Chile.

The following year he published his first novel, *La serpiente de oro,* which was published in English as *The Golden Serpent* in 1943. The book portrays the harsh existence of Indians living beside a river in the Huamachuco province, where Alegría grew up. He followed this with *Los perros hambrientos* (The Hungry Dogs) in 1938, which describes the life of Indian sheepherders, and *El mundo es ancho y ajeno* (Broad and Alien Is the World) in 1941, which concerns a group of Indian villagers trying to save their land from white usurpers. *Broad and Alien Is the World* gained him fame in the United States, and he moved there in 1941. In 1948 he was allowed to return to Peru, where he became a politician. He died in Lima, Peru, on February 17, 1967. (Early 1980)

See also *Broad and Alien Is the World;* Exiles

Aleramo, Sibilla

Sibilla Aleramo is the pseudonym for Rina Pierangeli Faccio, author of the feminist novel *Una Donna* (A Woman). Published in Italy in 1906 and as an English translation in 1908, it is the semiautobiographical story of one woman's domination by the men in her life and of her struggles to achieve freedom in a country that regards her as the legal property of her husband.

Aleramo was born in Milan, Italy, in 1876. She moved to southern Italy in 1887 after her father became the manager of a glassworks factory in the town of Porto Civitanova. Shortly thereafter Aleramo began working in his office, and when she was fifteen one of his employees raped her. She was forced to marry the man to preserve her honor. Her new husband proved to be intensely jealous and controlling, and Aleramo became so despondent that she tried to kill herself. Later she assuaged her loneliness by writing short stories about tragic heroines. After she gave birth to a son, her child became the focus of her life.

Then in 1898 Aleramo read a book about feminism and socialism that discussed the typically loveless nature of Italian marriages, and she decided to write her own articles on these issues. By 1899 she had gained national recognition for her work. That same year her husband was fired from his job, and Aleramo convinced him to move to Milan, where she became an editor at a feminist magazine. However, she often quarreled with the magazine's male executive editor, and she resigned her position in January 1900. Her husband then decided to move the family back to Porto Civitanova. By this time Aleramo was having an affair with the poet Guglielmo Felice Damiani and did not want to leave Milan. She begged her husband for a separation; he told her that if she left him, she would lose all contact with her son, who was then six years old. After some indecision Aleramo chose freedom over motherhood.

Aleramo wrote *A Woman* to justify this decision. The novel is a chronicle of her marital unhappiness, although on the advice of her second lover, the poet Giovanni Cena, it omits her affair with Damiani. According to Richard Drake in the introduction to a 1980 edition of the novel, Aleramo regretted this omission. Drake (xv–xvi) explains:

Cena sensed correctly that the moral force of *A Woman* would be diminished if public attention were distracted by the all-too-familiar device in Italian fiction of an adulterous triangle. He strongly urged her to end the novel on a lofty moral tone, revealing the "naked relentless conscience of a woman facing herself, with a duty toward herself." Aleramo yielded to her lover on this point with extreme reluctance, remembering in 1939 that "by mutilating the truth" she had experienced a sense of committing a sin.

Thirteen years after the publication of *A Woman*, Aleramo corrected her omission in her second novel, *Il passaggio*. Published in 1919, it revisited the memories of *A Woman* but revealed her affair. This novel was a commercial and critical failure. Similarly, her 1924 play *Endimione* was performed only once. Impoverished, Aleramo had to rely on government support. She also continued to write articles about feminist and political issues, as well as poetry. Although none of her writing was ever as well received as *A Woman*, in later years she did regain some of her earlier financial success.

In 1945 she published some of her memoirs as *From My Diary: 1940–1944* (Dal mio diario: 1940–1944), in which she discussed her conversion to Marxism and her love affair with a young poet, Franco Matacotta. During her lifetime she had many affairs with well-known Italian poets, authors, and artists, including Vincenzo Cardarelli, Gabriele D'Annunzio, and Dino Campana. In 1952 she published a collection of her letters to Campana, *Dino Campana-Sibilla Aleramo: Lettere*, and at the end of her life she published the rest of her memoirs as *Diario di una donna: Inediti 1945–1960* (Diary of a Woman: Unedited 1945–1960). She died in Italy on January 11, 1960. (Aleramo 1983)

See also Feminism; Socialism; *Woman, A*

Alessandro

Alessandro is one of the main characters in Helen Hunt Jackson's 1885 novel *Ramona*, which shows the injustices perpetrated against American Indians in California. A Native American, Alessandro is a skilled, hard-working sheepshearer. He is also brave, kind, and handsome, and he is an excellent singer and violinist. Nonetheless, society treats him as an inferior individual. Each time he tries to better himself, white settlers take away his property and his land. Finally he begins to lose his mind. One on occasion he becomes slightly confused and accidentally takes the wrong horse home from the town corral. Its owner tracks Alessandro down and shoots him. (Jackson 1988)

See also Jackson, Helen Hunt; *Ramona*

Allende, Isabel

Born in Lima, Peru, on August 2, 1942, Isabel Allende grew up in Chile, where her Marxist uncle, Salvador Allende Gossens, was president. She worked as a journalist there until 1973. At that time Allende's uncle was assassinated; his government was replaced with a military dictatorship led by General Augusto Pinochet Ugarte, and Allende fled the country for Venezuela. However, her grandfather remained in Chile, and her writings to him eventually became the basis of her first novel, the international bestseller *La casa de los espíritus* (1982). Published in English as *The House of the Spirits* in 1985, it explores interpersonal relationships against a backdrop of political unrest. In 1984 Allende published the novel *De amor y de sombra* (Of Love and Shadows), followed by *Eva Luna* in 1987; both of these novels deal with feminist issues as well as revolutionary politics. Allende moved to the United States in 1988, where she wrote *El plan infinito* (The Infinite Plan) in 1991 and a collection of short stories, *Cuentos de Eva Luna* (The Stories of Eva Luna), in 1990. (Hart 1989; Rojas and Rehbein 1991)

Isabel Allende (Horst Tappe/Archive Photos)

See also *Eva Luna;* Exiles; Feminism; *House of the Spirits, The;* Socialism

Amenabar, Don Alvaro

In Ciro Alegría's 1941 Peruvian novel *Broad and Alien Is the World* Don Alvaro Amenabar is a nonnative rancher who hates Indians and wants to enslave them. He manipulates the government and legal system to falsely imprison anyone who opposes him and arranges for his son Oscar to become a congressman. At one point Don Alvaro says, "I think . . . that these ignorant Indians are no good to the country, and that they should be handed over to men of enterprise, the men who make their countries great" (Alegría 1941, 165). He believes that "Peru needs men of enterprise who will make people work. What's the good of all this cheap humanitarianism? It's work and more work, and so that there will be work there must be men who will make the masses work" (165). Eventually he takes over the Indian village of Rumi and destroys the lives of its inhabitants, either through enslavement, imprisonment, or murder. (Alegría 1941)

See also Alegría, Ciro; *Broad and Alien Is the World;* Castro, Benito; Justice; Maqui, Rosendo

American Tragedy, An

Theodore Dreiser's novel *An American Tragedy* (1925) criticizes the U.S. economic system of the 1920s, which created social divisions based on wealth. Its main character, Clyde Griffiths, is a poor man who struggles but fails to be equal with those who are born rich.

The novel is divided into three parts, Books One, Two, and Three. Book One opens in Kansas City with Clyde as a young boy. His parents are itinerant preachers who force him to participate in street-corner prayer meetings. Embarrassed at their religious fervor, he begins working in a soda shop, and at sixteen he takes a job as a hotel bellhop. His tips are large, and with money he discovers a wild lifestyle. One night he and some friends are out driving in a stolen car when they accidentally hit and kill a little girl. The police spot them and give chase. The car crashes and

Clyde runs off in a panic, leaving Kansas City for Chicago.

Book Two opens in Chicago, where Clyde learns he is wanted by the police. He goes into hiding for almost two years, working at a variety of odd jobs under an assumed name. Finally he decides that the trouble has blown over. He once again uses his real name and gets a job at an exclusive meeting place called the Union League Club, where he eventually encounters his rich uncle, Samuel Griffiths. Griffiths hires Clyde to work at his factory in New York, where Clyde assumes he will receive preferential treatment. However, his cousin Gilbert, whom Clyde greatly resembles, takes an instant dislike to him. Gilbert is in charge of factory assignments, and he gives Clyde a low-level job. Later Clyde's uncle recognizes his son's jealousy and moves Clyde to a better position. However, he himself is not inclined to socialize with his poorer relation.

In the new job as a supervisor Clyde meets Roberta Alden, a young factory worker from a poor background. Company rules forbid him to date an employee. Nonetheless, he asks her out and eventually convinces her to become his mistress. Meanwhile Sondra Finchley, who belongs to Gilbert Griffith's circle of friends, asks Clyde to attend some of their group's parties. Originally she invites him to make Gilbert mad, but when Clyde proves popular, she starts to fall in love with him. Soon the Griffiths are forced to include him in their social invitations.

Clyde envisions a bright future for himself. Then Roberta tells him she is pregnant. He finds her a doctor he believes is an abortionist, but the man refuses to end her pregnancy. Roberta wants Clyde to marry her, but he refuses. Finally she threatens to expose him. Imagining a ruined reputation, he chances upon a newspaper article about a boating accident and decides to drown Roberta. After taking her to a remote resort on the pretense that they will get married there, he coaxes her out on a deserted lake. Once they are on the water, however, he finds himself in turmoil over the thought of killing her. She notices that he is upset and moves toward him, but he pushes her away. In his hand is a camera; it accidentally strikes her in the head, and she falls out of the boat, which then capsizes. Now Roberta is gone, and Clyde swims to shore.

Book Three opens with the discovery of Roberta's body. The police believe that there were two drowning victims, a man and his wife. Then they realize that only the woman was killed. They discover a letter in Roberta's pocket about her impending lakeside marriage, and upon further investigation it leads them to Clyde. He is arrested for the crime, and despite some clever manipulations by his lawyers, he is eventually sentenced to death and executed.

An American Tragedy is based on a real-life murder case. Dreiser had long wanted to do a book related to crime, partly because he admired Fyodor Dostoyevsky's novel *Crime and Punishment* (1866). Dreiser's notes reveal that he tried to develop a novel from several contemporary homicide cases before settling on the 1906 murder of a pregnant factory girl, Grace ("Billy") Brown, by her social-climbing boyfriend, Chester Gillette. He chose the Gillette case specifically because of its relationship to class structure and ambition and incorporated most of its details into his novel. However, he made Clyde far less cold-hearted and sophisticated than Gillette because he wanted *An American Tragedy* to say more about society in general than about the nature of an individual murderer. (Dreiser 1964; Geismar 1953; Kazin and Shapiro 1955; Moers 1969)

See also Class, Social; Dostoyevsky, Fyodor; Dreiser, Theodore; Finchley, Sondra; Griffiths, Clyde; *Possessed, The;* Poverty

Anand, Mulk Raj

Mulk Raj Anand depicted the plight of the lower classes in his native India in novels, short stories, and essays. According to scholar Margaret Berry (1971, 25), his work expresses ideas that "can be found in contemporary movements associated with nationalism, social reform, economic Communism and Socialism, and political democracy." Berry explains that "Anand's attacks on political, as well as social and economic institutions, are carried out mainly on behalf of India's poor, in the effort to destroy forces inimical to their development, and to build a world of freedom and equality where human potential can flourish" (72). Moreover, Anand (1940, 37) himself once said that an author must seek "the real courage to create a literature of protest, which can reveal the insults, humiliations and injustices sought to be perpetrated in our society by the inheritors of privileges who seek everything without offering sacrifices equal to those offered by less privileged people."

Anand was born in Peshawar, a northwest province of India, on December 12, 1905. His mother was a Sikh peasant, and his father was a member of the Thathiar caste (silver- and coppersmiths) who learned English and became the head clerk in a military regiment. Anand was well educated himself. He graduated from the University of Punjab in 1924 and subsequently studied philosophy at University College in London, earning his doctoral degree in 1929.

He continued to live in London for several years, during which he began to write books on Indian culture, including *The Hindu View of Art* in 1933. He also became involved in Indian politics. In one magazine interview, he was quoted as saying that writers should "align themselves with the vanguard of the Indian struggle for political and economic emancipation" (Berry 1971, 30). This attitude led him to write his first novel, *Untouchable,* which depicts life among members of the lowest caste in Hindu society, the Untouchables, who are responsible for cleaning latrines and sweeping dung. *Untouchable* was rejected by 19 publishers before being printed in England in 1935, and it was subsequently banned by the British government in India, as were most of Anand's later works, including *Coolie* (1936), which concerns India's poor, and *Two Leaves and a Bud* (1937), which deals with tea plantations.

Anand wrote several other novels in his career, including *The Village* (1939), *Across the Black Waters* (1940), *The Sword and the Sickle* (1942), *The Big Heart* (1945), and *The Private life of an Indian Prince* (1953). He also worked from 1939 to 1942 as a documentary filmmaker for the British Broadcasting Corporation and Ministry of Information during World War II. In 1945 he returned to India to become a professor at the University of Punjab. He continued his involvement in Indian culture and politics and published several autobiographical novels, including *Seven Summers* (1950), *Morning Face* (1968), *Confession of a Lover* (1972), and *The Bubble* (1988).

In summarizing Anand's career, Berry (1971, 97) says:

What, finally, is the value of Mulk Raj Anand's novels? It is the witness they offer of India's agonizing attempt to break out of massive stagnation and create a society in which men and women are free and equal, in which they can, therefore, live dynamically and creatively. It is the testimony they give of a generation of Indians familiar with the best and the worst of the West and with the best and the worst of India. It is the evidence they afford of the modern educated Indian's struggle to identify himself and his country in the context of modern world society and to find roots that yet live in a mouldering heritage. It is the search they pursue for a center, a principle of unity, which the West, theoretically, has found in the virtue of charity and which Anand knows as *bhakti* [devotion]. The critic can only regret that with such noble matter, Anand's considerable talents and energies should so early and so long have operated in the restrictive climate of a doctrinaire aesthetic.

(Anand 1940; Berry 1971)

See also Bakha; Capitalism; Class, Social; Poverty; Socialism; *Untouchable*

Anarchism

The term *anarchism* means "without a ruler." It refers to an ideology that supports personal freedom and opposes all forms of authority. Proponents of anarchism, called anarchists, advocate the elimination of gov-

Famous U.S. anarchist Emma Goldman (Archive Photos)

ernment and other controlling social and political institutions.

Anarchism as a social movement had its beginnings in the works of William Godwin, an eighteenth-century English political theorist. He argued that because humans are rational beings, they are capable of behaving in an orderly fashion without any government or legal restrictions. During the nineteenth century this concept inspired the formation of anarchist groups throughout Europe, and many poets began advocating anarchism. By the early twentieth century the anarchist movement had become particularly strong in Russia and was given voice through such periodicals as *The Stormy Petrel*. Russian author Maxim Gorky alluded to this periodical in his 1901 poem "Song of the Stormy Petrel." That same year an anarchist assassinated U.S. president William McKinley.

Anarchism was prevalent in U.S. immigrant communities and came to more widespread attention through the lectures of Emma Goldman (1869–1940), a Russian-born activist who was deported from the United States to

her native country in 1919. Goldman publicly condemned acts of violence but was involved with an anarchist group that attempted to assassinate millionaire industrialist Henry Clay Frick in 1892.

Goldman and many other anarchists advocated the eventual establishment of a communist society. Anarchism has much in common not only with communism but also with socialism; all three of these ideologies oppose capitalism and class structure. However, only anarchists believe that absolutely no hierarchical structure is necessary to organize society. Anarchists express complete faith in an individual's ability to behave well in the absence of an authority figure. This faith has been criticized in social protest literature, most notably in Eugene O'Neill's 1939 play *The Iceman Cometh* and William Golding's novel *Lord of the Flies*. *The Iceman Cometh* depicts an anarchist who betrays his own mother, and *Lord of the Flies* shows a society of boys who turn savage when stranded on an island without adults. (Carter 1971; Egbert 1967; Read 1947; Woodcock 1962)

See also Capitalism; Class, Social; Communism; Golding, William; *Iceman Cometh, The*; *Lord of the Flies*; Marxism; O'Neill, Eugene; Socialism

And Still I Rise

And Still I Rise is a collection of poetry by Maya Angelou. It was first published as a single volume in 1978 and then as part of *The Complete Collected Poems of Maya Angelou* in 1994. The poem that gives the collection its title, "Still I Rise," speaks of racism and sexism from the female African-American perspective, saying, "Out of the huts of history's shame / I rise / Up from a past that's routed in pain / I rise" (Angelou 1994, 164). Similarly, "One More Round" declares, "I was born to work up to my grave / But I was not born / To be a slave" (155), and "My Arkansas" protests the social system of the Old South, where "Old hates and / ante-bellum lace are rent / but not discarded" (143). Other poems illuminate social problems within the African-American community. For example, "A Kind

Maya Angelou reads her poem "On the Pulse of Morning" at President Clinton's inauguration in 1992. (Reuters/ Gary Hershom/Archive Photos)

of Love, Some Say" is in the voice of a battered woman, whereas "Momma Welfare Roll" is from the viewpoint of a welfare recipient, who says, "They don't give me welfare / I take it" (148). Most of the thirty-two poems in the collection deal with some form of oppression, whether economic, racial, or sexual. (Angelou 1994; Elliot 1989; Hagen 1996; McPherson 1990)

> See also Angelou, Maya; Feminism; Poverty; Racism

Angelou, Maya

African-American poet Maya Annie Angelou uses images of her painful upbringing in much of her poetry, which often focuses on racial, sexual, or economic oppression in the African-American community. Born Marguerite Johnson on April 4, 1928, in St. Louis, Missouri, and raised by her grand-

mother in Stamps, Arkansas, Angelou was raped at the age of eight by her mother's boyfriend. The trauma caused by this experience, and by the man's trial, conviction, and subsequent lynching, led Angelou to fall mute for five years. After her recovery she moved to California, where at age 16 she bore a son, and then to New York, where she joined the Harlem Writers Guild and began her career as a writer. She also worked as a singer, both in nightclubs and on stage.

During the 1960s Angelou was an activist for civil rights both in the United States and abroad. She spent several years in Ghana, Africa, editing a magazine called *African Review.* At the request of Martin Luther King Jr. she returned to the United States to become the northern coordinator of the Southern Christian Leadership Conference.

In 1970 she published an autobiography, *I*

Know Why the Caged Bird Sings, that focused on her childhood. She wrote about subsequent periods of her life in *Gather Together in My Name* (1974), *The Heart of a Woman* (1981), and *All God's Children Need Traveling Shoes* (1986). She also wrote screenplays and teleplays related to African-American life in the United States, as well as five collections of poetry: *Just Give Me a Cool Drink of Water 'fore I Diiie* (1971); *Oh Pray My Wings Are Gonna Fit Me Well* (1975); *And Still I Rise* (1978); *Shaker, Why Don't You Sing?* (1983); and *I Shall Not Be Moved* (1990). On January 20, 1993, she delivered her poem "On the Pulse of Morning" at the inauguration of President William Jefferson Clinton, and in 1994 she published *Wouldn't Take Nothing for My Journey Now,* a collection of personal essays.

Angelou has received numerous awards and honorary degrees and is on the board of the American Film Institute. In addition, she is currently the Reynolds Professor of American Studies at Wake Forest University in North Carolina. (Elliot 1989; McPherson 1990)

See also *And Still I Rise;* Feminism; Poverty; Racism

Animal Farm

The 1945 novel *Animal Farm* has been called a political tract, but it is also a commentary on human nature and society. Its author, George Orwell, was a British socialist who intended the work to be a cautionary tale against Soviet socialism, which he deplored. On one occasion he (1996, x) wrote: "I understood, more clearly than ever, the negative influence of the Soviet myth upon the western socialist movement. . . . It was of the utmost importance to me that people in western Europe should see the Soviet regime for what it really was."

In *Animal Farm* Orwell depicts the Soviet regime using animal characters. The novel's setting is Manor Farm, where a cruel farmer abuses his animals to excess. One day they rebel and chase him off his land. They then take over management of the farm themselves. At first they are guided by a grand ideology. They create a list of commandments, which

state that anyone on two legs is an enemy and that no animal shall wear clothes, sleep in a bed, drink alcohol, or kill another animal. Their most important principle is that all animals are created equal. After a short time, however, two pigs begin to fight over control of the farm. One of them, Napoleon, quickly takes over and becomes a brutal dictator. He and his loyal assistants, all of whom are pigs, eventually break all of the farm's commandments. They wear clothes, carry whips, walk on two legs, associate with humans, and exploit the other animals, killing those who oppose them or are no longer able to work. In the end their faces become indistinguishable from those of the men who were their former enemies.

Throughout the novel the animals refer to one another as "comrades," just as Soviet communists do. In this way Orwell emphasizes the connection between the animal's farm and the communist system. His work is a pessimistic view of that system's ability to maintain equality and avoid corruption among its leaders. (Crick 1980; Orwell 1996; Williams 1974)

See also Communism; Labor Issues; Orwell, George

Another Country

Published in 1960 when segregation was still prevalent in the United States, *Another Country,* by African-American writer James Baldwin, shows how racism corrupts interpersonal relationships. According to biographer David Leeming (1994, 200), Baldwin once explained that the book's characters "are on desperate searches for the self-knowledge and self-esteem—the identity—without which real love is impossible. Without such love people are unable to learn to see real human beings behind the categories, labels and prejudices created by the loveless, and the horrifying results of such blindness are evident in the history of the twentieth century."

Set in New York City with some minor scenes in Paris, the novel is divided into three parts. Book One, entitled "Easy Rider," introduces all of the book's African-American characters and is primarily concerned with racial prejudice. Book Two, entitled "Any Day Now," contrasts a loving homosexual relationship with a deteriorating white heterosexual one; its themes involve homosexuality and white elitism. Book Three, "Toward Bethlehem," offers a brief conclusion showing how each main character has resolved or succumbed to his or her particular struggles. In all three books the author shifts viewpoints among the novel's eight major characters.

The story begins with Rufus Scott, a young African-American man who was once a jazz drummer but is now out of work and homeless. Rufus feels he has been betrayed by society. Seven months earlier he was in love with a white woman named Leona, but neither blacks nor whites could accept this relationship. The couple continually "encountered the big world when they went out into the Sunday streets. It stared unsympathetically out at them from the eyes of the passing people; and Rufus realized that he had not thought at all about this world and its power to hate and destroy" (Baldwin 1962, 27). Rufus internalized this hatred, and in his anger he began to berate and beat Leona. Eventually she left him. Now she is in a mental institution, and Rufus is wracked with guilt. He commits suicide by jumping off the George Washington Bridge.

Rufus's best friend, an Irish American named Daniel Vivaldo Moore, feels partly responsible for the suicide because he saw Rufus the night before and did not realize how troubled the man was. Daniel tries to help Rufus's family and falls in love with Rufus's sister Ida. But this interracial relationship has its own difficulties, both from without and within. Not only does society frown on the couple, but also Ida herself has problems accepting her love for Vivaldo. She blames all white people for her brother's death.

Ida tells Vivaldo that when Rufus died, "I felt that I'd been robbed . . . by a group of people too cowardly even to know what they had done. And it didn't seem to me that they deserved any better than what they'd given me. I didn't care what happened to them, just

so they suffered" (417). She also explains that she decided not to end up like Rufus, saying, "I was going to get through the world, and get what I needed out of it, no matter how" (417). This attitude leads her to have an affair with an important white man just to further her career as a singer. However, in the end she realizes that this affair is destroying her soul. She confesses everything to Vivaldo, who still loves her.

Similarly, Vivaldo's friend Eric Jones risks destroying his homosexual relationship with a young Parisian named Yves by having an affair with Cass Silenski, a married mother of two. Eric met Yves while living in France and is waiting for him to come to the United States. When Eric becomes involved with Cass, he warns her that he does not love her, but Cass does not care. She admires Eric, an actor who has been asked to play the part of Stavrogin in a movie version of Fyodor Dostoyevsky's novel *The Possessed.* In contrast, she is disappointed in her husband, Richard, who has become famous for writing a popular novel that she considers insignificant. Eventually Richard finds out about the affair and threatens to divorce Cass and keep her away from her children. At the same time Eric ends their affair, partly because Yves is about to arrive and partly because he has just reconnected with his homosexuality by sleeping with Vivaldo. The novel ends with Yves arriving in New York, full of hopeful expectation about the wonders of this new country. (Baldwin 1962; Eckman 1966; Leeming 1994; Macebuh 1973)

See also Baldwin, James; Gay and Lesbian Issues; Jones, Eric; Moore, Daniel Vivaldo; Poverty; Racism; Scott, Ida and Rufus

Anthony, John

John Anthony appears in John Galsworthy's 1928 play *Strife,* which concerns a factory workers' strike at the Trenartha Tin Plate Works. As the founder of the company and the chair of its board of directors, Anthony stubbornly refuses to listen to the workers' demands. He refuses all attempts at compromise and believes that his employees should be treated as inferiors. At one point he says:

It has been said that times have changed; if they have, I have not changed with them. Neither will I. It has been said that masters and men are equal! Cant! There can only be one master in a house! Where two men meet the better man will rule. It has been said that Capital and Labour have the same interests. Cant! Their interests are as wide asunder as the poles. It has been said that the Board is only part of a machine. Cant! We *are* the machine; its brains and sinews, it is for us to lead and to determine what is to be done, and to do it without fear of favour. (Galsworthy 1928, 101)

(Galsworthy 1928)

See also Galsworthy, John; *Strife*

"Antiquity of Freedom, The"

Written by social reformer William Cullen Bryant, the short poem "The Antiquity of Freedom" (1821) depicts freedom as "a bearded man, armed to the teeth" who is "strong from struggling." Even when "Merciless Power" has created a dungeon and chains for him, he is not vanquished. Instead, he rises up out of his imprisonment and calls for nations to help him destroy the "pale oppressor" (Sinclair 1996, 167). (Sinclair 1996; Sturges 1968)

See also Bryant, William Cullen

Anti-Semitism

Anti-Semitism is a term generally used to refer to discrimination against Jewish people, either as a religious group or an ethnic group. This discrimination has taken many forms throughout the centuries. For example, in ancient times Jews were persecuted for refusing to worship pagan gods and were typically denied Roman citizenship. During the fifteenth century they were thrown out of Spain unless they agreed to convert to Christianity, and in the sixteenth century European cities began requiring them to live in walled communities called ghettos, which were locked at night and during Christian festivals.

Most countries had abolished forced segregation of the Jews by the late nineteenth century, although this practice was revived by the Nazis during World War II. However, because of continuing anti-Semitism among Europe's predominantly Christian population, many European Jews continued to live in ghettos even when they were no longer required to do so. Israel Zangwill depicts this type of anti-Semitism in his 1892 novel *Children of the Ghetto,* a work that focuses on the religious differences between Christians and Jews in nineteenth-century London.

Other writers have dealt with anti-Semitism as a form of racism. For example, Yevgeny Yevtushenko's 1961 poem "Babii Yar" concerns a racist Nazi massacre of Ukranian Jews, and Doris Lessing's novels about racism in South Africa include several persecuted Jewish characters. Novelists Jean-Paul Sartre and Émile Zola have protested this type of anti-Semitism in France, as have many political protest writers throughout history. (Flannery 1965; McWilliams 1948; Pulzer 1964)

See also "Babii Yar"; *Children of the Ghetto;* Lessing, Doris; Racism; Sartre, Jean-Paul; Yevtushenko, Yevgeny; Zangwill, Israel; Zola, Émile

Apartheid

The term *apartheid* is derived from an Afrikaans word meaning "apartness." It refers to legal and political policies of racial segregation established in South Africa during the late 1940s. Under apartheid, individuals were classified as white, Bantu (black), or coloured (mixed-race). Later, officials added the classification of Asian. Each race was required to live and do business in certain areas, and a variety of laws sprung up to further segregate one race from another. For example, interracial marriages were forbidden, and nonwhites could not participate in the national government. There were also restrictions regarding what types of jobs each race could hold.

Many authors protested South Africa's social policies. The most notable of these are Alan Paton, Peter Abrahams, Breyten Breytenbach, and Doris Lessing. As the result of such protest, the South African government gradually began relaxing apartheid laws during the 1980s, and official discrimination ended completely in 1994. Nonetheless, the country still struggles against racism in the private sector. (La Guma 1972)

See also Abrahams, Peter; Breytenbach, Breyten; Lessing, Doris; Paton, Alan

Archanians, The

The Archanians, by Aristophanes, is the first in a series of three Greek comedies written during the Peloponnesian War (431–404 B.C.) between the rival Greek city-states of Athens and Sparta. The play's initial performance was in January 426 B.C., when it won first prize at the Lenaean Festival. It was followed by *Peace* in 422 B.C. and *Lysistrata* in 411 B.C.

Aristophanes's goal in writing the series was to criticize the war and the people who perpetuated it. In *The Archanians* an Athenian agriculturist named Dicaeopolis argues for peace in a public forum. When no one listens to him, he sends his representative Amphitheus to negotiate a private peace between himself and the Lacedaemonians of Sparta. Amphitheus returns with three possible treaties, symbolized by three types of wine. Dicaeopolis samples each one and chooses the best tasting: 30 years of peace on land and sea. This displeases the Archanians, a chorus of "old dotards" (Aristophanes 1930, 97) who do not believe Dicaeopolis when he argues that the Lacedaemonians are not responsible for all of Athens's troubles. However, eventually the chorus reports that "convinced by this man's speech, the folk have changed their view and approve him for having concluded peace" (117), and after conducting a series of unusual business deals, Dicaeopolis is invited to a feast. (Aristophanes 1930; Murray 1933)

See also Aristophanes; *Lysistrata; Peace;* Peace

Archer, Newland

A young New York attorney during the 1870s, Newland Archer appears in Edith Wharton's novel *The Age of Innocence* (1986). He struggles with the rigid social codes of his day, often expressing his distaste for conformity, and falls in love with a very unconventional woman. He considers leaving his wife for her, but in the end he succumbs to society's expectations and remains married. He never sees his beloved again. (Wharton, 1986)

See also *Age of Innocence, The*

Aristophanes

Aristophanes was a Greek comedic playwright who lived from approximately 444 to 385 B.C. and wrote more than 40 plays. Only eleven survive today, including *The Archanians* (425 B.C.), *The Knights* (424 B.C.), *The Clouds* (423 B.C.), *The Wasps* (422 B.C.), *Peace* (421 B.C.), and *Lysistrata* (411 B.C.). In these and other comedies, Aristophanes uses humor to criticize the social and political institutions of his time. In particular, he attacks those who threaten traditional democracy in Athens, and he is highly critical of Athens's 27-year war with Sparta. Scholars know very little about Aristophanes's personal life, but they suspect that he was born in Athens and had ties to the island of Aegina. (Aristophanes 1930; Murray 1933)

See also *Archanians, The; Lysistrata; Peace;* Peace

Ariyoshi, Sawako

Born in Wakayama, Japan, on January 20, 1931, Sawako Ariyoshi is noted for her novels describing domestic life in Japan, in which she criticizes certain aspects of modern society. She studied literature and drama at the Tokyo Women's Christian College and began her writing career while working for a publishing company. Her first publications were primarily literary articles and short stories, although she also wrote scripts for radio, movies, television, and stage productions. Her plays are still popular in Japan. In 1959 she published the novel *Kinokawa* (The River Ki), which traces the lives of three generations of Japanese women. Her next novel, *Hanaoka Seishu no tsuma* (The Doctor's Wife), concerns the family of a nineteenth-century Japanese surgeon. It was published in 1967 and translated into French in 1981, becoming a best-seller in France. In 1964 she published the novel *Hishoku* (Without Color), which focused on racism in the United States, followed in 1972 by *Kokotso no hito* (The Twilight Years), which deals with ageism in Japan and sold over a million copies in its first year of publication. Her novel *Fukogo osen* (The Compound Pollution), published in 1975, criticizes environmental pollution. Ariyoshi also wrote a historical novel, *Kazu no miyasama otome* (Her Highness Princess Kazu) in 1978 and a travelogue, *Chugoku repoto* (China Report) in 1979. She died in Tokyo, Japan, on August 30, 1984. (Ariyoshi 1987)

See also Ageism; Feminism; *Twilight Years, The*

Asian-American Literature

Asian Americans have primarily expressed social protest through nonfiction rather than fiction, but not necessarily by choice. As Elaine H. Kim explains in her chapter on Asian-American Literature in the *Columbia Literary History of the United States* (Elliott 1988, 811–812):

Autobiography has been a popular genre among Asian-American writers, largely because it has been the most marketable. Given the popular image of Asian Americans as perpetual foreigners, some publishers preferred writings with anthropological appeal over fiction. Others encouraged Asian-American writers to present their work as autobiographical even when it was not. Carlos Bulosan was persuaded to write *America Is in the Heart* (1946) as personal history because it seemed likely to sell best that way. Although Maxine Hong Kingston's *The Woman Warrior* (1975) is fiction, it has been classified and sold as autobiography, or more broadly as nonfiction.

In discussing such works, Kim says that early examples, such as Lee Yan Phou's *When I Was a Boy in China* (1887) and New Il-Han's *When I Was a Boy in Korea* (1928), focused on "superficialities of food and dress, or ceremonies and customs, to appeal to the benign curiosity of Western readers" (812). For the most part, these books did not reflect the true problems of the Asian people. According to Kim (812):

These early autobiographical works disclose a marked dissociation between the authors and the common people of both Asia and the West. Even their tentative apologetic pleas for racial tolerance are made primarily for members of the author's own privileged class. Publishers and readers accepted them as representing all Asian Americans, but with few exceptions these works ignored the large numbers of laborers recruited for agricultural and construction work in Hawaii and the American West between 1840 and 1924.

Kim reports that the exception to this lack of realism was *America Is in the Heart*, by migrant farmworker Carlos Bulosan. This semiautobiographical book describes the lives of Asian-American farmworkers and cannery workers during the 1920s and 1930s; it is not a criticism of American labor institutions but a testament to democracy.

Kim believes that publishers "discouraged or even suppressed writers" who in any way criticized America's treatment of Asians (813). In part, this was because throughout the years, the marketplace continued to support only the most pleasant portrayals of the Asian-American experience. For example, she says: "Both Lin Yutang's *Chinatown Family* (1948) and Chin Yang Lee's *Flower Drum Song* (1957) present euphemistic portraits of Chinatown, and both quickly earned popular and financial success. By contrast, Louis Chu's *Eat a Bowl of Tea* (1961) offers a more realistic insider's view of the daily life, manners, attitudes, and problems of the Chinese American community—and it failed to gain readers or make money" (815).

Moreover, Kim says that Asian Americans' isolation from mainstream culture influenced the nature of their autobiographical material, explaining: "In many stories that portray Asian-American community life, there are no white characters at all simply because segregated existence excluded them. As a result, issues of racism and race relations are submerged" (814). Therefore there are no major social protest novels by Asian Americans.

However, modern Asian-American authors have expressed social protest concerns through a rich body of poetry, much of which has been privately published. Kim cites several examples of Asian-American verse, including "A Homecoming" (1972) by Korean immigrant Kinchung Kim. This work addresses the difficulties of a young Korean returning to his country after ten years in the United States.

Elaine Kim (820) also states that regardless of genre:

> the quest for a place in American life is a recurrent theme in Asian-American literature. Contemporary writers . . . focus not on accommodation or racial self-negation but on the ideal that Carlos Bulosan articulated in the 1940s, of an America of the heart, where it is possible to be both American and nonwhite. Indeed, several contemporary Asian-American writers express kinship with other nonwhite Americans, especially blacks and Native Americans, who frequently appear in their works.

(Elliot 1988)

See also Native American Issues

Atkins, Homer

Homer Atkins appears in the 1958 novel *The Ugly American,* by William Lederer and Eugene Burdick. He is an engineer who travels to Asia as a consultant to the U.S. and French governments on the building of dams and military roads. However, he quickly realizes that the region has more important needs and recommends that the two governments spend their money instead on local projects such as canning and brick factories, which would help make the Asian people self-sufficient. After his opinion is rudely rejected, he decides to help the Asians on his own. He works with an Asian mechanic to invent a water pump that will direct water to hillside crops, and the two men open a factory to mass-produce these machines. They also make their design available to anyone who wants to make his own machine. Atkins therefore represents the authors' position that what is needed in Asia is simple, basic help. In an epilogue to their novel, Lederer and Burdick (1958, 281–282) say:

> Most American technicians abroad are involved in the planning and execution of "big" projects: dams, highways, irrigation systems. The result is that we often develop huge technical complexes, which some day may pay dividends but which at this moment in Asian development are neither needed nor wanted except by a few local politicians who see such projects as a means to power and wealth. Technicians who want to work on smaller and more manageable projects are not encouraged. The authors of this book gathered statements from native economists of what projects were "most urgently needed" in various Asian countries. These included improvement of chicken and pig breeding, small pumps which did not need expensive replacement parts, knowledge on commercial fishing, canning of food, . . . and the development of small industries. These are the projects which would not only make friends, while costing little, but are also prerequisite to industrialization and economic independence for Asia.

(Lederer and Burdick 1958)

See also Burdick, Eugene; Knox, Tom; Lederer, William J.; *Ugly American, The*

Atlas Shrugged

Atlas Shrugged, by Ayn Rand, presents its author's views on capitalism, government regulation, and individual drive. Published in 1957, the novel depicts an American society that punishes the rich for being rich. The fictional U.S. government passes a series of laws that make it difficult for entrepreneurs to profit from their own efforts, and what money they do make is redirected into the hands of people who are mediocre, shiftless, or manipulative. The worst members of society are feeding off of the best and making the best feel guilty for their success. Of this situation, one character says:

Men who have no courage, pride or self-esteem, men who have no moral sense of their right to their money and are not willing to defend it as they defend their life, men who apologize for being rich—will not remain rich for long. They are the natural bait for the swarms of looters that stay under rocks for centuries, but come crawling out at the first smell of a man who begs to be forgiven for the guilt of owning wealth. They will hasten to relieve him of the guilt—and of his life, as he deserves.

Then you will see the rise of the men of the double standard—the men who live by force, yet count on those who live by trade to crate the value of their looted money—the men who are the hitchhikers of virtue. . . . Money is the barometer of a society's virtue. When you see . . . that in order to produce, you need to obtain permission from men who deal, not in goods, but in favors—when you see that men get richer by graft and by pull than by work, and your laws don't protect you against them, but protect them against you—when you see corruption being rewarded and honesty becoming a self-sacrifice—you may know that your society is doomed. (Rand 1992, 385)

Gradually the most successful industrialists decide that they are no longer willing to live in a society where they represent the mythical figure of Atlas, shouldering the burdens of the world. They "shrug"—or in other words, they go on strike. One by one they destroy or abandon their businesses and disappear, leaving the world without the products they used to produce. But strangely no one can figure out where these industrialists have gone.

Then one person, Dagny Taggert, begins to suspect that there is something sinister involved. Taggert is in charge of her family's railroad line, Taggert Transcontinental, and many of the missing industrialists are her friends. As a dedicated businesswoman she cannot understand how these men could have abandoned their life's work. She beings to investigate the situation and discovers that a mysterious stranger has been leading these men away just when their businesses are the most threatened by government interference.

Taggert wonders whether she will be next. Her railroad is in serious financial trouble, partially because its tracks are in disrepair, and she decides to construct a new line using an untested metal that is cheaper, yet stronger than steel. Government officials insist that this metal will crack, and they publicly accuse Dagny of trying to kill people. They also attack the metal's inventor, Hank Reardon, saying that he is more interested in money than in the people's welfare. Nonetheless, Taggert and Reardon build the railroad, and it proves successful. The two industrialists then begin having an affair.

Later this affair is used against them. The government passes a new law that reads, in part, "All patents and copyrights, pertaining to any devices, inventions, formulas, processes and works of any nature whatsoever, shall be turned over to the nation as a patriotic emergency gift by means of Gift Certificates to be signed voluntarily by the owners of all such patents and copyrights" (499). The authorities want Reardon to sign the Gift Certificate, giving away all of his rights to his special metal, but he refuses. Then they tell him that they know about the affair and will make it public if he refuses to sign. Not wanting Taggert to get hurt, he agrees. But this plan backfires when she finds out about his sacrifice, and during a live radio interview in which she is supposed to express support for the government, she tells the public about the blackmail. The government cuts her microphone, but the damage has already been done. People now realize how corrupt their society has become.

By this time Taggert has learned the whereabouts of the disappearing industrialists. While following a promising young inventor, she discovered a secret valley in the Rocky Mountains of Colorado. All of her missing friends are there, waiting for the time when they can once again profit from their own efforts. Also in the valley is her former lover, Francisco D'Anconia. Head of the largest copper company in the world, he has been gradually destroying the profitability of his copper mines in order to punish those who are planning to take them away. Moreover, D'Anconia was one of the first individuals to join forces with the group's founder, John Galt, a brilliant inventor who walked away from a company that sought to reward other employees for his hard work.

Taggert immediately falls in love with Galt, and he and the other members of the group ask her to stay with them in the valley. She refuses because she is not yet ready to abandon her railroad company. After promising not to reveal their existence or their plans, she returns home, where society has begun to deteriorate. Without the industrialists to work the mines, ship the goods, and create new products, life has become very difficult. Food and heating materials are scarce, and angry mobs are becoming more common. The leaders of the country have begun to fear the public. Nonetheless, they continue to oppress the remaining industrialists, particularly Hank Reardon. Finally he decides to join with Galt's group. Meanwhile Dagny Taggert continues to hope that she will not have to abandon her railroad, but she begins to change her mind after Galt makes a rousing radio speech to the public to reveal his philosophy in full. After this the government tracks him down, captures him, and tortures him to make him support the society. Taggert now decides to abandon her railroad. She helps Galt's group rescue him, and together they go to the valley, where they make plans to rebuild the country.

In discussing this novel, which had an original working title of *The Strike*, Ayn Rand (Rand 1992, 2–3) said: "I start with *the fantastic premise of the prime movers going on strike*. This is the actual heart and center of the novel. A distinction carefully to be observed here; I do not set out to glorify the prime mover. . . . I set out to show how desperately the world needs prime movers, and how viciously it treats them." She intended the work to be a statement of her philosophical principles, which collectively became known as Objectivism and attracted a large

Margaret Atwood, March 22, 1989 (Reuters/Gary Hershom/Archive Photos)

number of followers. (Baker 1987; Rand 1992)

See also Capitalism; Galt, John; Justice; Labor Issues; Rand, Ayn; Reardon, Hank; Taggert, Dagny

Atwood, Margaret

Margaret Eleanor Atwood is the author of several important feminist novels, including *The Edible Woman* (1969) and *The Handmaid's Tale* (1985). Born on November 18, 1939, in Ottawa, Canada, she began her writing career as a poet. Her first poem was published when she was nineteen and her first poetry collection when she was twenty-one. At that time she was attending the University of Toronto, where she received a B.A. in 1961. She received an M.A. from Radcliffe College in Cambridge, Massachusetts, in 1962 and later studied at Harvard University. She has traveled extensively throughout the world.

In 1966 her poetry collection *The Circle Game* was awarded a prestigious national prize, the Canadian Governor General's Award for Poetry. Her novel *The Handmaid's Tale* won the same award for fiction in 1986. Her first novel was *The Edible Woman;* subsequent novels include *Surfacing* (1972), *Bodily Harm* (1981), *Cat's Eye* (1988), and *The Robber Bride* (1993). She has also written short stories, articles, and children's books. (Davidson 1981; Grace 1980; Rosenberg 1984)

See also *Edible Woman, The;* Feminism; *Handmaid's Tale, The*

Autobiography of an Ex-Colored Man, The

The 1912 novel *The Autobiography of an Ex-Colored Man* was first published anonymously in order to make it seem like a true story. Its author, James Weldon Johnson, was a black man who experienced American racism, but unlike his book's unnamed narrator, he did not abandon his heritage. This fictional narrator is so light-skinned that many people mistakenly believe he is a white man. He is also a skilled musician who dreams of becoming a great composer; by so doing, he hopes to prove that blacks are not an inferior race. One day he decides to travel throughout the South listening to black music for inspiration. There he sees a group of white men set a black man on fire, and from that moment on he pretends to be white. Eventually he marries a white woman, who dies giving birth to his second child. He continues to pretend he is white and becomes a prosperous man. However, he concludes, "My love for my children makes me glad that I am what I am and keeps me from desiring to be otherwise; and yet, when I sometimes open a little box in which I still keep my fast yellowing [music] manuscripts, the only tangible remnants of a vanished dream, a dead ambition, a sacrificed talent, I cannot repress the thought that, after all, I have chosen the lesser part, that I have sold my birthright for a mess of pottage" (Johnson 1990, 154).

In writing about the novel in a 1990 introduction to Johnson's work, scholar William Andrews (xxvii) says that this ending does not mean that the narrator's life was meaningless:

Were the heritage and communal expression of black America to be consigned to this sort of private oblivion, this novel would seem indeed to culminate in tragedy. But through the ex-colored man's acknowledgement of his failure as a composer, Johnson allows him to succeed as a writer. The *Autobiography*'s unprecedented analysis of the social causes and artistic consequences of a black man's denial of the best within himself constitutes perhaps

James Weldon Johnson's greatest service to African-American culture.

But Johnson does not just comment on the black experience. Because his novel's narrator has also lived as a white man, Johnson has the opportunity to discuss the effect that racism has on white society. For example, the narrator says:

I am sure it would be safe to wager that no group of Southern white men could get together and talk for sixty minutes without bringing up the "race question." If a Northern white man happened to be in the group, the time could be safely cut to thirty minutes. In this respect I consider the conditions of the whites more to be deplored than that of the blacks. Here, a truly great people, a people that produced a majority of the great historic Americans from Washington to Lincoln, now forced to use up its energies in a conflict as lamentable as it is violent. (55)

Johnson also discusses the social protest novel *Uncle Tom's Cabin*. He complains about successful attempts to ban the book in school libraries and calls Harriet Beecher Stowe's novel "a fair and truthful panorama of slavery" (Johnson 1990, 29). (Johnson 1990; Levy 1973; Price and Oliver 1997)

See also Johnson, James Weldon; Racism; Stowe, Harriet Beecher; *Uncle Tom's Cabin*

Autobiography of Miss Jane Pittman, The

Published in 1971, *The Autobiography of Miss Jane Pittman,* by Ernest J. Gaines, protests racism in American society by tracing the life of a fictional black woman during 100 years of history, from the Civil War to the beginning of the civil rights movement. In the novel's introduction a fictional historian explains that in 1962 he interviewed a 110-year-old woman named Jane Pittman and tape-recorded her recollections. The rest of the book is the first-person narration of her life story.

Her narration begins when she is ten or eleven years old. At that time she answers to the name "Ticey." One day she encounters some Yankee soldiers passing through her Louisiana plantation during the Civil War. One of them tells her that Ticey is a slave name. Explaining that she will soon be set free, the soldier renames her "Jane," after his girlfriend in Ohio, and gives her his own last name, "Brown." After the soldiers have left, Jane refuses to answer to the name Ticey anymore. Her owners beat her. A year later the war ends and Jane heads north with several other slaves. Along the way some racist white men kill all of her traveling companions, except for one small boy named Ned. Jane becomes his mother. Together the two try to get to Ohio to find Mr. Brown, but Louisiana is a big state, and they soon give up all hope of leaving it.

Jane finds work on a plantation that has a school for Ned, and for a while life is good. Then a racist takes control of the place. The school is closed and life becomes as bad as it was under slavery. When Ned reaches the age of 17 or 18, he heads north to Kansas. Jane remains in Louisiana and moves in with Joe Pittman, who is an expert at breaking horses. One day he is killed while rounding up a wild stallion. Jane is distraught but goes on with her life. She is delighted when Ned returns to Louisiana to set up a school, but she fears for his life. Racist groups are prevalent in the South. But despite Jane's warnings, Ned refuses to give up his teaching. He believes in its importance, saying: "I want my children to be men. . . . I want my children to fight. Fight for all—not just for a corner. The black man or white man who tell you to stay in a corner want to keep your mind in a corner too. I'm building that school so you'll have a chance to get from out of that corner" (Gaines 1972, 110). Ned is soon murdered for his views, and even though there are several witnesses to the crime, the police make no effort to arrest the killer.

Shortly thereafter Jane moves seven miles north to another plantation, where she lives out the rest of her life. The plantation is owned by Robert Sampson, who has two sons. The oldest, Timmy, is half black and il-

legitimate. The other, Tee Bob, is white and legitimate. Robert treats both boys well, but he is particularly close to Timmy, who acts the most like him. Nonetheless, when Timmy grows too arrogant, Robert sends him away. Later Tee Bob falls in love with a half-black girl. When she refuses to marry him, he kills himself.

By this time the workers on the plantation have become convinced that one of their young people, Jimmy, will become a great man. They want him to be a preacher, but instead he becomes an activist. Jane disagrees with his methods, saying that he is moving too fast. She explains:

> You talk of freedom, Jimmy. Freedom here is able to make a little living and have the white folks say you good. . . . [Your people] want you, Jimmy, but now you here they don't understand nothing you telling them. You see, Jimmy, they want you to cure the ache, but they want you to do it and don't give them pain. And the worse pain, Jimmy, you can inflict is what you doing now—that's trying to make them see they good as the other man. You see, Jimmy, they been told from the cradle they wasn't—that they wasn't much better than the mule. You keep telling them this over and over, for hundreds and hundreds of years, they start thinking that way. (236)

Jane warns him that it could take a long time to change people. Nonetheless, Jimmy organizes a protest in the nearby city of Bayonne, where a black girl has been arrested for drinking from a "whites-only" water fountain. Before the protest can take place, he is killed. Jane then defies Robert Sampson's orders and makes plans to attend the protest with her friends, saying that, although Jimmy is gone, "just a little piece of him is dead. . . . The rest of him is waiting for us in Bayonne" (245).

The Autobiography of Miss Jane Pittman was a powerful statement against racism. However, a television movie based on the novel made Jane Pittman an even stronger advocate of civil rights; it ended with her drinking from the whites-only fountain herself. Televised in 1974, the show earned nine Emmy awards. (Babb 1991; Estes 1994; Gaines 1972)

See also Gaines, Ernest J.; Pittman, Jane Brown; Racism; Slavery

Avery, Shug

Shug Avery appears in Alice Walker's 1982 novel *The Color Purple*. A black singer, she helps the main character, Celie, develop self-respect. Shug encourages her friend to stand up to her oppressive husband, become independent, and start her own clothing business. Eventually Shug also becomes Celie's lover, and the two live together. In turn, Celie teaches Shug to quilt. With their friend Sophia they use quilting to become more deeply connected to one another. *The Color Purple* uses this symbol to show that communal solidarity can enhance personal growth. (Walker 1986)

See also *Color Purple, The;* Walker, Alice

B

Babbitt

Published in 1922, *Babbitt,* by Sinclair Lewis, tells the story of a 46-year-old real estate salesman who leads a successful but unsatisfying life. As the novel progresses, George F. Babbitt's unhappiness grows, and he begins to challenge many of the social conventions he once valued.

The novel begins in April 1920 in the midwestern American town of Zenith. It is a place where people conform in both behavior and thought. Anyone who expresses a different opinion from the masses is suspect. Babbitt himself suspects such nonconformists. For example, he questions the morals of his neighbors, who drink alcohol despite the Prohibition laws then in effect. He also scathingly attacks labor unions that want to change the status quo, saying:

> A good labor union is of value because it keeps out radical unions, which would destroy property. No one ought to be forced to belong to a union, however. All labor agitators who try to force men to join a union should be hanged. In fact, just between ourselves, there oughtn't to be any unions allowed at all; and as it's the best way of fighting the unions, every businessman ought to belong to an employers'- association and to the Chamber of Commerce. In union there is strength. So any selfish hog who doesn't join the Chamber of Commerce ought to be forced to.
> (Lewis 1950, 44)

Babbitt does not hear the hypocrisy in his words. He parrots his beliefs without seeming to understand them. He also lacks self-awareness. For example, he believes himself to be a reputable businessman, yet many of his real estate practices are unethical, and some border on the illegal. His main goal is to increase his standing in the community.

However, Babbitt begins to experience self-doubt when his best friend and former college roommate, Paul Reisling, goes through a personal crisis. Reisling always wanted to be a violinist, but his artistic career was cut short by marriage. To support his wife, Zilla, he took a job as a roofing salesman, and now he is profoundly unhappy, not only because of his lost dreams but also because Zilla berates him constantly. Babbitt is mildly unhappy at home himself; he feels that his wife, Myra, and children Ted, Verona, and Tinka value him only for his paycheck. Therefore, he suggests that he and Paul go on a fishing trip to Maine to get away from their heavy responsibilities for a while. They have a good time together, but when they return to Zenith, their lives are still the same.

Babbitt finds himself increasingly bored at work. Meanwhile Paul begins having an affair. Eventually he grows so angry with Zilla that he tries to kill her, shooting her in the shoulder. She recovers, but he is sent to prison. This event propels Babbitt into his own personal crisis. He begins to question his values and beliefs and makes some changes in his life. At first these changes are small. For example, he goes to see a movie in the middle of a business day. He expresses admiration for an old college friend, Seneca Doane, who is a hated social reformer, and when a labor strike occurs in town, he expresses sympathy for the strikers and the union leaders. However, eventually Babbitt's nonconformity becomes more extreme. He starts having an affair and spends much of his time drinking with a group of liberal thinkers, particularly when his wife is out of town visiting relatives. His friends and business associates warn him to behave better; when Babbitt does not listen to them, they shun him in public. He bemoans the loss of their respect, yet when they insist he join their newly formed Good Citizen's League, dedicated to preserving conservative thought in Zenith, he stubbornly refuses. Then his wife falls ill. Babbitt watches the townspeople offer her deep emotional support, and he realizes how lonely he has been as a nonconformist. He joins the Good Citizen's League and is once again warmly accepted into the community.

However, he is not quite the same man as he was at the beginning of the novel. When his son Ted tells the family that he and his girlfriend have eloped, and that he is going to leave college and take the job he has always wanted—as an auto mechanic—to support them, Babbitt encourages him to follow his dreams and never let society wear him down. Of this speech, scholar Martin Light (1975, 84) says: "It is impossible . . . to read Babbitt's last speech—his advice to his son to do what he wants to do—without realizing that Lewis had allowed Babbitt to know to a small extent what his experience of rebellion has meant. But George is still very much a Babbitt, frightened,

guilty, and conformist, and both his way of addressing his son and that son's character itself leave little confidence of growth." Babbitt's son Ted displays as little self-awareness as Babbit himself.

Soon after the novel was published, the word *Babbittry* came to mean blind support for the status quo, and the character of Babbitt was taken as a symbol for a broader part of society. Scholar Sheldon Grebstein (1962, 82) explains: "By means of this Babbitt, Lewis uses the book as a vehicle for satire and social history, the portrayal of a whole way of life in a representative American city. In this context Lewis gives us . . . [an] account of the conditions of life in an industrial and commercial society, which is dominated by the profit motive and acquiescent to the pressure toward sameness and standardization." Moreover, according to Grebstein (85), the book "summarized every criticism advanced against the middle class in the 1920's, and it rendered a superb account of the devastating effects of a material culture." It therefore engendered much discussion and criticism and as Grebstein reports has often been called "the outstanding social satire of its generation" (85). (Grebstein 1962; Lewis 1950; Schorer 1962)

See also Doane, Seneca; Labor Issues; Lewis, Sinclair; Reisling, Paul; Socialism

"Babii Yar"

"Babii Yar," by Yevgeny Yevtushenko, is the Russian poet's most famous work. This 1961 poem (also spelled "Baby Yar" or "Babi Yar") opens by lamenting the fact that there is no monument at Babii Yar, where thousands of Ukranian Jews were once massacred by the Nazis. It then protests current anti-Semitism in the Soviet Union, saying: "How vile these anti-Semites—without a qualm / they pompously call themselves / 'The Union of the Russian People'!" (Yevtushenko 1989, 147). The poem is extremely direct, a quality that scholar George Reavey believes caused its success. In discussing "Babii Yar" in a 1989 introduction to the work, Reavey (xii) says: "Yevtushenko's direct treatment of the subject [of anti-Semitism] was very forthright and brave. It was this poem more than anything else that gave him such immediate worldwide publicity. 'Babii Yar' . . . was certainly a most effective poem, rousing both emotions and passions, stirring many dovecots and thus demonstrating the potential power of the poetic world." Reavey (xii) adds that the poem therefore was subjected to "a whole barrage of rather savage attacks." Nonetheless, its great popularity abroad made it difficult for the Soviet authorities to punish Yevtushenko for writing the work. (Yevtushenko 1989)

See also Anti-Semitism; Yevtushenko, Yevgeny

Bakha

The main character from Mulk Raj Anand's 1935 novel *Untouchable*, Bakha is a member of India's Untouchables—the lowest caste in Hindu society. As such he is responsible for cleaning latrines and sweeping dung. He bemoans his place in society and agrees with an Indian poet who says that "we must destroy caste, we must destroy the inequalities of birth and unalterable vocations. We must recognise an equality of rights, privileges and opportunities for everyone" (Anand 1940, 155). (Anand 1940)

See also Anand, Mulk Raj; Class, Social; *Untouchable*

Baldwin, James

In novels and essays African-American author James Arthur Baldwin advocated civil rights activism and spoke against racism and sexism. Biographer David Leeming (1994, xiii) explains that Baldwin personally "took the side of those who were made into exiles and outcasts by barriers of race, sex, and class or who turned away from safety and chose the honorable path of tearing down such barriers. [He also] mourned for those who had created the barriers and had unwittingly allowed themselves to be destroyed by them."

Baldwin was born in Harlem, New York City, on August 2, 1924. His mother, Berdis Jones, was unmarried at the time of his birth, but when he was two years old she wed a minister, David Baldwin, who was the son of a

James Baldwin (Walter Daran/Archive Photos)

slave. According to Leeming (3), "illegitimacy and an almost obsessive preoccupation with his stepfather were constant themes in [his] life and work" (3). Baldwin did not respect his stepfather because of the man's "bitter subservience to bill collectors, landlords, and other whites" and considered him "the archetypal black father, one generation removed from slavery, prevented by the ever-present shadow and the frequently present effects of racial discrimination from providing his family with what they needed most—their birthright, their identity as individuals rather than as members of a class or a race" (5). Moreover, as a result of his stepfather's frustration with life, Baldwin's household was filled with "an arbitrary and puritanical discipline and a depressing air of bitter frustration which did nothing to alleviate the pain of poverty and oppression" (5).

Fortunately, the young Baldwin found a mentor in Countee Cullen, a well-known poet who had become a teacher in Harlem. Baldwin considered Cullen "living proof that a black man could be a writer" (22). Nonetheless, upon graduating from junior high school at age 14, Baldwin became not a writer but a minister, preaching in a small evangelical church. There he learned to use language effectively, and the rhythm of his writing would later reflect this experience. After three years in the ministry he left the church and his childhood home in Harlem for Greenwich Village, the bohemian section of New York City, where he became the protégé of Beauford Delany, a black artist. Baldwin also held a series of odd jobs.

Baldwin's writing career began in 1945 when he and a friend started a literary magazine, *This Generation.* At this time Baldwin was working on a novel called *In My Father's House;* he published a portion of it in the magazine as a short story. He also gave readings of *In My Father's House* at writers' gatherings. One of his listeners introduced him to author Richard Wright, then famous for his novel *Native Son,* who shared Baldwin's unfinished manuscript with his editor. As a result, Baldwin received a fellowship and grant money to finish his novel, which was published in 1953 as *Go Tell It on the Mountain.* He also continued to publish short stories and essays. In 1948 he moved to Europe, where he came to terms with his homosexuality. His 1956 novel *Giovanni's Room* reflects this experience.

Baldwin returned to the United States in 1957. By this time, in addition to his first novel, he had published a collection of essays entitled *Notes of a Native Son* (1955). It was followed by two more books of essays, *Nobody Knows My Name* (1961) and *The Fire Next Time* (1963), and the novels *Tell Me How Long the Train's Been Gone* (1968) and *Just Above My Head* (1979). Baldwin also wrote several plays, including *The Amen Corner* (1955), *Blues for Mister Charlie* (1964), and *The Women at the Well* (1972). He died on December 1, 1987, in Saint-Paul, France. (Eckman 1966; Leeming 1994; Macebuh 1973)

See also *Another Country;* Cullen, Countee; Gay and Lesbian Issues; *If Beale Street Could Talk; Native Son;* Poverty; Racism; Wright, Richard

"Ballad of Reading Gaol, The"

"The Ballad of Reading Gaol" is a semiautobiographical poem by Oscar Wilde that draws on his experiences as a prisoner in Reading Gaol, where he served two years for sodomy. Originally published under the pseudonym C.3.3., which was Wilde's cell number, it is the story of a prisoner sentenced to death for murdering his lover. The poem is a lengthy work that not only criticizes society's response to homosexuality but also attacks its legal systems and the hypocrisy of traditional religions. Regarding the latter, for example, the poem says, "That every prison that men build / Is built with bricks of shame, / And bound with bars lest Christ should see / How men their brothers maim" (Sinclair 1996, 115). (Aldington 1946; Ellman 1969; Sinclair 1996)

See also Gay and Lesbian Issues; Prison Reform; Wilde, Oscar

Balzac, Honoré de

Honoré de Balzac is the author of *La Comédie humaine* (The Human Comedy), a series of approximately 90 novels and novellas published in France between 1829 and 1847. Set between 1308 and 1846, these works show the political and social changes that occurred in the country during those years in order to criticize French society and offer insights into the causes and impact of the French Revolution.

Balzac, whose original last name was Balssa, was born on May 20, 1799, in Tours, France. He was educated in the cities of Vendôme and Paris and became a law clerk at age 16. At that time he began writing both plays and novels under a pseudonym. All of his works failed, and for a brief time he became a businessman. This career almost led him to ruin; he amassed many debts that he would struggle to repay for the rest of his life.

However, when Balzac was 30, his luck changed. In 1829, under his own name, he published the novel *Les Chouans* (The Chouans) about a band of peasants who supported the Royalist cause during the French Revolution, as well as the comedy *Les Physiologie du mariage* (The Physiology of Marriage), about marriage and adultery. Both of these books were a success, which scholar Samuel Rogers attributes to a change in

Balzac's politics. Rogers (1953, 15) explains: "Politically . . . his views began to change about his thirtieth year, and . . . he abandoned once and for all the bourgeois liberalism that had been the tradition of his family. Throughout the rest of his life, with minor shifts produced by political events and by new contacts with either people or books, he supported the royalist party and the Catholic Church."

Balzac continued to write novels for the rest of his life. By 1834 he had already decided to group his individual works, both past and future, into *The Human Comedy*. They include *Le Medicine de campagne* (The Country Doctor, 1833), *Le Père Goriot* (Father Goriot, 1835), *La Cousine Bette* (Cousin Bette, 1846), and *Le Cousin Pons* (Cousin Pons, 1847), which was his last novel. He died in Paris, France, on August 18, 1850. (Butler 1983; Marceau 1966; Oliver 1965; Rogers 1953)

See also Class, Social; *Human Comedy, The*

Beat Movement

The term *Beat movement* refers to a literary and social movement that began in the United States during the late 1950s and continued throughout the 1960s. It was led by a group of writers that included Jack Kerouac, William Burroughs, and Gary Snyder, all of whom rejected consumerism and embraced mysticism and drug use. Gary Snyder also became an environmental activist.

Beat writers experimented with literary form and often attempted to recreate the sound of jazz music in their poetry. However, they were largely apolitical and apathetic—or beat, meaning "weary." (Later beat came to refer to these writers' interest in musical beats or in "beatific" or spiritual pursuits.) However, some important social protest works did come out of the movement, most notably Allen Ginsberg's long poem *Howl*. An indictment of many aspects of contemporary society, it contains obscenities and references to homosexuality. It was banned from publication under censorship laws, and its publisher, poet Lawrence Ferlinghetti, was put on trial for distributing it. Ferlinghetti's acquittal in 1957

is considered one of the most important legal rulings on censorship in the United States. (Hickey 1990; Miles 1995)

See also Censorship; Environmentalism; Ferlinghetti, Lawrence; Ginsberg, Allen; *Howl*

Beatty, Captain

As a fire chief in Ray Bradbury's 1953 futuristic novel *Fahrenheit 451,* Captain Beatty's job is to burn books, which are banned in his society. However, Beatty is conflicted about his work. He often quotes from books himself and admits to having read them long ago. He also expresses understanding when another fireman, Guy Montag, questions the morality of their job. After Montag kills Beatty during a conflict over book-burning, Montag wonders whether Beatty *wanted* to be killed.

Although *Fahrenheit 451* never reveals the source of Beatty's unhappiness, its author has suggested a reason. In an afterword to a 1996 edition of the novel Bradbury says that the fire chief was once a scholar and still has a fine book collection. Unable to destroy his books, but wanting to remain within the law, he never reads them. He is therefore a tormented man. (Bradbury 1996)

See also Bradbury, Ray; *Fahrenheit 451;* Montag, Guy

Beauvoir, Simone de

Born on January 9, 1908, in Paris, France, Simone Bertrand de Beauvoir is best known for her nonfiction books. Her most famous works in this regard are *Le Deuxième Sexe* (The Second Sex, 1949), which discusses feminism, and *Old Age* (La Vieillesse, 1970), which discusses ageism. However, she also wrote fiction that reflected her concern with social issues. For example, her 1954 novel *Les Mandarins* (The Mandarins) is the story of a group of intellectuals who begin to engage in political activism. This work is semiautobiographical and includes a character believed to represent the novelist Jean-Paul Sartre.

Beauvoir and Sartre met while studying at the Sorbonne, and in 1945 they founded a monthly magazine, *Les Temps Modernes* (Modern Times). They remained together until

Simone de Beauvoir (UPI/Corbis-Bettmann)

Sartre's death. Beauvoir wrote about their relationship in her memoirs and in a book entitled *La Cérémonie des adieux* (Adieux: A Farewell to Sartre), which was published in 1981. Her other works include philosophy books, travel books, and essay collections. Beauvoir died in Paris on April 14, 1986. (Madsen 1977)

See also Ageism; Feminism; Sartre, Jean-Paul

Behn, Aphra

Aphra Behn is the author of *Oroonoko: or, The Royal Slave,* a book published in 1688. It concerns an African prince named Oroonoko who was captured and made into a slave at the European colony of Surinam in South America. Behn lived in Surinam for a time, and she presented her story as fact. In an introduction to Behn's work, scholar Lore Metzger says that as a result, "during her own time there were rumors that Aphra Behn had had a love affair with the black hero of her story" (Behn 1973, x). Today, however, some scholars consider *Oroonoko* to be a work of fiction.

Much of Behn's own life is also a mystery. She was born in 1640, probably in Kent, England, and as a child she traveled to Surinam,

then a colony of England. (Later it was taken over by the Dutch.) At some point she returned to England to marry a merchant named Behn. Some scholars report that this occurred during 1658, others in 1663. She then moved to the Netherlands, where she worked as a spy for England's King Charles II. When she returned to her own country, she was imprisoned for debt and started writing plays to pay her bills. Her first play, *The Forc'd Marriage,* was performed in 1671; a successful comedy, *The Rover,* was published in two parts in 1677 and 1681. In later years she wrote several popular novels, including *Oroonoko,* and was reputed to have had many affairs. However, Metzger suggests that these stories might have been mere rumors, probably the result of the unusual freedom she experienced as a writer. Metzger (ix) says:

The fiction she produced has been supplemented for two and a half centuries by a considerable amount of fiction about her. The facts of her life are so few yet so colorful that they quickly evoked sensational embellishment, insinuation, and speculation about her voyage to [Surinam], her love affairs, and her activities as a spy. The few facts suffice to establish Aphra Behn's opportunities for experience of the world of politics and art as larger and more varied than those open to any woman writer of the eighteenth or nineteenth century.

Aphra Behn died on April 16, 1689 and was buried in Westminster Abbey. (Behn 1973; Goreau 1980; Link 1968)

See also *Oroonoko;* Racism; Slavery

Bellamy, Edward

Author of the novel *Looking Backward, 2000–1887,* Edward Bellamy expresses his ideas for social reform through the character of Julian West, a fictional resident of both the nineteenth and twentieth centuries. West offers harsh comments about the realities of the late 1880s along with a utopian vision of the year 2000, embodying what Robert Shurter (xvii), in his introduction to a 1951 edition of the book, calls Bellamy's "intense hatred of social injustice in any form and his complete sincerity in attempting to strike a blow at the inequities of our social and economic system."

Bellamy had long been interested in social reform issues. The son of a Baptist minister, he was born on March 26, 1850, in Chicopee Falls, Massachusetts, where, according to scholar Cecelia Tichi (9) in her introduction to a 1982 edition, "all the problems involved in late-nineteenth-century industrialization were on view: crowded tenements, unemployment, sickness, strikes, an unstable population of laborers. One newspaper even reported families living in holes dug in the riverbank." Bellamy's social conscience was further heightened during the winter of 1868–1869 when he traveled through Europe with his cousin and began to study German socialism. Of this trip he (1951, xi) later said: "It was in the great cities of Europe and among the hovels of the peasantry that my eyes were first fully opened to the extent and consequences of 'man's inhumanity to man.'"

Upon returning to the United States, Bellamy studied law and opened his own law office, but he quit the profession after his first case, which required him to evict a widow for nonpayment of rent. He then became a newspaper journalist, first as a staff writer for the *New York Evening Post* and later as a book reviewer and editorialist for the *Springfield Daily Union* in Massachusetts. He left the *Union* in 1877 because of poor health and traveled to the Sandwich Islands, subsequently writing two short stories based on his vacation: *Deserted* in 1879 and *A Tale of the South Pacific* in 1880. Between 1878 to 1889 he published a total of 23 short stories in the leading magazines of his time, including *Atlantic Monthly* and *Harper's*. He also continued to write editorials wherein, according to Tichi (Bellamy 1982, 11), he "analyzed the social and economic issues that would dominate the novel *Looking Backward*."

His career as a novelist began with *Six to One: A Nantucket Idyll* in 1878, followed by *The Duke of Stockbridge* in 1879 and *Dr. Heidenhoff's Process* in 1880. In 1882 he married Emma Sanderson and later fathered two children: Paul, who was born in 1884, and Marion, who was born in 1886. His novel *Looking Backward, 2000–1887* was published in 1887. It was a time of great labor unrest in the United States, and Bellamy (1951, xiii) later wrote that his novel had been intended as "a vehicle of a definite scheme of industrial reorganization." In Bellamy's idealized future society all public services have been nationalized.

This concept, called Nationalism, soon became quite popular. By 1890, after approximately 400,000 copies of *Looking Backward* had been sold, there were 162 "Nationalist Clubs," also called "Bellamy Clubs," in the United States dedicated to promoting Bellamy's social reform concepts; club members eventually formed a Nationalist political party. Bellamy himself supported the Nationalist movement through lecture tours and as editor of two periodicals, the monthly *Nationalist* (1889–1891) and the weekly *New Nation* (1891–1894).

In 1897 he published a sequel to *Looking Backward*. Entitled *Equality*, it never achieved the same level of popularity as its predecessor, perhaps because it was more of an essay on economics than a novel. *Equality* was Bellamy's last work, although two collections of essays and letters were published posthumously: *Edward Bellamy Speaks Again!* in 1937 and *Talks on Nationalism* in 1938. The author died of tuberculosis on March 22, 1898.

Without Bellamy's influence, the Nationalism movement ended soon after his death. However, *Looking Backward* continued to influence social reformers for many years. Shurter (Bellamy 1951, xv) explains that in 1935 several independent lists still noted it as one of the most influential books in America, and Tichi (Bellamy 1982, 27) says that "one century after its publication, *Looking Backward* holds its own as a work of contemporary relevance." Shurter (Bellamy 1951, xxi) believes that the novel's endurance is related to Bellamy's character, concluding that Bellamy's "life and his book have lent a dignity to reform movements, for his sincerity cannot be questioned, his high-minded intentions cannot be doubted." (Bellamy 1951, 1982; Bowman 1962, 1979, 1986; Lipow 1982)

See also Capitalism; Labor Issues; *Looking Backward, 2000–1887;* Poverty; Socialism; West, Julian

Beloved

Beloved, by Toni Morrison, is set in Kentucky and Ohio during the late nineteenth century. When the novel was first published in 1987, reviewers compared it to *Uncle Tom's Cabin,* by Harriet Beecher Stowe, because it condemns slavery. Ann Snitow of the *Village Voice* also called it "holocaust writing" because it describes atrocities committed by one race on another (Gates and Appiah 1993c, 26). Morrison based the story on a real-life incident from 1856: upon capture a runaway slave killed her child to protect it from slavery. A similar incident occurs in Aphra Behn's novel *Oroonoko,* which might be based on a true story.

The main character of *Beloved* is Sethe, a former slave, who lives with her daughter Denver in a haunted house. Their ghost is Denver's older sister, who died as a two-year-old baby. One day an old friend, Paul D, comes to stay with them, and he shouts at the ghost to go away. Mysteriously the house becomes quiet.

Later a strange twenty-year-old woman shows up at the door. Her name is Beloved, and she seems in poor health. Sethe takes her in and cares for her. Paul D considers the girl strange and soon finds himself doing things against his will. One day he starts sleeping in the backyard shed, where Beloved comes to seduce him. Meanwhile first Denver and then Sethe realize that Beloved is their ghost, somehow made into flesh, who has taken her name from the only word on her tombstone. They do not reveal Beloved's true identity to Paul D, but Sethe does tell him how her baby daughter died. As a mistreated slave Sethe ran away, and when her white master came for her, she tried to kill her children to keep them safe from his cruelties. Sethe's two boys survived their mother's attack, as did her infant,

Denver. But the two-year-old child died because Sethe had sliced her neck with a handsaw. Sethe was arrested for the crime but later set free.

Paul D cannot handle this truth, and he leaves the house. Beloved immediately takes over, demanding that Sethe wait on her all day long. Happy to have her daughter and guilty over the past, Sethe obliges. Eventually Denver becomes worried about her mother, and she tells another woman about her troubles. That woman tells another and another, and soon thirty women are gathered to drive the ghost from Sethe's house. They arrive to pray there just as a white man drives up in his buggy. Sethe and Beloved are on the doorstep; Beloved is naked and pregnant. Suddenly Sethe flashes back to the time when another white man came to take her child away. She runs toward the man with a knife, but the women stop her. The ghost disappears, and later Paul D returns to comfort a grieving Sethe. When she says that she has lost her "best thing," he responds: "You your best thing, Sethe. You are" (Morrison 1987, 272–273).

Scholar Trudier Harris believes that this ending reflects the novel's main theme, which relates to personal worth. In an essay entitled "Escaping Slavery but Not Its Images," Harris (Gates and Appiah 1993c, 340) says: "Making another human being one's own 'best thing,' then, is ultimately to devolve into a condition worse than slavery. . . . Human freedom, finally, is not about ownership or possession; it is about responsibility, caretaking, and . . . [grace]."

Harris points out that in stressing this theme, *Beloved* uses a great deal of monetary/coin imagery. Moreover,

> the ownership-subservience tied to the coinage imagery occurs at important decision-making points in the novel, where characters have the option of moving forward to the future or returning to the past. All of these points presumably occur where human interaction is voluntary rather than forced, yet the characters

frequently continue the forced interactions of previous conditions. Thus the question becomes one of how to confront the past, make one's peace with it, and move on into the future. (339–340)

It is therefore interesting to note that, whereas in the past Sethe attacked her children to spare them from the whites, by the end of the novel she is able to attack the white man himself. (Gates and Appiah 1993c; Morrison 1987)

See also Behn, Aphra; Feminism; Morrison, Toni; *Oroonoko;* Racism; Sethe; Slavery

Berger, Thomas

Novelist Thomas Louis Berger uses irony and parody to point out how human thought influences action. As Berger biographer Brooks Landon (1989, 118) explains:

Berger's novels strongly suggest that many of the problems of human existence stem from . . . verbal constructs and from the consequent confusion of language with the referential world. . . . Consequently, [his] novels focus not so much on ideas or themes (although they swell with both) as on the relationship between language and thought. . . . Again and again, Berger's novels find new ways to suggest that the structures and institutions that order and give meaning to existence are much less important than the ways we talk about them, and that the ways we talk about those organizing beliefs have inevitably been designed by someone to influence the perception and judgment of someone else.

Born in Cincinnati, Ohio, on July 20, 1924, Berger grew up in Lockland, Ohio. He attended two years of college before leaving school to enlist in the army. His tour of duty, which lasted from 1943 to 1946, took him to England, France, and Germany. When he returned to the United States, he finished his education at the University of Cincinnati, receiving his B.A. in 1948. That same year he moved to New York and became a librarian at the Rand School of Social Science. He also attended writers' workshops and began taking graduate classes in English at Columbia University. In 1951 he worked as a staff member of the *New York Times Index,* and in 1952 he became a copy editor for *Popular Science Monthly.* The following year he left his job to become a freelance copy editor and proofreader.

His first novel, entitled *Crazy in Berlin,* was published in 1958. According to Landon (1989, 19), it focuses on a German American named Reinhart who is upset over German atrocities against the Jews during World War II and realizes "that nazism was a human rather than a German phenomenon." A sequel to *Crazy in Berlin,* entitled *Reinhart in Love,* was published in 1962.

Two years later Berger published his most famous work, *Little Big Man,* which concerns the plight of the Plains Indians in the post–Civil War United States. In discussing this novel, which was made into a movie in 1970, Landon (31) quotes scholar L. L. Lee as observing: "This is a most American novel. Not just in its subject, its setting, its story (these are common matters), but in its thematic structures, in its dialectic: savagery and civilization, indeed, but also the virgin land and the city, nature and the machine, individualism and community, democracy and hierarchy, innocence and knowledge, all the divisive and unifying themes of the American experience, or, more precisely, of the American 'myth.'"

Berger's subsequent works include two more sequels to *Crazy in Berlin,* entitled *Vital Parts* (1970) and *Reinhart's Women* (1981), as well as the novels *Killing Time* (1967), about a mass murderer, and *Arthur Rex* (1978), which concerns Arthurian legend. Berger also parodied detective and spy novels, respectively, in *Who Is Teddy Villanova?* (1977) and *Nowhere* (1985). In late 1997 he was reported to be working on a sequel to *Little Big Man.* (Landon 1989)

See also *Little Big Man;* Native American Issues; Racism

Beyond Our Power

Beyond Our Power

The Norwegian play *Over Aevne* (Beyond Our Power), also translated as *Beyond Human Power* or *Beyond Human Might,* was written in two parts, the first in 1883 and the second in 1895. Its author, Björnstjerne Björnson, was a poet, playwright, novelist, and politician who wrote his country's national anthem, "Ja, vi elsker dette landet" (Yes, We Love This Country), in 1859.

According to Björnson translator Edwin Björkman (Björnson 1916, 12), Björnson wrote both parts of *Beyond Our Power* to show, as one of the play's characters says, "that the day will come when mankind must discover that there lies more greatness and poetry in what is natural and possible—however insignificant it may frequently appear—than in the world's whole store of supernaturalism, from the first sun-myth down to the latest sermon preached about it."

The first part of *Beyond Our Power* focuses on the limits of organized religion. Its main characters are Pastor Adolph Sang and his wife, Clara, who does not believe in her husband's ability to perform miracles because he cannot improve her health. However, when his prayers appear to divert a landslide so that it misses his church, she accepts that miracles can happen and is cured. Overcome by the power of what has happened, she and her husband die in each other's arms.

The second part of *Beyond Our Power* is a sequel to the first, but it focuses on Adolph's son and daughter, depicting life in their valley village. According to scholar Harold Larson (1944, 140), the play is a wish for "social peace," that depicts "with stark simplicity the deep social cleavage in the capitalistic world between the slaves of industry living miserably in a sunless valley and the masters of industry dwelling luxuriously upon the sunlit heights." He adds that "arbitration was hinted at in the play by a deputation of workers who spoke of future legislation to provide for the settlement of disputes. But the poet's own program for industrial peace was only visionary socialism, including new inventions to make life more agreeable" (1944, 140).

Björkman (Björnson 1916, 13) believes that *Beyond Our Power, Part Two* "did for social superstition what the earlier play had done for that element in religion which Björnson had come to regard as lying 'beyond the limits of man.' It is one of the most powerful portrayals of the modern struggle between capital and labour which western literature has produced so far." (Björnson 1916; Larson 1944)

See also Björnson, Björnstjerne; Capitalism; Religion

Bibbett, Billy

In Ken Kesey's 1962 novel *One Flew over the Cuckoo's Nest,* 31-year-old Billy Bibbett is a patient in a mental hospital controlled by Nurse Ratched, a friend of his mother's. Both women are emasculating and treat Billy like a child. Consequently, he stutters and is afraid to leave the hospital even though he is sane. When he finally begins to gain strength, flout authority, and express his sexuality, Nurse Ratched ridicules him so severely that he commits suicide. Billy is a victim of a society that requires the suppression of natural urges. (Kesey 1964)

See also Kesey, Ken; *One Flew over the Cuckoo's Nest*; Ratched, Nurse

Biglow Papers, The

The Biglow Papers is a series of satirical poetry by American poet, essayist, and abolitionist James Russell Lowell. The first half of the series was published in the *Boston Courier* newspaper from 1846 to 1848 and in book form in 1849. The second half was published in the *Atlantic Monthly* during the Civil War and in book form in 1867. All of the poems oppose slavery. Therefore, when they appeared in print, they created much controversy, particularly in the South. For example, one critic wrote, "Mr. Lowell is one of the most rabid of the Abolition fanatics; and no Southerner who does not wish to be insulted, and at the same time revolted by a bigotry the most obstinately blind and deaf, should ever touch a volume by this author" (Wortham 1977, xxviii).

Björnstjerne Björnson, the Norwegian poet, novelist, and political leader (Corbis-Bettmann)

Each poem is accompanied by a lengthy, satirical introduction by a fictitious scholar. The verse itself is also written by a fictitious character, the poet Hosea Biglow, in rustic New England dialect. For example, one of these poems says: "Slavery aint o' nary color, / 'Taint the hide thet makes it wus, / All it keers fer in a feller / 'S jest to make him fill its pus" (52). In addition to this antislavery position, *The Biglow Papers* opposes the Mexican War and other forms of U.S. expansionism that would promote the spread of slavery. Another fictitious character, Birdofredum Sawin, reports on the war in several "letters." Lowell also used satire to criticize politicians, editors, and the upper classes. (Duberman 1966; Wortham 1977)

See also Lowell, James Russell; Racism; Slavery

Björnson, Björnstjerne

Poet, playwright, and novelist Björnstjerne Martinius Björnson was born on December 8, 1832, in Kvikne, Norway. He grew up in his country's Romsdal district on the Atlantic coast, but when he was 11, his father, a pastor who valued education, sent him away to school in the nearby town of Molde. At age 18 Björnson began attending a university preparatory school in Christiania (now Oslo), Norway. There he wrote his first play, a historical saga, when he was only 20. The Christiania Theater decided to produce his work; however, feeling that his play was inferior, Björnson asked them not to perform it. Four years later he produced what was, according to scholar and translator Edwin Borkman (Björnson 1916, 4), "his first dramatic work of lasting value," a historical play about the Norwegian civil wars entitled *Between the Battles* (Mellem Slagene), also translated as *Between Blows*.

Björnson would go on to write 20 more plays between 1858 and 1909, including *En handske* (The Gauntlet, 1883), which Borkman (9) calls "one of the main impulses for the Scandinavian feminist movement," and a two-part play entitled *Beyond Our Power* (part one in 1883 and part two in 1895), which criticizes modern spirituality and capitalism, respectively. In addition, he wrote novels critical of certain aspects of Norwegian society; for example, *Det flager i byen og på havnen* (The Heritage of the Kurts, 1884) attacks Christianity, and *På Guds veje* (In God's Way, 1889) focuses on the educational system. In 1903 he won the Nobel Prize in literature.

In addition to writing plays and novels, Björnson worked to revive Norwegian patriotism by encouraging public interest in Norwegian history and legends. As director of the Bergen Theater from 1857 to 1859 and the Christiania Theater from 1863 to 1867, he tried to eliminate Danish influence in Norwegian theater. He was also Norway's national poet, and in 1859 he wrote his country's national anthem, "Ja, vi elsker dette landet" (Yes, We Love This Country). A passionate supporter of Norwegian causes, he wrote articles advocating Norway's political independence from Sweden, with which it had been united since 1814, and according to scholars Eva and Einar Haugen (1978), Björnson was "Norway's most fiery orator and platform personality" (3). The Haugens explain that Björnson "never sought or held office, but throughout his life he was a powerful political force, in the forefront of every fray, opinionated and stubborn, impulsive and generous. The adulation of his admirers and the venom of his opponents left him untouched, as Norway's 'uncrowned king.' Hotly detested and warmly admired, he could not leave anyone indifferent, but in the long run he won respect for his honesty and his unswerving faith in progress and the future of his country" (3). (Björnson 1916; Haugen and Haugen 1978)

See also *Beyond Our Power; Capitalism; Feminism; Religion*

Bleak House

An extremely large and complicated work, *Bleak House,* by British author Charles Dickens, criticizes the law for causing needless suffering in Victorian society. It also depicts social reformers and philanthropists as being more interested in problems in distant lands than in problems in their native England. For example, a minor character, Mrs. Jellyby, is so devoted to African charities that she neglects her own children; Mrs. Pardiggle is a social worker whose children are equally miserable.

The novel was first published in serialized form, appearing in monthly installments in the author's own magazine, *Household Words,* from March 1852 to September 1853. Set around 1850, its story takes place primarily in London, where the High Court of Chancery is hearing an elaborate legal case, Jarndyce and Jarndyce, that has dragged on for years. About this case, an omniscient narrator says:

The parties to it understand it least; but it has been observed that no two Chancery lawyers can talk about it for five minutes, without coming to a total disagreement as to all the premises. . . . Scores of persons have deliriously found themselves made parties in Jarndyce and Jarndyce, without knowing how or why; whole families have inherited legendary hatreds with the suit. The little plaintiff or defendant, who was promised a new rocking-horse when Jarndyce and Jarndyce should be settled, has grown up, possessed himself of a real horse, and trotted away into the other world. Fair wards of court have faded into mothers and grandmothers; a long procession of Chancellors has come and gone out; the legion of bills in the suit have been transformed into mere bills of mortality; there are not three Jarndyces left upon the earth perhaps, since old Tom Jarndyce in despair blew his brains out at a coffee-house in Chancery Lane; but Jarndyce and Jarndyce still drags its dreary length before the Court, perennially hopeless. (Dickens 1987a, 4)

One of the remaining parties in this case is John Jarndyce, who is appointed guardian of Esther Summerson after the death of the aunt who raised her. Esther travels to Jarndyce's home, Bleak House, in the company of his two other wards, Ada Clare and Richard Carstone. They are also parties in the Jarndyce and Jarndyce lawsuit, as is Lady Deadlock, wife of an aristocrat. One day Lady Deadlock receives legal papers related to the case, and she recognizes the handwriting of its copyist as that of a former lover, Captain Hawdon. Lady Deadlock had an illegitimate child with this man before marrying her husband, and no one knows her shame. Without revealing her past, she asks her attorney, Mr. Tulkinghorn, to find the scribe. Tulkinghorn soon discovers that the man, who went by the name Nemo, died penniless and alone. Shortly thereafter Lady Deadlock dresses like her maid and visits a street sweeper, Jo, who knew Nemo. She talks to Jo about her former lover's life among the poor. She also finds Nemo's grave.

Meanwhile Mr. Tulkinghorn, who is a corrupt and evil lawyer, has become suspicious of Lady Deadlock's interest in Nemo. Eventually he discovers Nemo's true identity and threatens to tell Lady Deadlock's husband, Sir Leicester, about her affair. By this time the woman has learned that, although her sister told her otherwise, her illegitimate child survived its birth and is still alive. That child is Esther. Lady Deadlock goes to her daughter and reveals their relationship, telling her to keep it a secret from Sir Leicester. Lady Deadlock is desperate to keep her husband from finding out about the affair. Therefore, when Mr. Tulkinghorn is found dead, the reader suspects Lady Deadlock of killing him. The novel then takes on elements of a classic murder mystery; several minor characters had reason to kill Tulkinghorn.

Afraid that she will be accused of the crime, Lady Deadlock leaves a note for her husband, confessing her past and professing her innocence, and she flees. Upon finding the note, her husband has a stroke. Afterward he hires a detective, Inspector Bucket, to track down his wife and offer her his forgiveness. Esther accompanies Bucket in his search, and eventually they find Lady Deadlock dead on her lover's grave. By this time Bucket has learned that Lady Deadlock was innocent of Tulkinghorn's murder. Instead, the deed was committed by her maid, Hortense, whom Tulkinghorn used to gather information about her mistress's affair.

After discovering her mother's body, Esther falls ill. She is cared for by Allan Woodcourt, a doctor she has known for some time. He asks Esther to marry him, but she refuses, explaining that she has already agreed to marry her guardian, Mr. Jarndyce. Later, however, Jarndyce realizes that Esther would be happier with Allan Woodcourt and releases her from their engagement. Meanwhile, Jarndyce's other two wards, Ada and Richard, have fallen in love and secretly married. Richard is a weak man who has tried several careers but been unable to stick with anything very long. He stakes his future on the Jarndyce and Jarndyce legal case, whose settlement he hopes will bring him a large inheritance. But when the case is finally resolved, Robert discovers that legal fees have exhausted the fortunes of both sides. Already sick from worry, he dies upon hearing this news. Shortly thereafter Ada gives birth to his son.

The novel concludes with Esther's description of her happy life as Allan's wife, seven years later. Throughout *Bleak House* Dickens intersperses his omniscient narration with Esther's first-person accounts of the story. (Dickens 1987a)

See also Dickens, Charles; Jellyby, Mrs.; Justice; Pardiggle, Mrs.; Poverty

Block

A character in Franz Kafka's 1925 novel *Der Prozess* (The Trial), Block is a tradesman who is awaiting trial before a mysterious court that operates outside of the traditional legal system. His case has dragged on for over five years despite his best efforts to end it. As a result, he has lost his business and his life's savings. He lives at the house of his official lawyer, who treats him badly and gives him little hope of success. At the same time Block secretly employs five disreputable, or "pettifogging," lawyers to attempt to influence the court, which is corrupt and unjust. (Kafka 1964)

See also Kafka, Franz; *Trial, The*

Blount, Gil

The character Gil Blount appears in Richard Wright's 1953 novel *The Outsider,* which concerns racism and communism in the United States during the early 1950s. Blount is a white Communist leader who attempts to recruit a black man, Cross Damon. In doing so, Blount demonstrates his misunderstanding of the black race in general and of Damon in particular. He also teaches Damon that the Communist Party is not about ideology but about power. Blount relishes his power and wields it to demoralize others. After watching him, Damon thinks to himself:

This thing of power . . . why had he overlooked it till now? . . . Well, he had not been in those areas of life where power had held forth or reigned openly. Excitement grew in him; he felt that he was beginning to look at the emotional skeleton of man. He understood now the hard Communist insistence on strict obedience in things that had no direct relation to politics proper or to their keeping tight grasp of the reins of power. Once a thorough system of sensual power as a way of life had gotten hold of a man's heart to the extent that it ordered and defined all of his relations, it was bound to codify and arrange all of his life's activities into one organic unity. This systematizing of the sensual impulses of man to be a god must needs be jealous of all rival systems of sensuality, even those found in poetry and music. . . . And now . . . he could understand why the Communists, instead of shooting the capitalists and bankers as they had so ardently sworn that they would do when they came to power, made instead with blood in their eyes straight for the school teachers, priests, writers, artists, poets, musicians, and the deposed bourgeois governmental rulers as the men who held for them the deadliest of threats to their keeping and extending their power. (Wright 1993b, 269)

Blount is a cold-hearted man, and in the end Damon decides to kill him. While Blount is fighting with a racist fascist, Damon clubs them both in the head. (Wright 1993b)

See also Communism; *Outsider, The;* Racism; Wright, Richard

Bluest Eye, The

Published in 1970 and set in 1941, *The Bluest Eye* is the first novel of author Toni Morrison, whose work focuses on black and/or feminist themes. It is the story of a group of black girls growing up in a United States that values white skin and blond hair. The main character, 11-year-old Pecola Breedlove, prays for blue eyes, so that she will be beautiful.

At the same time the story's first-person narrator, a younger girl named Claudia MacTeer, does not accept society's idea of beauty. Whenever someone gives her a traditional white doll, she destroys it, saying: "I had only one desire: to dismember it. To see of what it was made, to discover the dearness, to find the beauty, the desirability that had escaped me, but apparently only me. Adults, older girls, shops, magazines, newspapers, window signs—all the world had agreed that a blue-eyed, yellow-haired, pink-skinned doll was what every girl child treasured" (Morrison 1993, 20–21).

Claudia and her sister, Frieda, like Pecola, but Pecola does not like herself. She believes that she and the rest of her family are too ugly to have value. In fact, many people in the town consider the Breedloves ugly. Claudia explains why:

You looked at them and wondered why they were so ugly; you looked closely and could not find the source. Then you realized that it came from conviction, their conviction. It was as though some mysterious all-knowing master had given each one a cloak of ugliness to wear, and they had each accepted it without question. The master had said, "You are ugly people." They had looked about themselves and saw nothing to contradict the statement; saw, in fact, support for it leaning at them from every billboard, every movie, every glance. "Yes," they had said. "You are right." And they took the ugliness in their hands, threw it as a mantle over them, and went about the world with it. (39)

Pecola's father has let this ugliness destroy his soul. Whereas as a boy he was kind, now he is angry. He drinks heavily and fights with his wife. One day he rapes Pecola. She becomes pregnant, but the baby is born too early and dies. Afterward Pecola goes insane, convinced that her eyes have become blue.

Toni Morrison says that in the early 1960s, when she wrote *The Bluest Eye,* many blacks wanted to look like whites. She explains that her work was an attempt to explore how a child might learn this type of "racial self-loathing" (210). However, in a 1993 afterword to the novel, she reports that her message was poorly received, saying, "With very few exceptions, the initial publication of *The Bluest Eye* was like Pecola's life: dismissed, trivialized, misread" (216). For this reason, scholars often compare *The Bluest Eye* with Zora Neale Hurston's *Their Eyes Were Watching God,* which was similarly dismissed after its 1937 publication. Like Morrison, Hurston depicts black characters who want to appear white. (Gates and Appiah 1993c; Morrison 1993)

See also Breedlove, Cholly and Pauline; Feminism; Morrison, Toni; Racism

Bostonians, The

The Bostonians, by Henry James, concerns the U.S. suffragette movement during the 1870s. The novel criticizes some of the ideas behind the fight for women's rights and questions the motives of its social reformers. The story begins when a Bostonian feminist, Olive Chancellor, meets her Mississippi cousin, Basil Ransom, for the first time. The young woman is unimpressed with her guest, who has been practicing law in New York. Nonetheless, she invites him to a suffragette meeting that evening. He is against the women's rights movement, but he decides to attend as an amusement. Once there, he meets Verena Tarrant, the daughter of a well-known healer. When Verena is asked to speak at the meeting, both Olive and Basil find themselves physically attracted to the beautiful young woman. After Basil regretfully returns to New York, Olive convinces Verena to become her protégée. She influences Verena's opinions and guides her into becoming a regular speaker for the suffragette movement. She also makes Verena vow never to wed. But despite her friend's vow, Olive fears that Verena might succumb to a man's charms. Her fears intensify during a speaking engagement in New York. Basil Ransom shows up at the meeting, and Olive subsequently learns that he and Verena have been corresponding with each other. In fact, Verena is the one who invited him to the meeting, hoping to convert him to the cause. Shortly after the meeting Basil and Verena go on a date.

During their outing Verena learns Basil's views on the women's movement. Basil not only believes that women are inferior to men, but also suggests that men need to fight against the "feminization" of the world. He says:

The whole generation is womanized; the masculine tone is passing out of the world; it's a feminine, a nervous hysterical, chattering, canting age, an age of hollow phrases and false delicacy and exaggerated solicitudes and coddled sensibilities, which, if we don't soon look out, will usher in the reign of mediocrity, of the feeblest and flattest and the most pretentious that has ever been. The masculine character, the ability to dare and endure, to know and yet not fear reality, to look the world in the face and take it for what it is—a very queer and partly very base mixture—that is what I want to preserve, or rather, as I may say, to recover; and I must tell you that I don't in the least care what becomes of you ladies while I make the attempt! (James 1956, 343)

However, Basil also says: "I don't want to destroy you, any more than I want to save you. There has been far too much talk about you, and I want to leave you alone altogether. My interest is in my own sex; yours evidently can look after itself. That's all I want to save" (342). At the same time he expresses contempt for the "new old maids," such as Olive Chancellor, who have too little to do and must "wander about the world crying out for a vocation" (345). He points out that Verena has been manipulated by Olive, explaining: "You always want to please someone, and now you go lecturing about the country, trying to provoke demonstrations, in order to please Miss Chancellor. . . . It isn't *you*, the least in the world, but an inflated little figure . . . whom you have invented and set on its feet, pulling strings, behind it, to make it move and speak, while you try to conceal and efface yourself there" (346).

Upset over their conversation, Verena leaves Basil and returns to Boston. Later he travels there to see her. He had hoped that his discussion with her in New York might have changed her beliefs. Instead, he finds her rehearsing an important speech for the suffragette movement. Basil asks her to marry him, but she is indecisive because she knows that it will necessitate her abandoning her suffragette work. She goes off by herself to think about the proposal, and no one will tell Basil where she is. On the night of her big speech Basil goes to the auditorium and tries to get backstage to talk to her, but Olive has told the guard not to admit him. Meanwhile Verena has noticed Basil in the auditorium and realizes that she cannot speak in front of him. She refuses to go onstage. The crowd gets angry, and the organizers of the event plead for her to change her mind. Instead, she and Basil slip out of the auditorium, intending to get married. A defeated Olive stays behind to speak in Verena's place. The novel ends with Verena saying, "Ah, now I am glad!" However, at the same time the omniscient narrator notes: "But though she was glad, . . . beneath her hood, she was in tears. It is to be feared that with the union, so far from brilliant, into which she was about to enter, these were not the last she was destined to shed" (464).

The Bostonians was not well received when it was originally published, first as a 1885–1886 serial in *Century Illustrated Magazine* and then as a three-volume book in 1886. Some readers objected to Olive Chancellor's apparent lesbianism, and many Bostonians criticized the novel's portrayal of their city's society. According to scholar Irving Howe (vii), writing in a 1956 introduction to the work, the book's failure "hurt and bewildered James" and "may have hastened his turn from the social novel," which ended "his earlier ambition to become the American Balzac." However, Howe (vii) believes that James made the right decision in abandoning social protest, saying that the author "lacked that passionate absorption in the worlds of business and poetics which a social novelist must have." (Edel 1963; James 1956)

See also Balzac, Honoré de; Chancellor, Olive; Feminism; James, Henry; Ransom, Basil; Tarrant, Verena

Boulle, Pierre

French novelist Pierre Boulle is best known for two works, *Le Pont de la rivière Kwaï* (Bridge over the River Kwai, 1952) and *La Planète des singes* (Planet of the Apes, 1963). The latter is a science fiction novel that comments on human nature and society's shortcomings. Boulle was born on February 20, 1912, in Avignon, France. He spent several years of his adult life in Southeast Asia, where he was a planter and soldier, and wrote several novels based on his experiences there. Boulle died on January 30, 1994, in Paris, France. (Frackman 1996)

See also *Planet of the Apes;* Science Fiction and Fantasy

Bradbury, Ray

Raymond Douglas Bradbury has written articles, essays, and science fiction stories and novels. Some of his fiction contains elements of social protest. For example, his novel *Fahrenheit 451* (1953) depicts a future United States where people are forbidden to read books and individuality is discouraged.

Born in Waukegan, Illinois, on August 22, 1920, Bradbury was 27 when his first book of short stories, entitled *Dark Carnival,* was published. His second collection, *The Martian Chronicles* (1950), is considered a science fiction classic and was made into a movie in 1966. Other story collections include *The Illustrated Man* (1951), *The Machineries of Joy* (1964), and *I Sing the Body Electric!* (1969). He also wrote the screenplay for the movie *Moby Dick,* filmed by John Huston in 1956. Bradbury's other novels include *Dandelion Wine* (1957) and *Something Wicked This Way Comes* (1985). Bradbury currently lives in southern California, where he continues to write both fiction and nonfiction. (Nolan 1975)

See also Censorship; *Fahrenheit 451;* Science Fiction and Fantasy

Brave New World

Published in 1932, *Brave New World,* by Aldous Huxley, is the author's view of the future, based on the misuse of science and a breakdown of morality. The novel opens in the Central London Hatchery and Conditioning Center, where human beings are created in test tubes. In the laboratory fetuses are manipulated to make them fit into a specific intellectual category, from clever Alphas down to dim-witted Epsilons. Laboratory officials also use mind-control techniques and electric shocks to condition people to fit their assigned roles.

One day a center psychologist, Bernard Marx, takes a vacation to a Savage Reservation in New Mexico. He wants to study people who have not been created in test tubes and who live in nature. Bernard's world has become sterile and artificial, and he doesn't feel as though he fits in there. Accompanying Bernard on his trip is Lenina Crowne, a woman who likes modern conveniences and is dependent on soma, a stupor-inducing drug sanctioned by her society. She complains about the reservation's lack of sanitation and is repulsed by its old people, who have wrinkles and missing teeth. One old person, Linda, particularly offends her. When Linda meets the visitors, she rushes up to hug them, and Bernard realizes that she is the former girlfriend of his boss. While touring the reserva-

tion with him years ago, she became lost and was left behind. At the time she was pregnant, and because the reservation had no abortion centers she was forced to bear the child, whom she named John.

John is now a charming young man, and Bernard receives permission to bring him and his mother back to his modern world. John is excited, envisioning a "brave new world" with glorious people in it (Huxley 1989, 141). He has read the works of William Shakespeare and has an old-fashioned view of the world. Therefore, he is later shocked to discover that modern people engage in promiscuous sexual behavior, do not quote poetry, and spend most of their time in a haze. His own mother, Linda, uses massive doses of soma to keep herself in a stupor. When she dies from her drug use, John tries to stop people from getting their soma at a local dispensing center. He is brought before an official who tells him that, unlike Shakespeare's time,

> the world's stable now. People are happy;
> they get what they want, and they never
> want what they can't get. They're well off;
> they're safe; they're never ill; they're not
> afraid of death; they're blissfully ignorant
> of passion and old age; they're plagued
> with no mothers or fathers; they've got no
> wives, or children, or lovers to feel
> strongly about; they're so conditioned that
> they practically can't help behaving as they
> ought to behave. And if anything should
> go wrong, there's *soma.* Which you go and
> chuck out of the window in the name of
> liberty, Mr. Savage. *Liberty!* (226)

Because Bernard was in charge of John, the older man is exiled to Iceland after the young man's outbreak. John goes off to live by himself at an abandoned lighthouse. But the news media have been fascinated with his activities ever since he arrived in the modern world, and they refuse to leave him alone. Eventually John realizes he no longer wants to live in such a cruel, immoral world. He hangs himself in the lighthouse tower.

In writing about this work, Huxley says

that he regrets John's death but believes that after seeing the modern world, he would have been unable to return to the reservation. However, in an introduction to his work, Huxley (ix–x) adds that if he were to rewrite *Brave New World,* he would create a third choice for the young man:

> Between the utopian and the primitive horns of his dilemma would lie the possibility of sanity—a possibility already actualized, to some extent, in a community of exiles and refugees from the Brave New World, living within the borders of the Reservation. In this community economics would be decentralist and . . . cooperative. Science and technology would be used as though, like the Sabbath, they had been made for man, not (as at present and still more so in the Brave New World) as though man were to be adapted and enslaved to them.

Huxley (xi) also explains that the theme of his novel "is not the advancement of science as such; it is the advancement of science as it affects human individuals." He (xi) adds:

> The triumphs of physics, chemistry and engineering are tacitly taken for granted. The only scientific advances to be specifically described are those involving the application to human beings of the results of future research in biology, physiology, and psychology. It is only by means of the sciences of life that the quality of life can be radically changed. The sciences of matter can be applied in such a way that they will destroy life or make the living of it impossibly complex and uncomfortable; but, unless used as instruments by the biologists and psychologists, they can do nothing to modify the natural forms and expressions of life itself. The release of atomic energy marks a great revolution in human history, but not (unless we blow ourselves to bits and so put an end to history) the final and most searching revolution.

For this reason, *Brave New World* has more to say about the moral implications of scientific discovery than about its physical or technological impact. It also contrasts the sterility of the modern world with the passionate emotion that existed in Shakespeare's time. (Atkins 1968; Brander 1970; Huxley 1989; Watts 1969)

See also Censorship; Crowne, Lenina; Huxley, Aldous; Marx, Bernard; Science Fiction and Fantasy

Breedlove, Cholly and Pauline

Cholly and Pauline Breedlove are the parents of 11-year-old Pecola, the main character in Toni Morrison's 1970 novel *The Bluest Eye*. Like their daughter, they are blacks who believe themselves ugly because of their blackness. Pauline Breedlove finds her only joy in the white household where she works as a servant. The place is clean and orderly, and her employers praise her for keeping it that way. Caught up in this world, gradually "she neglected her house, her children, her man— they were like the afterthoughts one has just before sleep, the early-morning and late-evening edges of her day, the dark edges that made the daily life with [her white family] lighter, more delicate, more lovely" (Morrison 1993, 127). But whereas Pauline tries to escape ugliness, Cholly falls deeper into it. He becomes an abusive alcoholic, and one day he rapes his own daughter. He then disappears, leaving his family in ruin. (Gates and Appiah 1993c; Morrison 1993)

See also *Bluest Eye, The;* Morrison, Toni

Breytenbach, Breyten

South African author Breyten Breytenbach expresses antiapartheid views in poems, essays, and nonfiction books written in his native language of Afrikaans. Born on September 16, 1939, when he was 20 he left South Africa and eventually settled in Paris, where he became a painter and poet. He then married a Vietnamese woman, who was labeled "nonwhite" by the South African government. As such, she was not allowed to accompany her husband when he visited Johannesburg,

South Africa, in 1964 to accept a literary award. Breytenbach spoke out against this act of discrimination, turning it into an international incident, and he became involved in antiapartheid politics. In 1972 he again visited South Africa, and this time the government allowed his wife to accompany him, but only for three months.

In 1975 Breytenbach once again traveled to South Africa, this time using a false name and passport. The reason for his visit is unclear. However, the government arrested him for terrorist activities and sentenced him to seven years in prison. This experience led him to write three books: *'n Seisoen in die Paradys* (A Season in Paradise, 1981), about his 1972 visit to South Africa; *Mouroir: Bespieelende notas van 'n roman* (Mouroir: Mirrornotes of a Novel, 1984), which is a collection of essays about freedom; and *The True Confessions of an Albino Terrorist* (1985), about his life in prison. He also published a collection of poems, *In Africa Even the Flies Are Happy: Selected Poems, 1964–77* in 1986, and in 1993 he again discussed apartheid in his book *Return to Paradise.* (Breytenbach 1994; Jolly 1996)

See also Apartheid; Exiles; Racism; *Season in Paradise, A*

Broad and Alien Is the World

Ciro Alegría's novel *El mundo es ancho y ajeno* (Broad and Alien Is the World), published in both Spanish and English editions in 1941, depicts the suffering of Peruvian Indians in the valley village of Rumi between 1912 and 1926. Rumi borders the property of a nonnative landowner, Don Alvaro Amenabar y Roldan, who wants to take over the village so he can enslave its inhabitants on his ranch or at his nearby mining operation. He files a lawsuit falsely claiming that the Indians have built their village on his land, then bribes the judge, the regional governor, and many of Rumi's witnesses so that he wins the case. When the judge orders the Indians to vacate their land, they consider fighting, but they decide to relocate to the neighboring mountainside. Meanwhile they begin the process of appealing their case to Peru's Supreme Court.

However, the mountainside is rocky and steep, and the Indians find life in their new village difficult. Discouraged, many of them leave to find work elsewhere. They quickly become enslaved through debt to cruel nonnative bosses, who rape the women and force the men to gather rubber in the Amazon jungle or pick leaves on coca plantations. Many sicken and die from malaria. Others are bitten by poisonous snakes. But those who remain in the village do not fare much better. Having spent most of their money on legal fees, they have little left to buy supplies. When Don Amenabar steals their cattle, the Indians' well-respected mayor, an old man named Rosendo Maqui, tries to retrieve one of the village bulls and is arrested for cattle theft. Amenabar bribes the newspaper to say that Rosendo is in league with a notorious bandit, Fiero Vasquez, whose wife lives in Rosendo's village. Rosendo therefore has little hope of receiving justice. He has "always despised" the law because he has experienced it "only in the form of abuses and taxes" (Alegría 1941, 326), and he shares the belief of another villager that "as soon as a rich man starts talking about rights that means something crooked is afoot, and if law exists, it is only to do [the Indians] harm" (14).

In fact, Amenabar's attorney delays the case so that Rosendo must spend weeks in prison without a hearing. His living conditions are filthy, and the four walls of his small cell close in on him. Increasingly despondent, he thinks that "no prisoner, however guilty he may be, but feels in the [prison] wall the hardness of the human heart. . . . The sorriest animal, the most insignificant insect, can use his legs or wings freely, while man, who considers himself the superior of all, heartlessly buries his fellow man in a gloomy hole" (326).

Rosendo soon discovers that he is not the only Indian who has been falsely imprisoned. Others offer him their stories of hardship and abuse, and one prisoner, a blacksmith named Jacinto Prieto, argues that the president of the Republic of Peru cannot possibly know about the injustices being perpetrated against his country's poor Indians. Prieto smuggles a letter to the president and receives a polite reply, but the injustices continue. Prieto rails against the government, saying, "There is no justice, there is no country. Where are all the upright men the nation needs? They are all out for what they can get, bootlickers at the orders of the mighty. A rich man can kill and nothing happens to him. A poor man gives someone a stiff punch and they accuse him of attempted homicide. Where is the equality before the law?" (377).

Meanwhile the bandit Vasquez has learned about Amenabar's treachery, and he decides to take revenge on everyone who helped the landowner destroy the village of Rumi. Vasquez's men, some of whom are former villagers, rob the governor and rape his daughter. They also kill a local peddler who was an informant for Amenabar. They attack Amenabar's ranch, but although some of the overseers there are killed, the landowner himself escapes harm. Amenabar calls on the military for help, and eventually Vasquez is captured. He is placed in the same prison cell as Rosendo; the two are to be tried together for crimes against the government. When Vasquez escapes, the prison guards beat Rosendo, who refused to accompany Vasquez. Rosendo dies from the beating.

Shortly thereafter Benito Castro, whom Rosendo raised as his own son, returns to Rumi. Castro has been away in the military for many years and was unaware of Amenabar's treachery. He is outraged to find that his former village has been left in ruins, while its people try to exist on a difficult mountainside. Castro helps the villagers dynamite and drain a mountain lake to create more arable land. He also convinces them to set aside superstition and relocate their houses to a better, yet supposedly haunted site. When some of the villagers accuse him of going against tradition, Castro says that "the only reason he advocated progress was because in his opinion it was only through progress that the Indians could free themselves from slavery and make something of themselves" (418). He argues that the landowners had succeeded specifically because they were not superstitious, adding that "people can be judged by

their beliefs" (419). Eventually the villagers agree with Castro and elect him mayor.

For a while things go well for the villagers. Then the Supreme Court decides not only that Amenabar owns Rumi but also that he owns the land the Indians now occupy on the mountainside. At this news one villager laments that "the Indian is a Christ nailed to the cross of injustice. Oh, that damned cross! Oh, cross, whose hungry arms never tire!" (423). Some want to leave the village, but Castro encourages them to fight. In an impassioned speech he says: "Have no fear of defeat for it is better to die than be a slave. Maybe the government will come to understand that injustice is not good for a country. To justify taking away the communal lands from the Indian, they say they want to develop a sense of private property in him, and they begin by taking away the only thing he's got. We're defending our lives, villagers! We're defending our land!" (425). The villagers are convinced to battle the forces coming to evict them from their land, but in the end most are killed. Castro, who has been mortally wounded, returns to his wife to urge her to leave the village. As he dies, she wonders where she will go. This question was particularly significant to the book's Peruvian author, who wrote his novel while exiled to Chile because of his political activities. (Alegría 1941; Early 1980)

See also Alegría, Ciro; Amenabar, Don Alvaro; Castro, Benito; Exiles; Justice; Maqui, Rosendo; Racism; Slavery

Bromden, Chief

Chief Bromden is the narrator of Ken Kesey's 1962 novel *One Flew over the Cuckoo's Nest*. A Native American from Oregon, he is extremely tall and strong but believes himself to be small and weak. He is a patient in a mental hospital who has endured several years of shock treatments and heavy medication. However, with the encouragement of another patient, Randall Patrick McMurphy, he stops taking his medication and gradually his insanity dissipates. Moreover, McMurphy convinces him that he is growing physically stronger every day. When a sadistic nurse arranges for

McMurphy to have brain surgery that turns him into a vegetable, Bromden kills his friend and throws some heavy equipment through a window so that he can escape the hospital. In the end it is clear that Bromden has recovered his sanity by fighting against social oppression, conformity, and injustice. (Kesey 1964)

See also Kesey, Ken; McMurphy, Randall Patrick; *One Flew over the Cuckoo's Nest*

Brown, Jonathan

A character in the 1958 novel *The Ugly American,* by William Lederer and Eugene Burdick, Jonathan Brown is a U.S. senator who travels to Southeast Asia to assess the strength of U.S. policies there. The U.S. diplomats and military personnel in the region do not want him to learn that they have been losing their fight against communism, so they trick him into believing that things are going well. They incorrectly translate statements from natives who criticize U.S. policy and encourage the senator to spend much of his time at parties and dinners rather than among the Asian people. As a result, Brown returns to the United States with the false impression that democracy is strong in Southeast Asia. (Lederer and Burdick 1958)

See also Communism; *Ugly American, The*

Brown, William Wells

Sometime during the early 1800s William Wells Brown was born a slave near Lexington, Kentucky. Eventually he was sold to a tobacco plantation in St. Louis, Missouri, and on New Year's Day 1834 he gained emancipation by running away to Cincinnati, Ohio. He then gave himself a surname in honor of the Quaker Wells Brown, who had helped him escape.

As a free man Brown was incredibly successful. He became a popular lecturer for antislavery and temperance causes, both in the United States and abroad, and was a delegate to the 1849 World Peace Congress in Paris. He was also the first African American to earn a living as a writer. He wrote 16 books; his first, an autobiography entitled *Narrative of William W. Brown, a Fugitive Slave* (1847), sold 10,000 copies in the first two years alone. His other nonfiction works include *The Black Man*

(1863), *The Negro in the American Rebellion* (1867), and *My Southern Home* (1880). He also wrote the first published novel by an African American, *Clotel* (1853); the first published play by an African American, *The Escape; or, a Leap for Freedom* (1858); and the first published travel memoir by an African American, *Three Years in Europe* (1852). He died on November 6, 1884, in Chelsea, Massachusetts. (Farrison 1969; Gates 1990; Warner 1976)

See also *Clotel;* Racism; Slavery

Bryant, William Cullen

William Cullen Bryant was a social reformer who expressed his views through journalism and poetry. Born on November 3, 1794, in Cummington, Massachusetts, he entered college at the age of 16, eventually leaving to study law on his own. He was admitted to the Massachusetts bar in 1815 and began practicing law. Ten years later he moved to New York City to become an editor for a liberal newspaper, the *New York Evening Post.* He remained in that position for 50 years, eventually becoming editor in chief and part owner of the paper. During that time he promoted many liberal causes, supporting a worker's right to strike and voicing opposition to slavery and political corruption. He died on June 12, 1878, in New York, New York. (Godwin 1967; McLean 1964; Sturges 1968)

See also *Antiquity of Freedom, The;* Slavery

Burdick, Eugene

Eugene Burdick is the author of both nonfiction and fiction books, including the 1962 novel *Fail Safe*, which concerns the Cold War between the United States and the Soviet Union. However, he is best known for his 1958 novel *The Ugly American.* Coauthored by William Lederer, the book criticizes the behavior of Americans living and working in Southeast Asia. (Lederer and Burdick 1958)

See also Lederer, William J.; *Ugly American, The*

Burgess, Anthony

Anthony Burgess is the pseudonym for British author John Anthony Burgess Wilson, who

Anthony Burgess, 1980 (Hulton-Deutsch Collection/-Corbis)

also wrote under the name Joseph Kell. Born in Manchester, England, he became an English teacher in 1946. He also worked for the Ministry of Education in England from 1948 to 1950. From 1954 to 1959 he taught in Malaya and Borneo and began writing novels. He wrote 32 in all, including *The Wanting Seed* (1962), which concerns overpopulation, and *A Clockwork Orange* (1962), about violence in society. He also wrote 16 nonfiction books, primarily biographies, autobiographies, and literary criticism, as well as a volume of poetry, 2 plays, and several musical compositions. He died on November 22, 1993, in London, England. (Burgess 1986; De Vitis 1972)

See also *Clockwork Orange, A;* Science Fiction and Fantasy

Burns, Robert

Scottish poet Robert Burns wrote about life as a common man and supported the rights of the individual. Born on January 25, 1759, in Alloway, Ayrshire, Scotland, he was the son of a poor farmer, and eventually he became a farmer himself. Nonetheless, he received some education and continued to study English literature on his own. He also began writing poems. In 1786 he self-published his first works as *Poems, Chiefly in the Scottish Dialect,* which quickly became a critical success. A national celebrity, Burns spent a few years in the city of Edinburgh before returning to farming. He continued to write verse and songs for the remainder of his life. He also protested conventional eighteenth-century religious and moral beliefs. He died on July 21, 1796, in Dumfries, Dumfriesshire, Scotland. (Daiches 1966)

See also "Man's a Man for a' That, A"

C

Camus, Albert

Algerian author Albert Camus wrote articles, plays, novels, and essays in which he explored the nature of human beings as individuals and as members of society. According to biographer Germaine Brée (1961, 8), Camus's "major preoccupation" was "the daily life of human beings, their freedom and the human justice meted out to them on this earth." This concern brought him the 1957 Nobel Prize in literature, which commended him for "his important literary production, which with clear-sighted earnestness illuminates the problems of the human conscience of our time" (5).

Brée explains that Camus's time was an era when "the age-old questions of the significance of man's odyssey on this earth were being posed anew and no new satisfactory answers were being offered. But for many young Europeans it seemed essential to find an answer to the question Why live? . . . To some the only possible justification for life was participation in some form of social and political action" (26). This was true for Camus. Born in Mondovi, Algiers, on November 7, 1913, he joined the Communist Party at the age of 21. When World War II broke out in 1939, he was a journalist for the radical newspaper *Algier-Republic,* writing about social injustices in Algiers, but he soon became involved in the French underground resistance movement against the Nazis. In 1943 he began to edit and secretly distribute a daily newssheet called *Combat,* dedicated to countering Nazi propaganda, reporting accurate information about the war, and encouraging the hope of an Allied victory.

By this time Camus was already a well-known author. His first novel, *L'Etranger* (The Stranger), had been published in 1942, and it gained immediate recognition. That same year Camus published a philosophical essay, *Le Mythe de Sisyphe* (The Myth of Sisyphus). His previous essays included *L'Envers et l'endroit* (The Wrong Side and the Right Side), published in 1937, and *Noces* (Nuptuals), published in 1938. His second novel, *La Peste* (The Plague), appeared in 1947. Whereas *L'Etranger* concerns one man's isolation from society, *La Peste* shows the isolation of an entire town because of a plague. Brée explains that the plague causes a "stifling oppressiveness" in the town and represents "any force which systematically cuts human beings off from the living breath of life" (128). Camus continued his theme of human isolation in *La Chute* (The Fall), published in 1956. Among his other works are several plays, including *Caligula* (1944), as well as a collection of short stories entitled *L'Exil et le royaume* (The

Exile and the Kingdom, 1957) and a long essay entitled *L'Homme révolté* (The Rebel, 1951). In *L'Homme révolté*, which discusses political revolution, Camus (237) says, "We all carry within us our prisons, our crimes, our destructiveness. But to unleash them in the world is not our duty. Our duty consists in fighting them in ourselves and in others." He maintained this belief until his death in France on January 4, 1960. (Brée 1961)

See also Clamence, Jean-Baptiste; *Fall, The;* Justice; Meursault, Monsieur; *Stranger, The*

Cane

Published in 1923, *Cane,* by Jean Toomer, is a collection of short stories and poems loosely organized around a central theme. In writing about that theme, Toomer says that his book is intended to show the end of an era among blacks. He (1993, xxii) explains that when he conceived of the work,

> a family of back-country Negroes had only recently moved into a shack not too far away. They sang. And this was the first time I'd ever heard the folk-songs and spirituals. They were very rich and sad and joyous and beautiful. But I learned that the Negroes of the town objected to them. They called them "shouting." They had victrolas and player-pianos. So, I realized with deep regret, that the spirituals, meeting ridicule, would be certain to die out. With Negroes also the trend was towards the small town and then towards the city—and industry and commerce and machines. The folk-spirit was walking in to die on the modern desert. That spirit was so beautiful. Its death was so tragic. Just this seemed to sum life for me. And this was the feeling I put into "Cane." "Cane" was a swan-song. It was a song of an end.

In describing the passing of an era, *Cane* addresses issues of social conformity, racism, and sexism. The work is divided into three sections. The first, set in Georgia, focuses on women pressured to conform to society's ex-pectations. The second, set in the cities of Washington, D.C., and Chicago, shows the influence of the past on the present as people struggle to free themselves from childhood attitudes. The third section is a single story, "Kabnis." Its main character, Ralph Kabnis, is a northern-educated black man who has come to Georgia to teach. Once there he learns that the state is not as emancipated as he assumed. He hears stories of whites lynching blacks and fears for his safety. He also learns that southern blacks do not like northern ones unless they conform to the southern way of thinking. Sick at heart, he leaves his teaching position to become apprentice to a wagonmaker. He begins to drink heavily, engage in immoral behavior, and spend time with an aged deaf man, waiting for him to speak. In the end the old man says, "O th sin th white folks 'mitted when they made th Bible lie" (115).

Cane is considered one of the most important books to come out the Harlem Renaissance, a literary era in which black writings flourished. Toomer's work was well received and made him famous. However, he did not appreciate praise based on his race. As scholar Darwin Turner (x) explains in an introduction to a 1993 edition of the work:

> After *Cane,* Toomer resisted identification with any race except the new one—the American race—that he envisioned coming to birth on the North American continent. A mixture of several races and nationalities, an individual who could be identified as an Indian or a dark-skinned European, Toomer argued that a Black label or a white label restricted one's access to both groups and limited one's growth. As evidence he bitterly cited publishers' rejections of his writings after *Cane.* Identifying him as a Negro, he argued, they expected and desired nothing except a duplicate of his earlier work.

Toomer was unable to sell another book manuscript, and eventually he abandoned fiction altogether to concentrate on poetry, essays, and autobiographical works. (Benson and Dillard 1980; Toomer 1993)

See also Harlem Renaissance; Racism; Slavery; Toomer, Jean

Capitalism

Capitalism is an economic system of private ownership. In theory, it allows supply and demand to dictate how many goods are produced and at what price they are sold. However, modern capitalism depends on some level of government control to regulate prices. It also depends on the ability of businesses to borrow money, called capital, to finance their endeavors. In capitalistic countries profits dictate the success of a business and economic competition is intense.

Modern capitalism first began in the Middle Ages. At that time the European economy was based on manorialism, a system whereby peasants lived in agricultural communities owned by noblemen. This system was subject to abuse, and peasants eventually began migrating to cities for better opportunities. As populations became more urban, the economy shifted to one based on trade rather than agriculture, and capitalism replaced manorialism.

Eventually, however, there were abuses under the system of capitalism as well. Small business became large corporations, which then tried to eliminate their competition. Some of these corporations joined together into cooperative ventures called trusts to control entire industries by agreeing on certain prices and practices. During the late 1800s trusts developed to control the petroleum industry, the cotton oil industry, the whiskey industry, the sugar industry, the match industry, and the tobacco industry. At the same time American farmers organized into the Grange movement, which protested railroad monopolies that charged usurious rates for transporting grain to market. Frank Norris's 1901 social protest novel *The Octopus* deals with this issue as it relates to the wheat industry.

Because of trusts and other unfair business practices, capitalists have been the subject of much criticism, particularly in social protest literature dealing with poverty and labor issues.

Some examples of such works are *The Jungle,* by Upton Sinclair; *Yonnondio: From the Thirties,* by Tillie Olsen; *Life in the Iron Mills,* by Rebecca Harding Davis; *The Grapes of Wrath,* by John Steinbeck; and *Little Dorrit,* by Charles Dickens. Anticapitalism novels that advocate alternative systems such as socialism or communism include *Babbitt,* by Sinclair Lewis; *The Iron Heel,* by Jack London; and *Looking Backward, 2000–1887,* by Edward Bellamy, the latter of which describes a futuristic utopia. *Tono-Bungay,* by H. G. Wells, is also an indictment of capitalism, as are Theodore Dreiser's *An American Tragedy* and Henry Miller's *The Air-Conditioned Nightmare,* whereas *Atlas Shrugged,* by Ayn Rand, is a defense of it. (Landes 1966; Pruden 1968; Schumpeter 1950)

See also *Air-Conditioned Nightmare, The; American Tragedy, An; Atlas Shrugged; Babbitt;* Bellamy, Edward; Communism; Davis, Rebecca Harding; Dickens, Charles; Dreiser, Theodore; *Grapes of Wrath, The; Iron Heel, The; Jungle, The;* Labor Issues; Lewis, Sinclair; *Life in the Iron Mills; Little Dorrit;* London, Jack; *Looking Backward, 2000–1887;* Manorialism; Miller, Henry; Norris, Frank; *Octopus, The;* Olsen, Tillie; Poverty; Rand, Ayn; Sinclair, Upton; Socialism; Steinbeck, John; *Tono-Bungay;* Wells, H. G.; *Yonnondio: From the Thirties*

Carlé, Lukas

In Isabel Allende's 1987 novel *Eva Luna,* Lukas Carlé is a cruel Nazi from northern Austria. He believes that "man is made for war. History demonstrates that progress is never achieved without violence" (Allende 1988, 35). War had "failed to instill in him any desire for peace; instead, it had etched in his mind the conviction that only gunpowder and blood can produce men capable of steering the foundering ship of humanity to port—abandoning the weak and helpless on the high seas, in accordance with the implacable laws of nature" (35). When he returns from the war, Lukas tortures his wife with sexual sadism and berates his three children, Jochen, Katharina, and Rolf. A schoolmaster, Lukas also torments his students, five of whom eventually hang him during an outing in the woods; the local police quickly deem the death a suicide. (Allende 1988)

See also Allende, Isabel; Carlé, Rolf; *Eva Luna*; Naranjo, Huberto; Rodríguez, Colonel Tolomeo

Carlé, Rolf

Rolf Carlé appears in Isabel Allende's 1987 novel *Eva Luna*. As a child of ten he helped bury concentration-camp dead in his native northern Austria. This experience sensitized him to the cruelties and secrecies of war; as an adult he becomes a news cameraman and documentary filmmaker dedicated to exposing political and social truths. For example, during a South American revolution "he was the only person who dared carry his camera into the Security Force building to record firsthand the piles of dead and wounded, the dismembered agents. . . . He was also at the General's mansion to film the mobs destroying furnishings, slitting paintings, and dragging the First Lady's chinchilla coats and beaded ball gowns into the streets, and he was also present at the Palace when the new Junta composed of rebel officers and prominent citizens were formed" (Allende 1988, 177). (Allende 1988)

See also Allende, Isabel; Carlé, Lukas; *Eva Luna*; Naranjo, Huberto; Rodríguez, Colonel Tolomeo

Carlson, Georgiana

In the 1853 novel *Clotel*, by William Wells Brown, Georgiana Peck Carlson becomes an abolitionist while living on a southern plantation. Her father is a slave owner, and while growing up she argues with him over the morality of owning men and woman. When he dies and she inherits his property, she wants to set her slaves free. However, she realizes that many of them would not be able to get to the free states of the North on their own and would simply end up back in slavery. Therefore, she and her husband devise a plan. They begin paying their slaves a salary, which they put into trust for the future. When a slave has earned enough for passage to the North and a new life there, they give it to him

or her. In this way the freed slaves will have a good chance of staying free. Of Georgiana's eventual death from an illness, the narrator of the story says:

> If true greatness consists in doing good to mankind, then was Georgiana Carlton an ornament to human nature. Who can think of the broken hearts made whole, of sad and dejected countenances now beaming with contentment and joy, of the mother offering her free-born babe to heaven, and of the father whose cup of joy seems overflowing in the presence of his family, where none can molest or make him afraid. Oh, that God may give more such persons to take the whip-scarred Negro by the hand and raise him to a level with our common humanity! (Gates 1990, 170–171)

(Gates 1990)

See also Brown, William Wells; *Clotel*; Slavery

Castle Rackrent

The novella *Castle Rackrent*, by Maria Edgeworth, was first published anonymously in January 1800 when Ireland began its constitutional union with England, but the following year Edgeworth acknowledged authorship, and later editions bore her name. The novel was translated into German in 1802, and in subsequent years it was also published in Dublin, Ireland, and in the United States.

Castle Rackrent offers two distinct voices: that of Thady Quirk, an Irish servant who narrates the story of the Rackrent family, and a fictitious editor, an Englishman who provides the book's preface and glossary. Through this editor's condescending comments about Irish language and customs, Edgeworth demonstrates the lack of understanding between the two cultures. Through Thady, she criticizes Irish landlords and the feudal system, as well as nostalgia and blind loyalty.

The servant is so enamored with the past that he cannot accept the flaws of the feudal system, and he is so loyal to the Rackrents that he cannot talk about them objectively. Scholar Marilyn Butler (12–13), writing in an introduction to a 1992 edition of *Castle Rackrent*, says that Thady "is one of the classic instances of that device so brilliantly handled in eighteenth-century narrative, the unreliable first-person narrator." She compares him to the narrators of Jonathan Swift's *Gulliver's Travels* and *A Modest Proposal*, both of whom are equally unreliable, and calls Edgeworth "Swift's end-of-century counterpart" (13). Moreover, Butler explains that both Swift and Edgeworth use irony and sarcasm to criticize existing social systems, saying that whereas Swift "satirizes modern intellectual innovations, secularization, scientism and self-sufficiency," Edgeworth "satirizes nostalgia, sectarianism, parochialism and blind loyalty" (13).

Thady offers naïve commentary about four successive masters, but despite his reluctance to discuss their faults, it becomes clear that none of them behaves well. The first, Sir Patrick Rackrent, is fond of gambling, parties, and alcohol and dies during a drunken revel. His son, Sir Murtagh, inherits his father's debts but refuses to honor them. He is a stingy man who demands extra money and services from his tenants and spends his spare time filing frivolous lawsuits. When he dies, Castle Rackrent passes to his younger brother, Sir Kit, who raises the rent on its lands, squanders the money on a trip abroad, and is forced to marry for money. He keeps his wife locked in a room and continues to behave as a single man. After he is killed in a duel, Sir Conolly (Condy for short) Rackrent, a distant relative, inherits the estate. Sir Condy is a gambler and spendthrift who accumulates massive debt and eventually sells Castle Rackrent to Thady's son, Jason, a clever attorney. Even though his own son now owns the estate, Thady is upset to see it change hands, and he remains loyal to his master until Sir Condy dies during a drinking contest with another man.

However, some scholars question Thady's loyalty. Butler (8–9) points out that, although many people "agree in finding Thady plain, simple and above all loyal," others have begun to wonder whether he might actually be "a

thieving rogue, the accomplice of his son Jason, who ends up in possession of his master's estate." As an unreliable narrator, Thady would be capable of concealing his own role in Jason's triumph. But perhaps to emphasize his innocence, he concludes his story by saying: "As for all I have here set down from memory and hearsay of the family, there's nothing but truth in it from beginning to end: that you may depend upon; for where's the use of telling lies about the things which every body knows as well as I do?" (121).

Immediately thereafter the editor adds:

The Editor could have readily made the catastrophe of Sir Condy's history more dramatic and more pathetic, if he thought it allowable to varnish the plain round tale of faithful Thady. He lays it before the English reader as a specimen of manners and characters, which are, perhaps, unknown in England. . . . All the features in the foregoing sketch were taken from the life, and they are characteristic of that mixture of quickness, simplicity, cunning, carelessness, dissipation, disinterestedness, shrewdness, and blunder, which, in different forms, and with various success, has been brought upon the state, or delineated in novels. (121)

He then questions whether England's union with Ireland will help the country; however, he says that "the few gentlemen of education, who now reside in [Ireland], will resort to England: they are few, but they are in nothing inferior to men of the same rank in Great Britain. The best that can happen will be the introduction of British manufacturers in their places" (122). (Butler 1972; Edgeworth 1992)

See also Edgeworth, Maria; *Gulliver's Travels*; Manorialism; *Modest Proposal, A*; Quirk, Thady; Swift, Jonathan

Castorp, Hans

Hans Castorp is the main character of Thomas Mann's 1924 novel *Der Zauberberg* (The Magic Mountain). A young man from a middle-class German family, he embarks on a three-week visit to his cousin, Joachim Ziemssen, who is confined to a mountain sanitorium because of tuberculosis. The doctors there soon convince Hans that he is ill, and he decides to put himself under their care. He remains at the sanitorium for seven years, during which he learns about life from patients who represent different social ideologies. For example, Ludovico Settembrini is an Italian humanist and naturalist, Leo Naphta is a rigid Jesuit-trained Catholic converted from Judaism, and Mynheer Peeperkorn is a wealthy hedonist. In discussing Hans's exposure to these various points of view, Mann (1972, 729) explains that the character is "a searcher after the Holy Grail" who is trying to find "the idea of the human being, the conception of a future humanity that has passed through and survived the profoundest knowledge of disease and death." However, before Hans can discover this Grail, World War I breaks out in Europe, and, as Mann explains, he is "snatched downwards from his heights into the European catastrophe" (729). He becomes a soldier, and the novel ends with him on the battlefield, facing an uncertain future. (Mann 1972)

> See also *Magic Mountain*, The; Mann, Thomas; Settembrini, Ludovico; Ziemssen, Joachim

Castro, Benito

Benito Castro is a former Peruvian military officer in Ciro Alegría's 1941 novel *El mundo es ancho y ajeno* (Broad and Alien Is the World) who tries to defend his Indian village from nonnative usurpation. Although other villagers consider this a local fight, Castro envisions it as part of a broader social protest movement. He wants to ask all other poor Indians in Peru to join his rebellion against the country's unjust nonnative government. However, during the battle to protect his village, he is mortally wounded, and as he dies, he advises his wife to find another place to live. (Alegría 1941)

> See also Alegría, Ciro; Amenabar, Don Alvaro; *Broad and Alien Is the World;* Justice; Maqui, Rosendo

Catch-22

Published in 1961 and set during World War II, *Catch-22*, by Joseph Heller, criticizes many aspects of modern society, particularly the way it conducts its wars. The novel's story is set in two places—Rome and the fictional Italian island of Pianosa, where a U.S. Air Force bombing group is stationed—and is told in a disjointed fashion to reflect the unsettled nature of its main character, Captain John Yossarian. He is a bombadier who tries several tactics to get out of flying his missions. For example, he goes to the hospital complaining of a pain in his liver and remains there while doctors test him for jaundice. He also feigns insanity, engaging in various forms of irrational behavior. Then he learns about Catch-22, a rule that reflects the illogic of the entire military system. Catch-22 states that anyone who flies such dangerous missions must be insane, whereas any flier asking to be relieved of his duties must not be insane. Therefore, there is no way for Yossarian to petition for a medical leave based on insanity.

Consequently, he remains surrounded by death and madness. His superior officers behave irrationally or are corrupt, and when Yossarian goes on leave in Rome, he finds similar insanity and corruption there. The world depicted in *Catch-22* is senselessly violent, and in the end Yossarian decides to escape to neutral Sweden. (Heller 1994; Merrill 1987; Nagel 1984; Seed 1989)

> See also Heller, Joseph; Peace; Yossarian, Captain John

Celie

Celie is the main character in Alice Walker's 1982 novel *The Color Purple,* which is presented as a series of her letters. As a girl she is raped by a man she believes to be her father and develops a deep shame. Later she allows her husband to victimize her as well. Then her husband's mistress, Shug Avery, befriends Celie. Shug encourages Celie to become strong. Under her guidance, Celie develops self-respect, starts her own business, and leaves her husband. In the end Celie is a loving and

In this scene from the 1970 movie Catch 22, *Captain John Yossarian protests the illogical military system by refusing to wear his uniform. (Paramount/The Museum of Modern Art Film Stills Archive)*

loved person and no longer anyone's victim. (Walker 1986)

> See also Avery, Shug; *Color Purple, The*; Walker, Alice

Censorship

Censorship is the suppression of information, whether in written, visual, or oral form, by governments, public or private institutions, or individuals. Many works of social protest have been censored by governments wishing to hide social problems. For example, the works of Pramoedya Ananta Toer have been censored in Indonesia, Fyodor Dostoyevsky and Yevgeny Yevtushenko in Russia, and Milan Kundera in Czechoslovakia. In the United States during an era called McCarthyism in the 1950s writers were censored for discussing communism, but more often the reason given for American censorship was obscenity. In this regard Henry Miller's works were banned, Theodore Dreiser was attacked by antiobscenity groups, and Lawrence Ferlinghetti was put on trial for distributing the epic poem *Howl*, by Allen Ginsberg.

In addition, several science fiction novels depict futuristic societies in which books and ideas are censored. Of these, perhaps the most notable are *Fahrenheit 451*, by Ray Bradbury, and *Brave New World*, by Aldous Huxley. (Boyer 1968)

> See also Bradbury, Ray; *Brave New World*; Communism; Dostoyevsky, Fyodor; Dreiser, Theodore; Ferlinghetti, Lawrence; Ginsberg, Allen; *Howl*; Huxley, Aldous; Kundera, Milan; McCarthyism; Toer, Pramoedya Ananta; Yevtushenko, Yevgeny

Chancellor, Olive

Olive Chancellor is a feminist in Henry James's 1886 novel *The Bostonians*. She is one of the first lesbians to appear in American literature but is depicted unflatteringly. An activist in the suffragette movement, Olive vies with a chauvinistic southern gentleman, Basil Ransom, for the affections of a beautiful young woman named Verena Tarrant. Eventually Verena chooses to reject feminism and marry Basil. (James 1956)

> See also *Bostonians, The;* Feminism; Gay and Lesbian Issues; James, Henry; Ransom, Basil; Tarrant, Verena

Child of the Jago, A

Scholars often compare *A Child of the Jago,* by Arthur Morrison, to the works of Charles Dickens because both novelists call attention to problems among the poor in nineteenth-century England. *Jago* depicts life in a British slum called the Jago. Its publication in 1896 brought about changes in government housing laws, and the slum was soon cleared.

The novel is the third-person account of the life of Dicky Perrott, a young boy who grows to manhood in the Jago. Dicky's father, Josh Perrott, is a plasterer by trade but cannot find a job; he steals to support his family. Depressed over their reduced circumstances, his wife, Hannah, takes little interest in their children, Dicky and Dicky's baby sister, Looey, who soon dies from a head injury received when her mother gets into a fistfight with another woman in the street. Fights are constantly breaking out in the Jago, which is dominated by two warring families, the Ranns and the Learys.

Thievery is also common in the Jago, and eventually Dicky begins stealing, too. He fences his stolen goods with a local coffee shop owner, Aaron Weech, who pays Dicky a fraction of what the items are worth. One day a pastor, Reverend Henry Sturt, helps Dicky get a job as a shopkeeper's helper. Dicky is proud of his new job and envisions the day when he will own a shop of his own. But Weech, not wanting to lose one of his best thieves, tells Dicky's employer that the boy is planning to rob him, and Dicky is fired. He goes back to stealing merchandise for Weech. Meanwhile Dicky's father steals a gold watch and takes it to Weech to sell. Weech knows that the watch belongs to a prominent mobster, and wanting to get in the mobster's favor, he turns Josh Perrott in to the police. Perrott is sent to prison for five years.

Now Hannah must struggle to make a living by herself. She gets a job pasting matchboxes together, and Dicky continues to steal.

By this time he has a new sister, Em, and a brother, Josh Junior, is born while his father is in prison. The family is excited when at last the day comes for Josh Perrott to be released from prison. But as soon as he is released, he goes to Weech's place during the night and murders him. Perrott is arrested and hanged for the crime. Shortly thereafter Dicky is attacked and stabbed by another boy. He dies from his wound, saying he is glad to be out of the Jago. (Morrison 1995)

See also Class, Social; Dickens, Charles; Morrison, Arthur; Poverty

Children of the Ghetto

Children of the Ghetto: A Study of a Peculiar People, by Israel Zangwill, concerns the life of Jewish immigrants in a London ghetto. It was first published in 1892 in two volumes, *Children of the Ghetto* and *Grandchildren of the Ghetto*. The following year a one-volume edition of the works appeared, complete with a glossary of Yiddish words and phrases.

The novels include numerous characters who illustrate different approaches to Jewish immigrant life in a London ghetto. Some of the characters forget their heritage and become assimilated into the Christian culture outside the ghetto. Some observe Jewish traditions only when it is convenient to do so. Others become so rigid in their observance of Jewish rituals that they are more concerned with technicalities than with spirituality. A few become involved in a movement to reestablish a Jewish homeland in Palestine, but when one man travels there, he is disappointed to find it "scarce more than his London Ghetto transplanted, only grown filthier and narrower and more ragged, with cripples for beggars and lepers in lieu of hawkers. The magic of his dream-city was not here" (Zangwill 1895, 221).

Two of the most significant characters in the novel are Hannah Jacobs and Esther Ansell. The daughter of a rabbi, Hannah Jacobs attends a party where the participants are joking about an upcoming marriage. The bridegroom-to-be pretends to go through the marriage ceremony with Hannah instead of with his bride. Later he and Hannah learn that Jewish law does not recognize a joke and that they are truly married in the eyes of God.

Fortunately, no one outside of the family knows what has happened, and Hannah's father arranges for her to get a quiet divorce. Then Hannah meets and falls in love with a young *Cohen,* or Jewish priest. They want to get married, but Hannah's father explains that her divorce means she cannot marry a *Cohen*. Hannah insists that because her marriage was not a real one, her divorce should not be considered real either. She reminds her father that no one knows about the divorce. Nonetheless, the rabbi remains rigid. Finally Hannah and her beloved agree to run away to the United States together to get married. At the last minute, however, Hannah cannot leave her family or religion. She lets the young man go on without her and lives out the rest of her life as a bitter spinster.

Meanwhile Esther Ansell is a child from a poor family who barely has enough to eat. One day she wins a poetry prize and comes to the attention of a wealthy Jewish woman. The woman pays for Esther's family to emigrate to the United States and adopts the little girl as her own. Esther attends the best schools and has fine clothes and good food. Nonetheless, she is pained by the differences she sees between her life and that of her friends in the ghetto. When she becomes a young woman, she writes a book under a male pseudonym criticizing upper- and middle-class Jewish life. No one else knows she has written it, and she has to sit in silence as her adopted family talks about how horrible the book is. One day she realizes that she does not belong with this family, and she runs away to the ghetto. Eventually a young man from her old life seeks her out, having read and admired her book. The editor of a Jewish newspaper, he has been fired for writing articles that do not meet with his sponsors' approval. Soon he realizes that he is in love with Esther, and the two become engaged.

Through these two characters, *Children of the Ghetto* shows the difficulties of maintaining Jewish traditions in a land of modern ideas. The novel also concerns itself with religious hypocrisy and its relationship to social problems. For example, men who need jobs often ignore the Jewish restriction against working on the Sabbath (Saturday), and during a workers' strike they go to a socialist meeting rather than remaining home on a Friday night (the beginning of the Sabbath), which is also required by their religion. Consequently, the third-person omniscient narrator concludes that "ancient piety" cannot withstand "the stress of modern social problems" (241). Similarly, the leader of the meeting is an atheist who keeps his beliefs to himself, knowing that his lack of religion would anger the crowd. Whereas once he used to argue religious issues with everyone he met, the narrator explains that "like so many reformers who have started with blatant atheism, he was beginning to see the insignificance of irreligious dissent as compared with the solution of the social problem" (242). He knows that the best way for him to accomplish change is to appear traditional. Thus, his deception furthers the socialist cause. (Leftwich 1957; Zangwill 1895)

> **See also** Anti-Semitism; Immigrant Communities; Poverty; Religion; Zangwill, Israel

Children of Violence

Children of Violence is a series of five semiautobiographical novels by Doris Lessing: *Martha Quest* (1952), *A Proper Marriage* (1954), *A Ripple from the Storm* (1958), *Landlocked* (1965), and *The Four-Gated City* (1969). Set in Africa and England during the 1930s and 1940s, they trace the political and spiritual awakenings of Martha Quest, a British woman who does not share the racist, anti-Semitic views of other African colonists.

Martha Quest is brought up in a Central African colony. Her father, a weak-willed man, cannot stand up to his racist, anti-Semitic, domineering wife. In contrast, Martha is intelligent and independent, and she and her mother quarrel repeatedly. The household is so filled with tension that when Martha turns 17, her father asks her to leave.

She moves to a nearby city and dreams of becoming a writer, journalist, or political activist of some kind; she believes in equality for the black natives. But the only work she can find is as a secretary, and her dreams soon fade. She falls in with a wild crowd and dates several men. Eventually she marries one of them, Douglas Knowell, simply to conform to society's expectations. Douglas is a narrow-minded, childish man, and Martha immediately knows that she has made a mistake in becoming his wife. She wants a divorce, but her friends and relatives convince her that she is simply experiencing the doubts that all women feel about their husbands. As the years pass, however, her unhappiness grows, particularly after she gives birth to a daughter, Caroline, and realizes that she does not love the girl. Martha simply does she want to be a housewife and mother. When her husband enlists in the war and leaves town, she becomes involved with a Communist group and falls in love with one of its members, an air force officer named William. The two are not lovers, but her husband hears that they are. When Douglas is discharged from the service, he returns home to confront her about the affair. The two quarrel, and she decides to leave him. Douglas begs her to stay. He threatens to kill her or himself if she walks out on him, and he enlists the help of friends and relatives to convince her to keep the marriage intact. Nonetheless, she walks out on Douglas, leaving her daughter behind.

Once free of her marriage, she becomes involved in a Marxist group, exploring various political and social philosophies. Eventually she marries the group's leader, yet she remains unsatisfied and restless. Then she has an affair with a Jewish gardener who has psychic abilities. Through him she learns that she, too, has a psychic gift and begins to explore this inner power. She divorces her husband, and after her lover goes insane, she moves to England, where she experiments with different lifestyles. She lives among dockworkers and then with shopkeepers, finally taking a job as the assistant to a Communist writer and activist. Meanwhile she continues to explore her mental powers.

She also becomes involved with a group of psychics who sense that a nuclear war is coming. The group creates sanctuaries far from major cities, and when the war does happen, they survive to create a new race of people. Unfortunately, Martha is not a part of this new society, having died after exposure to nuclear radiation. (Brewster 1965; Lessing 1964; Lessing 1969; Sprague and Tiger 1986)

> See also Anti-Semitism; Feminism; Knowell, Douglas; Lessing, Doris; Quest, Martha; Racism; Socialism

Children's Hour, The

The Children's Hour is a three-act drama by playwright Lillian Hellman. First performed and published in 1934, it depicts prejudice against lesbians. It also shows the destructive nature of malicious gossip, and in this regard is very similar to another drama, *The Crucible,* by Arthur Miller, which concerns unfair persecution during the Salem witch trials. Both Miller and Hellman were victims of unfair persecution themselves during the era of McCarthyism, an anticommunist "witch-hunt" of the 1950s.

As in *The Crucible,* the events of *The Children's Hour* are set into motion by a young girl. Mary Tilford is a student at a New England boarding school, and she hates the school's owners and teachers, Karen Wright and Martha Dobie. After Mary is punished for lying, she retaliates by telling her grandmother, a school sponsor, that the two women are having a lesbian affair. Mrs. Tilford tells the other students' parents, who remove their children from the school. Karen and Martha sue for libel but lose their case. Bankrupt and ashamed, Karen ends her engagement to a man who has stood by her throughout her legal case. Shortly thereafter Martha realizes that she has had feelings of love for Karen, and in despair she kills herself. Mrs. Tilford then arrives to tell Karen she has learned her granddaughter was lying about the affair. (Hellman 1979; Wright 1986)

> See also *Crucible, The;* Hellman, Lillian; McCarthyism; Miller, Arthur

Civil Rights
See Racism

Clamence, Jean-Baptiste
Jean-Baptiste Clamence, the first-person narrator of Albert Camus's 1956 novel *La Chute* (The Fall), undergoes a shift in self-awareness and tells the story of this shift to an unnamed stranger in an Amsterdam bar. Clamence describes himself as a "judge-penitent" because he has judged his own faults and suffered for them; therefore he feels qualified to judge the faults of others. Years earlier as a lawyer in Paris he let a woman drown rather than trouble himself with rescuing her. This experience and other equally selfish acts eventually led him to reevaluate his life, the life of all human beings, and the structure of his society. (Camus 1958)

> See also Camus, Albert; *Fall, The;* Justice

Clark, Walter Van Tilburg
Author of the novel *The Ox-Bow Incident,* Walter Van Tilburg Clark used the western genre to write stories critical of human nature. In 1969 scholar Max Westbrook (1969, 138) deemed Clark's work relevant to the civil rights movement; Westbrook compared Clark to prominent African-American author James Baldwin because both men explore the "unspeakable" fears, longings, and prejudices that hide within the human heart.

Clark was born in East Orland, Maine, on August 3, 1909, but from the age of eight he grew up in Reno, Nevada. His father was president of the University of Nevada, and Clark received his B.A. and M.A. degrees there, specializing in both English literature and European and American philosophers. In 1931 he became a teaching assistant in American literature and Greek philosophers at the University of Vermont, and his first publication, a book of poetry entitled *Ten Women in Gale's House and Shorter Poems,* was published the following year. In October 1933 he married and accepted a teaching position in Cazenovia, New York.

But although he lived in the East, Clark never forgot his childhood in Nevada, and in

1938 he set his first novel, *The Ox-Bow Incident,* in the American West. The book was published two years later. It was a critical success, and in 1943 a major motion picture company, 20th Century Fox, made *The Ox-Bow Incident* into a movie, which was nominated for an Academy Award that same year; Clark did not write the movie script.

In 1945 Clark published his second novel, *The City of Trembling Leaves.* This book was also set in the American West, but according to Westbrook (68), critics considered it "juvenile" in comparison with the "mature craftsmanship" of *The Ox-Bow Incident.* Similarly, Clark's next novel, *The Track of the Cat* (1949), which Westbrook (93) believes "perhaps the finest Western novel written," never received the same level of critical acclaim as *The Ox-Bow Incident,* nor did *The City of Trembling Leaves* when it was republished as *Tim Hazard* in 1951.

By this time Clark had relocated his home to Nevada, but in 1953, three years after publishing his final work, *The Watchful Gods and Other Stories,* he left his teaching position at the University of Nevada after a dispute over administrative policy. He lectured in creative writing, first at the University of Oregon and later at the University of Washington, before becoming an assistant professor of English at the University of Montana in 1954. Two years later he joined the creative writing program at San Francisco State College.

In 1957 Clark testified as a witness for the defense at an important obscenity trial. The case concerned a collection of poetry by Allen Ginsberg entitled *Howl and Other Poems.* *Howl* was a work of social protest that both celebrated and criticized masculinity; its strong language in reference to homosexuality led its publisher, Lawrence Ferlinghetti, to be charged with distributing obscene material. Ferlinghetti's acquittal was considered a landmark decision in regard to First Amendment constitutional rights.

In 1960 Clark became a fellow in English at Wesleyan University in Connecticut, but in 1962 he decided to return to Nevada. He became writer in residence at the University of Nevada and an editor for the University of Nevada Press. He died in 1971 in Reno, Nevada, at the age of 62. (Westbrook 1969)

See also Baldwin, James; Croft, Art; Davies, Art; Ferlinghetti, Lawrence; Ginsberg, Allen; *Howl;* Justice; Martin, Donald; *Ox-Bow Incident, The;* Tetley, Gerald

Class, Social

A social class is a group of people united by economic and/or social commonalities. In some places and time periods a person's class is determined by the amount of money he or she has, whereas in others a person's class is hereditary. In all cases classes are hierarchical, which means that some groups are considered superior to others and have more rights. A great deal of social protest literature concerns the struggle of the lower classes to achieve the same benefits as the upper ones. For example, Theodore Dreiser's novel *An American Tragedy* deals with a middle-class man's desire to better himself by marrying an upper-class woman. *Castle Rackrent,* by Maria Edgeworth, concerns the inferiority of peasants amid the aristocracy in England, and Ivan Turgenev's *A Sportsman's Sketches* addresses the same issue in Russia. The works of Honoré de Balzac, Charles Dickens, John Galsworthy, Victor Hugo, Henry James, Arthur Morrison, George Bernard Shaw, Émile Verhaeren, Edith Wharton, Israel Zangwill, and Émile Zola also depict difficulties between upper and lower economic classes. Some of these authors also include discussions of socialism and/or communism, which do not have the same emphasis on class structure and wealth as capitalism.

As for hereditary class systems, Mulk Raj Anand shows the problems of India's caste system in his novel *Untouchable,* and Pramoedya Ananta Toer shows the inferior social position of concubinage in his Indonesian novel *This Earth of Mankind,* which was banned in his native country. In addition, early feminists typically depicted women as belonging to a separate and inferior social class, regardless of their economic position. (Cole 1976; Crompton 1978; Szymanski 1983)

See also *American Tragedy, An;* Anand, Mulk Raj; Balzac, Honoré de; Capitalism; *Castle Rackrent;* Censorship; Communism; Dickens, Charles; Dreiser, Theodore; Edgeworth, Maria; Feminism; Galsworthy, John; Hugo, Victor; James, Henry; Morrison, Arthur; Poverty; Shaw, George Bernard; Socialism; *Sportsman's Sketches, A; This Earth of Mankind;* Toer, Pramoedya Ananta; Turgenev, Ivan; *Untouchable;* Verhaeren, Émile; Wharton, Edith; Zangwill, Israel; Zola, Émile

Clifton, Tod

A character from Ralph Ellison's 1952 novel *Invisible Man,* Tod Clifton is a confused black man who becomes the pawn of a white-run Communist organization called the Brotherhood. He believes in the Brotherhood, and when the group abandons its support for the black community, he is shattered. He goes into hiding and eventually reappears on a Harlem, New York, street corner selling politically incorrect dancing black dolls. Shortly thereafter he is killed by police, and the Brotherhood refuses to protest his unjust death. (Ellison 1952)

See also Ellison, Ralph; *Invisible Man*

Clockwork Orange, A

A Clockwork Orange, by Anthony Burgess, concerns a person's right to choose whether to be good or evil. Set in the future, the novel depicts a society where youths have become extremely violent and rival gangs roam the streets each night. Its first-person narrator, Alex, is the 15-year-old leader of one such gang. In a unique slang he explains that he and his friends Pete, Georgie, and Dim consider it fun to rob stores and houses, rape women, and brutalize people in their neighborhood. The only nonviolent thing that Alex enjoys is classical music.

One day Georgie decides to fight him over leadership of his group. Alex wins the fight and assumes they are once again friends. But later, while the gang is robbing a house, Georgie attacks him and leaves him for the police to find. Alex is sentenced to many years in prison. To reduce his time he volunteers for a new rehabilitation program in which doctors inject him with a special drug and force him to watch violent movies accompanied by classical music. The drug causes him to become sick at the sight of violence. After a while, even without the drug, he becomes sick at just the thought of violence. Unfortunately, he also becomes sick whenever he hears classical music.

Once Alex's reconditioning is complete, the government displays him to the media and sets him free. He quickly finds it difficult to survive as a pacifist. He is beaten up and brutalized both by his former victims and his former friends, and his parents do not want him to live with them anymore. Eventually he ends up at the house of a government protester and noted author, F. Alexander. He recognizes Alex from his picture in the newspaper. Alex also recognizes Alexander as one of his former victims. Wearing masks, Alex and his gang once broke into the writer's house, beat him, and repeatedly raped his wife, who later died from the attack. They also destroyed one of his manuscripts, *A Clockwork Orange,* which argued that men, like oranges, are natural objects that should not be mechanized.

Fortunately, F. Alexander does not seem to recognize Alex's voice, and he decides to use him to criticize the government. He writes an article using Alex's name, bemoaning his poor treatment in the antiviolence program, and calls in the members of an antigovernment group. This group tells Alex he will soon be a famous public speaker. They leave him at a strange apartment to sleep. When he awakes, classical music is blaring from the walls. He says:

Then it all came over me, the start of the pain and the sickness, and I began to groan deep down in my keeshkas. And then there I was, me who had loved music so much, crawling off the bed and going oh oh oh to myself, and then bang bang banging on the wall creeching: "Stop, stop it, turn it off!" But it went on and it seemed to be like louder. So I crashed at the wall till my knuckles were all red red

A teenage gang terrorizes one of its victims in the 1971 movie A Clockwork Orange. *(Warner/The Museum of Modern Art Film Stills Archive)*

drovvy and torn skin, creeching and creeching but the music did not stop . . . like it was a deliberate torture. (Burgess 1986, 167)

Alex then sees an open window and jumps, intending to kill himself. He wakes up in a government hospital, covered with bandages, and learns that the antigovernment group intended for him to die to promote its cause; F. Alexander did recognize his voice. After his attempted suicide, the newspaper headlines read: "Boy Victim of Criminal Reform Scheme and Government as Murderer" (172).

Now the government wants to make amends. It returns his mind to its former, violent condition and gives him a job upon his release from the hospital. His parents take him back, and his life is as before. However, in a final chapter Alex expresses dissatisfaction at what he has become. He has just turned 19 and meets his former gang-friend Pete, who is married and respectable. Alex starts thinking about the wife and son he'd like to have himself and seems relieved that his childhood is at an end.

When *A Clockwork Orange* was published

in 1962, this last chapter appeared in the British version of the novel but not in the American one. Author Anthony Burgess (Burgess 1986, viii) says his New York publisher omitted it because it "was a sellout. . . . It was bland and it showed . . . [an] unwillingness to accept that a human being could be a model of unregenerable evil." However, Burgess (viii) believes that the last chapter "gives the novel the quality of genuine fiction, an art founded on the principle that human beings change. There is, in fact, not much point in writing a novel unless you can show the possibility of moral transformation, or an increase in wisdom, operating in your chief character or characters." Burgess restored the chapter to the American version of *A Clockwork Orange* in a 1986 reprinting.

In an introduction to that edition, he (ix) discusses the social philosophy behind the plot, saying:

A human being is endowed with free will. He can use this to choose between good and evil. If he can only perform good or only perform evil, then he is a clockwork orange—meaning that he has the appearance of an organism lovely with colour and juice but is in fact only a clockwork toy to be wound up by God or the Devil or (since this is increasingly replacing both) the Almighty State. It is as inhuman to be totally good as it is to be totally evil. The important thing is moral choice.

Therefore, the novel presents government and antigovernment groups in the same negative light, as entities that want to eliminate free choice. (Burgess 1986; De Vitis 1972)

See also Burgess, Anthony; Peace; Science Fiction and Fantasy

Close Sesame

Published in 1983, *Close Sesame* is the final book of a trilogy known as *Variations on the Theme of an African Dictatorship,* which includes the novels *Sweet and Sour Milk* (1979) and *Sardines* (1981). The author of these works, Nuruddin Farah, is from the Republic of Somalia and writes about political and social oppression in that country. In *Close Sesame* Farah depicts the African dictatorship established by Somali natives as being just as corrupt and oppressive as the Italian and British colonial governments that preceded it. The novel's main character is an old man named Deeriye, who is one of the most respected people in the country. As a young man he refused to cooperate with the Italian government and was imprisoned for several years. Now he is a symbol of the liberation movement that established the native-run government. Meanwhile Deeriye's adult son, Mursal, has become involved in a plot to assassinate the general, the country's dictator. One day Mursal's friend Mahad tries to carry out the plot and fails. He is thrown into prison. Later Mahad's uncle, Deeriye's friend Rooble, is arrested after government officials trick him into disobeying a law regarding public assemblies.

Rooble's family is of a different clan from the general's, and the dictator wants the public to believe that the assassination attempt was based on clan rivalries rather than political ideologies. Thus, a campaign of misinfor-

mation begins. Regarding this campaign, the third-person narrator of the story says:

Information, Deeriye was thinking to himself, is the garden the common man in Somalia or anywhere else is not allowed to enter, sit in its shady trees, drink from its streams and eat its delicious fruits; information, or the access to that power and knowledge: power prepared to protect power; keep the populace underinformed so you can rule them; keep them apart by informing them separately; build bars of ignorance around them, imprison them with shackles of uninformedness and they are easy to govern; feed them with the wrong information, give them poisonous bits of what does not count, a piece of gossip here, a rumour there, an unconfirmed report. Keep them waiting; *let them not know;* let them not know what you are up to and where you might spring from again. (Farah 1992, 74)

Because Deeriye has become a symbol for freedom and justice, the government does not want him to become involved in the current situation. Moreover, since Deeriye is not in good health, his family members suggest that he leave the country rather than overtire himself with politics. Nonetheless, Deeriye remains, even after the government begins to harass him, and has long conversations with friends and relatives on various political and social issues in the country. Many of these issues are intertwined. For example, when the father of a young man named Mukhtaar, who was a coconspirator in the assassination attempt, kills his son and gets away with it, Deeriye and Mursal discuss the event's relationship to the traditional customs of the people. Mursal says:

A father can beat his son to madness in full public view and the son is expected not to raise a hand but to receive the beating in total silence. The son is not allowed to question the wisdom of his parent's statements, must never answer back, never raise his voice or head. A daughter is not, of course, expected to refuse or challenge her material worth: she is worth as much dowry as she can obtain for her parents—not more or less than that. As for public justice being confused with private justice, what would happen if Mukhtaar were to receive a fatal blow on the head and die? Nothing. Nothing would happen to avenge Mukhtaar's life and his father would not be submitted to questioning: after all, it is the prerogative of a parent what to do with the life and property of an offspring, in the same way as it is the prerogative of the husband what to do with the life and property of a wife for whom he has paid the necessary dowry. (120–121)

Throughout the novel, private events are related to public ones. Even the assassination attempt has a corresponding event in Deeriye's personal life. On the same day a young neighbor boy who dislikes Deeriye throws a stone at his head and injures him. Deeriye's forgiveness is in sharp contrast to the general's retaliation against his would-be assassins. Every person involved in the plot is eventually killed, including Mursal. When Deeriye hears of his son's death, he decides to kill the general himself. However, at the crucial moment he pulls rosary beads from his pocket instead of a gun and is shot dead by the general's guards. Some believe his act was a mark of insanity, whereas others consider it heroic. (Farah 1992; Wright 1994)

See also Farah, Nuruddin; Justice

Clotel

The 1853 novel *Clotel: or, The President's Daughter* was the first published work of an African American in the United States. Its author, William Wells Brown, was a southern slave who escaped to freedom in the North, and his story concerns the injustice of slavery. The novel's main character is Clotel, the daughter of a slave named Currer and the president of the United States, Thomas Jefferson. Currer was Jefferson's housekeeper in Virginia, and shortly after he left for Washington, D.C., she was sold at a slave auction, along with Clotel, age 16, and her sister Althesa, age 14. Both girls look white.

At the auction Currer and Althesa are sold to a slave trader, who then sells them to a Methodist minister and a bank teller, respectively, for use as housekeepers. Clotel is sold to Horatio Green, who takes her as his mistress. He and Clotel soon have a daughter, Mary, who is white and beautiful. The three are happy together until Horatio decides to marry into a politically prominent family. His new wife finds out about his mistress and orders her sold south. The woman then takes Mary as her servant—to humiliate the child and punish Horatio.

Clotel eventually ends up in the hands of another man who wants her as his mistress. Before he can take advantage of her, however, she escapes with the help of another slave, William. The two dress Clotel as a white man and pretend that she is William's master; in this way they travel north without suspicion. Once in the North William goes on to Canada, and Clotel heads to Virginia to rescue her daughter Mary. She is soon captured but escapes the jail. As she is about to be caught again, she plunges off a bridge into the Potomac River and dies.

Meanwhile Clotel's sister, Althesa, has married a white man who believes that all slaves should be free. They move to a place where everyone believes Althesa is white, too, and there they have two daughters. The two girls receive the finest education. Then Althesa and her husband both succumb to an illness, and after their death the truth about Althesa's background is revealed. Her two daughters are sold into slavery as part of the estate. They die shortly thereafter, one by killing herself with poison and the other by wasting away from despair.

By this time Clotel's mother, Currer, has died of an illness. However, she was treated well in the last part of her life. Her mistress, Georgiana Peck Carlson, inherited her slaves from her father but wants them set free. She and her husband have devised a plan whereby the slaves work for wages that are credited to an account. When a slave has earned a certain amount, he or she is given the money and sent north to freedom. Georgiana regrets Currer's death because she would have liked to reunite her with her two daughters. No one in the Carlson household knows what became of them.

Currer, Clotel, and Althesa have all died slaves, despite their connection to Jefferson, who has been advocating the abolition of slavery. However, Clotel's daughter Mary does eventually become free. In Horatio Green's household she meets a slave named George and falls in love with him. One day he participates in a slave rebellion, during which he is arrested and sentenced to death. Before his execution Mary visits the jail and changes clothes with him. He then walks out pretending to be her and quickly heads north to Canada. From there he travels to Europe, where he becomes a prosperous businessman. As punishment for helping George escape, Mary is sold south, but while traveling there by boat, she is helped to escape by a young Frenchman. He takes her to Paris and marries her. Sometime later, after her husband has died of an illness, Mary sees George sitting in a park. The two are joyfully reunited. They marry and continue to live in Europe as free human beings. Thus, the novel concludes, "We can but blush for our country's shame when we recall to mind the fact, that while George and Mary Green, and numbers of other fugitives from American slavery, can receive protection from any of the governments of Europe, they cannot return to their native land without becoming slaves" (Gates 1990, 221).

In addition to following the lives of Jefferson's enslaved offspring, *Clotel* offers various anecdotes about other slaves by way of illustrating the injustices of slavery. It also comments on the hypocrisy of American beliefs in regard to freedom. For example, at one point the novel points out that the founders of the country believed in "freedom and liberty for all" and yet instituted slavery almost immediately upon their arrival on American shores.

The narrator says that on the same day in 1620 two very different ships set forth, explaining:

The May-flower brought the seed-wheat of states and empire. . . . Here in this ship are great and good men. Justice, mercy, humanity, respect for the rights of all; each man honoured, as he was useful to himself and others; labour respected, law-abiding men, constitution-making and respecting men; men, whom no tyrant could conquer, or hardship overcome, with the high commission sealed by a Spirit divine, to establish religious and political liberty for all. . . . But look far in the South-east, and you behold on the same day . . . a low rakish ship hastening from the tropics, solitary and alone, to the New World. What is she? She is freighted with the elements of unmixed evil. Hark! Hear those rattling chains, hear that cry of despair and wail of anguish, as they die away in the unpitying distance. Listen to those shocking oaths, the crack of that flesh-cutting whip. Ah! it is the first cargo of slaves on their way to Jamestown, Virginia. (165–166)

The novel includes abolitionist poetry, as well as a concluding chapter that states that the author personally witnessed many of the events in the story. This conclusion gives statistics regarding how many Christians of different sects own slaves and says: "Let no Christian association be maintained with those who traffic in the blood and bones of those whom God has made of one flesh as yourselves" (223). (Farrison 1969; Gates 1990; Warner 1976)

See also Brown, William Wells; Carlson, Georgiana; Green, Horatio; Racism; Slavery

Cohen, Joss and Solly
Joss and Solly Cohen are brothers who appear in Doris Lessing's five-novel series *Children of Violence*. They grow up as the only Jews in a British colony of Central Africa and experience a great deal of prejudice, not only because

of their religion but also because of their liberal politics. Their only friend in the community is Martha Quest, with whom they share books on philosophy, sociology, psychology, and politics. Because of their influence, Martha rejects the conservative views of her parents and becomes a Communist. (Lessing 1964)

See also *Children of Violence;* Lessing, Doris; Quest, Martha

Color

Color was the first collection of poems by noted African-American author Countee (Porter) Cullen. Published in 1925, it presents many aspects of the black experience in the United States, including Cullen's experiences with racism. In one of the most powerful poems in the collection, "The Shroud of Color," Cullen says: "My color shrouds me in, I am as dirt / Beneath my brother's heel; there is a hurt" and later speaks of a racist beating after which "somehow it was borne upon my brain / How being dark, and living through the pain / Of it, is courage more than angels have" (Cullen 1991, 101–102). In another poem, "Heritage," he talks about being disconnected from his African heritage, saying, "What is Africa to me? . . . A book one thumbs / Listlessly, till slumber comes" (104–105). Cullen has inspired many black authors, including Peter Abrahams, who used a line from the Cullen poem "Tableau" as the title of his social protest novel *The Path of Thunder.* In Cullen's work the phrase refers to two young men, one black and one white, who arouse the ire of their communities by daring to walk together; he refers to their walk as creating "a path of thunder" (86). (Cullen 1991)

See also Abrahams, Peter; Cullen, Countee; *Path of Thunder, The;* Racism

Color Purple, The

The Color Purple, by Alice Walker, concerns the struggle of an African-American woman, Celie, to develop and strengthen her self-respect in a racist, sexist society. The novel was published in 1982, won a Pulitzer Prize in 1983, and became a major motion picture in 1985. The book is written in epistolary form, using Celie's letters to God and her younger sister Nettie, as well as Nettie's letters to Celie, to tell the story. Set in the early twentieth century, it begins when Celie is 14 and living in rural Georgia with her mother and her stepfather, Alphonso. Alphonso repeatedly rapes her, and she bears two of his children, which he takes away. When Celie's mother dies, Alphonso remarries and forces Celie to wed a man named Albert, who really wanted Nettie instead. Albert treats Celie badly and tries to seduce Nettie. Nettie leaves town, and Albert hides her subsequent letters to Celie. Then Albert moves his mistress, Shug Avery, into his house. Shug is a strong individual, and at first she feels contempt for Celie. Eventually, however, the two women become friends and lovers. Shug helps Celie develop self-respect and encourages her to start her own clothing business. Later Celie leaves Albert to move in with Shug. By this time Celie has discovered Nettie's letters. They reveal that Nettie is now living in Africa with the Olinkan tribe, and she has found Celie's lost children, Adam and Olivia, who were adopted by a black missionary named Samuel and his wife, Corinne. When Corinne dies, Nettie marries Samuel.

Meanwhile Alphonso has died, and Celie inherits his home. She moves there with Shug and makes peace with Albert. She has many friends, including Albert's oldest son, Harpo, and his wife, Sofia. A headstrong woman, Sofia once left Harpo because she found him too bossy. However, she soon encountered worse oppression from white men, and she was jailed for refusing to work for the mayor's wife. After her release Sophie reunites with Harpo, and together they join with Celie and Shug to celebrate Nettie's arrival. With her are Olivia, Adam, and Adam's Olinkan bride, Tashi. In the end all of the characters are reunited and reconciled, having matured and discovered their best selves with the help of their friends' support.

Because of the book's black folk dialect and feminist theme, *The Color Purple* has often been compared to the novel *Their Eyes Were Watching God,* by Zora Neale Hurston. This theme is revisited in much of Alice Walker's work, including *The Temple of My Familiar,* which includes some of the same characters as *The Color Purple.* (Gates and Appiah 1993a; Walker 1986; Winchell 1992)

See also Avery, Shug; Celie; Feminism; Gay and Lesbian Issues; Racism; Walker, Alice

Communism

Communism is a political and socioeconomic system related to socialism. Although many of the principles of communism developed in ancient times, the modern Communist movement did not begin until 1848 when German socialist Karl Marx published a work entitled *The Communist Manifesto,* in which he and coauthor Friedrich Engels suggested that socialism would develop from capitalism just as capitalism had developed from manorialism. The authors explained that communism would then develop from socialism after a revolutionary struggle between the upper classes, or bourgeoisie, and working classes, or proletariat.

Marx's ideology soon spread throughout Europe, but during and after the Russian Revolution of 1917 it split into several factions, most notably Marxism and Leninism. Communist groups also appeared in England and the United States, where many writers began advocating communism as an alternative to capitalism. In the 1950s U.S. senator Joseph McCarthy led a crusade against such writers; this crusade became known as McCarthyism.

Authors who discuss communism or depict Communist characters in their works include Isabel Allende, Carlos Fuentes, Graham Greene, Milan Kundera, Doris Lessing, Jack London, Jean-Paul Sartre, and William Lederer and Eugene Burdick. Black American authors Ralph Ellison and Richard Wright depict communism as an unsatisfactory way to combat racism in the United States. (Aaron 1961; Cohen 1962; Ruhle 1969; Williams 1977)

See also Allende, Isabel; Capitalism; Class, Social; Ellison, Ralph; Fuentes, Carlos; Greene, Graham; Kundera, Milan; Lessing, Doris; London, Jack; McCarthyism; Racism; Sartre, Jean-Paul; Socialism; Wright, Richard

Cosette

One of the main characters of Victor Hugo's 1862 novel *Les Misérables,* Cosette is an illegitimate child whose mother leaves her in the care of an innkeeper. Although the innkeeper has been paid to care for the little girl, he keeps her in rags and buys her no toys. When she is five, he makes her into a servant and treats her cruelly. Hugo (1987, 157) uses this incident to discuss the poor treatment of lower-class children throughout France, saying: "Five years old! It will be said that's hard to believe, but it's true; social suffering can begin at any age. Didn't we see recently the trial of Dumollard, an orphan turned bandit, who, from the age of five, say the official documents, being alone in the world, 'worked for his living and stole'!" Eventually, however, Cosette's circumstances improve. She is rescued by a wealthy benefactor, Jean Valjean; grows into a beautiful young woman; and marries a member of the upper classes despite her illegitimate past. (Hugo 1987; Swinburne 1970)

See also Hugo, Victor; Justice; *Misérables, Les;* Poverty; Valjean, Jean

Crabbe, George

Born on December 24, 1754, in the small seaside village of Aldeburgh in Suffolk, England, George Crabbe wrote poetry about the plight of the rural poor. He originally worked as a surgeon in Aldeburgh, writing poems as a hobby. Then he decided to stop practicing medicine and become a full-time author. In 1780 he moved to London, where he lived in poverty until he found a wealthy patron, Edmund Burke. He introduced Crabbe to many important men of the time and helped him publish a poem entitled *The Library* in 1781. Now a success, Crabbe decided to study theology. He was ordained as a cleric in 1782 and worked in that capacity for the remainder of his life. He also continued to write poetry. His most famous works are *The Village* (1783), a realistic poem about rural poverty, and *The Parish Register* (1807), in which he traced the life of a rural village through its marriage, birth, and death records. He died on February

3, 1832, in Trowbridge, Wiltshire, England. (Chamberlain 1965)

See also "Parish Workhouse, The"; Poverty

Crabbe, Jack

Jack Crabbe is the 111-year-old first-person narrator of *Little Big Man,* Thomas Berger's 1964 novel about the mistreatment of Native Americans during the 1800s. Although white, Jack spends his childhood among the Cheyenne Indians. As a man he lives in the white world, but eventually he returns to his tribe, where people are more honest and straightforward. Then soldiers from the U.S. Cavalry destroy his village. Vowing revenge on their general, George Armstrong Custer, Jack becomes a civilian employee in his army and is present at the Battle of the Little Big Horn. However, by this time he has realized that killing Custer will not stop the mistreatment of the Indians. (Berger 1964; Landon 1989)

See also Berger, Thomas; *Little Big Man;* Native American Issues; Old Lodge Skins; Racism

Crawford, Janie

The main character of Zora Neale Hurston's 1937 novel *Their Eyes Were Watching God,* Janie Crawford expresses feminist views that are unpopular in her black community. She marries three times, the first to please her grandmother, the second to gain respect, and the third to enjoy life. Her story is about self-awareness and personal empowerment. (Hemenway 1977; Hurston 1990)

See also Hurston, Zora Neale; Stark, Joe; Tea Cake; *Their Eyes Were Watching God*

Croft, Art

The narrator of Walter Van Tilburg Clark's western novel *The Ox-Bow Incident,* Art Croft joins a lynching party out of a misguided sense of loyalty to his fellow cowboys. However, throughout the novel he questions his participation in the group. Scholar Max Westbrook (1969, 60) believes that Art "is moving towards an acceptance of ethical responsibilities" and "wants to think outside himself, to a reality more objective than the personal projects

of the romanticized individualist." But despite doubts about the group's validity, both Art and his friend Gil Carter stay with the lynching party, and in the end they discover they have hung three innocent men. (Westbrook 1969)

See also Clark, Walter Van Tilberg; Davies, Art; Justice; Martin, Donald; *Ox-Bow Incident, The;* Tetley, Gerald

Crowne, Lenina

The character Lenina Crowne appears in Aldous Huxley's 1932 novel *Brave New World.* Living in the distant future, she has become completely cut off from nature. In her society women no longer give birth. Children are created in test tubes and raised in large centers, and adults are encouraged to have promiscuous fun. Therefore, when Lenina meets John, a young man from a more primitive world, and finds herself attracted to him, she immediately tries to have sex with him. He is repulsed and becomes violent, whereupon she locks herself in the bathroom. She never understands his response. (Atkins 1968; Brander 1970; Huxley 1989)

See also *Brave New World;* Huxley, Aldous

Crucible, The

The Crucible, by Arthur Miller, is a play about mass hysteria and the persecution of the innocent. Set in Salem, Massachusetts, in 1692, it begins when a girl falls ill after participating in a secret ceremony with her friends, during which they danced and brewed a love potion. Soon the townspeople learn what happened. They condemn it as witchcraft, a practice punishable by death. The girls, to save themselves, insist they did not join the ceremony willingly; agents of the Devil made them do it. They then begin to name these agents: neighbors they dislike. When doubted, the girls twitch and shriek as though tormented by witchcraft, and soon the town leaders believe them. One by one the good people of Salem are arrested, tried, and executed. Only those who confess and repent are spared.

The final victim is John Proctor. He had a brief affair with one of the accusers, a girl named Abigail Williams. At the beginning of the play he has just ended his relationship with Abby and reconciled with his wife. No one in town knows about the affair. However, after Abigail accuses his wife of witchcraft in the hopes of having him to herself, Proctor confesses his shame. He tells the town leaders that Abby has been lying and that there are no witches in Salem. But because he has not been going to church lately, he is immediately accused of being a witch himself. Right before his execution, he considers confessing to save his life. Then he realizes that his honor is more important and that if he confesses, it will imply that his friends are guilty, too. He accepts his fate and dies bravely.

In discussing this conclusion, scholar John Ferres (1972, 8) says, "Miller believes a man must be true to himself and to his fellows, even though being untrue may be the only way to stay alive," adding that this truth is only discovered through "the ordeal of the personal crucible." Similarly, scholar Leonard Moss (1967, 64) identifies the play's theme as having two parts, one of which is "the achievement of moral honesty"; the other, "the generation of hysteria."

Miller wanted to write about mass hysteria because of the historical period in which he lived. *The Crucible* was first performed in New York at the Martin Beck Theater on January 22, 1953. By that time Senator Joseph McCarthy had begun the public persecution of anyone he believed to be a Communist. Called McCarthyism, this witch-hunt destroyed many people's lives, and just as in *The Crucible*, anyone who disagreed with McCarthy was attacked. For example, in 1952 Senator William Benton of Connecticut tried to expel McCarthy from the U.S. Senate; McCarthy then suggested that Benton himself might be a communist and called for an in-depth investigation into his background and lifestyle. In an article called "The Meaning of McCarthyism," Earl Latham (Ferres 1972, 26) writes: "From 1950 to 1954, the activities of Senator McCarthy were an oppressive weight and pain to tens of thousands in government, politics, and the professions specifically, and within the ar-

ticulate and better educated circles of society generally. In America and abroad he became a symbol of mortal danger to liberal values and democratic processes."

Miller believed that McCarthyism was "a kind of personification of [moral] disintegration" (Moss 1967, 59). Moreover, in discussing his decision to write *The Crucible*, Miller (59–60) said: "It was not only the rise of 'McCarthyism' that moved me, but something which seemed much more weird and mysterious. It was the fact that a political, objective, knowledgeable campaign from the far Right was capable of creating not only a terror, but a new subjective reality, a veritable mystique which was gradually assuming even a holy resonance. . . . The terror in these people was being knowingly planned and consciously engineered, and yet all they knew was terror" (Moss 1967). Interestingly, after the play's production Miller himself was accused of being a Communist and had to defend himself before the U.S. Congress. (Corrigan 1969; Ferres 1972; Miller 1954; Moss 1967)

See also Censorship; McCarthyism; Miller, Arthur

Cruz, Artemio

The main character of Carlos Fuentes's 1964 novel *La muerte de Artemio Cruz* (The Death of Artemio Cruz), Artemio Cruz is a wealthy and powerful man who owns land, sulfur mines, hotels, a fish business, and a newspaper in Mexico City. However, he is also extremely dishonest. He frequently bribes government officials, and he uses his newspaper to manipulate public opinion. He has no loyalty to anyone but himself. Artemio Cruz therefore represents human corruption in the Mexican political and economic system. (Fuentes 1964)

See also Fuentes, Carlos; *Hydra Head, The*

Cry for Justice, The

The Cry for Justice is an anthology of social protest literature compiled by Upton Sinclair, whose novel *The Jungle* is itself an important work of social protest. The anthology presents a large body of poems as well as excerpts from longer works, both fiction and nonfiction. It was first published in 1915 and updated by Sinclair in 1963. In a 1915 introduction, Jack London writes that by reading social protest literature, a person learns

> that his fair world so brutally unfair, is not decreed by the will of God nor by any iron law of Nature. He will learn that the world can be fashioned a fair world indeed by the humans who inhabit it, by the very simple, and yet most difficult process of coming to an understanding of the world. Understanding, after all, is merely sympathy in its fine correct sense. And such sympathy, in its genuineness, makes toward unselfishness. Unselfishness inevitably connotes service. And service is the solution of the entire vexatious problem of man. (Sinclair 1996, 9)

(Sinclair 1996)

See also *Jungle, The;* Justice; London, Jack; Sinclair, Upton

Cry, the Beloved Country

Cry, the Beloved Country, by Alan Paton, was published in 1948. Set in South Africa, it depicts the deterioration of black society as its young people forsake rural communities to live in the city. The novel's main character is Stephen Kumalo, a black priest in the tribal village of Ixopo. One day he leaves his home to search for his son, Absalom; his sister, Gertrude; and Gertrude's little boy, who have moved to Johannesburg and never write him anymore. Stephen soon finds Gertrude and her son but is dismayed to learn that she has become a prostitute. It takes him much longer to locate his son, Absalom. Finally, with the help of another priest, Stephen locates the young man in jail, where Absalom has confessed to killing a white man, Arthur Jarvis, during the commission of a robbery. The murder has shocked both blacks and whites in Johannesburg because Jarvis was a social reformer who worked tirelessly to help the black community. Absalom insists that the shooting was an accident. Nonetheless, he

is sentenced to death for the crime, and Stephen leaves Johannesburg with Gertrude's son and Absalom's pregnant wife. Back in Ixopo, he finds it difficult to speak with Arthur Jarvis's father, who lives in the area. Eventually, however, the two come together in grief and concern for the village. Jarvis donates milk to the starving children of Ixopo, starts building a dam to provide needed water to the area, and brings in an agricultural expert to help improve the crops. He also gives Stephen money to build a new church. Jarvis has been reading his son's writings on equal rights and human compassion and has realized how much the black people need and deserve his help. Unfortunately, there are some blacks who do not appreciate Jarvis's efforts, and Stephen recalls the words of another black priest: "I have one great fear in my heart, that one day when they turn to loving they will find we are turned to hating" (Paton 1987, 276).

In a 1987 introduction to *Cry, the Beloved Country,* Edward Callen (xxvi–xxvii) points out that "zealous revolutionaries would scorn the personal actions taken by its characters to restore the village church and the land." However, he says that Alan Paton believed in the importance of such actions. Moreover, the novel portrays the political activism of organized groups as susceptible to corruption. Stephen Kumalo's brother, John, is a leading Johannesburg black activist who is cowardly and dishonest. John also supports violence, and it is his son who leads Absalom into a life of crime.

When *Cry, the Beloved Country* was published, it was not well received in South Africa. Callen (xxiv) reports that the prime minister's wife told its author: "Surely, Mr. Paton, you don't really think things are like that?" Nonetheless, the book was an international best-seller. It was translated into approximately twenty languages, including Zulu and Afrikaans, and was made into a musical, *Lost in the Stars,* and then a movie. (Callan 1982; Paton 1987)

See also Apartheid; Jurgis, Arthur; Kumalo, Stephen; Paton, Alan; Racism

Countee Cullen, circa 1930's–mid 1940's (Corbis-Bettmann)

Cullen, Countee

Countee Porter Cullen was a black American poet whose works expressed pride in his African heritage. Born on May 30, 1903, either in Louisville, Kentucky, or New York, New York, he was raised first by an elderly relative and then by a family friend, Reverend F. A. Cullen. Countee began writing poetry in childhood, winning prizes and publication for his work. As an undergraduate at New York University he received the Witter Bynner Poetry Prize and published his first volume of poetry, *Color* (1925), which was a critical success. He went on to receive a master's degree from Harvard in 1926, and two years later he studied in France under a Guggenheim Fellowship. He also continued to write poetry. His published works include *Copper Sun* (1927), *The Ballad of the Brown Girl* (1928), and *The Black Christ and Other Poems* (1929). In 1934 he became a New York public school teacher, a position he held until his death on January 9, 1946. (Cullen 1991; Ferguson 1966; Shucard 1984)

See also Baldwin, James; *Color;* Harlem Renaissance; *Path of Thunder, The;* Racism

D

Damon, Cross

Cross Damon is the main character in Richard Wright's 1953 novel *The Outsider,* which concerns black alienation within white American society during the early 1950s. Cross is an intellectual who chooses to take a job as a postal worker, and throughout the novel he is continually denying various aspects of his past and his identity. He is a perpetual outsider, a role he discusses with a white district attorney, Ely Houston, who is interested in understanding the black experience. In talking about racism, Damon says:

> After many of the restraints have been lifted from the Negro's movements, and after certain psychological inhibitions have been overcome on his part, then the problem of the Negro in America really starts, not only for whites who will have to become acquainted with Negroes, but mainly for Negroes themselves. Perhaps not many Negroes, even, are aware of this today. But time will make them increasingly conscious of it. Once the Negro has won his so-called rights, he is going to be confronted with a truly knotty problem. . . . Will he be able to settle down and live the normal, vulgar, day-to-day life of the average white American? Or

will he still cling to his sense of outsidedness? (Wright 1993b, 164–165)

In the end Damon cannot lose his own outsidedness. He becomes the ultimate outsider—a lawless murderer without a reasonable motive—and is eventually murdered himself. (Wright 1993b)

See also Houston, Ely; *Outsider, The;* Racism; Wright, Richard

Davies, Art

In the 1940 western novel *The Ox-Bow Incident,* by Walter Van Tilburg Clark, Art Davies tries to persuade a lynching party not to hang three men suspected of murder and cattle rustling. He believes in the legal system and tells the narrator of the story, cowboy Art Croft, that mob justice can "weaken the conscience of the nation" by committing a "sin against society" (Clark 1960, 48). However, scholar Max Westbrook (1969, 57) points out that Davies and another character who objects to the lynching, Gerald Tetley, "are repeatedly associated—both in language and action—with a degrading femininity" and are therefore not taken seriously. Davies also displays weakness by emotionally collapsing after he discovers that the hanging victims were innocent men. (Clark 1960; Westbrook 1969)

See also Clark, Walter Van Tilburg; Croft, Art; Justice; Martin, Donald; *Ox-Bow Incident, The;* Tetley, Gerald

Davis, Rebecca Harding

Born in 1831, novelist Rebecca Harding Davis was the author of several works of social protest. They include *Waiting for the Verdict* (1868), which concerns racism, and *John Andross* (1874), which is about political corruption. However, Davis's most famous work is the 1861 novella *Life in the Iron Mills.* Originally serialized in the *Atlantic Monthly* magazine, the novella heightened public awareness of working-class problems. It is based on Davis's experiences in the mill town of Wheeling, Virginia, where she moved when she was five years old. The book received critical acclaim and brought Davis to the attention of journalist Lemuel Clark Davis, who married her in 1863. Shortly thereafter Davis began raising a family but continued to write novels. She also worked on the editorial staff of the *New York Tribune* from 1869 to the mid-1870s. Davis died in 1910. (Harris 1991; Rose 1993; Wagner-Martin and Davidson 1995)

See also Labor Issues; *Life in the Iron Mills*

Days to Come

First performed in December 1936, the three-act drama *Days to Come,* by American playwright Lillian Hellman, concerns a factory strike in a small Ohio town where everyone gets along well. The factory owner, Andrew Rodman, wants to cut his workers' salaries because he is going bankrupt. Unable to survive on less money, his employees strike, and after they have been off the job for three weeks, Rodman pays for strikebreakers to come in. Rodman believes the strikebreakers will take his workers' place at the machines. Instead, they try to start a fight with the strikers, so that the law can be called in to end the strike forcibly. Eventually violence erupts, and an innocent girl is shot. The strikers decide to go back to work. However, now they hate their employer, and Rodman is afraid to walk through the town he once loved. (Hellman 1979)

See also Hellman, Lillian; Labor Issues

De Satigny, Alba Trueba

One of the narrators of Isabel Allende's 1982 novel *La casa de los espíritus* (The House of the Spirits), Alba Trueba de Satigny is the daughter of Blanca Trueba and her lover, socialist activist Pedro Tecero García. However, for many years Alba believes that her father is Count Jean de Satigny, whom Blanca was forced to marry to make Alba legitimate. Like Pedro Tecero, both Blanca and Alba are involved in socialist causes; like her mother, Alba takes a revolutionary, Miguel, as a lover. Eventually Alba is arrested for her political activities. While in prison she is tortured and raped, but she refuses to become bitter, even after she learns she is pregnant. At the end of the novel she says: "I want to think that my task is life and that my mission is not to prolong hatred but simply to fill these pages while I wait for Miguel, . . . while I wait for better times to come, while I carry this child in my womb, the daughter of so many rapes or perhaps of Miguel, but above all, my own daughter" (Allende 1985, 368). (Allende 1985)

See also Allende, Isabel; Del Valle, Clara; Feminism; García, Esteban; García, Pedro Tecero; *House of the Spirits, The;* Socialism; Trueba, Esteban

Death of Artemio Cruz, The

First published in Spanish in 1962, *La muerte de Artemio Cruz* (The Death of Artemio Cruz), by Carlos Fuentes, shows the transformation of a poor but honest boy into a wealthy but dishonest man. Its main character is 71-year-old Artemio Cruz, who controls a newspaper in Mexico City. After Cruz becomes bedridden with a fatal illness, he begins to flash back to important dates in his personal history. The novel alternates among these memories, which are written in the third person; Cruz's thoughts about the people surrounding his deathbed, which are written in the first person; and his speculations on what will be or might have been, which are written in the second person. Through all three techniques, Fuentes uses Cruz's life to comment on Mexican political issues and government corruption.

Cruz was born on April 9, 1889, as a result of his mother's rape by a wealthy landowner. Raised by a poor tobacco picker, he does not know the identity of his father, and he accidentally kills his paternal uncle. Ten years later while fighting on the side of the Rebels in the Mexican Revolution, he flees an important battle but is mistakenly labeled a hero. At the same time he learns that his lover, Regina, has been killed by his enemies, the Federals. He becomes crazed with revenge and fights heroically in the next battle.

Eventually he is captured by the Federals and is condemned to die. He shares a cell with a young lawyer named Gonzalo Bernal, who has also been condemned. Gonzalo tells him about his sister, Catalina Bernal, and his father, Don Gamaliel Bernal, an aristocratic landowner. The next morning Gonzalo is executed while Cruz is bargaining for his freedom with his captors. He agrees to give them information in exchange for his freedom. The information is false, but before the Federals can discover this, the Rebels defeat them and the war ends.

Cruz immediately seeks out Gonzalo's father and sister. He portrays himself as a friend of his former cellmate. Through clever tactics he takes over the management of Don Bernal's land and frightens away Catalina's boyfriend. He then marries Catalina himself, and they have two children, a boy named Lorenzo and a girl named Teresa. However, Catalina does not love Cruz and makes his life miserable, even as he is becoming more powerful and more corrupt. Teresa also does not love him, and at Cruz's deathbed she makes disparaging comments about him. Both women blame Cruz for the death of Lorenzo, who decided to fight in World War II and was killed by Italian bombers in Spain. Cruz believes that Lorenzo's life is the one he was meant to live. Instead, he is left to die of a gangrenous intestine, surrounded by people who are interested only in his last will and testament. (Fuentes 1964)

See also Cruz, Artemio; Fuentes, Carlos; Justice

Deeriye

Deeriye is the main character in Nuruddin Farah's 1983 Somalian novel *Close Sesame*. Once imprisoned for fighting against his country's oppression by colonial Italians and British, he has become a symbol of Somali freedom fighting. However, he eventually realizes that the new native government run by his people is as corrupt and oppressive as the colonial government once was. He attempts to assassinate the dictator of Somali and is killed. Later his daughter envisions that his epitaph will read, "Here lies dead a hero whose vision and faith in Africa remained unshaken" (Farah 1992, 237). (Farah 1992)

See also *Close Sesame*; Farah, Nuruddin; Justice

Del Valle, Clara

Clara del Valle is a clairvoyant whose journals allow her granddaughter to narrate the story of her life in Isabel Allende's 1982 novel *La casa de los espíritus* (The House of the Spirits). Clara's mother, Nívea del Valle, was an early supporter of women's rights in South America, and Clara encourages her own children to think for themselves. As a result, all three Trueba youngsters grow up to become active in socialist politics and charity work. Meanwhile as Clara ages, she becomes less involved in the world. She pursues the occult and speaks to the spirits until finally she decides she has lived long enough. She soon dies; according to her doctors, her death was due to her own will rather than an illness. (Allende 1985)

See also Allende, Isabel; De Satigny, Alba Trueba; Feminism; García, Esteban; García, Pedro Tecero; *House of the Spirits, The*; Socialism; Trueba, Esteban

Delarue, Mathieu

Mathieu Delarue is the main character in Jean-Paul Sartre's novel *L'Âge de raison* (The Age of Reason). A professor of philosophy, he advocates living a life of freedom and shuns the conventionality of marriage. Therefore, when his mistress tells him she is pregnant, he decides to pay for her to have an illegal abortion. But this decision troubles him. He is not as free of his conscience or upbringing as he would like to be. In fact, in all areas of his life he has difficulty reconciling his philosophy with his actions. As his brother Jacques points out to him during an argument:

> I should myself have thought . . . that freedom consisted in frankly confronting situations into which one has deliberately entered, and accepting all one's responsibilities. But that, no doubt, is not your view: you condemn capitalist society, and yet you are an official in that society; you display an abstract sympathy with Communists, but you take care not to commit yourself, you have never voted. You despise the bourgeois class, and yet you are a bourgeois, son and brother of a bourgeois, and you live like a bourgeois. (Sartre 1947, 138)

Mathieu is a symbol of hypocrisy. (Sartre 1947)

See also *Age of Reason, The;* Communism; Sartre, Jean-Paul

Dickens, Charles

Charles John Huffam Dickens was born February 7, 1812, in Portsmouth, Hampshire, England, but spent his early childhood in Chatham, England. His father, a navy clerk who often squandered his money, went to debtor's prison in 1824. By this time the family was living in London, and Dickens was forced to leave school to take a factory job there. He remained at work until his father's release from prison, whereupon he returned to school. At age 15, however, Dickens again left his studies, this time to become a law clerk. He later worked as a newspaper reporter, becoming involved in the liberal politics of his day. In 1833 he had several stories and essays published in various periodicals; in 1836 they were reprinted in a collection, *Sketches by "Boz."* Dickens also used the Boz pseudonym to publish installments of a serialized novel, *Pickwick Papers,* during 1836 and 1837. This work was extremely popular and appeared in book form in 1837. Dickens followed it with

Oliver Twist (1838), *Nicholas Nickelby* (1839), *The Old Curiosity Shop* (1841), and *Barnaby Rudge* (1841). All were published first in installments and then in book form. During this time Dickens also became a magazine editor, married, and started a family. He was to have nine children in all, but eventually he left his wife for another woman.

Dickens's later works include *A Christmas Carol* (1843), *Martin Chuzzlewit* (1844), *David Copperfield* (1850), and *A Tale of Two Cities* (1859). All of his novels contain elements of social protest. However, five books are particularly critical of Victorian society: *Bleak House* (1853), *Hard Times* (1854), *Little Dorrit* (1857), *Great Expectations* (1861), and *Our Mutual Friend* (1865). In addition to novels, Dickens wrote plays, poetry, essays, and articles. He also enjoyed giving public readings of his work. His performances were extremely popular, but unfortunately they strained his health. Dickens died on June 9, 1870, after falling ill during one of these tours. He left behind one unfinished novel, *Edwin Drood.* (Cruikshank 1949; Fielding 1958; Gissing 1924; Hibbert 1967)

See also *Bleak House;* Class, Social; *Great Expectations; Hard Times; Little Dorrit;* Poverty

Doane, Seneca

A minor character in the 1922 novel *Babbitt,* by Sinclair Lewis, Seneca Doane represents the author's own views about the value of nonconformity in American society. Doane is a highly intelligent, logical lawyer working as a social reformer. He persistently fights against government corruption, supports labor unions and their strikes, and openly advocates freedom of speech. When he was in college, Doane's goal was to be a rich man; in later years he came to view the enrichment of humanity as more important. Conversely, in college the novel's main character, George F. Babbitt, wanted to be a lawyer and help the poor; instead he became an unethical real estate salesman concerned with wealth and social standing. (Grebstein 1962; Lewis 1950)

See also *Babbitt;* Labor Issues; Lewis, Sinclair; Reisling, Paul

Doll's House, A

The 1879 three-act play *A Doll's House*, originally published in Norwegian as *Et dukkehjem* by Henrik Ibsen, concerns the emancipation of a housewife, Nora Helmer, whose husband treats her like a child. Years earlier, Nora's husband Torvald fell ill and required a vacation to a warmer climate. However, the couple was poor at the time, so Nora forged her father's name on a document in order to obtain a private loan. (Women were not allowed to conduct business transactions on their own.) Now the man who loaned her the money is using the document to blackmail her; he works for Torvald and wants Nora to convince her husband not to fire him. Meanwhile, Nora considers a variety of ways to keep Torvald from discovering the truth, and it becomes clear that the two have a highly dysfunctional marriage. Torvald treats Nora as though she were incompetent, while Nora submerges her own intellect in order to make him happy. Their life is built on illusions. When Torvald finally discovers Nora's deceit, he behaves badly and she realizes that he is not the man she thought him to be. She also realizes that she is not the woman she ought to be. She says (Ibsen 1978, 85–87):

> When I was at home with papa, he told me his opinion about everything, and so I had the same opinions; and if I differed from him I concealed the fact, because he would not have liked it. He called me his doll-child, and he played with me just as I used to play with my dolls. And when I came to live with you . . . I was simply transferred from papa's hands into yours. You arranged everything according to your own taste, and so I got the same tastes as you—or else I pretended to, I am really not quite sure which . . . [Now] I must try and educate myself—you are not the man to help me in that. I must do that for myself. And that is why I am going to leave you now.

Despite the fact that society will frown on her decision to leave her husband and children, Nora walks out on Torvald. When he begs her to remember her responsibilities, saying "before all else, you are a wife and a mother," she replies (88): "I don't believe that any longer. I believe that before all else I am a reasonable human being, just as you are—or, at all events, that I must try and become one. I know quite well, Torvald, that most people would think you right, and that views of that kind are to be found in books, but I can no longer content myself with what most people say, or with what is found in books. I must think over things for myself and get to understand them."

Because of its strong feminist statement, *A Doll's House* engendered much controversy when it was first produced. The work was also misunderstood. According to H. L. Mencken, writing in an introduction to the work (x), "the German middle classes mistook *A Doll's House* for a revolutionary document against monogamy." In other words, they saw it as an indictment of *all* marriage, rather than an indictment of a particular *type* of marriage. (Ibsen 1978)

See also Feminism; Ibsen, Henrik

Dostoyevsky, Fyodor

Russian author Fyodor Mikhaylovich Dostoyevsky wrote novels about human behavior and beliefs, many of which criticized Russian society. His most famous works are *Prestuplenie i nakazanie* (Crime and Punishment, 1866), *The Idiot* (1868), *Besy* (The Possessed, 1871–1872), and *Bratya Karamazovy* (Brothers Karamazov, 1880).

Dostoyevsky was born in Moscow, Russia, on November 11, 1821. His mother died when he was 16, and two years later his widowed father, a physician, was murdered by serfs. Dostoyevsky then went to St. Petersburg, where he studied at the Military Engineering College. He graduated in 1843 as an officer but soon began to write. His first published short story, "Bednye Lyudi" (Poor Folk), appeared in 1846 and gained him critical acclaim.

In 1849, however, he was arrested for his membership in the Petrashevsky Circle, an underground political organization. At first he was condemned to death, but later his sentence was commuted to confinement in a Siberian prison. He remained there until 1854. After his release he wrote *Zapiski iz myortvovo doma* (1861–1862), which later appeared in English as *Buried Alive; or, Ten Years of Penal Servitude in Siberia* (1881). In 1867 he married Anna Grigorievna Snitkina, and the two lived abroad until 1871, when Dostoyevsky returned to Russia to become a journal editor. He also continued to write novels. He died on February 9, 1881 in St. Petersburg, Russia. (Dostoyevsky 1936; Dostoyevsky 1968)

See also Censorship; *Possessed, The;* Verhovensky, Pyotr Stepanovitch

Dreiser, Theodore

American novelist Theodore Dreiser was lauded as a social reformer after the publication of his novel *An American Tragedy* in 1925. Because the book criticizes a society that bases class divisions on economics, some people believed that Dreiser intended it as an argument in favor of communism. However, this was not the case. Biographer Ellen Moers (1969, 240) explains:

> Soon after the publication of *An American Tragedy,* the Russian critic Sergei Dinamov wrote to its author to say that he had noted Dreiser's bitter criticism of the inequities and hypocrisies of American capitalism and to inquire what system the novelist believed should take its place. Dreiser wrote in reply that he had "no theories about life, or the solution of economic and political problems. Life, as I see it, is an organized process about which we can do nothing in the final analysis." He wished the Russian experiment well, but he thought there was no plan, from the Christian to the Communist, "that can be more than a theory. And dealing with man is a practical thing—not a theoretical one. Nothing can alter his emotions, his primitive and animal reactions to life."

Dreiser's interest in economic inequity originated not in his politics but in his upbringing. He was born in Terre Haute, Indiana, on August 27, 1871, as the eleventh of twelve children. Because his German-immigrant parents were extremely poor, he could not afford a good education. However, a high school teacher decided to help him, paying one year's tuition at Indiana University. When her support ran out, he left college to become a journalist.

Dreiser worked for newspapers in several major cities before settling in New York, where he eventually became a magazine editor-in-chief. In 1900 he wrote his first novel, *Sister Carrie,* about a woman who attains economic success in life by becoming a mistress. At the time this was not a popular topic; the novel appeared in print only because Frank Norris, a prominent social protest author, urged his publisher to support the project. Nonetheless, the book was not a commercial success, and so Dreiser continued working as an editor. In 1910 he was forced to resign his position because of a scandal involving an office romance. He then became a freelance writer, publishing collections of short stories, essays, and plays as well as autobiographical works. He also continued to write novels, including *The Financier* (1912) and *The Titan* (1914), which are the fictionalized story of a real-life American businessman. In 1915 he published the semiautobiographical *The 'Genius,'* which describes the love affairs of an immoral man. This book was censured by the New York Society for the Suppression of Vice, but the ban was lifted a year later after it was protested by many other prominent authors. Dreiser's next novel, *An American Tragedy,* appeared ten years later and was his most famous work. When he died on December 28, 1945, in Hollywood, California, he was working on a sequel to *The Titan* entitled *The Stoic,* which was published posthumously. (Geismar 1953; Gerber 1964; Kazin and Shapiro 1955; Moers 1969)

See also *American Tragedy, An;* Censorship; Norris, Frank

Dufrenoy, Michel

The main character in Jules Verne's 1863 novel *Paris au XXe Siècle* (Paris in the Twentieth Century). Michel Dufrenoy is a poet struggling to earn a living in a society that values only science and technology. In the end he falls into poverty and despair, collapsing in the snow of a Paris cemetery. (Verne 1996)

> See also *Paris in the Twentieth Century;* Science Fiction and Fantasy; Verne, Jules

Dunbar-Nelson, Alice

Alice Dunbar-Nelson was an African-American author who wrote short stories and articles about racial prejudice. Born Alice Ruth Moore in 1875, she attended the University of Pennsylvania and Cornell University and married black poet Paul Laurence Dunbar, who was the son of slaves. The couple eventually divorced. In 1916 Alice Dunbar married publisher Robert John Nelson and became a high school teacher in Wilmington, Delaware. She was fired from this position in 1920 because of her political views. Dunbar-Nelson was involved with the National Association of Colored Women and later the American Interracial Peace Committee. She also worked toward the establishment of a school for troubled black girls. After losing her teaching position, she became a magazine editor and newspaper columnist. Her diary was published in 1984 and a collection of her works in 1988. Dunbar-Nelson died in 1935. (Roses and Randolph 1996)

> See also Harlem Renaissance; "Hope Deferred"

E

Edgeworth, Maria

Maria Edgeworth was born January 1, 1767, in Oxfordshire, England. She was the oldest daughter of an Irish inventor and landowner, Richard Lovell Edgeworth. Schooled in England, she began living on her father's estate in Edgeworthtown, Ireland, at the age of 15, where she became governess to his 21 other children from four successive marriages. Her first published work, a collection of stories called *The Parent's Assistant* (1796), was based on her experiences with her half brothers and half sisters.

Castle Rackrent, written in 1800, was her first novel. It criticizes the Irish feudal system and highlights the differences between Irish and English culture. Edgeworth originally published it anonymously in England, but the following year she acknowledged authorship, and subsequent editions bore her name. It garnered the praise of both King George III and his prime minister, as well as such authors as Sir Walter Scott, who credited its influence on his own novel, *Waverly*. Similarly, Edgeworth's next novel, *Belinda* (1801), was praised by author Jane Austen.

Following *Belinda*, Edgeworth published a six-volume novel series entitled *Tales of Fashionable Life* (1809–1812). This series included *The Absentee* (1812), which criticizes absentee English landlords. She followed her series with three more novels. All of these, like their predecessors, were edited by her father, who maintained a great deal of influence over her life. She died on May 22, 1849. (Butler 1972; Edgeworth 1992)

See also *Castle Rackrent;* Class, Social

Edible Woman, The

The Edible Woman, by Margaret Atwood, was written in 1964 at the beginning of second-wave feminism but was not published until 1969. At that time reviewers did not appreciate the novel, but today it is considered an important work of feminist literature. Its theme concerns the struggle for self-identity in a depersonalized world; its main character is a woman who gradually subjugates herself to her boyfriend. This subjugation is expressed through extended metaphors and literary allusions, most of which relate to food consumption.

At the beginning of the novel Marian MacAlpin narrates her story in the first person. She tells of her work at a product test-marketing company, where she designs research questionnaires on food preferences, and offers mundane details about her life. Marian lunches every day with three coworkers, virgins named Emmy, Lucy, and Millie, and develops a friendship with one of her research subjects, Duncan, a painfully thin and neurotic graduate student. Marian also has a roommate, Ainsley Tewce, who is her exact opposite. Whereas Marian is staid and conventional, Ainsley is promiscuous and liberated.

One day Ainsley decides that she wants to have a baby. As she makes plans to trick Marian's friend Len Slank into having sex with her at the appropriate time, Marian grows angry but says little. She also does not warn Len of Ainsley's upcoming trickery. In fact, Marian increasingly finds herself unable to express her own views, particularly around her boyfriend, Peter. On one occasion when she and Peter are visiting with Len and Ainsley, Marian feels so insignificant that she hides under the bed, literally making herself invisible to the others. It takes her friends a while to notice she is missing. This upsets her and she runs away. When Peter finds her, he asks her to marry him, and she agrees without much feeling. She begins to plan her wedding, and the novel changes abruptly from first person to third, so that Marian no longer narrates her own story.

At the same time Marian begins to have a problem with food. Whenever she realizes that something was once alive, she cannot eat it. In the beginning only foods that look like animal parts disturb her: hunks of cow or pig, for example. Later she cannot stand the sight of ground meats. Eventually she also stops eating eggs, because they remind her of embryonic chickens, and vegetables, because they were once alive and growing. When she tastes a piece of cake and realizes that it is "spongy and ceullar against her tongue, like the bursting of thousands of tiny lungs," she cannot eat that either (Atwood 1996, 227).

By this time Peter has completely consumed her life, and during their engagement party she realizes she has to escape their future together. She sneaks away from the party and spends the night with Duncan, who refuses to help her solve her problems. The next morning Marian decides to end her engagement. She invites Peter over, and while waiting, she bakes him an elaborate cake shaped and decorated to look like a woman. When he arrives, she serves it to him, saying: "You've been trying to destroy me, haven't you. . . . You've been trying to assimilate me. But I've made you a substitute, something you'll like much better. This is what you really wanted all along, isn't it?" (299–300). Embarrassed, Peter leaves, and suddenly Marian is starving. She begins eating the cake, and after she severs its head, the novel's narration returns to the first person. Marian then finishes her story, telling of Ainsley's decision to marry a strange man just to give her baby a father and of Duncan visiting her house and sharing the rest of the cake with her. She is pleased by his obvious enjoyment of the cake, yet discomfitted by the determination with which he consumes it.

Because of this ending, scholars typically discuss *The Edible Woman* in terms of its obvious feminism. However, Robert Lecker, in his article "Janus Through the Looking Glass: Atwood's First Three Novels," points out that the novel has a significant message for men. He (Davidson and Davidson 1981, 186) says that *The Edible Woman* is a "comedy of manners which comments tragically on a contemporary world in which even the semblance of identity has disappeared and men (and women) are seen only as faceless nonentities in a zombified crowd. In such a world, the hope that one can find one's 'true identity' can only lead to the 'sinking feeling' which plagues Marian at the end of *The Edible Woman*." Atwood's male characters are as unhappy as her female ones. Peter doubts whether he will make a good husband, Len does not want to be a father, and Duncan questions his purpose as a graduate student. Defined by roles rather than individual traits, these people all struggle against society's expectations for them. (Atwood 1996; Davidson and Davidson 1981)

See also Atwood, Margaret; Feminism; MacAlpin, Marian; Tewce, Ainsley

El Saadawi, Nawal

A noted feminist, Nawal El Saadawi was born on October 27, 1931, in Kafr Tahia, Egypt, and received a medical degree at Cairo University in 1955. In 1966 she received a master's degree in public health from Columbia University in New York City. As a physician at Cairo University, she became the editor of *Health* magazine, and eventually she was named Egypt's director of public health. However, in 1972 she was dismissed from that position after writing a nonfiction book called *Woman and Sex*, in which she expressed a feminist viewpoint. Undeterred, she wrote several novels that argued against the oppression of women, including *Mawt al-rajul al-wahid 'ala 'l-ard* (God Dies by the Nile, 1974), *Imra'ah 'ind nuqtat al-sifr* (Women at Point Zero, 1975), *Al-wajh al-'ārī lil-mar'ah al-'Arabiyyah* (The Hidden Face of Eve, 1977), and *Jannât wa-Iblîs* (The Innocence of the Devil, 1992). In 1981 the Egyptian government, led by Anwar Sadat, imprisoned El Saadawi for two months as punishment for her feminist beliefs. (El Saadawi 1990; Malti-Douglas 1995)

See also Feminism; *God Dies by the Nile*

Ellison, Ralph

Ralph Waldo Ellison is the author of *Invisible Man,* published in 1952. The novel examines the role of black men in American society during the late 1940s. Born in Oklahoma City, Oklahoma, on March 1, 1914, Ellison originally wanted to be a musician, and in 1933 he began studying music at Alabama's Tuskegee Institute. Then he decided to pursue a career in writing. In 1936 he left Tuskegee to join the Federal Writer's Project in New York City, New York, where he met novelist Richard Wright. With Wright's encouragement, Ellison began contributing short stories and articles to a variety of magazines, and after a stint of service in the merchant marine during World War II, he started writing *Invisible Man.* Upon its publication in 1952, it was an immediate success, winning the National Book Award in 1953. Ellison then became a university lecturer on writing and American black culture. His subsequent books were two essay collections, *Shadow and Act* (1964) and *Going to the Territory* (1986), and a collection of short stories, *Flying Home: And Other Stories*

Ralph Ellison (right) presenting the Howells Medal for Fiction to John Cheever, May 19, 1965. (UPI/Corbis-Bettmann)

(1994), published posthumously. At the time of his death on April 16, 1994, he was working on a second novel. (Hersey 1974)

See also *Invisible Man;* Racism; Wright, Richard

Elmer Gantry

Elmer Gantry (1927), by Sinclair Lewis, is an attack on religious institutions and beliefs in the early twentieth century. Its main character, Elmer Gantry, is a minister who engages in immoral behavior, and its most moral character, a fellow minister named Frank Shallard, is secretly an atheist.

The novel begins in the year 1902. Elmer Gantry is a 22-year-old student at a Baptist college in Kansas. However, he is more interested in drinking, fighting, and having sex than he is in studying. But very quickly Elmer's life changes. One day in town he sees a theology student being heckled while trying to preach, and Elmer defends the man's right to speak. Believing that Elmer has been inspired by God, religious leaders at the college try to convince him to join the Baptist Church and become a minister. Meanwhile his best friend, Jim, an avowed atheist, argues against it. After some internal struggle Elmer is caught up with emotion during a prayer session and does indeed become a convert to the Baptist faith. Afterward he gives a moving speech about the power of love; no one but Jim knows that he has plagiarized it from the works of a great social reformer of the time, Robert G. Ingersoll.

Elmer then begins studying for the ministry. In addition to biblical facts, he learns various techniques for increasing church donations and improving his public speaking skills. At the same time he secretly continues to drink and smoke, and when he is sent to preach at a nearby church, he seduces a young Sunday school teacher. Her father finds out and complains to the college; as a result, Elmer is forced to propose to the girl. But just before the marriage, he tricks her father into believing she is seeing another man, and the engagement is broken. Elmer is sent to another town to preach, but along the way he gets drunk and is kicked out of the ministry.

After a brief time as a salesman, he realizes he misses the adulation of the crowd that he used to feel when he preached. He becomes the assistant to a woman evangelist, Sharon Falconer, and travels the country with her preaching. He also becomes her lover, and together they engage in various immoral behaviors. Elmer soon learns that much about Sharon is false, even her name. However, when a fire breaks out while she is preaching, she tests her faith in God by remaining inside to lead people through the flames while Elmer runs out through a back door. He survives; Sharon dies.

Elmer tries to continue alone as an evangelist, but he fails to attract crowds. He then learns enough Hindu beliefs to promote mysticism, but he finds it does not pay well enough. He ingratiates himself with a bishop in the Methodist Church, converts, and becomes a Methodist minister. When he learns that he will get a better church appointment if married, he chooses a wife whom he believes will reflect well on his position. He does not love her.

He advances quickly as a minister, moving to larger and larger towns. At last he is sent to head the Methodist Church in the town of Zenith, which has a population of 400,000. There he vows to clean up sin and corruption, staging several "vice raids" and gaining a great deal of publicity. His church thrives. At the same time, to better his own position, he accuses a former friend and fellow minister, Frank Shallard, of being an atheist. This accusation is true. Frank does have doubts about God, but he is otherwise an outstanding minister, helping the sick and guiding his parishioners to make wise, moral decisions in life. Nonetheless, he loses his job. Meanwhile Elmer has two affairs, one with his former fiancée, who is now married. At the end of the novel a third mistress publicizes his infidelity, and for a brief time his parishioners suspect his true nature. But when Elmer has the woman's private life investigated and threatens to ruin her, she recants her story, and the townspeople reaffirm their faith in their minister.

Elmer remains unchanged at the end of the novel, as does the view of religion offered by author Sinclair Lewis. Throughout *Elmer Gantry* churchmen are depicted as hypocritical people more interested in commerce than in spirituality. The two characters with the highest morals, Jim Lefferts and Frank Shallard, are atheists. Moreover, when Sharon the evangelist rises above her hypocrisy and expresses her faith in God, He fails her.

Many scholars believe that the character of Sharon was modeled after a real-life evangelist of the time, Aimee Semple McPherson. They also note similarities between Elmer Gantry and real-life preacher Billy Sunday. Sunday, like Gantry, plagiarized one of his speeches from social reformer Robert Ingersoll. In addition, according to Sheldon Grebstein (1962, 100–101), "the boisterous activities of Sharon's evangelist troupe are based on 1915 court proceedings in which a Philadelphia landlord sued Sunday for the damage caused to his house by Sunday's party of assistants." Grebstein (105) adds: "We must . . . remember, in judging *Elmer Gantry*, that Lewis was writing in the most hotly charged religious atmosphere in America since the Salem witch burnings." It was a time when people were debating whether the science of evolution, instead of or in addition to biblical creationism, should be taught in the public schools. The publication of *Elmer Gantry* was perceived as yet one more attack on the Christian religion. Grebstein (106) reports:

> The novel sold over two hundred thousand copies in the first ten weeks after publication, and it provoked dozens of incidents as well. . . . A well-known Los Angeles minister invited Lewis to visit the city, promising he would personally lead a lynching party in the novelist's honor; at the same time another clergyman started proceedings in New Hampshire to jail Lewis for writing *Elmer Gantry*. . . . For a time it seemed that Lewis's prediction that he would be thrown out of the country for *Elmer Gantry* might be coming true. But at least he had calculated correctly on one point. He had wanted the book to make the nation take notice, and he was not disappointed. With all its faults, *Elmer Gantry* continues to remind us of the bitterness of the struggle in Lewis's generation between religious liberalism and literalism, modernism and fundamentalism; and it remains to this day one of the two or three best American novels centered upon religion.

(Grebstein 1962; Lewis 1970; Schorer 1962)

See also Falconer, Sharon; Lewis, Sinclair; Religion; Shallard, Frank

Endō, Shūsaku

Shūsaku Endō is noted for writing novels that examine the differences between Japanese and Western cultures and morality. He was born in Tokyo, Japan, on March 27, 1923. His family urged him to become a Roman Catholic when he was 11 years old. He never became completely comfortable with this religion and consequently explored his sense of conflict through his work. His first fiction was published in 1955 as two short-story collections: *Shiroi hito* (White Man) and *Kiiroi hito* (Yellow Man). His most internationally well-

Shūsaku Endō, 13 December 1993 (AP Photo/Masahiro Yokota)

known novel, *Chimmoku* (Silence), was published in 1966; it concerns the persecution of Japanese Christians in seventeenth-century Japan. Shūsaku Endō's other novels include *Umi to dokuyaku* (The Sea and Poison, 1957) and *Samurai* (1980). He has also written essays, plays, and a biography. (Endō 1980)

See also Religion; *Silence*

Environmentalism

Environmentalism is a concern for the health of the earth, and it is expressed in a large body of environmental literature, most of it nonfiction. However, a few novelists and poets have addressed environmental issues. In fact, one of the most famous works of environmental literature is the novel *The Monkey Wrench Gang*, by Edward Abbey. The poets of the Beat movement also criticized attitudes in American society that contributed to environmental destruction. In addition, many works of science fiction depict a future of severe pollution, thereby protesting antienvironmental practices of the present.

See also Abbey, Edward; Beat Movement; *Monkey Wrench Gang, The;* Science Fiction and Fantasy

Erlone, Jan

The character of Jan Erlone appears in Richard Wright's 1940 novel *Native Son,* which concerns American racism. He is a Communist who believes that all men deserve respect. He treats the novel's main character, a black man named Bigger Thomas, as an equal and does not understand why this makes the man hate him. After Bigger kills Jan's girlfriend and tries unsuccessfully to blame Jan for the crime, Jan is angry. Then he realizes he has not understood the full depth of the black experience. He visits Bigger in jail and says:

> Though this thing hurt me, I got something out of it. . . . It taught me that it's your right to hate me, Bigger. I see now that you couldn't do anything else but that; it was all you had.. . . . I'm not trying to make up to you, Bigger. I didn't come here to feel sorry for you. . . . I'm here because I'm trying to live up to this thing as I see it. . . . I was . . . grieving for Mary and then I thought of all the black men who've been killed, the black men who had to grieve when their people were snatched from them in slavery and since slavery. I thought that if they could stand it, then I ought to. (Wright 1993, 332)

Jan helps Bigger get an attorney and fight for white justice. Unfortunately, his efforts fail and Bigger is condemned to death. (Wright 1993)

See also Communism; *Native Son;* Racism; Thomas, Bigger

Eva Luna

Published in Spain in 1987 and the United States in 1988, *Eva Luna,* by Isabel Allende, is set against a background of political unrest in an unnamed South American country where the government is moving from dictatorship to democracy. As guerrilla forces try to turn the people toward socialism, the novel's first-person narrator, Eva Luna, eventually realizes that for the revolutionaries, "the people" are "composed exclusively of men; we women should contribute to the struggle but were excluded from decision-making and power" (Allende 1988, 233).

Eva is a strong woman at a time when feminism is virtually unknown in her country. She lives with her friend Mimi, a beautiful actress who began life as a transsexual named Melesio. Mimi encourages Eva to become a writer and helps her sell a telenovela series, or soap opera, to the director of national television. In the series Eva uses her fiction to expose many of her country's real problems and political events, causing one military leader, Colonel Tolomeo Rodríguez, to warn her that revealing such truths to the public can be dangerous. Eva has been getting her political information from two people: a guerrilla leader named Huberto Naranjo, who is also her lover, and a filmmaker named Rolf Carlé, who at the end of the novel becomes her husband.

Throughout *Eva Luna* Eva tells Rolf's life story along with her own. Born in northern Austria, he grows up with a cruel father, Lukas Carlé, a schoolteacher who so torments his students that they hang him during a school outing. After his father's death Rolf goes to live with his aunt and uncle in South America, where he eventually becomes a famous cameraman and documentary filmmaker. He meets Eva while filming a guerrilla revolutionary group led by Naranjo.

Eva first meets Naranjo while roaming the streets of the city. Her mother died when she was six, and she has spent the seven years since then working as a servant in a series of homes. Naranjo arranges for her to stay in a house of prostitution, where she lives sheltered from all sexual activities until the house is raided by the police. She escapes the raid and goes to work for Riad Halabí, a Turkish shopkeeper. Riad loves his adopted country because, whereas in Turkey "there are many castes and many codes [and a] man dies right where he is born," in South America there is "a single class, a single people. Everyone thinks he's king of the mountain, free of social ranks and rules—no one better than anyone else either by birth or money" (211).

When Riad's wife, Zulema, commits suicide, Eva is arrested for the murder and is beaten by police. Riad bribes them to set her free, and Eva returns to the city, where she encounters Mimi and begins a career as a writer. Eva also runs into Naranjo, who has become the famous guerrilla leader Comandante Rogelio. Mimi warns Eva not to become Naranjo's lover, telling Eva that his guerrilla revolution will fail, but that even if Naranjo "wins his revolution, . . . in a very short time he would be acting with the arrogance of every man who attains power" (267). Mimi argues that all men "operate on the same principal: authority, competitiveness, greed, repression—it's always the same" (268). Nonetheless, Eva helps Naranjo liberate a group of political prisoners from a guarded fortress before leaving the city with Rolf, who has filmed the prison raid. (Allende 1988)

See also Allende, Isabel; Carlé, Lukas; Carlé, Rolf; Naranjo, Huberto; Rodríguez, Colonel Tolomeo; Socialism

Everhard, Avis

Avis Everhard is the wife of revolutionary activist Ernest Everhard in Jack London's 1908 novel *The Iron Heel.* As the first-person narrator of his life story, she recounts his socialist speeches and describes his attempts to fight an oppressive American oligarchy called the Iron Heel. She is a strong woman and eventually becomes a spy to help her husband's cause. In an introduction to her manuscript a fictional scholar of the future, Anthony Meredith, tells of her fate:

It is quite clear that she intended the Manuscript for immediate publication, as soon as the Iron Heel was overthrown, so that her husband . . . should receive full credit for all that he had ventured and accomplished. Then came the frightful crushing of the Second Revolt, and it is probable that in the moment of danger, ere she fled or was captured by the Mercenaries, she hid the Manuscript. . . . Of

Avis Everhard there is no further record. Undoubtedly she was executed . . . and, as is well known, no record of such executions was kept by the Iron Heel. (London 1924, xi-xii)

(London 1924)

See also *Iron Heel, The;* London, Jack; Meredith, Anthony; Socialism

Ewell, Bob

In Harper Lee's 1960 novel *To Kill a Mockingbird,* Bob Ewell is a coward and bully who hates African Americans. He falsely accuses a black man of raping his daughter and threatens the lawyer who defends the man. Eventually he tries to kill the lawyer's children and is himself killed during the attack. (Lee 1993)

See also Lee, Harper; *To Kill a Mockingbird*

Exiles

An exile is a person who has been banished from his or her native country. The term also refers to those who have left their country voluntarily after a period of persecution, oppression, and/or censorship. Several social protest authors have been exiled, either forcibly or voluntarily, because of their work and beliefs. These include Ciro Alegría, Isabel Allende, Breyten Breytenbach, Nuruddin Farah, Anatole France, Maxim Gorky, Milan Kundera, and Aleksandr Solzhenitsyn.

Physical or emotional exiles are common characters in social protest literature. For example, in Aldous Huxley's *Brave New World* Bernard Marx is banished to an island for social misfits, and in Ayn Rand's *Atlas Shrugged* a group of revolutionaries exile themselves to a secret mountain community. In the works of Ralph Ellison and Richard Wright black men are depicted as exiles from white society, as are Native Americans in Helen Hunt Jackson's *Ramona.* In Edith Wharton's novel *The Age of Innocence* Countess Ellen Olenska escapes her husband's brutality by leaving Poland for the United States, where she finds herself not only physically but also emotionally exiled because of her failure to fit in with high society. Fictional revolutionaries, criminals, time-travelers, and explorers, such as Avis Everhard, Lemuel Gulliver, Jean Valjean, and Julian West, are shown to be exiles from their societies. (Tabori 1972)

See also *Age of Innocence, The;* Alegría, Ciro; Allende, Isabel; *Atlas Shrugged; Brave New World;* Breytenbach, Breyten; Ellison, Ralph; Everhard, Avis; Farah, Nuruddin; France, Anatole; Gorky, Maxim; *Gulliver's Travels;* Huxley, Aldous; Jackson, Helen Hunt; Kundera, Milan; Olenska, Countess Ellen; *Ramona;* Rand, Ayn; Solzhenitsyn, Aleksandr; Valjean, Jean; West, Julian; Wharton, Edith; Wright, Richard

F

Fahrenheit 451

First published in 1950 as a short story entitled "The Fire Man," the title of the 1953 novel *Fahrenheit 451,* by Ray Bradbury, refers to the temperature at which paper burns. The story is set in a future United States where it is a crime to own or read books. Independent thought is discouraged, and people spend most of their time watching television or speeding nowhere along fast highways. They lead uncaring lives in fireproof metal homes, and it is the job of firemen such as Guy Montag to burn books.

Montag enjoys this job until he meets a young neighbor who questions his decision to become a fireman. He starts reevaluating his life, and when he encounters a woman who would rather burn to death than leave her books, he wonders why they could be so important. He secretly steals several books for himself. His fire chief, Beatty, becomes suspicious, warning him that if he does have any books, he has 24 hours to turn them in. Beatty then tells Montag how book-burning came about. He says that at first it was individuals, not the government, who wanted books destroyed, explaining:

You must understand that our civilization is so vast that we can't have our minorities upset and stirred. Ask yourself, What do we want in this country, above all? People want to be happy, isn't that right? . . . That's what we live for, isn't it? . . . Colored people don't like *Little Black Sambo.*

Burn it. White people don't feel good about *Uncle Tom's Cabin.* Burn it. Someone's written a book on tobacco and cancer of the lungs? The cigarette people are weeping? Burn the book. Serenity, Montag. Peace, Montag. Take your fight outside. Better yet, into the incinerator. (Bradbury 1996, 59)

Later Montag considers turning the books in, but first he wants to read them. His wife, Mildred, is horrified. She doesn't want to know about books. She only wants to watch television. Disgusted with her, Montag goes to visit a man, Faber, he once suspected of owning books. He asks Faber to help him make copies of his books, and the two discuss ways to end book-burning in the United States. They also discuss the news that the country might soon be at war.

When Montag returns home, he discovers that Mildred has invited some friends over to watch her favorite television program. Montag begins reading them poetry instead. They leave upset, and Mildred soon follows. Later

The book burners raid a house in this scene from the 1966 movie Fahrenheit 451. *(Rank/The Museum of Modern Art Film Stills Archive)*

she turns him in to the fire department, and Captain Beatty tells Montag he must burn his own house. Montag refuses and burns Captain Beatty instead. Now wanted for murder, he runs to Faber's house, and with his friend's help he escapes the city to join up with a group of book-loving hobos. Montag soon learns that each one has memorized a different part of a book. As one man explains:

> It wasn't planned, at first. Each man had a book he wanted to remember, and did. Then, over a period of twenty years or so, we met each other, traveling, and got the loose network together and set out a plan. . . . We're nothing more than dust jackets for books, of no significance otherwise. Some of us live in small towns. Chapter One of Thoreau's *Walden* in Green River, Chapter Two in Willow Farm, Maine. . . . And when the war's over, someday, some year, the books can be written again, the people will be called in, one by one, to recite what they know and we'll set it up in type until another Dark Age, when we might have to do the whole damn thing over again. (153)

Montag remembers what he has read and agrees to join the group as the Book of Ecclesiastes from the Bible. Together with his new friends he sits on a hillside and watches as bombs strike and destroy the city.

In discussing *Fahrenheit 451* in a 1996 edition of the work, Bradbury argues that, although the novel was written in 1951, it is still an important work of social protest for today's society. He (176–178) states that special-interest groups continue to threaten books, saying:

> There is more than one way to burn a

book. And the world is full of people running around with lit matches. Every minority, be it Baptist/Unitarian, Irish/Italian/Octogenarian /Zen Buddhist, Zionist/ Seventh-day Adventist, Women's Lib/Republican/Mattachine/FourSquare Gospel feels it has the will, the right, the duty to douse the kerosene and light the fuse. . . . Fire-Captain Beatty . . . described how the books were burned first by minorities, each ripping a page or a paragraph from this book, then that, until the day came when the books were empty and the minds shut and the libraries closed forever. . . . [And today] it is a mad world and it will get madder if we allow the minorities, be they dwarf or giant, orangutan or dolphin, nuclear-head or water-conservationist, pro-computerologist or Neo-Luddite, simpleton or sage, to interfere with aesthetics. The real world is the playing ground for each and every group, to make or unmake laws. But the tip of the nose of my book or stories or poems is where their rights end and my territorial imperatives begin, run and rule. If Mormons do not like my plays let them write their own. . . . If the Chicano intellectuals wish to re-cut my "Wonderful Ice Cream Suit" so it shapes "Zoot," may the belt unravel and the pants fall.

(Bradbury 1996; Nolan 1975)

See also Beatty, Captain; Bradbury, Ray; Censorship; Montag, Guy; Science Fiction and Fantasy; *Uncle Tom's Cabin*

Falconer, Sharon

Sharon Falconer, a secondary character in the novel *Elmer Gantry,* by Sinclair Lewis, represents religious hypocrisy. She is a woman evangelist and was most likely modeled after Aimee Semple McPherson, a real-life evangelist of the 1920s. McPherson, who died of a drug overdose in 1944, lived a questionable lifestyle and was involved in several scandals. Similarly, Sharon Falconer indulges in wild parties and sexual adventures while professing her deep spirituality. She claims to be from an old, upstanding Virginia family, but her real name is Katie Jonas and her father is a simple bricklayer. She tells one follower: "Perhaps I'm a prophetess, a little bit, but I'm also a good liar. I picked out the name Sharon Falconer while I was a stenographer. . . . And yet I'm not a liar! . . . I *am* Sharon Falconer now! I've made her—by prayer and by having a right to be her!" (Lewis 1970, 182). She believes that her faith will sustain her, and when a fire breaks out at one of her spiritual gatherings, she tells people that together she and God will lead them through the flames. She dies both despite and because of her religion. (Lewis 1970)

See also *Elmer Gantry;* Religion

Fall, The

The 1956 novel *The Fall,* written in French by Algerian author Albert Camus and published in that language as *La Chute,* addresses a wide variety of human failings, but it particularly criticizes those who are self-serving and consider themselves superior to other human beings. The novel expresses this theme through former lawyer Jean-Baptiste Clamence, who relates the story of his life in a one-sided dialogue with an unnamed stranger, whom he calls a "cultured bourgeois" (Camus 1958, 9).

The two men first meet in an Amsterdam bar, and for the next five days Clamence confesses his past faults. Clamence explains that at one time "my popularity was great and my successes in society innumerable" (27). He lived in Paris, where he was particularly noted for his charitable acts. However, he performed these acts not because he wanted to help others but because he needed to feel superior. He says, "I was always bursting with vanity. I, I, I is the refrain of my whole life, which could be heard in everything I said. I could never talk without boasting" (48).

Because Clamence craved public recognition, he did not perform a good deed unless someone was there to notice it. When he heard a woman jump off a deserted bridge into the Seine River late one night, he did nothing to save her from drowning. "I have forgotten what I thought then," he says. "'Too late, too far . . .' or something of the sort" (70). This event and others eventually led Clamence to question his nature. "I had the suspicion that maybe I wasn't so admirable," he says (77).

Once Clamence judged himself to be flawed, he began to believe that others were judging him with equal harshness. He explains, "In my eyes my fellows ceased to be the respectful public to which I was accustomed. . . . The moment I grasped that there was something to judge in me, I realized that there was in them an irresistible vocation for judgment" (78). As a result of this attitude, Clamence started expressing uncharitable or otherwise outrageous opinions in public. He abused alcohol and indulged in immoral behavior; his career as a lawyer suffered.

Then one day while on an ocean liner he momentarily glimpsed a black speck on the sea. "I was on the point of shouting, of stupidly calling for help," he explains, "when I saw it again. It was one of those bits of refuse that ships leave behind them. Yet I had not been able to endure watching it; for I had thought at once of a drowning person" (108). At that point Clamence realized that the cry of the drowning woman he had failed to save would never leave him, and he admitted his guilt (109).

But this guilt is not Clamence's alone. He explains, "The more I accuse myself, the more I have a right to judge you. Even better, I provoke you into judging yourself, and this relieves me of that much of the burden" (140). Clamence calls himself a "judge-penitent" and points out flaws in both individuals and society as a whole, saying, "The portrait I hold out to my contemporaries becomes a mirror" (140).

In the end he encourages the stranger to talk about his own transgressions, saying that "we are odd, wretched creatures, and if we merely look back over our lives, there's no lack of occasions to amaze and horrify ourselves. Just try" (140). Clamence is sure that the stranger has encountered his own woman on the bridge and that he, too, has longed for a second chance to save her—while at the same time feeling fortunate that such a second chance is impossible because, after all, "the water's so cold!" (147). In this way *The Fall* suggests that all people experience a conflict between their desire to better humanity and their desire to remain selfish; the work is therefore a generalized criticism of human society rather than a specific call for social reform. (Camus 1958)

See also Camus, Albert; Clamence, Jean-Baptiste; Justice

Farah, Nuruddin

Born in 1945 in what is now the Republic of Somalia, novelist Nuruddin Farah is credited as being the first published novelist and first English-language author from his country. His works are political in nature. For example, his first novel, *From a Crooked Rib* (1970), deals with sexism, and his trilogy, comprising *Sweet and Sour Milk* (1979), *Sardines* (1981), and *Close Sesame* (1983), shows the oppression of an African dictatorship.

Although Farah is Somali, he has spent much of his time elsewhere. He attended schools in Ethiopia and India and has lived in several different countries for fear of persecution in his own. He received a German fellowship in 1990 and the Swedish Tucholsky Literary Award, which is awarded to exiles, in 1991. (Farah 1992; Wright 1994)

See also *Close Sesame;* Exiles

Fascism

Fascism is a form of totalitarian dictatorship that first appeared in the twentieth century. The term was coined in 1919 by Italian politician Benito Mussolini, who was referring to an ancient Roman power symbol called the fasces. Mussolini believed in the government's right to control and punish its citizens at will. When he seized the Italian government in 1922, he banned all political parties except the Fascist Party and eliminated labor unions and the right to strike.

From 1919 to 1945 fascism spread throughout Europe. Different countries embraced different types of fascism, but all forms had certain things in common. For example, fascists opposed individual freedom, capitalism, feminism, and the women's rights movement. Most were also racist and supported military action, domination, oppression, and censorship. Consequently, many authors, including Lillian Hellman, Sinclair Lewis, Upton Sinclair, and Richard Wright, spoke out against fascism. Others did not specifically criticize the fascist movement but attacked the attitudes that encouraged it. For example, Walter Van Tilburg Clark's *The Ox-Bow Incident*, which concerns an American lynching, is often interpreted as an antifascist novel. (Cohen 1962)

> See also Clark, Walter Van Tilburg; Hellman, Lillian; Lewis, Sinclair; *Ox-Bow Incident, The;* Sinclair, Upton; Wright, Richard

Fatheya

Fatheya appears in the 1974 Egyptian feminist novel *Mawt al-rajul al-wahid 'ala 'l-ard* (God Dies by the Nile), by Nawal El Saadawi. Her husband is the religious leader of the village, yet when he finds an illegitimate child on their doorstep, he wants to leave it to die. Fatheya insists that they keep the baby, even after the villagers decide it is bringing the town bad luck. When a mob comes to kill the boy, she tries to defend him with her own life, dying with his body in her arms. (El Saadawi 1990)

> See also El Saadawi, Nawal; *God Dies by the Nile*

Feminism

The term *feminism* refers to the belief that women should be treated as equals to men, not only politically but also economically and socially. A great deal of feminist literature is therefore also social protest literature. In nonfiction, such works include English author Mary Wollstonecraft's 1792 treatise *A Vindication of the Rights of Woman*, American author Betty Friedan's 1963 book *The Feminine Mystique*, and the speeches and writings of such notable early feminists as Susan B. Anthony, Elizabeth Cady Stanton, Julia Ward Howe, and Sojourner Truth. In fiction, feminist authors include Sibilla Aleramo, Isabel Allende, Maya Angelou, Sawako Ariyoshi, Margaret Atwood, Nawal El Saadawi, Miles Franklin, Zora Neale Hurston, Nella Larsen, Toni Morrison, Tillie Olsen, and Alice Walker. Many male social protest authors also deal with feminist issues in their work. For example, Henry James's novel *The Bostonians* concerns the women's rights movement in the United States, and Pramoedya Ananta Toer's novel *This Earth of Mankind* depicts the oppression of women in Indonesia. (Jenness 1972; Ramelson 1967; Schneir 1972)

> See also Aleramo, Sibilla; Allende, Isabel; Angelou, Maya; Ariyoshi, Sawako; Atwood, Margaret; *Bostonians, The;* El Saadawi, Nawal; Franklin, Miles; Howe, Julia Ward; Hurston, Zora Neale; James, Henry; Larsen, Nella; Morrison, Toni; Olsen, Tillie; *This Earth of Mankind;* Toer, Pramoedya Ananta; Walker, Alice

Ferlinghetti, Lawrence

Born on March 24, 1919 or 1920, in Yonkers, New York, Lawrence Ferlinghetti is a poet best known for fighting against censorship in the United States. He also founded a San Francisco bookstore, City Lights, where many writers of the Beat movement congregated, and he started his own publishing company, City Lights Books, to disseminate many of their works. The first publication of City Lights Books was Ferlinghetti's first book of poems, *Pictures of the Gone World* (1955). His second book, *A Coney Island of the Mind* (1958), is his most famous and has several short social protest poems. His subsequent works include *Landscapes of Living and Dying* (1979), *Wild Dreams of a New Beginning* (1988), and *These Are My Rivers, 1950–1993* (1993). (Cherkovski 1979; Ferlinghetti 1958)

> See also Beat Movement; Censorship

Ferreira, Christovao

Christovao Ferreira is one of the main characters in Shūsaku Endō's 1966 novel *Chimmoku* (Silence). A Portuguese priest sent to gain converts to Christianity in Japan, he is arrested by Japanese authorities who want to end the religion's spread. When Ferreira refuses to renounce his religion, he is cut and left to bleed to death, hung upside down in a pit with other dying men. In the end he rejects Christianity not to save himself but to save his fellow sufferers, believing that Jesus Christ would have done this, too. Nonetheless, after he is released from the pit and word of his actions reaches Portugal, he becomes an object of scorn there, and over time he becomes a dispirited man. He spends the rest of his life in Japan, living as a Japanese, writing anti-Christianity materials, and helping the authorities identify Christians for persecution. (Endō 1980)

See also Endō, Shūsaku; *Silence*

Finch, Jean Louise ("Scout")

Jean Louise Finch, nicknamed "Scout," is the first-person narrator of *To Kill a Mockingbird* (1960), by Harper Lee. She describes a series of events during her childhood that teach her about morals, courage, and prejudice. In her town of Maycomb, Alabama, she observes that most people associate only with those from their own social class and that whites discriminate against blacks. Her father, however, is different; he treats everyone with respect regardless of class or race. Eventually Scout learns to do this herself. (Lee 1993)

See also Lee, Harper; *To Kill a Mockingbird*

Finchley, Sondra

In Theodore Dreiser's 1925 novel *An American Tragedy*, Sondra Finchley is a rich girl who falls in love with Clyde Griffiths, a man of poor background. She originally begins dating him on a lark, but she later falls in love and wants to marry him despite her family's objections. However, when Clyde is arrested for killing a mistress whom he has impregnated, Sondra allows her parents to keep her away from him. The Finchleys fear for their reputation in the community, and Sondra is as much a prisoner of her social status as Clyde. (Dreiser 1964; Moers 1969)

See also *American Tragedy, An;* Dreiser, Theodore; Griffiths, Clyde

Finkelberg, Isaac

Son of a Jewish shopkeeper and a character from the 1948 South African novel *The Path of Thunder*, by Peter Abrahams, Isaac Finkelberg is an intellectual who discusses his country's racial policies with his friends, Mako and Lanny. Lanny is a mixed-race, or "coloured," man, whereas Mako is a Zulu native who tells Isaac that the situation of the Jewish people is similar to that of the coloureds because both live "in lands of other nations" and have "no independent nationality" (Abrahams 1975, 89). Isaac's father disagrees, saying that a man can be a Jew or a Zulu no matter where he lives and tells Isaac that he is a fool to associate with Mako and Lanny because the Dutch who control the area will persecute him for this association. Consequently, father and son quarrel, and Isaac concludes that the old man "seemed to have forgotten how to strike a blow for his own freedom and independence" (72). In fact, Isaac believes that all Jews have become "too civilized. Too humane. They were known for the peaceful arts. The creative arts. Scholarship. They were too . . . deeply steeped in the peaceful, commercial, and creatively gentle art of living. They knew how to build but they had forgotten how to destroy. And the foundations were rotten" (72). (Abrahams 1975; Ensor 1992)

See also Abrahams, Peter; Mako; *Path of Thunder, The;* Racism; Swartz, Lanny

France, Anatole

Anatole France was born Jacques-Anatole-François Thibault on April 16, 1844, in Paris, France. He wrote novels, plays, poems, essays, and literary criticism and commentary, including an introduction to Jack London's social protest novel *The Iron Heel*. France also dealt with social issues in some of his own works. For example, his 1903 three-act comedy *Crainquebille* depicts some of the beliefs that led France to embrace socialism, and his 1908 novel *L'Île des Pingouins* (Penguin Island) shows the development of civilization, industrialization, and pollution on an island of humanlike penguins.

France was also known for his involvement in the Dreyfus Affair. In 1894 Captain Alfred Dreyfus was falsely accused of treason, court-martialed by the military, and sent to prison on Devil's Island. His conviction was based not on evidence but on the fact that he was Jewish. Consequently, France and many other writers, including Émile Zola, began demanding Dreyfus's release, and in 1906 a civilian court finally declared Dreyfus innocent. France deals with this issue in his satirical novel *Monsieur Bergeret a Paris* (1901), which is the last volume in a trilogy known as *L'Histoire contemporaine* (1897–1901).

France was elected to the Academie Française in 1896 and received a Nobel Prize in literature in 1921. He died on October 12, 1924, in Saint-Cyr-sur-Loire, France. (May 1970; Vertanen 1968)

See also Anti-Semitism; Exiles; *Iron Heel, The;* London, Jack; Socialism; Zola, Émile

Franklin, Miles

Australian author Stella Maria Sarah Miles Franklin is known for her feminist novels, which include *My Brilliant Career* (1901) and its sequel, *My Career Goes Bung.* The latter was considered too controversial for publication until 1946. She also wrote under the pseudonyms Brent of Bin Bin and Mrs. Ogniblat l'Artsau. Born on October 14, 1879, in Talbingo, New South Wales, Australia, Franklin was raised in remote bush country. In 1906 she moved to the United States, where she worked as an editor, and nine years later to England. In 1927 she returned to Australia to write historical fiction set in her native country. These works include *Up the Country* (1929), *Prelude to Waking* (1950), and *Gentlemen at Gyang Gynag* (1956), all published under the name Brent of Bin Bin. This pseudonym was not recognized as hers until after her death on September 19, 1954, in Sydney, New South Wales. Additional works under her own name include *Some Everyday Folk and Dawn* (1909) and *All That Swagger* (1936). (Barnard 1967; Franklin 1965; Roderick 1982)

See also Feminism; *My Brilliant Career*

Fuentes, Carlos

Mexican writer Carlos Fuentes is best known for his novels exploring Mexican culture and politics in the twentieth century. However, he has also written short stories, plays, essays, and a television series entitled *El espejo enterrado* (The Buried Mirror), which concerns Mexican history and culture and was published in book form in English and Spanish in 1992.

Fuentes was born on November 11, 1928, in Mexico City, where he studied to be a lawyer. Eventually he became a diplomat, as was his father. He held several important posts, including cultural attaché at the Mexican Embassy in Geneva, Switzerland, from 1950 to 1952 and Mexican ambassador to France from 1975 to 1977.

His first published work appeared in 1954; it was a collection of short stories entitled *Los días enmascarados* (The Masked Days). His first novel, *La región transparente* (Where the Air Is Clear) was published in Spanish in 1958 and in English in 1960. It criticized many aspects of Mexican society and gained Fuentes recognition in his own country, as did

Carlos Fuentes, 21 April 1988 (Reuters/High Peralton/ Archive Photos)

his second and third novels, *Las buenas con-ciencias* (The Good Conscience, 1959) and *Aura* (1962). However, his third novel, *La muerte de Artemio Cruz* (The Death of Artemio Cruz), gained him international recognition. Published in Spanish in 1962 and in English in 1964, it, too, criticizes Mexican society as it presents the memories of a wealthy man on his deathbed.

Fuentes is the author of several more nov-els, including *La cabeza de la hidra* (The Hydra Head, 1978), a spy thriller about Mexican backroom politics, and *Una familia lejana* (Distant Relations, 1980), an experimental novel about alternate realities. He also wrote a work of literary criticism entitled *La nueva novela hispanoamericana* (The New Hispano-American Novel, 1969). (Faris 1983)

See also *Death of Artemio Cruz, The; Hydra Head, The*

G

Gaines, Ernest J.

African-American author Ernest James Gaines is best known for writing *The Autobiography of Miss Jane Pittman,* a novel about slavery and the civil rights movement. Published in 1971, the book was made into an award-winning television special in 1974.

Gaines was born on a plantation in Oscar, Louisiana, on January 15, 1933. As a boy he worked in the fields for 50 cents a day. When he was 15, he moved to California, where he graduated from San Francisco State College in 1957. He later received a writing fellowship at Stanford University. His first novel, *Catherine Carmier* (1964), won a prestigious award, the Joseph Henry Jackson Literary Prize. His other works include *In My Father's House* (1978), *A Gathering of Old Men* (1983), and *A Lesson before Dying* (1993). (Babb 1991; Estes 1994; Gaines 1972)

See also *Autobiography of Miss Jane Pittman, The;* Racism; Slavery

Galsworthy, John

English author John Galsworthy is best known for a series of novels entitled *The Forsyte Saga,* published together in 1922 and later made into a television drama. However, he also wrote important social protest plays, including *Strife* (1909), which deals with a la-bor strike, and *Justice* (1910), which led to prison reform in England.

Galsworthy was born in Kingston Hill, Surrey, England, on August 14, 1867. He grew up in a wealthy family and was educated at Harrow and New College, Oxford. In 1890 he became a lawyer, but he soon grew dissatisfied with the profession. He began to write, and in 1898 he self-published a collection of short stories and a novel, entitled *Jocelyn,* under the pseudonym John Sinjohn. It was not until 1904 that he published a novel, *The Island Pharisees,* under his own name. His other novels include *The Man of Property* (1906), *Chancery* (1920), and *To Let* (1921), which were later published collectively as *The Forsyte Saga,* as well as several sequels to the saga: *The White Monkey* (1924), *The Silver Spoon* (1926), *Swan Song* (1928), which were published collectively as *A Modern Comedy* in 1929, and *End of the Chapter* (1931–1932). Galsworthy died on January 31, 1933, in Grove Lodge, Hamstead, England. (Barker 1969)

See also Labor Issues; Prison Reform; *Strife*

Galt, John

Throughout Ayn Rand's novel *Atlas Shrugged* characters use the slang phrase "Who is John Galt?" to mean "Who knows?" There are various theories regarding the expression's origin, but eventually the truth is revealed. John Galt is an inventor who once worked for a motor-car company. One day the company decided that extra effort, creativity, and merit would no longer be rewarded. Every worker was to be treated equally, so that the industrious would actually be subsidizing the mediocre. Galt quickly realized that this approach was going to spread throughout the United States. He quit his job and announced that he would stop the motor of the world. He created a secret society that is fighting to preserve capitalism. By the end of the novel he has succeeded in destroying the government and is ready to lead a new society based on profit and individual effort. (Rand 1992)

See also *Atlas Shrugged*; Rand, Ayn

García, Esteban

In Isabel Allende's 1982 South American novel *La casa de los espíritus* (The House of the Spirits) Esteban García is a cruel policeman who enjoys torturing innocent people. The illegitimate grandson of wealthy conservative senator Esteban Trueba, he feels betrayed out of his rightful inheritance and seeks his revenge by punishing Trueba's granddaughter, Alba. After a military coup he arrests Alba for political crimes and subjects her to rapes, beatings, and electric shock treatments. (Allende 1985)

See also Allende, Isabel; De Satigny, Alba Trueba; Del Valle, Clara; García, Pedro Tecero; *House of the Spirits, The;* Trueba, Esteban

García, Pedro Tecero

In Isabel Allende's 1982 novel *La casa de los espíritus* (The House of the Spirits), Pedro Tecero García is a revolutionary who supports socialism in his South American homeland by handing out pamphlets and singing social protest songs. He works to overturn the conservative government, but the new socialist regime is short-lived. A military coup soon occurs, ushering in a dictatorship, and Pedro Tecero and his lover, Blanca Trueba, must escape the country with the help of her father, a disillusioned conservative politician. (Allende 1985)

See also Allende, Isabel; De Satigny, Alba Trueba; Del Valle, Clara; García, Esteban; *House of the Spirits, The;* Socialism; Trueba, Esteban

Gay and Lesbian Issues

Homosexuality involves a sexual relationship between members of the same sex. Gays and lesbians have been persecuted to varying degrees throughout history, and many authors have protested this persecution. They have also encouraged an understanding of gay and lesbian issues and lifestyle. For example, Jean-Paul Sartre and James Baldwin depict men struggling to accept their homosexuality in their novels *The Age of Reason* and *Another Country,* respectively, and Alice Walker shows a woman exploring lesbianism in her novel *The Color Purple.* Lillian Hellman examines the persecution of lesbians in her play *The Children's Hour,* and Allen Ginsberg provoked censorship for his mention of homosexuality in his poem *Howl.* (Galloway and Sabish 1982)

See also *Age of Reason, The; Another Country;* Baldwin, James; Censorship; *Children's Hour, The; Color Purple, The;* Ginsberg, Allen; Hellman, Lillian; *Howl;* Sartre, Jean-Paul; Walker, Alice

Ginsberg, Allen

American poet Allen Ginsberg was the author of the epic poem *Howl,* which protests society's suppression of individuality and personal exploration. Published in 1956, it created immediate controversy for its raw language, and its publisher was arrested for distributing obscenity. The American Civil Liberties Union defended the book and its publisher in the resulting obscenity trial, eventually winning the case.

Ginsberg was born on June 3, 1926, in Newark, New Jersey. His mother was a Russian immigrant, his father a poet and schoolteacher. At age 17 he began attending Columbia University, but he was expelled in 1945 for bad behavior. He then worked at a variety of odd jobs, including dishwasher, night porter, copy boy, and literary agent, before being readmitted to Columbia in 1948. He graduated

Allen Ginsberg (Russell Reif/Archive Photos)

Street (1891). Named for the literary district of London, it presents the desperation of the poor in Victorian England.

In his early years as a writer Gissing himself lived in poverty. The son of a pharmacist, he fell in love with a woman suspected of being a prostitute while he was away at college. To support her, he stole money from coat pockets. He was soon expelled, and his family disowned him. Later he married the woman, and despite his prolific writing career, he remained relatively poor until her death in 1888, when he was able to live more economically. However, although Gissing discusses the economic disadvantages of marriage in *New Grub Street,* the year it was published he married another lower-class woman. The two eventually separated, and he lived in France with a mistress until his death in 1903. Two of Gissing's books, *Commonplace Book* (1962) and *The Diary of George Gissing, Novelist* (1982), were published posthumously. (Gissing 1926; Goode 1979; Selig 1983)

See also Class, Social; *New Grub Street;* Poverty

that same year with a bachelor of arts degree and entered into graduate study. In 1949 he spent two months in a state hospital for psychiatric problems. He also began experimenting with drugs.

In 1954 he moved to San Francisco, where he wrote *Howl and Other Poems* and became involved in the Beat movement, a counterculture social and literary movement that took place in the United States during the late 1950s and early 1960s. He published a great deal of poetry during this period, including *Kaddish and Other Poems* (1961) and *Reality Sandwiches* (1963). His recent works include *Cosmopolitan Greetings: Poems 1986–1992* (1994) and *Journals Mid-Fifties, 1954–1958* (1995). He died on April 5, 1997, in New York City. (Merrill 1969; Miles 1995)

See also Beat Movement; Censorship; *Howl*

Gissing, George

Born in 1857, English novelist George Robert Gissing was one of the most productive authors of his time. He published 19 novels, many of them written in three volumes. Perhaps the most famous of these was *New Grub*

Glass Bead Game, The

Published as *Magister Ludi* in a 1949 English translation, the 1943 novel *Das Glasperlenspiel* (The Glass Bead Game), by Hermann Hesse, examines the compartmentalization of society and the conflict that occurs within people who do not lead a balanced life. It is the fictional biography of Joseph Knecht, a man of the twenty-third century, as told by a twenty-fifty-century scholar. As a young boy Knecht is identified as a talented musician and asked to join an elite order of intellectuals. This order is supported by the government and segregated from the rest of society. Its members are not allowed to marry or participate in worldly activities, and although they learn meditation, they do not practice a religion. They also do not study history or politics, believing them to be too worldly and common. Knecht has mixed feelings about joining this order, but eventually becomes one of its leaders, or Magisters, and is placed in charge of the Glass Bead Game. The game is an important mental exercise for those in the order. The narrator's description of it is vague, but it appears to be a meditative pursuit in which players use music, mathematics, and other intellectual disciplines to make complex mental connections between various objects and concepts. Constantly evolving and changing, the game's many variations and strategies are recorded in a great archive in the province of Castalia, which is overseen by Knecht in his position as Magister Ludi.

This position is the pinnacle of success in the order, but after several years Knecht becomes dissatisfied with it. He realizes that if he remains isolated from the rest of his society, he will never learn or grow as an individual. Moreover, after studying history and politics, he decides that the outside world will eventually stop supporting the order unless it makes some fundamental changes. When its governing board refuses to heed his warnings, Knecht resigns his position and becomes a tutor for a young man from a politically powerful family. Knecht believes that his influence on this man will ultimately benefit society, and he is full of hope for the future. Unfortunately, he drowns in a swimming accident shortly after meeting his new pupil. Nonetheless, the young man's perception of the world and his role in it have been altered by his contact with Joseph Knecht.

Although set in the future, *The Glass Bead Game* is actually a statement on contemporary society. As scholar Theodore Ziolkowsky (xv) points out in a 1986 introduction to the novel, Knecht's order "has more than a little in common with the intellectual and cultural institutions of the sixties, to the extent that they have become autonomous empires cut off from the social needs of mankind and cultivating their own Glass Bead Games in glorious isolation." The novel portrays not only the order but also the world outside the order as being dysfunctional, suggesting that both halves of society suffer from the separation of intellectual and nonintellectual pursuits. (Hesse 1986; Ziolkowski 1965)

See also Hesse, Hermann; Knecht, Joseph

God Dies by the Nile

The novel *God Dies by the Nile,* which first appeared in Arabic in 1974 as *Mawt al-rajul al-wahid 'ala 'l-ard,* concerns the oppression of women in modern-day Egypt. Its author, Nawal El Saadawi, is a noted Egyptian feminist.

The story is set in Kafr El Teen, a small town beside the Nile River, where the mayor completely controls the lives of the peasants. On a whim he taxes people until they forfeit their land or arrests them on contrived charges. He uses three men as his spies and henchmen: Sheikh Zaran, who is chief of the Village Guard; Sheikh Hamzawi, who is in charge of prayer at the mosque; and Haj Ismail, who is the village barber. These three help the mayor obtain peasant girls for his personal pleasure.

One day the mayor decides that he must have the beautiful young Nefissa. Haj Ismail convinces her father, Kafrawi, to force her to work as a servant in the mayor's house. Kafrawi is a poor widower who lives with his widowed sister, Zakeya. Neither he nor the other peasants suspect that the mayor, who is married, will rape Nefissa. In fact, even after she becomes pregnant and leaves the village, they believe the mayor is blameless. They do, however, think that Nefissa's baby is evil simply because it is illegitimate. When Sheikh Hamzawi finds the baby on his doorstep, they urge him to get rid of the child, and they are angry when his childless wife, Fatheya, takes the little one as her own.

By this time the mayor has decided that he wants Nefissa's younger sister, Zeinab. She refuses to come to his house, so he spreads the rumor that a peasant named Elwau fathered Nefissa's baby, then arranges Elwau's murder and frames Kafrawi for the crime. With her father in jail, Zeinab is left alone to care for her Aunt Zakeya, who has gone crazy with grief. Zeinab begs Sheikh Hamzawi to help her cure her aunt. He sends the two women to a great mosque in a nearby city, where a holy man gives them a message from God: to cure her aunt's mental illness, Zeinab must work in the house of the mayor. The two women return home, and Zeinab becomes the mayor's servant and mistress. No one in the village knows of her shame.

Meanwhile the town's crops have started to fail. The people blame Nefissa's illegitimate son for their bad fortune. They kill both the baby and Fatheya, who is trying to protect him. Shortly thereafter Zakeya's son, Galal, a soldier, returns home from a war on the Sinai Peninsula. He marries Zeinab, and she stops working as a servant girl. Angry that Zeinab no longer comes to his house, the mayor plants a bag of silver in Galal's home and has him arrested for theft. Zeinab goes to visit him at the jail and is kidnapped by a strange man. She is never seen again.

Now Zakeya realizes that the mayor must have told the holy man to send Zeinab to him. Alone and angry, she sees him coming out of his house. She takes a hoe and hammers him to death. After she is arrested, she tells another prisoner that God has now been buried on the banks of the Nile.

Zakeya's retribution brings the death of a tyrant. But although his destruction is the act of an individual, the novel makes it clear that that eventually the other peasants would have risen up against him. Near the end of *God Dies by the Nile* the chief of the Village Guard says: "People have changed. . . . The people who at one time could not look me in the eye, now look at me straight in the face, and no longer bow their heads to the ground when I pass by. Just yesterday, one of the villagers refused to pay his taxes and shouted, 'We work all the year round and all we end up with are debts to the government.' I never used to hear this kind of talk from any of them before" (El Saadawi 1990, 126–127). (El Saadawi 1990; Malti-Douglas 1995)

See also El Saadawi, Nawal; Fatheya; Feminism; Justice; Zakeya; Zeinab

Golding, William

English novelist Sir William Gerald Golding wrote primarily about human violence. His first and most famous work, *Lord of the Flies* (1954), concerns a group of schoolboys stranded on an island who quickly turn savage. His second novel, *The Inheritors* (1955), is set in prehistoric times among brutal Neanderthals. Subsequent novels include *Free Fall* (1959), *The Spire* (1964), *Rites of Passage* (1980), and *Fire Down Below* (1989).

Golding was born on September 19, 1911, near Newquay in Cornwall, England. The son of a teacher, he graduated from Brasenose College in Oxford in 1935 and became a teacher himself, working at Bishop Wordsworth's School in Salisbury. During World War II he joined the Royal Navy, and in 1941 he was present during the military campaign that sunk the German battleship *Bismarck*. After the war he returned to his teaching job, a position he held until 1961. In 1983 he won the Nobel Prize for Literature, and in 1988 he was knighted. He died on June 19, 1993, in Perranarworthal, Cornwall, England. (Baker 1965; Dick 1967; Hynes 1964)

See also *Lord of the Flies*

Gorky, Maxim

Maxim Gorky is the pseudonym for Russian novelist, short-story writer, and poet Aleksey Maksimovich Peshkov. The word *gorky* in Russian means "bitter one," and the author chose it to represent his difficult upbringing. Born in March 1868 in Nizhny Novgorod, Russia, Gorky grew up in his grandfather's home, his father having died when he was only five. When Gorky turned eight, his grandfather made him begin working at odd jobs, which continued into his adulthood. At various times he was an errand boy, a dishwasher, a bakery shop worker, a fisherman, a railroad worker, a clerk, a dockworker, and a night watchman. His life was so harsh that he once tried to commit suicide, and eventually he ended up a vagabond.

From his experiences as a tramp came several ideas for stories, sketches, and articles. His first published fiction appeared in 1892 in local newspapers, whereupon he attracted the attention of author and journalist Vladimir Korolenko. Korolenko helped Gorky get his work published in important journals, and Gorky quickly became famous. He went on to write plays and novels, the latter of which included *Ispoved* (A Confession, 1908) and *Mat* (Mother, 1906). He also established his own publishing house.

Gorky was a Marxist and used much of his income to support the Social Democratic Party and the Marxist movement. This made him unpopular with government officials. In 1901 he was arrested for writing a revolutionary poem, "Pesnya o burevestnike" (Song of the Stormy Petrel), and although he was soon released, he continued to have trouble with the government. In 1906 he was again arrested for his involvement with the Russian Revolution of the previous year. However, his international notoriety made it difficult for the government to keep him in jail, and once more his confinement was brief. After his release he toured the United States and then went into a self-imposed political exile on Italy's island of Capri.

In 1913 Gorky ended his exile and went back to Russia, where he protested some of Vladimir I. Lenin's policies. Lenin then censored Gorky's writings, and eventually Gorky ended his protests. Except for a period in Italy from 1921 to 1928, he lived the rest of his life in Russia. He wrote several more novels, including an autobiography in three volumes, and in 1934 he founded the Soviet Writers' Union. His later work addressed the decline of the merchant families and the intelligentsia in Russia. He died suddenly and mysteriously in 1936, and many scholars suspect that Gorky's death was actually a murder ordered by Joseph Stalin. (Levin 1965)

See also Exiles; "Song of the Stormy Petrel"

Grapes of Wrath, The

The Grapes of Wrath, by John Steinbeck, is the story of a poor farm family struggling for survival amid the harsh economic conditions of the 1930s. However, it is also a timeless protest against oppression and injustice in American society. Its title refers to a phrase from the lyrics of "The Battle Hymn of the Republic," written in 1862 by social reformist Julia Ward Howe.

The novel created a great deal of controversy when it was published in 1939. Some readers believed that Steinbeck was a revolu-

tionary who exaggerated the plight of working-class families in order to promote his political views. Others recognized that the novel realistically portrays the hardships of migrant farmworkers during the period. The author lived among such people while doing research for his work, and reporters later confirmed that he accurately depicted these lives. *The Grapes of Wrath* was awarded the Pulitzer Prize in 1940 and was made into a movie the same year.

The novel alternates omniscient discussions about the plight of migrant farmworkers in general with a narrative about the Joad family of Oklahoma in particular. At the beginning of the narrative Tom Joad Jr. has just been released from prison, where he served four years for killing a man in self-defense. On his way home Tom meets Jim Casy, who was once his preacher but has lost his faith and left the church. Together the two travel to Tom's family farm through land wasted by drought. The Joads have been tenants on the farm for a long time, but when the two men reach it, they find the farm deserted. Another farmer tells them that the Joads are at a relative's house getting ready to leave for California. Because of the drought, tenant farming throughout the Midwest has become unprofitable, and the landowners have decided to either sell their property or turn to mechanized farming. The tenant farmers, or sharecroppers, are therefore being forced to move, but not before selling their furniture and equipment at reduced prices and buying used cars at inflated ones.

Tom and Jim find the Joads at an uncle's house. The family includes Pa and Ma Joad; their sons Noah and Al; their pregnant teenage daughter Rose of Sharon (referred to as Rosasharn) and her husband Connie Rivers; the Joads' two youngest children, Ruthie and Winfield; and Granma and Grampa Joad. Glad to see Tom, they tell him about a handbill advertising for farmworkers in California. They have bought an old truck to carry them there and ask Jim to accompany them. He gladly agrees. But the trip across the country is hard, and along the way Grampa dies of a stroke. The family buries him by the side of the road. Later the truck breaks down

Tom Joad kneels to check on the family truck in a scene from the 1940 movie The Grapes of Wrath. *(Library of Congress/Corbis)*

and must be repaired. Finally the family crosses the California border. The Joads camp by a river where some other migrant families are gathered and learn that work in California is hard to find. They also discover that migrants are not treated well in California. One person tells them that Californians "hate you 'cause they're scairt. They know a hungry fella gonna get food even if he got to take it" (Steinbeck 1972, 225). This man then explains that all migrant workers are called "Okies," saying: "Okie use' ta mean you was from Oklahoma. Now it means you're . . . scum. Don't mean nothing itself, it's the way they say it. But I can't tell you nothin'. You got to go there. I hear there's three hunderd thousan' of our people there—an' livin' like hogs, 'cause ever'thing in California is owned. They ain't nothin' left. An' them people that owns it is gonna hang onto it if they got ta kill ever'-body in the worl' to do it" (225–226).

Later the omniscient narrator also discusses the fears of the owners, saying:

And the great owners, who must lose their land in an upheaval, the great owners with access to history, with eyes to real history and to know the great fact; when property accumulates in too few hands it is taken away. And that companion fact: when a majority of the people are hungry and cold they will take by force what they need. And the little screaming fact that sounds through all history: repression works only to strengthen and knit the repressed. The great owners ignored the three cries of history. The land fell into fewer hands, the number of the dispossessed increased, and every effort of the great owners was directed at repression. The money was spent for arms, for gas to protect the great holdings, and spies were sent to catch the murmuring of revolt so that it might be stamped out. The changing economy was ignored, plans for the change ignored; and only means to destroy revolt were considered, while the causes of revolt went on. (262)

The Joads are warned several times that they might starve in California, but they know they cannot return to Oklahoma. While they rest at the river camp, they plan their journey across the desert to the fertile land around Bakersfield. Suddenly Noah decides that he will not continue with the group. He tells Tom that he plans to stay by the river and eat fish, then disappears. Shortly thereafter a policeman arrives and orders the family to move on. The Joads head west, and Granma dies in the desert. The family leaves her body with the coroner in Bakersfield and heads to a migrant camp on the outskirts of town. There Tom gets into a fight with a cruel police deputy who is harassing an innocent man. Jim knocks the deputy out and tells Tom to hide. He reminds Tom that as a newly released convict, he was supposed to have stayed in Oklahoma, has therefore violated his parole, and will undoubtedly be sent back to prison. Tom runs away, and when the rest of the police arrive, Jim takes full blame for the incident. He is arrested and taken to jail.

When Tom returns, he discovers that Connie, who has been complaining about their harsh living conditions, has deserted his family. The Joads decide to relocate to a government-run camp, where no deputies will bother them. There they are pleased to find that the camp has good sanitary conditions and is governed with fairness by a committee of its residents. Then Tom learns that the townspeople have a plan to shut down the camp. They intend to start a fight at a camp dance, so that deputies can come in and clear the place out. Tom warns the other residents, and the troublemakers are stopped before they can do any damage. The camp remains open.

Unfortunately, the Joads cannot find enough work in the area, so they head north to a large farm that needs peach pickers. They must enter the gate with a police escort, past an angry mob protesting the farm's unfair wages. Once inside, the Joads spend all day picking peaches for five cents a box; even though every member of the family is working, they earn only enough money for one meal. Not only are wages low, but also the goods at the company store are overpriced. That night Tom goes for a walk, crawls under the fence, and encounters the protesters. To his surprise, he discovers that Jim Casy is among them. Jim explains that the protesters are former employees of the farm who went on strike when their wages were cut from a dollar and a half per box of peaches picked to two and a half cents a box. Jim asks Tom to convince the strikebreakers to join their protest. While the two are talking, some strangers attack them. Jim is killed, and Tom kills one of the attackers. He returns to the farm and asks his family to hide him until he can escape.

But Ma Joad is unwilling to let him leave them. Instead, she decides that the entire family will move on, hiding Tom under a mattress in the truck as they drive away. Her plan works. Eventually they come upon a group of migrants camped in some abandoned boxcars. They make camp and get jobs picking cotton. Tom remains in hiding. Then Ruthie tells another girl about him, and Ma Joad realizes that Tom is now in danger of being caught. She tells him to leave. He agrees, vowing to spend his life fighting against injustice. He says: "Wherever they's a fight so hungry people can eat, I'll be there. Wherever they's a cop beatin' up a guy, I'll be there. . . . I'll be in the way guys yell when they're made an'—I'll be in the way kids laugh when they're hungry an' they know supper's ready. An' when our folks eat the stuff they raise an' live in the houses they build—why, I'll be there" (463).

After Tom is gone, a heavy rainstorm causes a stream to overflow and flood the camp, despite the migrants' efforts to prevent it. At the same time Rose of Sharon delivers a stillborn baby. Eventually the waters rise so high that the Joads' car will not work, and the family must flee on foot. They find a barn, where a

Man in a soup kitchen, New York City, 1938 (Library of Congress)

man is starving to death. Rose of Sharon feeds him with her breast milk. In this way the poor nourish their own and life goes on.

Throughout the novel those in power either neglect or mistreat the downtrodden. Police, bank managers, and landowners are depicted as either cruel or easily intimidated by those with more power. For example, one landowner does not want to reduce his farmworkers' pay; however, the bank has threatened to foreclose on his loan if he refuses to do so. Similarly, some townspeople want to destroy the government-run migrant camps, which provide toilets and hot water. One man says that the migrants do not deserve hot water, adding: "We ain't gonna have no peace till we wipe them camps out. They'll be wantin' clean sheets, first thing we know" (417). Faced with such discrimination, the Joads develop a social conscience. At the beginning of the novel they are highly individualistic. However, as the story progresses, they begin to show concern for other migrants and to recognize that their problems are everyone's problems. This concern for the greater good is

also shared by the former preacher, Jim Casy. Having lost his faith in traditional religion, he discovers a new religious fervor through his fight for justice among the farmworkers. He dies protesting their mistreatment. (Moore 1968; Steinbeck 1972)

See also Great Depression; Immigrant Communities; Joad Family; Poverty; Steinbeck, John

Great Depression

The Great Depression was a time of economic hardship that developed during the 1930s throughout the world. In the United States one in every four workers lost his or her job. Stocks decreased in value, businesses failed, and many affluent people were thrown into poverty. At the same time farmers in the Dust Bowl region of the country, which includes the Oklahoma and Texas panhandles and parts of Colorado, Kansas, and New Mexico, experienced a drought and began migrating to other areas looking for work. In major cities they competed with immigrants from other countries who had come to the United States hoping for an end to their poverty. One of the most famous American social protest novels, *The Grapes of Wrath,* by John Steinbeck, was inspired by this situation. Another significant social protest novel of the period was *Yonnondio: From the Thirties,* by Tillie Olsen. (Shannon 1960; Swados 1966)

See also *Grapes of Wrath, The;* Olsen, Tillie; Poverty; Steinbeck, John; *Yonnondio: From the Thirties*

Great Expectations

Great Expectations, by Charles Dickens, was first published in serialized form in a weekly periodical, *All the Year Round,* from 1860 to 1861. The novel was published in book form in 1861. It is the first-person narrative of Phillip Pirrip, known as Pip. As a child Pip is orphaned and raised by his sister, who is cruel, and her husband, Joe, who is kind. One day the boy meets an escaped prisoner who asks him for food. Pip brings him a pork pie and a file to cut the chain from his leg. The man promises he will repay Pip someday for his kindness.

Meanwhile Pip's sister makes him visit an old woman, Miss Haversham, each day. Miss Haversham is bitter because her fiancé disappeared on her wedding day, and she is teaching her young ward, Estella, to be cruel to men. Consequently, Estella often teases Pip. Nonetheless, when a lawyer approaches Pip and tells him that a benefactor has arranged for him to go to London, the young man assumes that Miss Haversham is behind his good fortune. He assumes that she wants him to become a gentleman, so that he can marry Estella. Later Miss Haversham encourages this belief.

While in London Pip moves among the upper classes and becomes conceited. Consequently, when Estella visits London and he falls in love with her, she rejects him for another man. Then Pip discovers that his benefactor was not Miss Haversham but Abel Magwitch, the convict he once helped. Shortly after Pip rescued him from hunger, Magwitch was recaptured and exiled to New South Wales, where he made a fortune as a sheep farmer. He returned to England specifically to help Pip, even though this was against the law.

Pip confronts Miss Haversham with her deceit and learns that Estella is about to be married. Later he visits Miss Haversham again and discovers that her house is on fire. He tries to save the old woman but fails. By this time he knows that Magwitch's long-standing enemy, Arthur Compeyson, is plotting to kill the former convict and that Compeyson is the man who once jilted Miss Haversham. Pip has also discovered that Magwitch is Estella's father. The young man tries to get his benefactor out of England to safety. During the escape Compeyson attacks Magwitch and Magwitch kills him. The old man is captured and sent to prison, where he dies before his trial. Pip now reunites with a widowed Joe, loses the last of his conceit, and goes into business with a pleasant young man named Herbert Pocket. Eleven years later he also reunites with Estella, whose husband has died.

The story of *Great Expectations* is primarily a romance and a mystery, but there are elements of social protest in Pip's rise through the social classes. Pip's moral corruption as he gains wealth reflects Dickens's view of the upper classes in general. This theme appears in many of his works and is particularly prominent in *Little Dorrit.* (Dickens 1963; Fielding 1958; Hibbert 1967)

See also Class, Social; Dickens, Charles; *Little Dorrit;* Poverty

Green, Horatio

Horatio Green is a character in the 1853 novel *Clotel,* by William Wells Brown, which concerns slavery in the United States during the 1800s. He falls in love with a young slave, Clotel, and takes her to be his mistress. They live together as man and wife and have a beautiful young daughter. Nonetheless, society does not recognize Clotel as anything but Horatio's slave. Moreover, when Horatio decides that he wants to become politically powerful, he finds it easy to abandon his love for Clotel and marry a white woman from a well-connected family. He allows his new wife to sell

Clotel and make her daughter a house slave, and he lives out the rest of his life as an unhappy man. (Gates 1990)

See also *Clotel*

Greene, Graham

The works of English novelist Henry Graham Greene deal with human corruption and decay in contemporary political settings. Many of his novels are set in countries with unstable governments. For example, *The Quiet American* (1956) takes place in Vietnam during the 1950s; *Our Man in Havana* (1958) in Cuba just prior to the Communist revolution. One of his most famous novels, *The Power and the Glory* (1940), concerns religious persecution in Mexico under a revolutionary government. Graham's other novels include *Stamboul Train*, also titled *Orient Express* (1932), *Brighton Rock* (1938), *The Heart of the Matter* (1948), *A Burnt-Out Case* (1961), *The Comedians* (1966), and *The Tenth Man* (1985). He also wrote several collections of short stories, as well as plays, essays, and memoirs.

Greene was born in Berkhamsted, Hertfordshire, England, on October 2, 1904. The son of a teacher, he ran away from school and was later sent to live with a psychoanalyst in London. He attended Balliol College in Oxford and became a Roman Catholic in 1926. The following year he moved back to London and became a copy editor for *The Times* newspaper. His first published novel, *The Man Within,* appeared in 1929, and because of its success, he quit his job to become a film critic and literary editor for *The Spectator,* a position he held until 1940. He died on April 3, 1991, in Vevey, Switzerland. (De Vitis 1964; Pryce-Jones 1968)

See also Exiles; Justice; *Power and the Glory, The;* Religion

Griffiths, Clyde

As the main character of Theodore Dreiser's 1925 novel *An American Tragedy,* Clyde Griffiths is more concerned with social climbing than morality. He was raised in poverty but wants to be a rich man. Therefore, he is over-joyed when a girl from a prominent New York family becomes romantically interested in him. There is just once problem: he already has a girlfriend, Roberta Alden. When Roberta tells Clyde she is pregnant and threatens to expose him as a cad unless he marries her, he decides to murder her. At the last minute he changes his mind but accidentally kills her anyway. This is not the first accident in Clyde's life; he is often the victim of chance or circumstance because Dreiser wanted to show human beings as victims of their backgrounds, social roles, and passions. Nonetheless, Clyde receives full punishment for Roberta's death from a legal system that considers outcome more important than intent. Eventually he is executed for murder. (Dreiser 1964; Moers 1969)

See also *American Tragedy, An;* Dreiser, Theodore; Finchley, Sondra

Gulliver's Travels

Gulliver's Travels, by Jonathan Swift, was published in 1726 as *Travels into Several Remote Nations of the World, by Lemuel Gulliver.* A satirical novel, it criticizes various aspects of British society in particular and human nature in general. The story takes place from 1699 to 1713. During this time the main character, Lemuel Gulliver, journeys to four different lands: Lilliput, Brobdingnag, Laputa, and Houyhnhnmland. In each place he compares and contrasts various social and political institutions with those in his native England.

Gulliver's adventure begins when he signs on as a ship's doctor. After setting sail for the South Seas, the vessel encounters a storm and is wrecked. Gulliver then swims to the nearest shore and collapses with exhaustion. When he wakes up, he finds himself tied with tiny ropes and learns that he is in a world ruled by six-inch-tall people. His captors, the Lilliputians, make him their prisoner, but when Gulliver behaves well and learns their language, he is set free. Later he helps them fight and defeat their enemies, the Blefuscudians. The Blefuscudians were once Lilliputians but fled to the nearby island of Blefuscu over a matter of principle: Lilliputian law declares that they must break eggs on the small end before eating them, whereas Blefuscudian tradition is to break eggs on the large end.

After Gulliver captures the Blefuscudian fleet, the Lilliputians' emperor wants to make the Blefuscudians into slaves. Gulliver convinces the Lilliputian Parliament to oppose the emperor. This makes Gulliver unpopular with the royal court but popular in Blefuscu. Later the emperor of Blefuscu alerts Gulliver to a plot against him. Gulliver escapes to Blefuscu and discovers a wrecked ship of his size there. The people of Blefuscu help him repair it, and he sails home.

Gulliver then embarks on a ship to India. The vessel is blown off course, and its sailors go ashore in a strange land to find food. Gulliver accompanies them but becomes separated from the group. He is captured by a giant farmer and becomes the pet of the man's nine-year-old daughter, who is 40 feet tall. Later the farmer displays Gulliver in the city, where the queen buys him. Gulliver and the king discuss the social, political, and philosophical differences between the giant land, Brobdingnag, and Great Britain. In addition, Gulliver experiences many dangers because of his small size. For example, he has to fight off giant rats and wasps. One day a giant bird picks up his tiny home and drops it in the sea, where a ship finds him.

Gulliver is soon back in England. Once again he signs up as a ship's doctor, and this time his vessel is attacked by pirates. He is set adrift, alone in a small boat, and lands on yet another strange shore. Shortly thereafter he notices a flying island hovering above the land. He receives permission to climb up to it and meets the people of Laputa. The Laputans are unrealistic, absentminded intellectuals, and Gulliver quickly grows tired of them. The Laputans lower him down to the continent of Balnibarbi, where he visits an academy where men work on impractical projects and inventions. From Balnibarbi Gulliver travels to the island of Glubbdubdrib, where many sorcerers live. They contact the spirit world and bring forth historical figures for Gulliver to question. He learns that he has been harboring many misconceptions about these people and says:

> I was chiefly disgusted with modern history. For having strictly examined all the persons of greatest name in the courts of princes for an hundred years past, I found how the world had been misled by prostitute writers, to ascribe the greatest exploits in war to cowards, the wisest counsel to fools, sincerity to flatterers, Roman virtue to betrayers of their country, piety to atheists, chastity to sodomites, truth to informers. How many innocent and excellent persons had been condemned to death or banishment, by the practising of great ministers upon the corruption of judges, and the malice of factions. How many villains had been exalted to the highest places of trust, power, dignity, and profit; how great a share in the motions and events of courts, councils, and senates might be challenged by bawds, whores, pimps, parasites, and buffoons. How low an opinion I had of human wisdom and integrity, when I was truly informed of the springs and motives of great enterprises and revolutions in the world, and of the contemptible accidents to which they owned their success. (Swift 1960, 216)

Gulliver soon sails from Glubbdubdrib to the land of Luggnagg, where he meets a race of immortals, the struldbrugs. These people lose their legal rights and estates at age 80 and their teeth and hair at age 90. They are ugly, melancholy people with extremely poor memories, and their society does not want them around. In fact, their situation is so hideous that Gulliver thinks "no tyrant could invent a death into which I would not run with pleasure from such a life" (232). However, he agrees with the struldbrugs' legal oppression, saying, "Otherwise, as avarice is the necessary consequent of old age, those immortals would in time become proprietors of the whole nation and engross the civil power, which, for want of abilities to manage, must end in the ruin of the public" (232).

In this illustration from Gulliver's Travels, *Lemuel Gulliver finds himself in the land of Lilliput after surviving a shipwreck (Archive Photos).* Gulliver's Travels *critiques British society by comparing it to several imaginary cultures.*

From Luggnagg Gulliver travels to Japan and then to England. After a brief time there, he again boards a ship for the South Seas, this time as its captain. En route the crew mutinies and Gulliver is set adrift. He lands in a world of rational horses, called Houyhnhnm, and irrational apelike men, called Yahoos. He lives with the Houyhnhnms and tells them about England. They are horrified to learn about its wars, legal system, and other cruel customs.

Eventually they tell Gulliver that he must either live among the Yahoos or leave. He builds a boat, sets sail, and is picked up by a Portuguese ship. Back in England, he finds himself unable to stand his fellow man. He spends most of his time among his horses.

Gulliver's Travels expresses a great deal of hatred for humankind, and upon the book's publication some people pronounced its author mentally ill. Indeed, Swift was repulsed by the uncleanness of the human body and bathed frequently. But in an introduction to the work, scholar Marcus Cunliffe (xviii–xx) argues that this does not mean the man was insane:

> While certainly an unusual man, Swift was far from being a monster. He was *not* mentally unbalanced, although he did become senile toward the end of his long life. . . . The man himself . . . is not particularly gross or grotesque. Nor is the lesson imparted by *Gulliver's Travels*. Not all mankind is portrayed as worthless and bestial. Swift has no fault to find, for example, with the Portuguese sea captain whom Gulliver meets after leaving the Yahoos. Swift may be an ironist but he is not a cynic: he cares too deeply. . . . Men are fallible: they have also made things steadily worse for themselves. In other words, Swift assumes that in a former, yeoman order men had the dignity of simplicity. This has been spoiled by kings and tyrants, courts, pride, wealth. To the curse of original sin has been added the subordinate curse of sophistication.

(Swift 1960)

See also Science Fiction and Fantasy; Swift, Jonathan

H

Haller, Harry

The main character of Hermann Hesse's 1927 novel *Steppenwolf*, Harry Haller has trouble fitting in with bourgeois society. He thinks of his personality as being split in two, into a human part and a wolf part. As the novel progresses, he struggles to suppress his natural urges and eventually learns how important it is to release them. However, he also learns that when this release is uncontrolled, it results in chaos, both for the individual and for society. (Hesse 1963)

See also Hesse, Hermann; *Steppenwolf*

Handmaid's Tale, The

Published in 1985, *The Handmaid's Tale,* by feminist Margaret Atwood, is a futuristic story about the suppression of women. It is set in the late twentieth century in the United States, where religious fundamentalists have created their own country, the Republic of Gilead.

In Gilead women have no rights. Men have divided them into different classes, each with its own designated clothing color and societal role. For example, the Marthas, who wear green, are household servants. The Unwomen, who dress in gray, are political rebels whose punishment is to work in the pollution-plagued colonies outside of Gilead. The Aunts, all in brown, indoctrinate the red-clad Handmaids in their duties as sexual surrogates for the blue-clad Wives, who are the spouses of Gilead's leaders, the Commanders.

Environmental pollution and unusual viruses have made most women sterile. Since procreation is vital for the survival of the government, the Commanders have designated all fertile women as Handmaids. This idea was taken from the biblical story of Rachel, who cannot have a child but tells her husband, Jacob: "Behold my maid Bilhah, go into her; and she shall bear upon my knees, that I may also have children by her" (Genesis 30:1–3). Each Commander can therefore have both a Handmaid and a Wife, who is sterile. However, the two women are treated differently. Wives are highly esteemed in the community; Handmaids are considered vital but unworthy of respect. Moreover, once a baby is born, it becomes the Wife's child, and when the infant is three months old and weaned, the Handmaid is sent to another household.

The first-person narrator of *The Handmaid's Tale* has been forced to become a Handmaid against her will. Taken from her husband and daughter during the revolution that created Gilead, she is trained as a Handmaid and sent first to one Commander's home and then another. Like all Handmaids, she is given a name representative of the Commander to whom she belongs. The story begins with her as Offred, the new Handmaid of Commander Fred.

The Commander's Wife is a former television evangelist named Serena Joy. Serena hates Offred but suffers her presence because she desperately wants the status that comes with having a child. Serena also breaks some of Gilead's rules to try increasing Offred's chances of becoming pregnant. For example, a Handmaid's couplings with a Commander are supposed to take place only during a particular biblical ritual, with the Wife lying with the Handmaid on the bed. However, Serena encourages Offred and the Commander to meet more frequently in private. During these meetings the Commander offers Offred forbidden items, such as old magazines and scented soaps, and tells her that he wants her life to be bearable because her predecessor hanged herself. Offred believes that the Commander really wants an intimacy that she cannot give.

As time passes and Offred fails to get pregnant, Serena secretly arranges for her to have sex with the Commander's chauffeur, Nick. Offred and Nick develop a close relationship, and later they sneak off to meet on their own. In addition, the Commander smuggles Offred into a brothel to try exciting her. There she meets a former friend, Moira, who is now a prostitute. Moira talks about escaping Gilead. By this time Offred has discovered that another Handmaid, Ofglen, is a member of an underground antigovernment group called Mayday. One day she hears that Ofglen's activities have been discovered and that she has killed herself rather than be arrested. Offred falls into despair. Then some men in a government van come to arrest her. She is frightened until Nick whispers that they are actually members of Mayday, as is he, and have come to help her escape. She leaves hoping he is telling her the truth.

The novel ends with a section entitled "Historical Notes," which is "a partial transcript of the proceedings of the Twelfth Symposium on Gileadean Studies," dated June 25, 2195 (Atwood 1986, 299). In it keynote speaker James Pieixoto of Cambridge University reports that *The Handmaid's Tale* was transcribed from some ancient tapes discovered in a buried footlocker. Pieixoto then discusses Gilead as a historical era, comparing it to the restrictive regime of Iran during the same time period, and explains that an Underground Femaleroad helped women escape from Gilead into Canada. During this discussion he makes derogatory jokes about women, and his male audience laughs appropriately.

The Handmaid's Tale does not tell Offred's ultimate fate, nor does it say what became of Offred's husband when she became a Handmaid. At one point in the novel she says that she wants to believe he escaped capture. However, she fears that he was executed along with others who oppose Gilead's brutal theocracy. The novel makes it clear that in this new society men are as oppressed and unhappy as women; even Commander Fred wonders whether his elite group made the right decisions in creating Gilead.

The Handmaid's Tale also serves as a cautionary tale regarding the cashless, paperless society of the United States. The revolution that created Gilead succeeded largely because it took over the country's computers, including Compubank. One of the first actions of the new leaders was to cut off people's access to their savings accounts, making them dependent on their government for food and other necessities. Offred says: "If there had still been portable money, it would have been more difficult" (174). This kind of government control also appears in the novel *1984,* by George Orwell, another political novel set in the future, to which scholars often compare *The Handmaid's Tale.* (Atwood 1986; Grace 1980; McCombs 1988)

See also Atwood, Margaret; Feminism; Joy, Serena; *1984;* Offred; Orwell, George

Hansberry, Lorraine

Lorraine Hansberry wrote the first play by a black woman ever performed on Broadway. Entitled *A Raisin in the Sun,* it won numerous awards for its portrayal of a black working-class family rediscovering pride in its African heritage.

Hansberry was born on May 19, 1930, in Chicago, Illinois. Her father was a real estate agent who decided to take a stand against racist housing laws by moving the family into an all-white neighborhood. He eventually won a lawsuit to keep them there, but the struggle soured him on living in the United States, and he relocated the family to Mexico. Hansberry studied art there as well as in the United States. She also spent two years at the University of Wisconsin. In 1950 she settled in New York, where she began to write while working at a variety of odd jobs. With the production of *A Raisin in the Sun,* her success seemed assured; she was only 29, the youngest professional playwright in the United States. But while her second play, *The Sign in Sidney Brustein's Window,* was appearing on Broadway, she developed cancer. She died in New York on January 12, 1965, at the age of 35. (Cheney 1984; Hansberry 1994)

See also Racism; *Raisin in the Sun, A*

Hard Times

Hard Times (1854), by Charles Dickens, protests unfair living conditions among the working classes in nineteenth-century England. It also depicts narrow-mindedness among the aristocracy and middle class and shows how this type of thinking leads to unhappiness. The novel's main character, Thomas Gradgrind, runs a school in Coketown, England, that teaches nothing but facts. He abhors flights of fancy and is appalled to discover two of his children, Tom Jr. and Louisa, spying on some circus people. When this happens, he wonders what his friend Mr. Bounderby would think. Bounderby, a wealthy factory owner and banker, is very opinionated. He tells Gradgrind that the children's interest in the circus is the fault of their playmate, Sissy Jupe, whose father is a clown. After Sissy's father deserts her in order to give her a chance at a better life, Gradgrind takes the girl into his own household in hopes of reforming her.

Meanwhile Stephen Blackpool, a power-loom weaver at Bounderby's mill, is leading a miserable life. Dickens's portrait of Blackpool's oppression is an indictment of laws he believed unfair to the labor class. These laws result not only in harsh working conditions but also in difficult social problems. For example, although Blackpool's wife is a drunk, he does not have enough money to divorce her, and if he were to leave her, he would be judged too immoral to deserve a job. This situation makes Blackpool so desperate that for a brief moment he considers giving his wife poison.

Hard Times then jumps several years into the future. Tom Jr. is an employee at Bounderby's bank, and Bounderby has convinced Louisa to marry him. Shortly thereafter social unrest spreads through the town. A labor-union agitator, Slackbridge, tries to lead the workers, but he is just as corrupt as their employers. Blackpool is the only one who realizes this. Therefore, when he refuses to join the union, his fellow workers shun him. Blackpool is then summoned before Bounderby, who questions him about Slackbridge's activities. Blackpool tells him about the workers' problems, saying:

> Look round town—so rich as 'tis—and see the numbers o' people as has been broughten into bein heer, fur to weave, an' to card, an' to piece out a livin', aw the same one way, somehows, 'twixt their cradles and their graves. Look how we live, an' wheer we live, an' in what numbers, an' by what chances, and wi' what sameness; and look how the mills is awlus a goin, and how they never works us no nigher to onny dis'ant object—ceptin awlus, Death. Look how you considers of us, and writes of us, and talks of us, and goes up wi' yor deputations to Secretaries o' State 'bout us, and how you are awlus right, and how we are awlus wrong, and never had'n no reason in us sin ever we were born. Look how this ha' growen an' growen, Sir, bigger an' bigger, broader an' broader, harder and harder fro year to year, fro generation unto generation. Who can look on 't, Sir, and fairly tell a man 'tis not a muddle? (Dickens 1966, 114)

Bounderby's response is to say that he will have all agitators arrested. He then fires Blackpool for complaining about working conditions and labor politics.

After Blackpool leaves, Louisa, who has heard his conversation with her husband, goes to his house. Tom Jr. accompanies her. Louisa has never been among the poor before, and she has always thought of them as objects. Now she sees them as real people. Horrified by Blackpool's suffering, she gives him money. Then Tom Jr. pulls Blackpool aside and tells him he might be able to get the young man a bank job. Tom tells Blackpool to wait outside the bank each evening to be ready for his chance. Later the bank is robbed, and Stephen is suspected of the crime. Unfortunately, he cannot be found.

Meanwhile Louisa has met a young man, James Harthouse, who tries to woo her. He makes her realize how sterile her life with Mr. Bounderby really is. Upset, she goes to her father's house and asks Sissy to talk to Mr. Harthouse for her. Sissy convinces the man to leave Louisa alone, and he leaves town. Bounderby thinks that Louisa has left with him, and when he finds her at her father's house, he is angry. He tells her that their marriage will be over if she does not return home immediately. She remains with her father.

Now a bachelor again, Bounderby puts all his effort into finding the bank robber. He offers a reward for Blackpool's arrest. Eventually the young man is found lying at the bottom of an abandoned mine shaft. He has fallen in and been trapped there for several days. The townspeople pull him out, but it is clear he is dying. He professes his innocence, tells about Tom's request that he wait outside the bank, expresses his love for humankind, and dies. When Gradgrind hears about Tom's plot, he is disappointed in his son and the educational system that produced him. He finds Tom hiding at the circus and says he is going to send him away. A young man, Blitzer, interferes. Blitzer intends to take Tom back to Bounderby, not because he believes in justice but because it will earn him a promotion. Blitzer tells Gradgrind: "I am sure you know that the whole social system is a question of self-interest" (218). Nonetheless, the circus people help Tom escape. A final chapter forecasts the future of the characters, predicting a lonely death for Tom, a happy marriage for Sissy, and a life of social concern for Louisa.

When *Hard Times* was published, critics disagreed on its merit and significance. In a critical edition of the work, scholars George Ford and Sylvere Monod (330) report: "About none of [Dickens's] novels has there been less agreement. Some writers who generally admire Dickens, such as . . . [George Bernard] Shaw, have found *Hard Times* to be one of his most successful works; others, such as George Gissing, consider it a sorry failure. In one of his books on Dickens, Gissing remarks: 'Of *Hard Times*, I have said nothing; it is practically a forgotten book, and little in it demands attention.' This verdict, published in 1898, has been shared by many otherwise enthusiastic Dickensians" (330).

But in 1912 George Bernard Shaw wrote that *Hard Times* is far superior to another of Dickens's social protest novels, *Bleak House*, because it demonstrates a better understanding of Victorian social problems and the possible solutions for them. About these solutions, and Dickens's view of them, Shaw (334) writes:

Whereas formerly men said to the victim of society who ventured to complain, "Go and reform yourself before you pretend to reform Society," it now has to admit that until Society is reformed, no man can reform himself except in the most insignificantly small ways. He may cease picking your pocket of half crowns; but he cannot cease taking a quarter of a million a year from the community for nothing at one end of the scale, or living under conditions in which health, decency, and gentleness are impossible at the other, if he happens to be born to such a lot.

In addition, Shaw refers to the "mercilessly faithful and penetrating exposures of English social, industrial, and political life" in *Hard*

Times and *Bleak House* (335). He says that Dickens assaults "the conscience of the governing class," adding, "*Hard Times* was written to make you uncomfortable" (335). (Cruikshank 1949; Dickens 1966; Fielding 1958; Gissing 1924; Hibbert 1967)

See also *Bleak House;* Dickens, Charles; Gissing, George; Labor Issues; Poverty; Shaw, George Bernard

"Harlem, Montana: Just Off the Reservation"

The poem "Harlem, Montana: Just Off the Reservation," by Native American author James Welch, first appeared in his 1971 poetry collection *Riding the Earthboy 40.* It depicts the life of Native Americans in a town near a reservation, showing the prevalence of alcoholism, discrimination, and hopelessness. In Harlem "money is free if you're poor enough," and "booze is law" (Velie 1991, 238). (Velie 1991)

See also Native American Issues; Welch, James

Harlem Renaissance

The term *Harlem Renaissance* refers to a period in American literary history from the 1920s to the early 1930s. At that time African-American authors, most of whom lived in the Harlem district of New York City, began writing about life in the United States from the black perspective, exploring issues of white racism and black pride. These authors include Countee Cullen, Alice Dunbar-Nelson, Lorraine Hansberry, Langston Hughes, Zora Neale Hurston, Nella Larsen, James Weldon Johnson, Eloise Bibb Thompson, and Jean Toomer. Their works were initially published by black magazines, but eventually they were supported by major publishing houses as well. Unfortunately, the economic hardships of the Great Depression decreased sales of black literature, effectively ending the Harlem Renaissance. (Huggins 1971)

See also Cullen, Countee; Dunbar-Nelson, Alice; Great Depression; Hansberry, Lorraine; Hughes, Langston; Hurston, Zora Neale; Johnson, James Weldon; Larsen, Nella; Thompson, Eloise Bibb; Toomer, Jean

Heller, Joseph

Joseph Heller is the author of *Catch-22* (1961), a satirical antiwar novel set during World War II. He participated in this war himself as a bombardier for the U.S. Air Force. Born on May 1, 1923, in Brooklyn, New York, he received a master's degree at Columbia University in 1949 and studied at Oxford University as a Fulbright scholar from 1949 to 1950. He then taught for two years at Pennsylvania State University. Shortly thereafter he began writing advertisements for magazines. With the publication of *Catch-22* he became a freelance author. His subsequent works include the novels *Something Happened* (1974), *Good as Gold* (1979), and *God Knows* (1984), as well as the play *We Bombed in New Haven* (1968). In 1998 he published his memoirs entitled *Now and Then: From Coney Island to Here.* (Merrill 1987; Seed 1989)

See also *Catch-22;* Peace

Hellman, Lillian

Lillian Hellman was a playwright and screenwriter who often used her work to protest prejudice and injustice in American society. Born on June 20, 1905, in New Orleans, Louisiana, she was married to playwright Arthur Kober from 1925 to 1932, but she divorced him because of her involvement with writer Dashiell Hammett, who became famous for his detective novels. Hellman first became famous herself for *The Children's Hour* (1934), a play concerning society's prejudice against lesbians. It was made into a movie in both 1936 and 1962. Hellman's subsequent social protest plays, which include *Days to Come* (1936), *The Little Foxes* (1939), and *Watch on the Rhine* (1941; film 1943), were also extremely popular. In addition to plays, Hellman edited story and letter collections and wrote several memoirs. One of these, *Scoundrel Time* (1976), tells of the persecution that she and other writers experienced during the McCarthy era. Hellman died on June 30, 1984, at Martha's Vineyard, Massachusetts. (Lederer 1979; Rollyson 1988; Wright 1986)

See also *Children's Hour, The; Days to Come;* McCarthyism; *Watch on the Rhine*

Lillian Hellman receiving the Gold Medal of The National Institute of Arts and Letters, May 20, 1964 (Archive Photos)

Hesse, Hermann

German-Swiss author Hermann Hesse primarily wrote about the relationship between the individual and society. In doing so, he criticized many aspects of modern life. Born on July 2, 1877, in Calw, Germany, Hesse entered a seminary as a young man but left there to become a factory apprentice. Later he began working in a bookstore. In 1904 he became a freelance author and published his first novel, *Peter Camenzind.* His subsequent novels include *Unterm Rad* (Beneath the Wheel, 1906), *Demian* (1919), and *Siddhartha* (1922). During World War II Hesse moved to Switzerland, where he wrote essays and articles protesting German ideology and arguing for peace. In 1923 he became a naturalized citizen of Switzerland. After the publication of *Das Glaperlenspiel* (The Glass Bead Game) in 1943, Hesse abandoned long fiction and began writing essays, letters, poems, and short stories instead, and in 1946 he won the Nobel Prize in literature. He died on August 9, 1962, in Montagnola, Switzerland. (Hesse 1986; Ziolkowski 1965)

See also *Glass Bead Game, The;* Peace

Holbrook Family

An American pre-Depression-era family in Tillie Olsen's novel *Yonnondio: From the Thirties* (1974), the Holbrooks must deal with poverty on a daily basis. Jim, the head of the household, holds a series of jobs that place him in difficult working conditions, yet offer little income. His wife, Anna, suffers from poor health and despair. His daughter, Mazie, and sons, Will, Ben, Jim Junior, and Bess, have little hope for the future. There is barely enough money to feed them; their clothes are ragged, and they cannot afford an education. Moreover, Jim and Anna teach their children the common view of their time regarding sexual stereotypes: men and woman have different roles in life. As Deborah Rosenfelt says in her essay "From the Thirties: Tillie Olsen and the Radical Tradition" (Nelson and Huse 1994, 84–85):

The conditioning of children to accept limiting sex roles is an important theme in *Yonnondio.* . . . Anna, full of her own repressed longings, imparts the lessons of sex roles to her children. "Boys get to do that," she tells Benjy wistfully, talking of travel by trains and boats, "not girls" (113). And when Mazie asks her, "Why is it always me that has to help? How come Will gets to play?" Anna can only answer, "Willie's a boy" (142). Olsen, then, suggests throughout *Yonnondio* that both women and men are circumstanced to certain social roles, and that these roles, while placing impossible burdens of responsibility on working-class men, constrict the lives of women in particularly damaging ways.

(Nelson and Huse 1994; Olsen 1980)

See also Feminism; Great Depression; Labor Issues; Olsen, Tillie; *Yonnondio: From the Thirties*

Hood, Thomas

English poet Thomas Hood is the author of two of the most famous social protest poems ever written, "The Song of the Shirt" and "The Lay of the Labourer" (both 1825), which concern labor abuses and unemployment. Born in London, England, on May 23, 1799, Hood worked as a book engraver and then as a magazine editor before publishing his first volume of poetry, *The Plea of the Midsummer Fairies,* in 1827. His subsequent works include the humorous *Odes and Addresses to Great People* (1825). He died in London on May 3, 1845. (Walter 1968)

See also Labor Issues; Poverty; "Song of the Shirt, The"

"Hope Deferred"

The short story "Hope Deferred," by African-American author Alice Dunbar-Nelson, was originally published in the magazine *Source: The Crisis* in September 1914. Its main character is Louis Edwards, a civil engineer. Unable to find work because he is black, he becomes a waiter and endures abuse from the people he waits on. One day he loses his temper and attacks a man. He is arrested and sent to a county workhouse. Meanwhile the restaurant puts up a sign: "Waiters Wanted. None but White Men Need Apply" (Roses and Randolph 1996, 90). "Hope Deferred" is representative of the author's work, which sought to depict racial prejudice and injustice in the United States. (Roses and Randolph 1996)

See also Dunbar-Nelson, Alice; Harlem Renaissance; Racism

House of the Spirits, The

The House of the Spirits, by Chilean author Isabel Allende, was originally published in Spain as *La casa de los espíritus* in 1982. Reprinted in the United States in 1985, the novel follows the lives of several members of the Trueba family, who live during a time of political turmoil in an unnamed South American country. The story is narrated by two characters: Esteban Trueba, who writes in the first person, and his granddaughter, who offers a third-person narrative based on the journals of her deceased grandmother, Esteban's wife, Clara.

Clara, daughter of politician Severo del Valle and his suffragette wife, Nívea, is a clairvoyant who can predict the future, speak with spirits, and make objects float into the air. She falls mute after witnessing the autopsy of her older sister, Rosa, who was killed by drinking poisoned wine meant for her father. Clara remains silent for nine years, until the day she announces that she is destined to marry Rosa's former fiancé, Esteban Trueba.

In the years since Rosa's death, Esteban, who grew up in poverty, has inherited an abandoned family ranch, Tres Marías, and turned it into a profitable enterprise. He spends much of his time raping young peasant women, including Pancha, the sister of his foreman, Pedro Segundo García. When Pancha becomes pregnant, Esteban becomes uninterested in her and decides to take a wife from his own social class. Returning to his hometown, he meets and marries Clara. Esteban and Clara have three children: Jaime, Nicolás, and Blanca. Esteban does not get along well with any of them, particularly after he becomes a senator from the Conservative Party, because they are involved in socialist activities. When

Jaime becomes a doctor for the poor, Esteban calls him a "hopeless loser" who has "no sense of reality" and has "put [his] faith in utopian values that don't even exist" (Allende 1985, 252). When Nicolás forms his own religious group and begins holding protests for religious freedom and civil rights, Esteban makes him leave the country. When Blanca becomes pregnant by socialist singer Pedro Tecero García, the son of her father's foreman, Esteban becomes enraged and attacks Pedro Tecero, cutting off three of the young man's fingers. He also beats Blanca and forces her to marry a French count, Jean de Satigny, but the marriage breaks up before Blanca's daughter, Alba, is born.

Alba does not learn the identity of her real father until she is a young woman. By this time she has become involved in socialist activities herself. Esteban, who is now a widower, ignores these activities because he loves his granddaughter dearly. However, he continues to be a vocal opponent of socialism, and when the Liberal Party defeats his Conservative Party in a major election, he works secretly to encourage a military coup. He believes that the military leaders will seize the government and return it to the conservative politicians. During the coup Esteban realizes he was wrong and that "this was not the best way to overthrow Marxism" (320). The military leaders prove themselves cruel and power-hungry; they assassinate the president and kill Esteban's son Jaime, who had become the president's friend and doctor. They also take Alba away for questioning because she has become the girlfriend of a socialist leader. Alba's interrogation is handled by Esteban García, the grandson of Pancha García and Esteban Trueba, who is angry that Alba has taken his place as Esteban Trueba's acknowledged grandchild. Esteban García therefore tortures Alba unnecessarily. He and his men continually rape and abuse her until her grandfather finally arranges for her release. Now pregnant, she returns to live with Esteban Trueba, who dies shortly after writing his life story in the presence of his wife's spirit. Alba is alone because her mother has left the country with Pedro Tecero García,

yet she is comforted by reading her grandmother's journals. She begins to recite her story, and the last line of *The House of the Spirits* is therefore the same as the first.

Although the novel primarily focuses on family relationships, there are social protest elements throughout. Clara's suffragette mother, who would "chain herself with other ladies to the gates of Congress and the Supreme Court" (58), is a vocal supporter of women's rights. Clara's husband opposes such activities, considering them "a degrading spectacle that made all their husbands look ridiculous" (58). Esteban also criticizes socialism, communism, and Marxism, which he calls a "cancer" that must be stopped (260). In addition, he argues that the poor do not deserve charity because "those people don't even try. It's very easy to stretch out your hand and beg for alms!" He says he believes only "in effort and reward" (117).

Moreover, when Esteban discovers that Pedro Tecero García has been handing out pamphlets to the peasants of Tres Marías advocating "Sundays off, a minimum wage, retirement and health plans, maternity leave for women, elections without coercion, and . . . a peasant organization that would confront the owners," he whips him (133). But Pedro Tecero will not stop distributing his socialist literature. By this time World War II is under way, and Pedro tells Blanca "about what was going on the rest of the world and in the country, about the distant war that had sent half of humanity into a hail of shrapnel, and an agony of concentration camps, and produced a flood of widows and orphans. He spoke of the workers of Europe and the United States, whose rights were respected because the slaughter of organizers and Socialists of the preceding decades has led to laws that were more just and republics that were governed properly" (147).

The novel's most powerful social protest passages come after the socialists gain power and are destroyed by the conservative-supported military coup. At that time "the upper middle class and the economic right, who had favored the coup, were euphoric. . . . They thought the loss of democratic freedom would be temporary and that it was possible to go without individual or collective rights for a while so long as the regime respected the tenets of free enterprise" (326). However, they soon realized that the military regime wanted to remain in power forever and had no concern for human rights. In the concluding chapters, entitled "The Terror" and "The Hour of Truth," and the "Epilogue," *The House of the Spirits* offers vivid descriptions of military cruelty, torture, and murder. (Allende 1985; Hart 1989; Rojas and Rehbein, 1991)

See also Allende, Isabel; Communism; De Satigny, Alba Trueba; Del Valle, Clara; Feminism; García, Esteban; García, Pedro Tecero; Socialism; Trueba, Esteban

Houston, Ely

The character Ely Houston appears in Richard Wright's 1953 novel *The Outsider*. A white district attorney in New York, he is trying to understand racism and the black experience. He questions a black intellectual, Cross Damon, about this, and the two have many interesting discussions. For example, Houston says:

> The way Negroes were transported to this country and sold into slavery, then stripped of their tribal culture and held in bondage; and then allowed, so teasingly and over so long a period of time, to be sucked into our way of life is something which resembles the rise of all men from whatever it was we all came from. . . . We are not now keeping the Negro on such a short chain and they are slowly entering into our cultures. But that is not the end of this problem. It is the beginning. . . . Negroes, as they enter our culture, are going to inherit the problems we have, but with a difference. They are outsiders and they are going to *know* that they have these problems. They are going to be self-conscious; they are going to be gifted with a double vision, for, being Negroes, they are going to be both *inside* and *outside* of our culture at the same time. Every emo-

tional and cultural convulsion that ever shook the heart and soul of Western man will shake them. Negroes will develop unique and specially defined psychological types. They will become psychological men, like the Jews. . . . They will not only be Americans or Negroes; they will be centers of *knowing,* so to speak. (Wright 1993b, 164–165)

Houston remains fascinated by Cross Damon throughout the novel, and when he learns that Damon is a murderer, he is even more fascinated by what has become of this intellectual outsider. As Damon is dying of a bullet wound, Houston continues to quiz him about the nature of his experience. (Wright 1993b)

See also Damon, Cross; *Outsider, The;* Wright, Richard

Howe, Julia Ward

Julia Ward Howe was a poet and social reformer best known for writing "The Battle Hymn of the Republic." This hymn, which was adopted as a marching song for the North during the U.S. Civil War, was first published

Julia Ward Howe, mid-nineteenth century (Photo by J. E. Purdy/Library of Congress)

in the magazine *Atlantic Monthly* in February 1862. Howe was born in New York City on May 27, 1819. She and her husband, Samuel Grinley Howe, edited a Boston newspaper, *Commonwealth,* that advocated the end of slavery. Howe was also dedicated to promoting women's rights. In this regard she served as president of both the New England Woman Suffrage Association and the Association for the Advancement of Women. In her later years she became an activist for prison reform and world peace. In addition to her lectures and essays on social reform issues, she continued to write poetry and was the first woman elected to the American Academy of Arts and Letters. She died on October 17, 1910, in Newport, Rhode Island. (Clifford 1979)

See also Feminism; Slavery

Howl

Published in 1956, *Howl* is American poet Allen Ginsberg's outcry against society's suppression of individuality and personal exploration. The poem is divided into three parts, the first of which is a listing of the different ways that people look for excitement and meaning through sex, drugs, music, and religion. Its second part, which Ginsberg admits he wrote while under the influence of drugs, is an indictment of a society that makes people feel insane for wanting to satisfy their natural urges. Its third section is an expression of unity with an individual, Carl Solomon, driven mad by society and confined to a mental institution.

In a letter discussing this work, Ginsberg (Miles 1995, 152) writes that, contrary to many people's opinions, *Howl* is not a "negative howl of protest." He explains:

> The title notwithstanding, the poem itself is an act of sympathy, not rejection. In it I am leaping *out* of a preconceived notion of social "values," following my own heart's instincts—*allowing* myself to follow my own heart's instincts, overturning any notion of propriety, moral "value," superficial "maturity," . . . and exposing my true feelings—of sympathy and identification

with the rejected, mystical, individual even "mad."

> I am saying that what seems "mad" in America is our expression of natural ecstasy . . . which suppressed, finds no social form organization background frame of reference or rapport or validation from the outside and so the "patient" gets confused thinks he is mad and really goes off rocker. I am paying homage to mystical mysteries in the forms in which they actually occur here in the U.S. in our environment.

> I have taken a leap of detachment from the Artificial preoccupations and preconceptions of what is acceptable and normal and given my yea to the specific types of madness listed in the [first part of the poem].

Ginsberg catalogs this madness in passionate, raw language—language that led to the arrest of the poem's publisher, Lawrence Ferlinghetti, on charges of distributing obscenity. During Ferlinghetti's trial lawyers from the American Civil Liberties Union defended the poem's literary value, and eventually it was judged not to be an obscene work; Ferlinghetti was found not guilty. (Merrill 1969; Miles 1995)

See also Beat Movement; Censorship; Ferlinghetti, Lawrence; Ginsberg, Allen

Hughes, Langston

James Mercer Langston Hughes was an African-American poet who protested racism in much of his work. Born on February 1, 1902, in Joplin, Missouri, he was raised by his mother and lived in several different cities. He graduated from a Cleveland, Ohio, high school in 1921, the same year his first poem, "The Negro Speaks of Rivers," was published in the magazine *Crisis.* Hughes then began attending New York's Columbia University, but he left there after only one year to become a ship's steward. After traveling to Africa and back, he became a busboy in Washington, D.C. One day he left some of his poems at the table of American poet Vachel Lindsay, and the next morning the newspapers were report-

Langston Hughes (Archive Photos)

ing Lindsay's praise for Hughes's work. As a result, Hughes received a scholarship to Lincoln University in Pennsylvania. He graduated in 1929, by which time he had already published two books of verse, *The Weary Blues* (1926) and *Fine Clothes to the Jew* (1927). In 1930 he published his first prose work, *Not without Laughter* (1930), and in 1931 he coauthored a play, *Mule Bone,* with Zora Neale Hurston. He published a collection of short stories, *The Ways of White Folks,* in 1934 and an autobiography in 1940.

In later years he not only continued to write poetry, stories, and plays, but also authored essays, anthology collections, poetry translations, song lyrics, a history book, and a newspaper column. Hughes traveled extensively throughout the world, and in 1937 he reported on the Spanish Civil War as a newspaper correspondent. His most famous work, however, was the poem "Harlem," published in 1951 as part of a poetry collection entitled *Montage of a Dream Deferred.* This collection addresses various aspects of life in the black community of Harlem, New York. Despite his travels, Hughes remained very attached to this community throughout his life. He died in New York, New York, on May 22, 1967. (Emanuel 1967; Hughes 1958; Muller 1986; O'Daniel 1971)

See also Harlem Renaissance; Hurston, Zora Neale; *Montage of a Dream Deferred;* Racism

Hugo, Victor

Born on February 26, 1802, in Besançon, France, Victor Hugo originally intended to be a lawyer. He attended law school in Paris but had a difficult time with his studies. In 1819 he founded a literary review, *Conservateur Litteraire,* and began contributing essays and articles to it. He published a book of poetry in 1822. It expressed his royalist views and therefore earned the praise of King Louis XVIII, who awarded Hugo a pension.

In 1823 Hugo began publishing novels as well as poems and plays. His best-known novels are *Notre-Dame de Paris* (The Hunchback of Notre-Dame, 1831) and *Les Misérables* (1862), but the amount of creative work he produced during his lifetime is extremely large. He was also a politician and political writer who protested many aspects of French society, including censorship and capital punishment. In 1841 he was elected to the French Academy, but ten years later he fled France when the government changed hands. He lived first in Brussels and then on the island of Jersey in the English Channel. Later he moved to the neighboring island of Guernsey.

Hugo returned to Paris in 1871 when the French Third Republic began, having added considerably to his body of work while in exile. His writings during this time include a great deal of poetry, much of it political in nature. In Paris he had become a national hero, and he was elected senator. However, his personal life was marked by tragedies. While a young man, he had married and had five children; one died in 1843, another in 1871, and another in 1873. His wife died in 1868 and his mistress in 1885. Hugo himself died in 1885 after suffering from cerebral palsy for seven years. He was buried in the Pantheon during a national funeral. (Houston 1975; Richardson 1976; Swinburne 1970)

See also *Misérables, Les*

Human Comedy, The

Published in France as *La Comédie humaine* between 1829 and 1847, *The Human Comedy,* by Honoré de Balzac, is a collection of approximately 90 novels and novellas that take place between 1308 and 1846. In writing them, Balzac wanted to trace the social and political history of France and show how the French Revolution affected the life of the country rather than the lives of individuals. He therefore set his stories among many types of people. According to scholar Felicien Marceau (1966, 12), Balzac used 2,472 characters to "depict the whole of society, town and country, Court and commerce, the world of high finance and the world of the press, of the law courts, of the moneylenders, of the drapers and of the tarts."

The individual novels of *The Human Comedy* can be read in any order. As Marceau (6) explains: "To Balzac, each one of his novels had its own separate meaning and internal unity. In each one of them, we are always provided with all the indispensable data necessary to understand it." However, characters do recur, and sometimes secondary characters in one novel become main characters in another. Therefore, Marceau (7) says that each novel "is a novel with windows onto a larger world—a novel with avenues, prospects, paths continually leading out of it if we choose to take them."

Balzac himself said that his novels fall into three general categories: *études analytiques* (analytic studies), which deal with the principles of human society; *études philosophiques* (philosophical studies), which deal with the reasons behind human activities; and *études de moeurs* (studies of manners), which show the results of human activities. In each of these categories Balzac criticizes social conventions. Scholar Samuel Rogers (1953, ix) explains that Balzac "lived through and described an exceptionally crowded and interesting period. The air was full of social and political, religious and aesthetic ideas and systems, merging into each other or struggling against each other. There is hardly one of these that is not reflected in *La Comédie humaine.*"

Balzac's novels protest many aspects of the social system prevalent in postrevolutionary France. For example, Balzac particularly objected to the demise of the aristocracy, believing that only through wealth could intellectualism and great art thrive. Many of his novels therefore present ambitious, yet poor men who find it difficult to succeed in an increasingly materialistic world. (Butler 1983; Marceau 1966; Rogers 1953)

See also Balzac, Honoré de; Class, Social

Hunt, Alonzo ("Fonny")

A 22-year-old black man in James Baldwin's 1974 novel *If Beale Street Could Talk,* Fonny Hunt has been falsely imprisoned for a crime he did not commit. While in prison awaiting trial, he gains strength from the love of his

19-year-old pregnant fiancée, Clementine "Tish" Rivers. According to Baldwin biographer David Leeming (1994, 122), Fonny represents "victims who have nonetheless found some reason for remaining alive in the social prison in which they find themselves." In addition, Leeming compares Fonny, who is a gifted sculptor, to Tish's unborn child, saying, "The baby in Tish's womb is a prisoner yearning to be free as surely as her lover is a man in bondage longing to become himself through his love and his art" (325). (Baldwin 1988; Leeming 1994)

> See also Baldwin, James; *If Beale Street Could Talk;* Racism; Rivers, Clementine ("Tish")

Hurston, Zora Neale

Zora Neale Hurston is the author of what many scholars consider to be the first African-American feminist novel. She was born in Eatonville, Florida, on January 7 sometime between 1898 and 1903. (Records are unclear, and Hurston herself refused to reveal her true age.) Her mother died when she was 9, and her father, a carpenter and Baptist preacher, quickly remarried. Hurston hated her stepmother and began living with other relatives. At 16 she joined a Gilbert and Sullivan traveling theater group as a wardrobe girl. She left the troupe 18 months later, in Baltimore, when she decided she needed an education. In 1920 she received an associate degree from Howard University. The following year, while continuing her education, she published her first short story, "John Redding Goes to Sea," in a campus literary magazine. She then began submitting stories to *Opportunity: A Journal of Negro Life,* which was published by the National Urban League. Her work was not only published but also won her awards in the magazine's literary contest.

In 1925 Hurston decided to become a full-time writer and moved to New York, the home of many prominent black literary figures. She also became a student at Barnard College on a full scholarship. Always before Hurston had struggled to pay for her tuition, working as a manicurist, waitress, or secretary. Now she could completely devote herself to her educa-

tion. She quickly became fascinated with the social sciences and chose to perform research studies for anthropologist Franz Boas. She began to collect black folklore not only in New York but also in the South. Meanwhile, she continued to publish many more short stories, as well as articles about black history. In 1930 she collaborated on a play, *Mule Bone,* with noted black author Langston Hughes; however, the two quarreled and the play was left unfinished until after their deaths.

Hurston's first novel, *Jonah's Gourd Vine,* was published in 1934, followed by a collection of folktales, *Of Mules and Men,* in 1935. She then went to Haiti to study Haitian folklore and voodoo. While there she wrote her most famous novel, *Their Eyes Were Watching God,* which was published after her return to the United States in 1937. Over the next several years Hurston wrote more novels, short stories, and plays. She worked as a college drama teacher in 1939 and as a story consultant for Paramount Pictures in 1941. She also became involved in race-related politics. In 1942 she published her autobiography, *Dust Tracks on a Road,* which received the Anisfield-Wolf Book Award in Race Relations. But despite her success, Hurston was experiencing financial difficulties and remained poor even after the publication of a new novel, *Seraph on the Suwanee* (1948). She started working as a maid, then a librarian, than a substitute teacher. In 1959 after suffering a stroke, she was forced to enter a welfare home in Florida, and after she died there on January 28, 1960, she was buried in an unmarked grave. In 1973 author Alice Walker searched for the grave and provided it with a headstone, subsequently publishing an article in *Ms.* magazine entitled "In Search of Zora Neale Hurston" (1975), which revived interest in Hurston's work. (Hemenway 1977; Hurston 1990; Lyons 1990)

> See also Feminism; Hughes, Langston; Racism; *Their Eyes Were Watching God;* Walker, Alice

Huxley, Aldous

English novelist Aldous Leonard Huxley is best known for his science fiction novel *Brave*

New World (1932), about a distant time when people are scientifically engineered to fulfill predetermined roles. By suggesting a dark future, the novel criticizes politics and technology in the twentieth century.

Huxley was born on July 26, 1894, in Godalming, Surrey, England. His grandfather was a noted biologist, his father a prominent biographer. In 1916 Aldous graduated from Balliol College in Oxford and began writing for the journal *Athenaeum*. He became a freelance writer in 1921. His first novel, *Chrome Yellow*, was published the same year. Subsequent works include *Antic Hay* (1923), *Eyeless in Gaza* (1936), and *The Devils of Loudun* (1952). He died on November 22, 1963, in Los Angeles, California. (Atkins 1968; Brander 1970; Watts 1969)

See also *Brave New World*

Hydra Head, The

Set in Mexico City, *La cabeza de la hidra* (The Hydra Head), by Carlos Fuentes, is a 1978 spy thriller that criticizes the backroom politics of Mexico and the Israeli-Palestinian conflict in the Middle East during the 1970s. Much of the intrigue in the novel revolves around Israel's desire to reclaim its ancient lands in Palestine. The atrocities that Israeli agents commit against the Palestinians is likened to those that Adolf Hitler committed against the Jewish people when he took over Germany.

The main character of *The Hydra Head* is Felix Maldonado, a Mexican convert to Judaism. Felix works as the chief of the Bureau of Cost Analysis for Mexico's Ministry of Economic Development and is an expert on the country's nationalized oil industry. One day a powerful government official, the director general of Mexico, tells him that his name will be used in conjunction with a crime. In exchange for his name, Felix will get a new identity and passport for himself and his wife, Ruth, as well as a great deal of money. Felix does not want to cooperate with the director general, but it is not clear whether he has a choice in the matter.

At the same time Felix is preparing to attend an important government function, an awards ceremony for the National Prizes in Arts and Sciences, where the president of Mexico will honor Felix's former economics professor, Professor Bernstein. The director general's henchman, an Arab named Simon Ayub, tells Felix not to go to the ceremony. Felix's wife, Ruth, asks him not to go because Sara Klein is going to be there. Felix was once in love with Sara, but he lost touch with her when she moved to Palestine to become a teacher. Felix is upset to learn that Sara is now Bernstein's lover.

Felix was also once sexually involved with a woman named Mary, who is now married to a wealthy man named Abie Benjamin. All of the people closest to Felix—Ruth, Mary, Sara, Abie, Professor Bernstein—are part of Mexico's Jewish community. It is Felix's connection to this community that caused the director general to want his identity. The director general has arranged for a sharpshooter to assassinate the president of Mexico at the precise moment that Felix steps forward to shake the man's hand during the awards ceremony. In the ensuing confusion someone from the crowd will put a gun in Felix's hand, and he will be accused of being an Israeli agent. He will then "die" in prison. The director general believes that this event will cause Mexico to cut all ties with the Israelis, who are battling with the Arabs over who should possess Palestine and that Mexico will then join the Organization of Petroleum Exporting Countries, which regulates oil production. Only a few years earlier, in 1973, scientists discovered a huge oil reserve in Mexico.

The director general's plan fails when Felix faints before reaching the president. No assassination occurs, but the director general still uses the incident to his advantage. He shows the president Felix's gun and tells him that the Israelis are trying to kill him. The still-unconscious Felix is taken to jail, where he is switched with a dead man of similar appearance and subjected to plastic surgery to change his face. When he awakes, he finds that his family and friends think him dead and have already attended his funeral.

Felix escapes from the hospital and learns that Sara Klein has been killed. Shortly thereafter he contacts a mysterious friend named Timon, who is the head of a new spy agency that operates in Mexico but is independent of the Mexican government. At this point the novel begins to use the first person, as Timon reveals that he is the one who provided the preceding third-person narration of Felix's predicament.

Felix is actually an agent working for Timon. In that capacity he proceeds to unravel the mystery surrounding Sarah's death and his own loss of identity. He learns that Professor Bernstein is working as a spy for the Israelis and has uncovered very detailed information about the Mexican oil fields. This information has been placed holographically in the large stone of Bernstein's ring, so that it can be delivered to spies in the United States. With this information, if the Arabs shut off oil to Israel and the United States, the United States would know where to find oil in Mexico. Professor Bernstein believes that with enough economic incentive, Mexico could be convinced to denationalize its oil industry, so that private industry could harvest this reserve.

Through some very complicated maneuvers that result in several deaths, Felix manages to retrieve the ring and get it to Timon. He also learns that Mary and Abie Benjamin, as well as his own wife, Ruth, are Israeli agents and were responsible for Sara Klein's death. Sara had learned that the Israelis were committing atrocities against the Palestinians, and she was planning to expose Bernstein's involvement in them. Sara had become intimate with the professor just to gather information. Her real boyfriend was a young Palestinian who was helping her in her efforts. He was killed and buried in Felix's grave.

Without friends and family Felix takes a new name and once again begins working as an economist at the Ministry of Economic Development. The director general believes that Felix will be acting as a spy for him, whereas Timon is convinced that Felix will continue to work as a spy for his independent agency. At the end of the novel Felix, now Diego Vasquez, is at a public ceremony, walking toward the president to shake his hand. (Faris 1983; Fuentes 1978)

See also Fuentes, Carlos; Justice; Maldonado, Felix

Hyer, Aunt Ri'

The character of Aunt Ri' Hyer appears in Helen Hunt Jackson's 1885 novel *Ramona,* which concerns the plight of California's Native Americans during the late 1880s. A settler from Tennessee, Aunt Ri' is prejudiced against all Indians, believing them to be lazy and ignorant. Then she meets Alessandro and Ramona, a young Indian couple who are good, hard-working, intelligent people. Slowly her perceptions begin to change. She becomes their friend and later visits an Indian village. Afterward she complains to an agent from the U.S. government that Native Americans deserve better treatment. (Jackson 1988)

See also Jackson, Helen Hunt; *Ramona*

I

Ibsen, Henrik

Norwegian playwright Henrik Ibsen criticized human nature and social conventions during the nineteenth century. His best-known work is *En dukkehjem* (A Doll's House, 1879), in which a wife keeps secrets from her husband meant to protect him and then leaves him when he castigates her for doing so. At the time the play was produced, this woman's declaration of independence shocked theater audiences.

Ibsen was born on March 20, 1828, in Skien, Norway. His father, once a prosperous merchant, went bankrupt in 1836. Seven years later the 15-year-old Ibsen left home to become apprentice to an apothecary. In 1850 he entered the university in Christiania (now Oslo) and became involved in its theater. The following year he was appointed the director and playwright for a theater in Bergen, Norway, and from 1857 to 1862 he took the same position at the Christiania Theater. (Roberts 1974; Rose 1973)

See also *Doll's House, A;* Feminism

Iceman Cometh, The

The Iceman Cometh is a four-act tragedy by Eugene O'Neill. Written in 1939, it was first produced and published in 1946. The play's main theme is that human beings need to deceive themselves about their lives and their natures; otherwise they will succumb to despair and self-destructive acts. However, in presenting this theme, *The Iceman Cometh* depicts an anarchist who acts not out of political convictions but for emotional reasons rooted in his childhood. This character is Don Parritt,

Henrik Ibsen, c. 1895 (Corbis-Bettmann)

whose mother has been involved with the anarchist movement since before he was born. One day his mother is arrested for participating in an anarchist bombing. Parritt, who says he is being sought by police himself, moves into a rooming house connected to a New York saloon. In the bar he encounters a group of friends who have gathered for a birthday party. One of these men, Theodore Hickman, confronts each party guest individually and forces all of them to see the reality of their lives. When Parritt is confronted, he admits that he turned in the bombing group to the law. He says:

> I want you to understand the reason. You see, I began studying American history. I got to admiring Washington and Jefferson and Jackson and Lincoln. I began to feel patriotic and love this country. I saw it was the best government in the world, where everybody was equal and had a chance. I saw that all the ideas behind the Movement came from a lot of Russians . . . and were meant for Europe, but we didn't need them here in a democracy where we were free already. I didn't want this country to be destroyed for a damned foreign pipe dream. After all, I'm from old American pioneer stock. I began to feel I was a traitor for helping a lot of cranks and bums and free women plot to overthrow our government. (O'Neill 1967, 686)

At the same time Parritt insists that he never thought his mother would be arrested, too, and that he feels terrible about it. Hickman does not accept this explanation, and Parritt soon changes his story. Now he says that he turned informant for money. Nevertheless, Hickman remains skeptical. In the end Parritt confesses that he became an informant specifically so his mother would get arrested. He has hated her all his life. Once this truth is revealed, he decides to commit suicide, saying: "I can see now it's the only possible way I can ever get free from her. I guess I've really known that all my life. . . . It ought

to comfort Mother a little, too. It'll give her the chance to play the great incorruptible Mother of the Revolution, whose only child is the Proletariat. She'll be able to say: 'Justice is done! So may all traitors die!' She'll be able to say: 'I am glad he's dead! Long live the Revolution!'" (751).

Parritt then hangs himself, and in so doing, he shows the weakness of any social or political movement: its members are flawed, emotional human beings with self-serving motives. Meanwhile Hickman reveals that he, too, is flawed, having just come from killing his own wife. (Clark 1947; O'Neill 1967)

See also Anarchism; O'Neill, Eugene

If Beale Street Could Talk

Written in 1974 by African-American author James Baldwin, *If Beale Street Could Talk* deals with racism and false imprisonment in Harlem, New York. According to biographer David Leeming (1994, 325), the novel was "Baldwin's answer in this period of his career to the deficiency in the protest novel, his attempt to 'make this tradition articulate. . . . For a tradition expresses . . . nothing more than the long and painful experience of a people; it comes out of the battle waged to maintain their integrity or . . . out of their struggle to survive.'"

In addition, Leeming (323) explains that Baldwin used prison as a metaphor: "Prisoners were those who were deprived of their birthright in the unfeeling and unseeing prison that was racism in America." Therefore, *If Beale Street Could Talk* was "the natural illustration and culmination of [Baldwin's] long meditation on psychological, emotional, and intellectual imprisonment" (323).

The novel's first-person narrator is Clementine "Tish" Rivers, a pregnant 19-year-old black woman whose 22-year-old fiancé, Alonzo "Fonny" Hunt, has been arrested for a crime he did not commit. Prior to his arrest, Fonny and Tish were being harassed by a racist white policeman, Officer Bell, who later insisted that he saw Fonny running away from the scene of a rape. Bell also convinced the victim that Fonny was her attacker, even though Fonny was not in the neighborhood when the crime occurred.

While Fonny is in prison awaiting trial, Tish and her family work to help with his defense. Tish visits him in prison every day, promising him that he will be free by the time their child is born, and Tish's sister, Ernestine, engages a young white lawyer, Mr. Hayward, to represent him. Tish's father, Joseph, and Fonny's father, Frank, both begin stealing to pay for Fonny's legal expenses. They keep their activities a secret from Fonny's mother and two sisters, who hate Fonny and undermine his case by telling the district attorney's office that he has always been a bad person.

As the trial approaches, Ernestine investigates Officer Bell's background. When she learns that he was transferred to Harlem from Manhattan because he had killed a 12-year-old black boy there, she believes that this information can be used to discredit him as a witness. At the same time Hayward asks Tish's mother, Sharon, to visit the victim, who is living in Puerto Rico until the trial. Sharon goes there but cannot convince the woman to change her story. However, under Sharon's pressure the woman suffers a miscarriage, goes insane, and disappears. Hayward therefore asks the district attorney to drop the case. He refuses, merely postponing the trial until the woman can be found; however, the judge does grant Hayward's request that Fonny be released on bail. Joseph, Frank, and Ernestine struggle to raise the bail money, but Frank is caught stealing and loses his job. Ashamed, he commits suicide as Tish goes into labor.

Fonny's dysfunctional father, mother, and sisters contrast harshly with Tish's family, who, according to Leeming (347), "through their African-American identity have achieved genuine strength in the face of the harsh realities of their life." In this regard the Rivers "represent community, the only possibility of survival in a hostile white world that cannot see humanity in blackness. . . . Never the sweet-talking victims exuding humility . . . they are angry, determined, hard-talking . . . people who . . . 'endure' . . . actively, by fighting back from the fortress of their self-respect

and their love for each other" (324). Leeming (325) concludes that they are "representative of Baldwin's private hopes and of the hope of all those strangers in the 'house of bondage.'" (Baldwin 1988; Leeming 1994)

See also Baldwin, James; Hunt, Alonzo ("Fonny"); Racism; Rivers, Clementine ("Tish")

Immigrant Communities

Throughout history residents of immigrant communities have had to struggle against poverty and racial discrimination. These struggles have been depicted in two important works of social protest, *The Jungle,* by Upton Sinclair, and *Children of the Ghetto,* by Israel Zangwill. John Steinbeck showed similar difficulties among migrant farmworkers in his novel *The Grapes of Wrath.*

See also Anti-Semitism; *Children of the Ghetto; Grapes of Wrath, The; Jungle, The;* Poverty; Racism; Sinclair, Upton; Steinbeck, John

Imoinda

Imoinda is the black heroine of the 1688 novel *Oroonoko* by Aphra Behn. She is beautiful, kind, and highly moral. One day an African prince, Oroonoko, asks her to marry him and she agrees. But before the ceremony can take place, Oroonoko's grandfather, the king, forces Imoinda to marry him instead. The king then sells her into slavery when he discovers she has given herself to Prince Oroonoko.

Later Oroonoko is also enslaved. At a South American slave colony he discovers Imoinda, called Clemene by her white masters, and marries her. Imoinda soon becomes pregnant, but she is unhappy that her child will not be born free. She and Prince Oroonoko run away from the colony. When the Europeans find them, Imoinda fights bravely beside her husband. Nonetheless, they are recaptured, and Imoinda allows her husband to kill her, so that their child will not be born a slave. (Behn 1973)

See also Behn, Aphra; *Oroonoko;* Racism

Indian Reservations

See Native American Issues

Intimation of Things Distant, An

An Intimation of Things Distant is a 1992 collection of short stories by Nella Larsen, who wrote about black women and racism at the time of the Harlem Renaissance. This collection contains two of her novellas, *Quicksand* and *Passing,* which were first published in 1928 and 1929, respectively. *Quicksand* is the story of Helga Crane, a mixed-race woman hated by her family because of her black skin. Throughout the novella Helga struggles with issues of self-acceptance and racism. *Passing* concerns a mixed-race woman, Clare Kendry, who cannot accept her color. She passes herself off as a white woman to gain acceptance in society.

An Intimation of Things Distant also includes the short stories "The Wrong Man" and "Freedom," which were first published in *Young's Magazine* in 1926. Neither of these concerns racism. However, another story, "Sanctuary," is the story of a black man, Jim Hammer, who asks a friend's mother, Annie Poole, to hide him from the police. She does so, and when the police arrive, she learns that they believe Jim has just murdered her son. Jim expects Annie to turn him in. Instead, she keeps his location a secret, and once the police have gone, she tells him to "nevah stop thankin' yo' Jesus he done gib you dat black face" (Roses and Randolph 1996, 14). Annie recognizes the need for racial solidarity regardless of its personal cost, and she has learned that a black man cannot be assumed guilty just because white lawmen are chasing him.

"Sanctuary" initially appeared in *Forum* magazine in 1931, but its publication brought Larsen a great deal of trouble. She was accused of plagiarizing the work and had to defend herself. Although she was eventually exonerated, none of her later stories was ever published. (Larsen 1992; Roses and Randolph 1996)

See also Feminism; Larsen, Nella; Racism

Invisible Man

Ralph Ellison's 1952 novel *Invisible Man* depicts the identity crisis of American blacks at the beginning of the civil rights movement. Set in Harlem, New York, during the late 1940s and early 1950s, it offers the first-person narrative of an unnamed small-town southern black whose idealism is gradually destroyed by the reality of big-city politics.

The novel opens with a prologue in which the narrator explains that he is literally invisible, not because of some "biochemical accident to [his] epidermis" but because his true self is unknown and therefore unrecognized by a predominantly white society (Ellison 1952, 3). He lives alone and friendless in a dark basement illuminated by 1,369 light bulbs, stealing his electricity through illegal wiring. For him these lights illuminate the truth.

The narrator then flashes back to the time of his high school graduation. A naïve young man in a small southern town, he gives a speech extolling humility and social responsibility to a group of racist local businessmen, who award him a scholarship to the State College for Negroes. There he gets into trouble by driving a white trustee past some lower-class black homes, even though the white man requested it. The college president, Mr. Bledsoe, believes that blacks should present a false image to whites, and he berates the narrator for showing the trustee a less-than-idealized version of black society. Moreover, he tells the young man that he is too honest and that "the only way to please a white man is to tell him a lie" (107).

Bledsoe then lies to the young man, telling him that he must leave the school but can return in the fall; actually, the narrator has been permanently expelled. Bledsoe sends him to Harlem with sealed letters that are supposed to help him get an executive job. However, after delivering the letters to several offices, the narrator discovers that Bledsoe is really warning employers not to hire him.

Nearly penniless, the young man is forced to take a menial job at a paint factory, where a boiler explodes and injures him. The factory doctors subject him to experimental shock treatments before firing him and paying him off. While out of work, he passes the site of an eviction, where he makes an impromptu speech that rallies a crowd to riot in protest. Consequently, a Communist organization, the Brotherhood, hires him as one of its speakers.

The leaders of the Brotherhood, all of whom are white, immediately insist that the narrator's speeches focus on Communist issues rather than black ones. They do not want to help blacks unless it benefits their own cause. As a result, the Brotherhood's support in the black community is tenuous, and the group's members are often physically attacked by the members of an all-black organization led by Ras the Destroyer. Ras is proud of his African heritage and does not understand why blacks would want to work with whites.

Nonetheless, the narrator continues to do whatever the Brotherhood wants him to do, until a former member, Tod Clifton, is shot by police. Clifton was selling black dancing dolls on a street corner when the police accosted him. Because these dolls are politically incorrect, the Brotherhood does not want any of its members to speak at Clifton's funeral, nor will they join the black protest against his death. When the narrator defies their wishes, the leaders of the Brotherhood reprimand him. At the same time they use Clifton's death to incite a race riot in the community. The narrator rushes to stop the riot, telling Ras that the white Communists "want this to happen. They planned it. They want the mobs to come uptown with machine guns and rifles. They want the streets to flow with blood; your blood, black blood and white blood, so that they can turn your death and sorrow and defeat into propaganda" (421). But Ras does not listen and tries to kill the narrator, who in turn kills him.

After the riot the narrator realizes that he has been suffering from a sickness, one that "came upon [him] slowly, like that strange disease that affects those black men whom you see turning slowly from black to albino, their pigment disappearing as under the radiation of some cruel, invisible ray" (434). He

traces his path from "being 'for' society and then 'against' it" (435) and decides that the only way to stay healthy is to stay entirely separate from society. It is for this reason that he has retreated to his basement hole, "because up above there's an increasing passion to make men conform to a pattern" (435). He bemoans this "passion toward conformity," saying that conformity would

> end up by forcing me, an invisible man, to become white, which is not a color but the lack of one. Must I strive toward colorlessness? But seriously, and without snobbery, think of what the world would lose if that should happen. America is woven of many strands. . . . Our fate is to become one, and yet many—This is not prophesy, but description. Thus one of the greatest jokes in the world is the spectacle of the whites busy escaping blackness and becoming blacker every day, and the blacks striving toward whiteness, becoming quite dull and gray. None of us seems to know who he is or where he's going. (435–436)

All at once he realizes that it is a "social crime" for him to stay in his hole too long because "there's a possibility that even an invisible man has a socially responsible role to play," and he decides to go out into the world again (439).

Eventually the narrator himself becomes disillusioned with the Brotherhood. He realizes that the group does not really care about blacks as people, saying, "What did they know of us, except that we numbered so many, worked on certain jobs, offered so many votes, and provided so many marchers for some protest parade of theirs?" (383).

The narrator's search for identity as a black man in a white society has led many scholars to compare *Invisible Man* to the novels of James Baldwin and Richard Wright, who wrote during the same period. In fact, Wright was Ellison's friend and encouraged him in his work. (Ellison 1952; Hersey 1974)

See also Baldwin, James; Communism; Ellison, Ralph; Racism; Wright, Richard

Iron Heel, The

The Iron Heel, by Jack London, traces the rise of a fictional oligarchy, the Iron Heel, in the United States during the years 1912–1917. Published in 1908, the novel is presented as a manuscript written by Avis Everhard, who offers a first-person narration of her life with her husband, Ernest, a famous revolutionary. This manuscript includes scholarly footnotes, written by a fictional historian approximately seven centuries in the future, to explain various terms and concepts, which are also clever commentaries on society's ills. For example, to explain the term *watchman,* the footnote says:

> In those days thievery was incredibly prevalent. Everybody stole property from everybody else. The lords of society stole legally or else legalized their stealing, while the poorer classes stole illegally. Nothing was safe unless guarded. Enormous numbers of men were employed as watchmen to protect property. The houses of the well-to-do were a combination of safe deposit vault and fortress. The appropriation of the personal belongings of others by our own children of to-day is looked upon as rudimentary survival of the theft-characteristic that in those early times was universal. (London 1924, 43–44)

The plot begins with Ernest and Avis's first meeting, at a dinner given by her father, John Cunningham, who is a respected scientist and professor at a university in Berkeley, California. During this meeting Ernest expounds on his socialist theories, argues that the ruling classes have too much power, and suggests that one day a revolution will take place. At subsequent speaking engagements throughout the city Ernest develops his ideas still further. He explains that the capitalists and trusts are a ruling oligarchy, which he calls the Iron Heel, and warns that this heel will eventually crush everyone beneath it. He suggests that the owners of small businesses join with the working classes before the Iron Heel stamps out not only their livelihoods but also their lives. Although many of these business owners

think that Ernest's opinions regarding socialism make sense, most will not accept his concept of the Iron Heel, and they refuse to believe that his predictions of a future working-class revolution will come true.

At first Avis also resists Ernest's views. Then he challenges her to investigate the case of a workman who lost his arm in an industrial accident and then was persecuted for it. She tracks down everyone involved in the incident, and learns that, even though the accident was not the man's fault, the company blamed him for it and refused to pay him any monetary compensation for his injury. The man's life was ruined. In addition, Avis learns that many other working-class people are not being treated fairly because of the oppression of the Iron Heel. She tries to get the newspapers to report on these injustices, but she soon discovers that the Iron Heel controls the media. She now believes in Ernest's philosophy.

Ernest makes another convert out of Bishop Morehouse by challenging this idealistic minister to study working-class life. Morehouse soon discovers that society is more cruel than he imagined. The minister tells Ernest that he will give a speech to his fellow clergymen, rousing them to do more to help the downtrodden. Ernest warns him against it, saying that he will be attacked for going against the best interests of the capitalistic class to which he belongs. Nonetheless, the minister follows through with his plans, preaching:

> Let each one of you who is prosperous take into his house some thief and treat him as his brother, some unfortunate and treat her as his sister, and San Francisco will need no police force and no magistrates; the prisons will be turned into hospitals, and the criminal will disappear with his crime. We must give ourselves and not our money alone. . . . You have hardened your hearts. You have closed your ears to the voices that are crying in the land—the voices of pain and sorrow that you will not hear but that some day will be heard. (115–116)

After his speech the minister is deemed insane and sentenced to a mental asylum. He pretends to "get well," is released, and secretly begins selling his property. When he has enough money, he changes his identity and disappears to work among the poor. The Iron Heel eventually finds him again, and he ends up back in a mental institution.

When Ernest and Avis get engaged, Ernest warns John Cunningham that he, too, will be persecuted for associating with revolutionary ideas. He urges his future father-in-law to leave the country. Cunningham decides to stay, and the Iron Heel pressures the university to give him a leave of absence from his job. The authorities then make up a false mortgage on his home, although he owns it free and clear, and foreclose on it. Cunningham loses everything, and like the Bishop, he goes to live among the working classes.

By this time Avis and Ernest are married, and she has become involved in his revolutionary activities. She participates in a general strike and a failed revolution, during which she pretends to be working for the government. Later Ernest is falsely accused of planting a bomb while giving a speech to Congress. Powerful members of the oligarchy have set him up, and they use the incident to accuse any congressman who opposes them of being a revolutionary. Over 30 men, including Ernest, are sent to prison. Meanwhile Avis goes into hiding, changes her identity, and awaits her husband's escape. The two are part of a large, growing underground organization seeking to overthrow the oligarchy. Eventually the couple is reunited to participate in a final action against the Iron Heel. The manuscript ends in midsentence, with a footnote remarking how unfortunate it is that the book was not completed because then it "would have cleared away the mystery that has shrouded for seven centuries the execution of Ernest Everhard" (354).

In writing about this novel in 1924, social protest author Anatole France argues that London's warning of socialism's demise is justified. France believes that if the powerful want socialism to disappear, then it will, saying: "There is no reason to believe that . . . be it sooner or later, Socialism will be crushed beneath the Heel of Iron and be drowned in blood" (xv). In this France disagrees with the prevailing view when the novel was published. He (xv–xvi) reports: "In 1907 Jack London was shouted at as a frightful pessimist. Even sincere socialists blamed him for casting terror into the party ranks. They were wrong; those who have the precious and rare gift of foreseeing the future are bound to reveal the dangers it presents." At the same time France agrees with London that, even if socialism is crushed, the oligarchy will not last forever. France (xvi–xvii) insists that the working classes will prevail, saying: "Already, in its very strength we can perceive signs of its ruin. It will perish because all caste government is vowed to death. It will perish because it is unjust. It will perish swollen with pride and at the height of its power, just as slavery and serfdom have perished. Even now if one observes it attentively one can see that it is decrepit." (London 1924; O'Conner 1964)

See also France, Anatole; London, Jack; Socialism

J

Jackson, Helen Hunt

Born on October 15, 1830, in Amherst, Massachusetts, Helen Hunt Jackson was a poet, novelist, and children's book writer who advocated better treatment for Native Americans, particularly those in California. She began writing in 1863 after the deaths of her husband and two sons, and her poetry received much acclaim. In 1875 she remarried and moved to Colorado, where she wrote *A Century of Dishonor* (1881). The book criticized government policies in regard to Native Americans, and its publication led to Hunt's appointment to a federal commission investigating the treatment of California's Mission Indians. This experience led Hunt to write her most famous work, *Ramona* (1885). The novel was extremely popular and aroused public sympathy for the plight of Native Americans everywhere. Hunt died on August 12, 1885, in San Francisco, California. (Banning 1973; Mathes 1990)

See also Native American Issues; Racism; *Ramona*

Jackson, Shirley

Novelist Shirley Hardie Jackson is best known for her short story "The Lottery" (1948), which depicts a town that holds a yearly lottery to select a sacrificial victim. Some schol-ars have interpreted the work as a protest against unexamined traditions. Jackson wrote several other short stories, as well as Gothic novels and fictionalized memoirs.

Born on December 14, 1916, in San Francisco, California, she attended Syracuse University in New York. After her graduation in 1940, she married literary critic Stanley Edgar Hyman, and in 1945 the couple moved to Bennington, Vermont. Jackson died there on August 8, 1965. (Friedman 1975)

See also "Lottery, The"

James, Henry

Novelist Henry James wrote primarily about the societal differences between Europeans and Americans. He was born on April 15, 1843, in New York, New York, into a family of prominent philosophers. As a child he and his brother had private tutors and traveled with their parents throughout Europe, intermittently returning to the eastern United States. In 1862 James began attending Harvard Law School. He also studied literature and wrote stories. His first story was published anonymously in 1864 in a New York magazine, the *Continental Monthly*. Shortly thereafter he became a regular contributor to the *Atlantic Monthly*. He also wrote book reviews for the *North American Review*.

Henry James (Archive Photos)

In 1875 James moved to Paris, France, where he published his first novel, *Roderick Hudson.* He also befriended the Russian social protest novelist Ivan Turgenev, whose work he admired, but James left Paris after a year to move to London, England. There he produced his most important novels, including *Daisy Miller* (1879), *The Portrait of a Lady* (1881), and two works concerning social and political reform, *The Bostonians* (1886) and *The Princess Casamassima* (1886), respectively. During his career James wrote a total of 20 novels, 12 plays, and over 100 stories. He also wrote articles, essays, criticisms, and travel literature. In 1915 he became an English citizen, and a year later, on February 28, 1916, he died in London, England. (McElderry 1965)

See also *Bostonians, The*

Javert

A police inspector in Victor Hugo's 1862 novel *Les Misérables,* Monsieur Javert is a narrow-minded man incapable of mercy. He pursues an escaped convict, Jean Valjean, for years, even though the man has reformed and does not deserve to be jailed. One day during a civil uprising Valjean saves Javert's life, and the police inspector realizes that he cannot arrest the man. Distraught over his failure to do his duty, Javert drowns himself in the Seine River. (Hugo 1987)

See also Hugo, Victor; *Misérables, Les;* Valjean, Jean

Jellyby, Mrs.

Mrs. Jellyby is a character in Charles Dickens's novel *Bleak House,* which first appeared in serialized form between 1852 and 1853. She is introduced in a chapter entitled "Telescopic Philanthropy" and described as a woman obsessed with philanthropic efforts. One of her friends explains: "Mrs. Jellyby . . . is a lady of very remarkable strength of character, who devotes herself entirely to the public. She has devoted herself to an extensive variety of public subjects, at various times, and is at present (until something else attracts her) devoted to the subject of Africa; with a view to the general cultivation of the coffee berry—*and* the natives—and the happy settlement, on the banks of the African rivers, of our superabundant home population" (Dickens 1987, 34).

However, it soon becomes apparent that Mrs. Jellyby is a bit too involved in her social reform efforts. One observer reports:

Mrs. Jellyby had very good hair, but was too much occupied with her African duties to brush it. . . . The room, which was strewn with papers and nearly filled by a great writing-table covered with similar litter, was, I must say, not only very untidy, but very dirty. . . . But what principally struck us was a jaded and unhealthy-looking . . . girl, at the writing-table, who sat biting the feather of her pen, and staring at us. I suppose nobody ever was in such a state of ink. And, from her tumbled hair to her pretty feet, which were disfigured with frayed and broken satin slippers trodden down at heel, she really seemed to have no article of dress upon her, from a pin upwards, that was in its proper condition or its right place. (37)

Mrs. Jellyby neglects her children and husband at home in order to participate in causes that will benefit people abroad. The term *telescopic* in the chapter's title means "distant." Charles Dickens often criticized activists for overlooking the suffering children in their own neighborhoods to concentrate on problems elsewhere. (Dickens 1987a)

See also *Bleak House;* Dickens, Charles

Joad Family

The Joad family is featured in John Steinbeck's 1939 novel *The Grapes of Wrath.* Composed of three generations, its members include Tom Joad Jr. and his siblings Rose of Sharon, Noah, Al, Ruthie, and Winfield; Tom's parents Tom Joad Sr. and Ma Joad; and Tom's grandparents Granma and Grampa Joad. They represent the thousands of tenant farmers in the American Midwest who were forced from their land during the 1930s. Like most other Oklahomans, they migrate to California expecting to find a better life. Instead, they find prejudice, injustice, and unfair working conditions. The family, which was once strong and unified, begins to break apart. Some members die; some drift away. Tom Joad Jr. commits a murder in self-defense and becomes a wanted man, but he vows to continue fighting for justice while on the run. Tom Joad Sr. works with a group of migrants to prevent a river from overflowing and learns that people must join together for the greater good. Meanwhile Ma Joad comes to view her family not as an individual unit but as a part of a whole. She sees life as "all one flow, like a stream, little eddies, little waterfalls" and says that, despite difficulties, "the river, it goes right on," adding: "We ain't gonna die out. People is goin' on—changin' a little, maybe, but goin' right on" (Steinbeck 1972, 467). The Joads's story suggests that the poor and downtrodden will always exist and will do what they have to do in order to survive. (Steinbeck 1972)

See also *Grapes of Wrath, The;* Great Depression; Immigrant Communities; Steinbeck, John

Johnson, James Weldon

James Weldon Johnson is best known today for his novel *The Autobiography of an Ex-Colored Man,* which he first published anonymously in 1912. The work did not appear under his own name until 1927, the same year he published a collection of poetry entitled *God's Trombones: Seven Negro Spirituals in Verse.*

Born June 17, 1871, in Jacksonville, Florida, Johnson attended Atlanta University before studying law at New York's Columbia University. He was the first black man admitted to the Florida bar. Nonetheless, in 1901 he and his brother became composers for the New York stage, and together they wrote over 200 songs for Broadway productions. In 1906 he accepted a diplomatic position, serving as a U.S. consul in Venezuela and Nicaragua. His diplomatic career ended in 1914, and shortly thereafter he began teaching creative writing at Fisk University in Tennessee. He also helped found the National Association for the Advancement of Colored People and acted as its secretary from 1916 to 1930. His other works include a poetry collection, *Fifty Years and Other Poems* (1917); an anthology, *Book of American Negro Poetry* (1922); and an autobiography, *Along This Way* (1933). Johnson died on June 26, 1938, in Wiscasset, Maine. (Levy 1973)

See also *Autobiography of an Ex-Colored Man;* Harlem Renaissance; Racism

Jones, Eric

Eric Jones appears in James Baldwin's 1960 novel *Another Country.* After a series of homosexual relationships, he has an affair with a married woman. He begins the affair in part because she is an old friend, but mostly because it would be easier for him to be heterosexual. However, in the end he realizes that, even though "the life you think you *should* want . . . is always the life that looks safest," in actuality "you've got to be truthful about the life you *have*" (Baldwin 1962, 336). He ends the affair and returns to homosexuality. (Baldwin 1962)

See also *Another Country;* Baldwin, James; Gay and Lesbian Issues; Moore, Daniel Vivaldo; Scott, Ida and Rufus

Joseph K.

Joseph K. is the main character in Franz Kafka's 1925 novel *Der Prozess* (The Trial). An ordinary bank clerk, he is accused of a crime by a mysterious court but allowed to remain free until his trial. Yet no one will tell him what he has done wrong, and although he struggles to obtain more information, he cannot find out much about the court or its officers. A year after his arrest two officers of the court execute him in a deserted field near a stone quarry. (Kafka 1964)

See also Kafka, Franz; *Trial, The*

Joy, Serena

The character Serena Joy appears in the futuristic novel *The Handmaid's Tale* (1985), by Margaret Atwood. A former television evangelist, Serena supported a rebellion that created Gilead, a country run by religious fundamentalists. Under this theocracy her assigned role as Wife of a Commander is to run the household, maintain the garden, and socialize with other Wives. She has great power over women in lesser roles, but she is ultimately powerless in a regime controlled by men. Moreover, as a barren woman who longs for a child, she is powerless in a more personal sense. Serena Joy is Atwood's caution to women of religious movements who are too eager to give away their power as individuals. (Atwood 1986; McCombs 1988)

See also Atwood, Margaret; Feminism; *Handmaid's Tale, The*; Offred

Jungle, The

Upton Sinclair's 1906 novel *The Jungle* exposes injustice and corruption in the U.S. meatpacking industry during the early twentieth century. Because of the book's emphasis on slavelike working conditions within the industry, in 1905 reviewer Jack London (Sinclair 1972, vii) compared it to the antislavery novel *Uncle Tom's Cabin* and called it an important socialist work, saying: "It will be read by every workingman. It will open countless ears that have been deaf to Socialism. It will plough the soil for the seed of our propaganda. It will make thousands of converts to our cause."

However, the public largely ignored the human injustices portrayed in the story, preferring instead to focus on what the book revealed about the unsanitary practices of food processing. As Sinclair (viii) himself explains: "I aimed at the public's heart and by accident I hit it in the stomach." As a result, President Theodore Roosevelt launched an investigation into the sanitation of meatpacking factories. This led to the enactment of new health laws, including the Pure Food and Drug Act.

Other laws to address poor working conditions were slower to arrive. In a 1946 introduction to the work Sinclair Lewis (viii) wrote:

> Forty years have passed [since *The Jungle* was published], and the workers throughout America have fought a bitter war for a share of control over their own destinies. . . . The labor of slaughtering animals is still hard and often dangerous; it is ill-paid and uncertain, as all labor must be so long as it is carried on under the profit system; but it is not so bad as it was forty years ago, and that much comfort can be offered to present-day readers of *The Jungle*.

The novel's story of social injustice is shown through the struggles of its main character, Jurgis Rudkus, and his family, which includes Jurgis's father, Antanas; Jurgis's fiancée, Ona; Ona's cousin Marija; Ona's stepmother, Elzbieta; Elzbieta's brother, Jonas; and Elzbieta's six children. Jurgis is a big, muscular Lithuanian peasant who does not understand English. Nonetheless, he takes his family to the United States, where he believes that people can make good money as laborers in the stockyards of Chicago. There he gets a job sweeping cattle entrails into a trap in the floor, and he is able to save up enough money to pay for his wedding. Meanwhile Marija finds work painting labels on cans of smoked beef.

The family lives in a crowded, dirty boardinghouse but soon decides to purchase a brand-new house. However, after the deed is signed, the Rudkuses learn that they have been cheated. The house is not new at all, only freshly painted, and in addition to regular payments they will be charged interest as well as additional sums for insurance and other expenses. Consequently, other members of the family are forced to find jobs. Antanas mops floors around vats of chemically treated beef, but because he is old, he must work for little money. Ona sews covers on hams, and Elzbieta's oldest son, 14-year-old Stanislovas, places cans on a lard-canning machine. His younger brothers sell newspapers on street corners.

In every case working conditions are unusually hard and business practices are unsanitary. Diseased hogs and cattle are slaughtered along with healthy ones, and spoiled food is doctored with colorants and chemicals to make it look edible. Employees are expected to work as quickly as possible until they drop. Under such conditions Antanas falls ill and dies. Shortly thereafter Marija's canning factory shuts down because of overproduction, and in the winter Jurgis's work hours are reduced. The family slips deeper into poverty. Ona, Jurgis, and Stanislaus can no longer afford to ride a streetcar to work; instead they must walk two miles each way through the snow. They also cannot afford much coal, and the house grows cold.

In the spring things seem to improve. Marija finds work as a beef trimmer, and Ona gives birth to a boy she names Antanas. However, she cannot take time off from work to recuperate from the birth, and her health deteriorates. Then Jurgis injures his ankle on the job and must go home to recuperate without pay. Although his injury heals, he is no longer as strong as before. He loses his job and has difficulty finding another. Finally he agrees to work in the fertilizer department, where conditions are so toxic that most workers are not expected to survive more than five years. Despondent, he begins to drink.

One day he discovers that Ona, who is pregnant again, has been forced to become her boss's mistress in order to save her job. Jurgis rushes to the factory, beats the man up, and is sentenced to 30 days in jail. Stanislaus visits him and reveals that Marija was injured

at work and has lost her job. Ona is also out of work, as is Stanislaus, because of what Jurgis did to the factory boss. The family is starving to death.

When Jurgis is released from jail, he learns that his family has been evicted. Everyone is back at the old boardinghouse, where a severely malnourished Ona has gone into premature labor. She and the child both die. Shortly thereafter baby Antanas drowns in a mucky street. Disgusted with the city, Jurgis hops a train to the country, where he becomes a hobo and occasional farmworker. Unfortunately he can find no work or shelter for the winter and he decides to return to Chicago, where he finds a job as a tunnel digger. When a runaway underground train engine injures his shoulder, he must become a beggar and a thief in order to survive. He begins to make friends among his fellow thieves, and eventually a corrupt politician gets him a job at his old factory, so that he can influence voters there. When the employees go out on strike, Jurgis keeps working and is promoted to foreman. One day he encounters the man who seduced Ona, beats him up again, and is arrested. While out on bail he leaves the district and again becomes a beggar. On the streets he learns that Marija has become a prostitute. He visits her, and she encourages him rejoin the family, now living near the house of prostitution. On the way to see them Jurgis attends a political meeting to get warm and hears an impassioned speech about socialism. He becomes involved in the socialist cause and begins working as a porter for a socialist hotel owner. His spirit is uplifted, and he anticipates converting many more workers to the cause.

The novel ends with a socialist speaker arguing that when the Democrats do not deliver on their election promises, they will lose power:

We shall have the sham reformers self-stultified and self-convicted; we shall have the radical Democracy left without a lie with which to cover its nakedness! And then will begin the rush that will never be checked, the tide that will never turn till it has reached its flood—that will be irresistible, overwhelming—the rallying of the outraged workingmen of Chicago to our standard! And we shall organize them, we shall drill them, we shall marshal them for the victory! We shall bear down the opposition, we shall sweep it before us—and Chicago will be ours! (Sinclair 1972, 342–343)

In discussing this speech, Sinclair Lewis explains that he heard similar orations during his own activities in support of the socialist cause and is surprised that more people have not been inspired by such words. He questions whether he has "placed far too high an estimate upon the intelligence of the human race, and its moral qualities." However, he is encouraged by the fact that the novel did bring about some reforms in both industry and politics and hopes that more will come in the future (Sinclair 1972, viii). (Bloodworth 1977; Mookerjee 1988; Sinclair 1972)

See also Labor Issues; London, Jack; Rudkus, Jurgis and Ona; Socialism; *Uncle Tom's Cabin*

Jurgis, Arthur

Arthur Jurgis is a character in Alan Paton's 1948 South African novel *Cry, the Beloved Country*. He does not appear in life; however, his writings feature prominently in the story after his death. Murdered by a black man during a burglary, Jurgis was a white activist who worked for black equality and often quoted Abraham Lincoln. After his funeral his grieving father studies his son's work and decides to help the blacks in his rural village. (Paton 1987)

See also *Cry, the Beloved Country;* Paton, Alan

Justice

Justice is a major concern of social protest authors. For example, Albert Camus, Charles Dickens, Victor Hugo, Franz Kafka, and Harper Lee criticize injustice in their countries' legal systems. Nuruddin Farah, Carlos Fuentes, and Milan Kundera protest political injustice. Ciro Alegría's novel *Broad and Alien Is the World* depicts both political and legal corruption, whereas Walter Van Tilburg Clark's *The Ox-Bow Incident* concerns the injustice of a lynch mob. Writers who deal with issues of apartheid, feminism, racism, homosexuality, anti-Semitism, Native American rights, and other forms of discrimination, particularly those involving labor issues and class structure, are also concerned with injustice.

See also Alegría, Ciro; Anti-Semitism; Apartheid; *Broad and Alien Is the World;* Camus, Albert; Clark, Walter Van Tilburg; Class, Social; Dickens, Charles; Farah, Nuruddin; Feminism; Fuentes, Carlos; Gay and Lesbian Issues; Hugo, Victor; Kafka, Franz; Kundera, Milan; Labor Issues; Lee, Harper; Native American Issues; *Ox-Bow Incident, The; Racism*

K

Kafka, Franz

Born on July 3, 1883, in Prague, Bohemia, Austria-Hungary (now part of the Czech Republic), Franz Kafka wrote fiction that concerned the modern person's alienation from society. This theme was inspired in part by his own alienation from society. As a Jewish man living in an anti-Semitic Germanic community, he had difficulty both fitting in and honoring his heritage. Eventually he broke off all connections to his past by becoming a socialist and an atheist. In 1906 Kafka received a doctorate, and from 1906 to 1922 he worked in the insurance industry. He left the business in 1923 to devote himself entirely to his writing. A year later, on June 3, 1924, he died of tuberculosis in a town near Vienna, Austria. Most of his writings were published posthumously, by his friend and promoter Max Brod, despite Kafka's expressed wish that they be destroyed. These works include the novels *Der Prozess* (The Trial, 1925) and *Der Schloss* (The Castle, 1926). Of the works published during Kafka's lifetime, the stories *Die Verwandlung* (The Metamorphosis 1915) and *In der Strafkolonie* (In the Penal Colony, 1919) are perhaps the best known. (Hamalian 1974; Spann 1976)

See also *Trial, The*

Franz Kafka, c. 1890's–1910's (Corbis-Bettmann)

Kesey, Ken

As a member of the 1960s Beat Movement in the United States, Ken Kesey wrote fiction and nonfiction critical of American culture.

His most significant novel in this regard was *One Flew over the Cuckoo's Nest*, published in 1962. The book was based in part on Kesey's experience testing psychedelic drugs as a paid volunteer at a veterans' hospital, where he later worked as an aide.

Born on September 17, 1935, in La Junta, Colorado, Kesey attended both the University of Oregon and Stanford University. He continues to write, although his works appear irregularly. His most recent books are *The Further Inquiry* (1990) and *Sailor Song* (1992).

See also Beat Movement; *One Flew Over the Cuckoo's Nest*

Knecht, Joseph

Joseph Knecht is the subject of Hermann Hesse's 1943 fictional biography *Das Glasperlenspiel* (The Glass Bead Game), also entitled *Magister Ludi*. He is a member of an elite intellectual order but gradually realizes that his isolation from nonintellectuals is hindering his personal growth. He resigns from his order to become a tutor to a young man from a politically powerful family, hoping to help change society. However, before Knecht can realize his goal he drowns in a swimming accident. (Hesse 1986)

See also *Glass Bead Game, The;* Hesse, Hermann

Knowell, Douglas

Douglas Knowell appears in Doris Lessing's five-novel series *Children of Violence*. Married to the main character, Martha Quest, he tries to prevent her from becoming involved in political activism, believing that women should be wives and mothers and little else. He also submerges his own political views, choosing to abandon his interest in communism to take a job in the civil service. He is an alcoholic, and when Martha tells him she wants a divorce, he threatens to kill either her or himself. (Lessing 1964)

See also *Children of Violence;* Lessing, Doris

Knox, Tom

A character in the 1958 novel *The Ugly American,* by William J. Lederer and Eugene Burdick, Tom Knox is an expert on poultry who travels to Asia as part of a group called the American Aid Mission. During a conference of American agricultural experts, he recommends that funds be allotted to buy chickens and sugarcane processing machines for local communities. But his superiors want to spend the money on a new canal and a large mechanized farm, which are far more impressive projects, and they ridicule Knox for his suggestions. As a result, he leaves for the United States, intending to protest their decision. However, his return trip has been arranged by Asian officials who will profit from the mechanized farm, and as he travels, they subtly convince him to abandon his complaints. Once home he forgets all about the problems of the Asian people. (Lederer and Burdick 1958)

See also *Ugly American, The*

Kumalo, Stephen

The main character of Alan Paton's 1948 South African novel *Cry, the Beloved Country,* Stephen Kumalo is a black priest from a rural village. His son, Absalom, moves to the city of Johannesburg; falls in with a bad crowd; and commits several crimes, including murder. When Absalom ends up in jail, he blames everyone else for his fate, but Stephen insists that his son take responsibility for his actions. At the same time the old priest recognizes that it is difficult for his people to maintain their morality when they become separated from their families and ancient customs. He works to improve life in his village, so that young people will not want to leave it. (Paton 1987)

See also *Cry, the Beloved Country;* Paton, Alan

Kundera, Milan

Czechoslovakian author Milan Kundera writes novels, short stories, plays, and poems, many of which include political and social criticism. Born on April 1, 1929, in the city of Brno, his first poetry collections were condemned by the Czechoslovakian government. After 1969 the government banned the publication of all of his work, including his internationally famous novel *Nesnesitelná lehkost bytí* (The Unbearable Lightness of Being,

1984). Most of his works therefore appeared first in translation.

Kundera was politically active in his country and participated in a liberalization movement during 1967–1968, which led authorities to fire him from his teaching positions and oust him from the Communist Party. In 1975 he left Czechoslovakia for France and took a teaching position at the University of Rennes. Four years later the Czech government revoked his citizenship, and his works remained banned in the Czech Republic until 1989. Kundera continues to live and write in France today. (Aji 1992; Kundera 1984)

See also Censorship; Communism; Exiles; *Unbearable Lightness of Being, The*

L

Labor Issues

Social protest authors have written about a wide variety of labor issues. For example, the works of Rebecca Harding Davis, Charles Dickens, and Tillie Olsen express concern for the poor quality of life among factory workers. Dickens's novels also protest child labor. Upton Sinclair and John Steinbeck expose unfair labor practices in the meatpacking and agricultural industries, respectively, in their novels *The Jungle* and *The Grapes of Wrath.* John Galsworthy and Lillian Hellman depict labor strikes in their respective plays *Strife* and *Days to Come.* Jack London's novel *The Iron Heel,* Ayn Rand's novel *Atlas Shrugged,* and H. G. Wells's novel *Tono-Bungay* examine labor issues as they relate to the differences between socialism and capitalism. Job satisfaction is the subject of Sinclair Lewis's novel *Babbitt* and is also a common subject for science fiction novels, including Edward Bellamy's *Looking Backward, 2000–1887;* Aldous Huxley's *Brave New World;* George Orwell's *1984;* Jules Verne's *Paris in the Twentieth Century;* and Kurt Vonnegut's *Player Piano.* In addition, writers who depict racism or other types of prejudice, such as anti-Semitism or antifeminism, often deal with discrimination in the workplace. (Wortman 1969)

See also Anti-Semitism; *Atlas Shrugged; Babbitt;* Bellamy, Edward; *Brave New World;* Capitalism; Davis, Rebecca Harding; *Days to Come;* Dickens, Charles; Feminism; Galsworthy, John; *Grapes of Wrath, The;* Hellman, Lillian; Huxley, Aldous; *Iron Heel, The; Jungle, The;* Lewis, Sinclair; London, Jack; *Looking Backward, 2000–1887; 1984;* Olsen, Tillie; Orwell, George; *Paris in the Twentieth Century; Player Piano;* Poverty; Racism; Rand, Ayn; Sinclair, Upton; Socialism; Steinbeck, John; *Strife; Tono-Bungay;* Verne, Jules; Vonnegut, Kurt; Wells, H. G.

Larsen, Nella

Born in 1891, probably in either Chicago, Illinois, or New York, New York, Nella Larsen wrote novels and short stories that drew on her own experiences with racism in the United States. She was of mixed race, having a mother who was Danish and a father who was a black West Indian. Although she gave different versions of her childhood, biographers believe that as a girl she was expelled from her family because of her color. In 1912 she began attending a nursing school in New York City, graduating in 1915. She worked as a nurse until 1921, when she took a job as a librarian and started writing fiction. By this time she lived in the Harlem district of New

York City. Her first publications were stories in black magazines. Her first novella, *Quicksand,* was published in 1928, and her second, *Passing,* in 1929. In 1992 these works and some of her short stories were republished in a collection entitled *An Intimation of Things Distant.*

In 1930 Larsen became the first black woman to win a Guggenheim fellowship. Unfortunately, she experienced personal difficulties soon afterward, and her writing suffered. None of her later works was ever published. Eventually she returned to nursing in New York City, where she died on March 30, 1964. (Davis 1994; Larson 1993)

See also Feminism; *Intimation of Things Distant, An;* Racism

Le Guin, Ursula

Science fiction and fantasy writer Ursula Le Guin often uses fictional worlds to comment on the failings of the real world. Born on October 21, 1929, in Berkeley, California, she attended Radcliffe College and Columbia University in New York. Her first novel was the first in a trilogy involving an alien society on the planet Hain, which established human life on Earth. She followed this trilogy with the first in a series of four children's books known as the Earthsea Quartet. At the same time she published several novels for adults, including *The Left Hand of Darkness* (1969), which comments on human sexuality and morality; *The Dispossessed* (1974), which depicts both an anarchist world and a world of capitalists and Communists; and *Malafrena* (1979), which concerns political and social oppression in a fictional nineteenth-century European country. Le Guin continues to write fiction, as well as essays on fiction, feminism, and other topics. (Spivack 1984)

See also Anarchism; *Malafrena;* Science Fiction and Fantasy

Lederer, William J.

William Julius Lederer is the author of several fiction and nonfiction books, but his best-known work is the novel *The Ugly American,* which he coauthored with Eugene Burdick. Published in 1958, the novel protests U.S. policies in Southeast Asia, as well as the behavior of U.S. and French military and diplomatic leaders in the region. (Lederer and Burdick 1958)

See also Burdick, Eugene; Justice; *Ugly American, The*

Lee, Harper

Nelle Harper Lee is the author of *To Kill a Mockingbird* (1960), a novel that protested racism in the southern United States. Born in Monroeville, Alabama, on April 28, 1926, she wanted to become a lawyer like her father. However, although she studied law at the University of Alabama from 1945 to 1949, she became an airline clerk instead. *To Kill a Mockingbird* was her only work. (Lee 1993)

See also *To Kill a Mockingbird*

Leete, Edith

Edith Leete, a character in the 1887 novel *Looking Backward, 2000–1887,* embodies author Edward Bellamy's vision of a twentieth-century woman. Writing from the perspective of the late 1880s, Bellamy made Edith not only compassionate, kind, and beautiful, but also rational, intelligent, and straightforward. In her society women are supposedly equal to men in every way. As Edith's father, Dr. Leete, explains, "No woman is heard nowadays wishing she were a man, nor parents desiring boy rather than girl children. Our girls are as full of ambition for their careers as our boys. Marriage, when it comes, does not mean incarceration for them, nor does it separate them in any way from the later interests of society" (Bellamy 1951, 212). However, scholar Cecelia Tichi (25), writing in an introduction to a 1982 edition, believes that "beneath the surface of Bellamy's feminist program . . . lies the sexual segregation of separate and unequal women's lives. The women's industrial army, which mirrors that of men, exists only through *noblesse oblige,* as Dr. Leete reveals when he says of women, 'We have given them a world of their own.'" Moreover, Edith "has

Actor Gregory Peck and novelist Harper Lee on the set of the Universal Pictures movie To Kill a Mockingbird, *1962 (UPI/Corbis-Bettmann)*

no discernible occupation apart from shopping and nurturing Julian West" (25) a visitor who was born in 1857 but, through an accident of hypnosis, slept for 113 years. At the end of the novel the two become engaged. (Bellamy 1951, 1982)

See also Bellamy, Edward; Feminism; *Looking Backward, 2000–1887;* West, Julian

Legal Issues
See Justice

Lessing, Doris
Doris Lessing writes novels and short stories that primarily concern characters trying to deal with social and political change. She was born Doris May Taylor in Persia (now Iran) on October 22, 1919, but was brought up on a farm in southern Rhodesia (now Zimbabwe). In 1949 she moved to England, and a year later she published her first book, *The*

Grass Is Singing, which is set in Africa. She has written many more novels in her career. Some scholars believe that her most important work is a five-novel series entitled *Children of Violence* (1952–1969), which concerns the issues of racism, feminism, socialism, and anti-Semitism, both in Africa and in England. Lessing's other works include *The Golden Notebook* (1962), *The Good Terrorist* (1986), and *The Fifth Child* (1988), as well as nonfiction books, essays, and science fiction stories. In 1995 she received an honorary degree from Harvard University and published the first volume of her autobiography, *Under My Skin.* The second volume, *Walking in the Shade,* appeared in 1997. (Brewster 1965; Sprague and Tiger 1986)

See also Anti-Semitism; *Children of Violence;* Feminism; Racism; Science Fiction and Fantasy; Socialism

Doris Lessing, 13 October 1992 (Reuters/Peter Morgan/Archive Photos)

Lewis, Sinclair

Harry Sinclair Lewis wrote several novels criticizing conventional middle-class beliefs regarding business, religion, and politics in the United States of the 1920s. His most famous work is *Babbitt* (1922), whose main character is a successful, yet dissatisfied real estate salesman. After the novel's publication the word *Babbittry* entered the vernacular, meaning mindless conformity to middle-class values.

Lewis was born on February 7, 1885, in Sauk Center, Minnesota. From 1901 to 1903 he worked as a typesetter for local newspapers, and in 1903 he moved to New Haven, Connecticut, to attend Yale University, where he edited the campus literary magazine. He graduated in 1908 and began traveling throughout the United States as a freelance editor and journalist. He also sold story ideas to fiction writer Jack London.

In 1910 Lewis returned to New York to work at a variety of publishing-related jobs and began writing novels in his spare time. His first novel, an adventure story for children called *Hike and the Aeroplane,* was published in 1912 under the pseudonym Tom Graham. Under his own name he published two novels for adult readers, *Our Mr. Wrenn* (1914) and *The Trail of the Hawk* (1915). In 1915 he became a full-time freelance writer. Over the next five years he wrote several short stories, a play, and three more novels, entitled *The Job*

(1917), *The Innocents* (1917), and *Free Air* (1919). However, these books did not attract much attention; it was his seventh novel that brought Lewis recognition.

Entitled *Main Street* (1920), it examines life in an American small town, where bigotry and ignorance are commonplace. Lewis's subsequent work, *Babbitt,* is set in a medium-sized town with the same faults. Both books were commercial successes. However, they were also severely criticized for their unflattering portrait of American middle-class culture.

Lewis went on to write 14 more novels, including *Elmer Gantry* (1927) and *It Can't Happen Here* (1935). *Elmer Gantry* concerns religious hypocrisy, whereas *It Can't Happen Here* is a cautionary tale about the spread of fascism. In 1926 Lewis was awarded the Pulitzer Prize for another novel, *Arrowsmith* (1925), which focuses on the problems of a medical researcher working within a materialistic society. However, Lewis refused the award, believing he should have won it for *Main Street* or *Babbitt* instead. In 1930 he did accept the Nobel Prize in literature as the first American so honored. By this time he had divorced his first wife to marry a well-known journalist, Dorothy Thompson, whom he divorced in 1942.

After receiving the Nobel Prize, Lewis continued to write novels, but none was as well received as his earlier works. In fact, Sheldon Norman Grebstein (1962, 7) says that "no writer has ever risen higher in our critical esteem and then dropped more precipitately. In 1930 he was by far the most famous and among the two or three most respected American novelists. By the time of his death twenty years later, despite two best-sellers published just a few years before, the critics had written him off."

Nonetheless, Lewis was active in the theater, not just as a playwright but as a director, producer, and actor, and he lectured about writing at several universities. According to Martin Light, Lewis often spoke about the influence other writers had on his work. He particularly praised novelists Honoré de Balzac and Charles Dickens, who "led him to understand that it was possible to be realistic in descriptions of . . . common people" (Light 1975, 20), as well as Theodore Dreiser, whom Lewis lauded in his Nobel Prize acceptance speech. Lewis also said that the social protest novel *Tono-Bungay* was perhaps the greatest book he had ever read; its author, H. G. Wells, was Lewis's friend and mentor.

Lewis spent the last years of his life traveling, and in 1951 he died in Rome, Italy, of heart disease. His final work, *World So Wide*, was published posthumously. (Grebstein 1962; Schorer 1962)

See also *Babbitt;* Balzac, Honoré de; Dreiser, Theodore; *Elmer Gantry; Tono-Bungay;* Wells, H. G.

Life in the Iron Mills

Rebecca Harding Davis's novella *Life in the Iron Mills* was originally published in the April 1861 issue of the magazine *Atlantic Monthly.* It garnered much acclaim and was published in book form that same year. Set in Virginia and told by an unnamed first-person narrator of indeterminate gender, the story concerns the fate of Hugh Wolfe, a young Welsh furnace-tender at an iron-rolling mill. One day he encounters a group of upper-class men inspecting the mill. They notice a beautiful carved statue of a woman, and Hugh admits that he carved it himself. The men praise the work, and one of them, a physician named Doctor May, tells Hugh: "Do you know, boy, that you have it in you to be a great sculptor, a great man? . . . A man may make himself anything he chooses. God has given you stronger powers than many men,— me, for instance" (Wagner-Martin and Davidson 1995, 212). Hugh then asks May for help in accomplishing this goal. The doctor replies that he does not have enough money to educate the young man. The other men agree that it takes a lot of money to achieve goals in the United States. They toss Hugh a few coins and leave.

Hugh's cousin Deborah has witnessed this event, and later she brings Hugh a wallet she pickpocketed from one of the men. It is filled with money, and Deborah tells Hugh it is his

right to keep it, to make a great man of himself. Hugh is tempted, but in the end he decides to return the money to its rightful owner. Before he can do so, he is arrested for theft, tried, and sentenced to 19 years of hard labor. Deborah is sentenced to 3 years as his accomplice. Shortly after his sentencing Hugh uses a scrap of tin to slit his wrists. A Quaker woman arrives at the jail to tend to his body, speaks with Deborah, and invites the young woman to live with her after her prison sentence has been served. Deborah accepts the offer and spends the rest of her life in a good home. The narrator concludes the story by admitting to be the current owner of Hugh's statue, "through which the spirit of the dead [sculptor] looks out, with its thwarted life, its mighty hunger, its unfinished work" (228). (Harris 1991; Rose 1993; Wagner-Martin and Davidson 1995)

See also Davis, Rebecca Harding; Labor Issues

Little Big Man

The 1964 novel *Little Big Man,* by Thomas Berger, depicts the social injustices perpetrated against Native Americans during the 1800s. Nonetheless, the author (Landon 1989, 30) himself once said: "I did not write *Little Big Man* as an exercise in social criticism. It was not intended as an indictment of the white man. I wrote it for the same motive that informs all my fiction: to amuse myself."

The novel opens with a foreword by a fictional journalist, Ralph Fielding Snell, who reports that during 1952 and 1953 he conducted a series of interviews with Jack Crabbe, an 111-year-old man in a nursing home. Jack claims to have been with General George Armstrong Custer at the Battle of the Little Big Horn. The rest of the novel is Jack's account of his life among both whites and Native Americans.

His story begins in 1852 when he is ten years old. While traveling west across the American plains to California, his family meets a group of Cheyenne Indians. Jack's father gives them whiskey and is killed in the ensuing drunken brawl. Because of a misunderstanding, Jack and his sister, Caroline, believe

Jack Crabbe and Old Lodge Skins ride together in a scene from the 1970 movie Little Big Man *(The Museum of Modern Art Film Stills Archive). The story depicts the conflicts between white and Native American people during the era of the American Indian Wars.*

they are now the Cheyenne's prisoners. Caroline later escapes her captors, but Jack remains with them throughout his childhood, living in the lodge of their chief, Old Lodge Skins.

When Jack is 15, he joins a Cheyenne raid on a Crow Indian camp. The Crow and the Cheyenne are always stealing ponies from each other. During this raid Jack is forced to kill a Crow to defend a fellow Cheyenne, Younger Bear. This shames Younger Bear but earns Jack full membership in the tribe and a Cheyenne name: Little Big Man. Old Lodge Skins chooses this name because Jack is short but has a big heart and because Little Big Man was a great warrior.

A brief while later Jack participates in a battle against the U.S. Cavalry. He is nearly killed before he convinces the soldiers that he is white. They take him to their fort, where he is adopted by the Reverend Silas Pendrake, an older man, and his beautiful young wife. Jack becomes infatuated with Mrs. Pendrake and tries to follow her teachings about morality. However, he soon discovers that she has been having affairs and lying to him. Disillusioned, he leaves town, but he cannot return to the Cheyenne because "being primitive ain't the easiest thing in the world to get used to if you know better. You get showed a more regular manner of obtaining your grub, for example, and it's pretty hard to return to a method that ain't guaranteed" (Berger 1964, 143).

He therefore takes on a series of roles in the white man's world: trader, mule skinner, buffalo hunter, drunkard, gunfighter, gambler, Indian scout. As a trader he marries a Swedish woman, Olga, and has a son, both of whom are later captured by Indians. As a drunkard he meets his sister, Caroline, who teaches him to shoot a gun. He also meets many famous people of his day, including Wild Bill Hickock, Wyatt Earp, and Calamity Jane.

Eventually Jack returns to the Cheyenne. He again lives with Old Lodge Skins's tribe and takes a woman named Sunshine as his wife. Later he discovers that Olga is with his old enemy, Younger Bear, and has become an ugly nag; she no longer recognizes Jack, and he is glad. Younger Bear also has another "wife," Yellow Horse, a homosexual. Jack explains that the Cheyenne do not stigmatize people according to their sexual preference, just as they do not consider a white man evil just because he is white. In this and many other ways he shows the Cheyenne to be fair and accepting people.

Meanwhile the whites are incredibly brutal. They decide to exterminate the Indians, and during one attack they kill many of Jack's friends and destroy their village. Afterward Sunshine is missing, and Jack vows revenge on the leader of the attack, George Armstrong Custer. After finding the general's encampment, however, he realizes that killing Custer will not stop the slaughter of the Indians. He therefore decides to act as a spy. He gets a job handling pack animals for Custer's troops and becomes an unwilling participant at the Battle of the Little Big Horn, where he is rescued by Younger Bear, who says: "You and I are even at last, and the next time we fight, I can kill you without becoming an evil person" (415). Jack then sees Old Lodge Skins again, and the two discuss the relationship between the whites and the Indians. Afterward Old Lodge Skins decides that he is old and has seen enough of life. Saying "It is a good day to die," he does (436). Journalist Snell then reports that Jack Crabbe himself died soon after telling this story, adding that the old man "was either the most neglected hero in the history of this country or a liar of insane proportions" (440). (Berger 1964; Landon 1989)

See also Berger, Thomas; Crabbe, Jack; Native American Issues; Old Lodge Skins; Racism

Little Dorrit

Little Dorrit, by Charles Dickens, was first published in serial form from 1855 to 1857 and in book form in 1857. The novel concerns the life of Amy Dorrit, whom everyone calls Little Dorrit. Her father was imprisoned for debt right before her birth, and Little Dorrit was born in a debtor's prison. After her mother dies, she begins taking care of her father. Her older brother and sister are selfish and do little to help. As a young woman Little Dorrit begins to earn money as a seamstress, and it is in this capacity that she meets Arthur Clennam. Arthur's mother has given Little Dorrit work, but he suspects there is a deeper connection between the two women. When his father died, the man seemed to refer to some wrong that he or his wife had committed. Arthur believes that Little Dorrit has something to do with this. Therefore, he begins giving Little Dorrit and her family money. However, after an investigator discovers that Little Dorrit's father is the heir to a wealthy estate, the woman's father, brother, and sister want nothing more to do with Arthur. They are ashamed of their background.

Released from prison, the Dorrit family begins traveling throughout Europe. Meanwhile Arthur makes a bad investment and loses his fortune. Now he is in debtor's prison, and Little Dorrit comes to stay with him. He refuses her help, saying that because he loves her, he cannot take her money. However, she reveals that she, too, lost her fortune in the same bad investment. Then it is revealed that Arthur's mother is not really his mother; his father had an affair with a young woman who was a friend of Little Dorrit's uncle. Moreover, in his will Arthur's father left a substantial sum of money to Arthur and Little Dorrit, but Mrs. Clennam concealed the document. Now Arthur and Little Dorrit both have fortunes, and they soon get married.

Little Dorrit is therefore both a romance and a mystery, but it also has many elements of social protest. In fact, playwright George Bernard Shaw credited the novel with converting him to socialism. The story not only offers a harsh portrayal of debtor's prisons but also severely criticizes the wealthy for ignoring the needs of the poor. Its characters include a seemingly philanthropic landowner who encourages his rent collector to harass his tenants and an apparently rich man who intentionally defrauds investors. Moreover, as Little Dorrit's father moves up in social class, he loses any endearing qualities he once had and becomes an unhappy man. At the end of his life he loses touch with reality and believes himself back in debtor's prison. (Dickens 1987b; Fielding 1958; Gissing 1924)

See also Class, Social; Dickens, Charles; Shaw, George Bernard

London, Jack

American writer Jack London is best known for his adventure stories and novels, which include *The Call of the Wild* (1903) and *White*

Jack London, American adventurer and writer (Archive Photos)

Fang (1906). However, he also wrote works of social protest. These include *The Iron Heel* (1907), which concerns a socialist revolution, and *The Valley of the Moon* (1913), which criticizes urbanization. London was born John Griffith Chaney on January 12, 1876, in San Francisco, California. As a boy he had a series of jobs related to the fishing industry, and at the age of 17 he became a sailor on a sealing schooner. A year later he became a hobo, traveling across the United States by rail. In 1893 he was arrested for being a vagrant and subsequently became a socialist. When he was 19, he decided to acquire an education. He became an avid reader and completed a four year high-school course in one year. He then briefly attended the University of California at Berkeley before going to the Klondike during the gold rush of 1897. During this time he began writing about his experiences. His first story, "To the Man on the Trail," was published in the *Overland Monthly* in 1899. His first book, a collection of stories entitled *The Son of the Wolf,* was published in 1900. He eventually published over 50 books, both fiction and nonfiction, and continued to live an adventurous life, sailing a ketch to the South Pacific and indulging in alcohol. He died of a drug overdose on November 22, 1916, in Glen Ellen, California. (O'Connor 1964)

See also *Iron Heel, The;* Socialism

Looking Backward, 2000–1887

Although published in 1887, *Looking Backward, 2000–1887* begins with a preface dated December 26, 2000. In it the book's author, Edward Bellamy, speaks as though he were a resident of the twentieth century. He explains that the object of *Looking Backward* is to help people "gain a more definite idea of the social contrasts between the nineteenth and twentieth centuries" (Bellamy 1951, xxv-xxvi). He then offers as fact the first-person narrative of a fictional character, Julian West, whom he says has lived in both time periods.

West was born on December 26, 1857. At the age of 30 he is a wealthy Bostonian engaged to a socially prominent young woman named Edith Bartlett, and the only difficulty in his life is his insomnia. West has so much trouble sleeping that he has constructed a special sleep chamber under the foundation of his house. In this subterranean room he meets regularly with Dr. Pillsbury, a "mesmerist" who hypnotizes him into sleep. No one else knows about the room except West's servant Sawyer, who has learned how to revive him.

But on May 30, 1887, something goes wrong. Dr. Pillsbury hypnotizes West into sleep, but Sawyer does not awaken him. Instead, when West regains consciousness, he finds himself in the company of Dr. and Mrs. Leete and their daughter, Edith, who reminds him of his fiancée. Dr. Leete tells West that they discovered him during an excavation of their garden. His subterranean room is all that remains of his house, which burned down the very night he fell asleep. That was 113 years ago; it is now 2000.

West reports that it feels as though he were asleep far longer because the differences between the nineteenth and twentieth centuries are so extreme. For example, there are no politicians and no lawyers, and the U.S. government is now run as "one great business corporation" (Bellamy 1951, 41). It manufactures and provides all goods through a national distribution system, and a sample of every available product is displayed in identical regional shops.

Citizens purchase these products not with money, which no longer exists, but with credits equal to each person's share of the annual gross national product. In return, after receiving an excellent education, every individual must work until retirement in a job for which the government has determined he or she is best suited. Young women can choose to leave their careers to have children, but anyone else who refuses to work is jailed.

Under this system all occupations are considered equally important. For example, as Dr. Leete tells West, "no difference is recognized between a waiter's functions and those of any other worker" because "the individual is never regarded, nor regards himself, as the servant of those he serves" (Bellamy 1951, 126). Instead, "it is always the nation which he is serving" (126). Therefore, there are no class distinctions and no labor disputes.

West contrasts this to the situation in 1887, when "the working classes had quite suddenly and very generally become infected with a profound discontent with their condition, and an idea that it could be greatly bettered if they only knew how to go about it. On every side, with one accord, they preferred demands for higher pay, shorter hours, better dwellings, better educational advantages, and a share in the refinements and luxuries of life" (8).

When he was living in the nineteenth century, West believed that these demands were unrealistic because the relationship between the rich and the poor was like "a prodigious coach which the masses of humanity were harnessed to and dragged toilsomely along a very hilly slope" while the rich sat on top of the coach in seats that were "very breezy and comfortable" (3). The coach's driver "was hunger, and permitted no lagging, though the pace was necessarily very slow" (3). Consequently, no one on top of the coach willingly gave up his or her seat, although they would occasionally "call down encouragingly to the toilers of the rope, exhorting them to patience, and holding out hopes of possible compensation in another world for the hardness of their lot, while others contributed to buy salves and liniments for the crippled and injured" (4).

West is relieved that this attitude no longer exists in the year 2000, and he is therefore extremely upset when, during a dream, he believes himself back in 1887. In the dream he berates the citizens of the nineteenth century in general and his fiancée and her family in particular for their treatment of the poor, saying, "Do you not know that close to your doors a great multitude of men and women, flesh of your flesh, live lives that are one agony from birth to death?" (267). He now knows that the solution to the nation's problems is to regulate the labor force "for the common good" (270).

When West reawakens in the year 2000 he is doubly grateful to have left his old life behind. By this time the government has already offered him a career as a historian specializing in the nineteenth century, a job for which it has deemed him perfectly suited. In addition, he is engaged to marry Edith Leete, whom he has learned is coincidentally the great-granddaughter of his former fiancée. Now he finds her in her garden, where he professes love for both her and the twentieth century.

West's relationship with Edith led Edward Bellamy, in a postscript to the 1889 edition of *Looking Backward,* to call the form of his novel "a fanciful romance." However, the author explains that the book's deeper intent is "as a forecast, in accordance with the principles of evolution, of the next stage in the industrial and social development of humanity" (273). Because this forecast is idyllic, scholars have designated *Looking Backward* a utopian novel.

However, Robert L. Shurter (vi) points out in an introduction to the 1951 edition of the book that *Looking Backward* is more importantly "a sincere attempt to chart a course for a better society." He explains that the book, which appeared at a time of great unemployment and labor unrest, "included most of the reform ideas of Bellamy's generation, expressed in a form so attractive and with a social system so seemingly capable of attainment that the book immediately became the focal point of innumerable idealistic schemes" (vii).

The book's publication resulted in a short-lived "Nationalist" movement dedicated to making Bellamy's national labor system a reality. According to Sylvia Bowman, members of this movement did not realize that Nationalism was similar to socialism; she believes that this is the reason for the success of *Looking Backward,* of which 400,000 copies were sold between 1888 and 1897. Bowman (1962, 32–33) explains that, "although *Looking Backward* appealed to its readers because of its graphic explanation of complex principles and because of its constructive, hopeful, and sincere message, its sale would probably have been greatly curtailed had . . . Bellamy not called his form of government Nationalism rather than socialism" because at the time "the ideas of socialists and philosophical anarchists were an anathema."

However, the book did generate some criticism, as did its 1897 sequel, *Equality*, which was more an economic treatise than a novel. Bowman (1979, 306) reports that Bellamy appreciated these attacks, believing that "all reformers would have to welcome opposition, since this would keep the issue before the public and open the way for discussion and debate." In fact, *Looking Backward* continued to generate discussion for many years after its publication, and Bellamy's ideas had a significant impact on social reformers of his era. Shurter (Bellamy 1951, vi-vii) therefore believes that "*Looking Backward* deserves to rank along with *Uncle Tom's Cabin* and *Ramona* as one of the most timely books ever to appear in America." (Bellamy 1951; Bowman, 1962, 1979, 1986)

See also Anarchism; Bellamy, Edward; Capitalism; Leete, Edith; *Ramona;* Socialism; *Uncle Tom's Cabin;* West, Julian

Piggy and Ralph consult on survival strategies in this scene from the 1963 movie Lord of the Flies. *(Allen-Hogden Productions/The Museum of Modern Art Film Stills Archive)*

Lord of the Flies

Lord of the Flies, by William Golding, suggests that human beings are inherently barbaric. The novel, which was published in 1954, concerns a group of British schoolboys whose plane is shot down during wartime. Stranded on a deserted island with no adults present, they establish their own system of rules and elect a leader, Ralph, a 12-year-old who is more charismatic than clever. Ralph relies on the advice of an intelligent, overweight, unpopular boy known as "Piggy," while another boy, Jack Merridew, takes charge of a group of hunters.

At first things go well. The children begin building shelters and maintain a signal fire to attract passing ships. But their enthusiasm for work does not last long, and most of the shelters are left unfinished. Meanwhile Jack becomes obsessed with killing pigs. He turns into a bloodthirsty savage, painting his face and leading his hunters in chants and rituals. One day the boys convince themselves that there is a beast on the island. When they disagree on how to handle the danger, Jack uses this as an opportunity to challenge Ralph's authority. He talks most of Ralph's followers into joining his group and establishes a new camp on the other side of the island. Shortly thereafter Jack's hunters mistake a member of Ralph's group for the beast and kill him.

The murderers feel no remorse. In fact, they grow even wilder, attacking Piggy and stealing his glasses, so that they can start their own fire. When Piggy tries to get the glasses back, they kill him and force Ralph's remaining followers to join their group. Jack then orders his group to hunt Ralph like a pig. They plan to kill him and put his head on a stake, but before they can catch him, they encounter a naval officer who has just landed on the beach. When the man sees Ralph being chased by boys in war paint, he assumes that the children are playing a game and is embarrassed when they all burst into tears.

In describing the meaning of his novel, Golding (1954, 204) writes:

The theme is an attempt to trace the defects of society back to the defects of human nature. The moral is that the shape of a society must depend on the ethical nature of the individual and not on any political system however apparently logical or respectable. The whole book is symbolic in nature except the rescue in the end where adult life appears, dignified and capable, but in reality enmeshed in the same evil as the symbolic life of the children on the island. The officer, having interrupted a man-hunt, prepares to take the children off the island in a cruiser which will presently be hunting its enemy in the same implacable way. And who will rescue the adult and his cruiser?

However, in an essay on the novel's symbolism published in the 1954 edition of the work, scholar E. L. Epstein says that this description is too simplistic. He suggests that each of the main characters represents a different aspect of the British political system. Ralph symbolizes "civilization with its parliaments and his brain trust (Piggy, the intellectual whose shattering spectacles mark the progressive decay of rational influence as the story progresses)," and Jack is "the leader of the forces of anarchy" (206). The struggle between the two boys symbolizes "the struggle in modern society between those same forces translated on a worldwide scale" (206). Epstein also discusses the central image of the book, the "lord of the flies." A pig's head on a stick, it is Jack's ritual offering to the imaginary beast. But Epstein notes that "lord of the flies" is a translation of *Ba'alzevuv* in Hebrew and *Beelzebub* in Greek, another name for the Devil. He believes that "this pungent and suggestive name for the Devil, a devil whose name suggests that he is devoted to decay, destruction, demoralization, hysteria and panic . . . fits in very well with Golding's theme" (205). (Golding 1954)

See also Anarchism; Golding, William; Merridew, Jack; Peace; Piggy; Ralph

"Lottery, The"

A short story by Shirley Jackson, "The Lottery" was first published in 1948 in *The New Yorker* magazine and was part of a 1949 short story collection called *The Lottery: or, The Adventures of James Harris*. It deals with social pressures and human sacrifice in a small New England town. Every year the town holds a lottery, a festive tradition that has been going on for generations. However, the reader does not learn the winner's reward until the end of the story. When Tessie Hutchinson draws the honor, she is stoned to death despite her protests. In discussing "The Lottery," scholars have provided various interpretations of the story's meaning. Among these is the suggestion that the work protests unexamined social customs and traditions. (Friedman 1975)

See also Jackson, Shirley

Lowell, James Russell

American poet and essayist James Russell Lowell was an abolitionist during the Civil War, and many of his works reflect his political position. Born on February 22, 1819, in Cambridge, Massachusetts, he graduated from Harvard University in Boston in 1838. In 1840 he received a law degree. Instead of becoming a lawyer, however, he became a writer. In 1841 he published a collection of poems, *A Year's Life*. He also began writing critical essays, particularly on the subject of slavery. In 1844 he married a noted abolitionist, the poet Maria White, and from 1845 to 1850 he wrote approximately 50 antislavery articles. He also began publishing one of his best-known works, an antislavery poetry series called *The Biglow Papers*. After his wife died in 1853, Lowell turned his attention to literary subjects, writing not only about literature and language but also about authors. He became a professor at Harvard University and a newspaper editor, first for the *Atlantic Monthly* and then for the *North American Review*. From 1877 to 1880 he was the U.S. ambassador to Spain and from 1880 to 1885 the ambassador to Great Britain. He died in Cambridge, Massachusetts, on August 12, 1891. (Duberman 1966; Wortham 1977)

See also *Biglow Papers, The;* Slavery

Lysistrata

Lysistrata, by Aristophanes, is the third play in a series of three comedies about the Peloponnesian War (431–404 B.C.) between the rival

Greek city-states of Athens and Sparta. First performed in 411 B.C., the play's predecessors were The *Archanians* (426 B.C.) and *Peace* (422 B.C.). *Lysistrata* is the most bawdy of the three; it concerns the decision of women throughout Greece to refuse sexual favors to their men until peace is declared. Led by an Athenian named Lysistrata, they ceremonially vow to resist temptation and, if forced to yield, to "be cold as ice, and never stir a limb . . . [or] aid him in any way," so that the men take no pleasure in their actions (Aristophanes 1930, 241). At the same time a group of older women takes over the Acropolis and its state treasury. Faced with such widespread insubordination, the frustrated men eventually agree to sign peace agreements. They then prepare for a celebration banquet marking the end of Grecian celibacy. (Aristophanes 1930; Murray 1933)

See also *Archanians, The;* Aristophanes; *Peace;* Peace

M

MacAlpin, Marian

Marian MacAlpin is the main character in Margaret Atwood's 1969 feminist novel *The Edible Woman*. Over the course of the story she subjugates herself to her fiancé, allowing him to control her life. At the same time she develops an eating disorder and cannot eat anything that was once alive and growing. In the end she refuses to allow him to consume her. She bakes him a cake shaped like a woman and tells him he should eat that instead. (Atwood 1996)

> See also Atwood, Margaret; *Edible Woman, The;* Feminism

MacWhite, Gilbert

Gilbert MacWhite is a character in the 1958 novel *The Ugly American,* by William J. Lederer and Eugene Burdick. After he is appointed U.S. ambassador to a small Asian country, he attempts to learn more about Asian culture and beliefs. Eventually he develops a deep understanding of the region's problems and tries to convince his superiors that a new approach to Asian politics is necessary. His suggestions are rejected, and the U.S. government removes him from his post. (Lederer and Burdick 1958)

> See also Burdick, Eugene; Lederer, William J.; *Ugly American, The*

Magic Mountain, The

Published in German in 1924 and English in 1927, *Der Zauberberg* (The Magic Mountain), by Thomas Mann, is set in a Swiss sanitorium during the early 1900s. Its main character, Hans Castorp, travels there to spend three weeks with his cousin, Joachim Ziemssen, who is being treated for tuberculosis. However, before his visit ends, Hans contracts a cold and a doctor convinces him that he also has tuberculosis. Hans therefore cancels his plans to leave the sanitorium, even though he has just taken a job as a ship engineer, and begins to revel in his illness. He also becomes fascinated with death. He studies science texts and arranges to visit the bedsides of the dying. At the same time he engages in deep philosophical discussions with various members of the sanitorium, each of whom represents a different ideology and approach to European life. For example, Ludovico Settembrini is an optimistic Italian humanist, Leo Naphta is a pessimistic Catholic convert, Mynheer Peeperkorn is a wealthy hedonist, and Ellen Brand is a spiritual medium. Hans learns from all of these people and eventually forms his own opinions about the world. He remains at the sanitorium even after his cousin's departure, subsequent return, and death, until seven years have passed. Then war breaks out in Europe, and Hans decides to leave the mountain and become a soldier. The novel ends with him on the battlefield facing a future as uncertain as Europe's.

The Magic Mountain examines the society of pre–World War I Europe, presenting its various ideologies and problems through somewhat one-dimensional characters at the sanitorium. It also illustrates the flaws inherent in any isolated and idle society. Various individuals react differently to their confinement, and Hans himself goes through a series of reactions to his situation, from resistance to acceptance to boredom to restlessness. In addition, on a more superficial level the novel criticizes the need for sanitoriums, which were prevalent when Mann began writing *The Magic Mountain* in 1912. As he (1972, 721) explains:

> You will have got from my book an idea of the narrowness of this charmed circle of isolation and invalidism. It is a sort of substitute existence, and it can, in a relatively short time, wholly wean a young person from actual and active life. Everything there, including the conception of time, is thought of on a luxurious scale. The cure is always a matter of several months, often of several years. But after the first six months the young person has not a single idea left save flirtation and the thermometer under his tongue. . . . Such institutions . . . were a typical prewar phenomenon. They were only possible in a capitalistic economy that was still functioning well and normally. Only under such a system was it possible for patients to remain there year after year at the family's expense. *The Magic Mountain* became the swan song of that form of existence.

Mann had firsthand knowledge of this existence, having spent three weeks at a sanitorium in Davos, Switzerland, when his wife was being treated there. As with Hans, the doctors tried to convince Mann that he was also ill and should remain under their care. He says: "If I had followed his advice, who knows, I might still be there! I wrote *The Magic Mountain* instead" (721). (Cleugh 1968; Hatfield 1964; Mann 1972)

See also Castorp, Hans; Mann, Thomas; Settembrini, Ludovico; Ziemssen Joachim

Major Barbara

A three-act play by Irish author George Bernard Shaw, *Major Barbara* is a satire involving religious hypocrisy and society's attitudes toward the poor. It was first performed in 1905 and published in 1907. Its title refers to one of its main characters, Barbara Undershaft, who is a major in the Salvation Army. She tries to save the souls of working-class men but finds many of them unreceptive to her words because they are out of work and more interested in food than religion.

Barbara is engaged to a young man named Adolphus Cusins, who is pretending to be a Salvationist in order to woo her. He is a poor scholar and can offer her little money. Therefore, Barbara's mother sends for her estranged husband, Andrew Undershaft, and asks him to give his daughter money. Shortly after Andrew arrives, he and Barbara's mother begin rehashing an old quarrel over the inheritance of their three children: Barbara; her sister, Sarah; and her brother, Stephen. Andrew is a wealthy manufacturer of armory and ammunition. A foundling, he received the business from a stranger who adopted him. This is a long-standing tradition in the munitions factory; each owner must choose a foundling as his successor, regardless of whether or not he has a son of his own. Andrew intends to uphold the tradition. His wife opposes it.

When Andrew is reunited with his children, whom he has not seen in years, he becomes fascinated with Barbara. The two debate various issues, and Barbara professes disgust for her father's profession. She says that no one of good moral character could make money from war. She vows to convert him to Salvationism, and in return Andrew vows to convert his daughter into a supporter of his munitions factory. He goes to the Salvation Army shelter where she works and easily convinces her superiors to accept a £5,000 donation of money from him. Disillusioned, Barbara quits her position. She then accompanies her father to his factory and its surrounding town and sees that the people there are well treated, happy, productive, and spiritual. When she asks him how he keeps such order without being oppressive, Andrew explains:

Practically, every man of them keeps the man just below him in his place. I never meddle with them. I never bully them. . . . I say that certain things are to be done; but I don't order anybody to do them. I don't say, mind you, that there is no ordering about and snubbing and even bullying. The men snub the boys and order them about; the carmen snub the sweepers; the artisans snub the unskilled laborers; the foremen drive and bully both the laborers and the artisans; the assistant engineers find fault with the foremen; the chief engineers drop on the assistants; the departmental managers worry the chiefs; and the clerks have tall hats and hymn-books and keep up the social tone by refusing to associate on equal terms with anybody. The result is a colossal profit, which comes to me. (Shaw 1962, 419)

But Barbara sees that much of that money has been spent on the workers. The factory workers' town is clean and well appointed, and their church is thriving. She now realizes that Andrew Undershaft has done more to uplift the lower classes than the Salvation Army ever did. This proves his earlier arguments concerning the importance of alleviating poverty, during which he explained:

Food, clothing, firing, rent, taxes, respectability and children. Nothing can lift those seven millstones from Man's neck but money; and the spirit cannot soar until the millstones are lifted. . . . [Poverty is] the worst of crimes. All other crimes are virtues beside it. . . . Poverty blights whole cities; spreads horrible pestilences; strikes dead the very souls of all who come

within sight, sound or smell of it. What you call crime is nothing: a murder here and a theft there. . . . But there are millions of poor people, abject people, dirty people, ill fed, ill clothed people. They poison us morally and physically: they kill the happiness of society: they force us to do away with our own liberties and to organize unnatural cruelties for fear they should rise against us and drag us down into their abyss. Only fools fear crime: we all fear poverty. (434)

Adolphus is impressed with Andrew's arguments. In turn, Andrew is impressed with his future son-in-law. When he learns that the young man is a foundling, he announces that he will leave the business to Adolphus. Adolphus accepts the offer, explaining to Barbara that he has no problem making money from manufacturing weapons because they help the common man fight his oppressors. He says: "I love the common people. I want to arm them against the lawyers, the doctors, the priests, the literary men, the professors, the artists, and the politicians, who, once in authority, are more disastrous and tyrannical than all the fools, rascals, and impostors. I want a power simple enough for common men to use, yet strong enough to force the intellectual oligarchy to use its genius for the general good" (442). In the end Barbara rejoices over Adolphus's new role in society, having realized that she can do more good for the people using her father's methods than the Salvation Army's.

Shaw (305–306) discusses this aspect of *Major Barbara* in a preface to the work:

In the millionaire Undershaft I have represented a man who has become intellectually and spiritually as well as practically conscious of the irresistible natural truth which we all abhor and repudiate: to wit, that the greatest of our evils, and the worst of our crimes is poverty, and that our first duty, to which every other consideration should be sacrificed, is not to be poor. . . . Security, the chief pretence of civilization, cannot exist where the worst of dangers, the danger of poverty, hangs over everyone's head, and where the alleged protection of our persons from violence is only an accidental result of the existence of a police force whose real business is to force the poor man to see his children starve whilst idle people overfeed pet dogs with the money that might feed and clothe them.

Shaw also criticizes class distinctions and snobbery in his preface, as well as the Salvation Army in particular and religion in general. He concludes that because of hypocrisy, "at present there is not a single credible established religion in the world" (339). Shaw criticizes religion in other writings as well. For example, in the preface to his play *Heartbreak House,* he calls the church "that stuffy, uncomfortable place of penance in which we suffer so much inconvenience on the slenderest chance of gaining a scrap of food for our starving souls" (482). As a socialist Shaw was a harsh critic of British society. In addition to his numerous plays, he wrote antiwar speeches and other political essays and tracts. (Hill 1978; McCabe 1974; Shaw 1962)

See also Poverty; Religion; Shaw, George Bernard; Undershaft, Andrew

Mako

This well-educated Zulu man from Peter Abrahams's 1948 novel *The Path of Thunder* believes in black nationalism. Mako criticizes South Africa's foreign rulers, who control all education and force native people "to assimilate many of their ways to survive" (Abrahams 1975, 91). He does not believe in interracial marriage if it is done as an attempt of the blacks to become more like the whites. However, if it is a union born out of true love, he supports it, saying that such intermarriage "is a mirror to the nationalism on a higher plane. There are those who say the world will not be free and happy—and I agree—until nations stop fighting the other nations and nations stop oppressing other nations. The national intermarriage, whether it is between white and black or between pink and red, is a mirror of this highest form of world nationalism

when man will really be free" (93). (Abrahams 1975; Ensor 1992)

See also Abrahams, Peter; Finkelberg, Isaac; *Path of Thunder, The;* Racism; Swartz, Lanny

Malafrena

Published in 1979, *Malafrena,* by Ursula Le Guin, concerns political and social oppression. The novel is set in the early nineteenth century in the fictional country of Orsinia, which is under the control of Austria. Its two main characters are Piera Valtoskar and Itale Sorde, who live in the Malafrena Valley. At the beginning of the story Piera is a young woman whose only thoughts are of falling in love. She is attracted to Itale, but when he shows no interest in her, she secretly becomes engaged to another man, then breaks off her engagement to become betrothed to someone else. Eventually, however, she breaks that engagement to take over the management of her ailing father's estate. No woman in Malafrena has ever done such a thing, but Piera proves herself as competent at the job as any man.

Meanwhile Itale has been examining his own role in society. He is heir to a large estate, and his father expects him to manage it. However, Itale is passionate about his political beliefs and moves to a nearby city, Krasnoy, to take part in revolutionary activities. He also has a secret affair with Baroness Luisa Paludeskar, a lady-in-waiting to the Grand Duchess. Eventually Itale is arrested by the Austrian police for his political activities, and Luisa uses her influence to have him freed. But after two years in prison he is not the same man. His health is poor, and he has lost his passion for revolution. Luisa realizes she is no longer attracted to him and ends their affair. Shortly thereafter Itale learns that the French have overthrown their king. His political passion returns, and he participates in a revolution against the Orsinian government. When the battle is lost, he flees to Malafrena, where he plans to live in exile. There he meets Piera Valtoskar. They express their friendship and go rowing together. (Le Guin 1979)

See also Le Guin, Ursula; Science Fiction and Fantasy; Sorde, Itale; Valtoskar, Piera

Maldonado, Felix

The main character of Carlos Fuentes's 1978 novel *La cabeza de la hidra* (The Hydra Head), Felix Maldonado is an agent of an independent Mexican spy organization that wants that country's oil industry to remain nationalized. Felix's father worked in the industry when it was still controlled by private corporations, and he considers it a terrible time in Mexico's history. Felix tells a friend that whenever his father went to talk to his British boss, "he never saw his face. Each time my father entered, this Englishman was sitting with his back to him. That was the custom; you received Mexican employees with your back turned, to make them feel they were inferior, like the Hindu employees of the British Raj" (Fuentes 1978, 218). However, after the oil companies were nationalized, there were "no more White Guards, the company's private army, stealing land and cutting off the ears of rural schoolteachers. And most important of all, people looked one another in the face" (218). Because of his emotions regarding Mexico's oil industry, Felix becomes involved in an intricate plot involving a large oil reserve whose existence is important to both the Israelis and the Arabs. Caught between these two factions, Felix eventually loses his identity and everyone he loves. (Fuentes 1978)

See also Fuentes, Carlos; *Hydra Head, The*

"Man with the Hoe, The"

Written in 1899 by American poet Edwin Markham, the poem "The Man with the Hoe" concerns the plight of the farmer, upon whose back rests "the burden of the world." Overworked, he is a "monstrous thing distorted and soul-quenched," and the poet calls upon the "masters, lords and rulers in all lands" to "straighten up this shape" and "rebuild in it the music and the dream," or fear the day "when whirlwinds of rebellion shake the world" (Sinclair 1996, 29–30). (Sinclair 1996)

See also Labor Issues; Markham, Edwin

Mann, Thomas

German novelist and essayist Thomas Mann often addressed political and social issues in his work, examining the nature of Western culture and its relationship to the human spirit. His novels include *Tristan* (1903), *Der Tod in Venedig* (Death in Venice, 1912), *Der Zauberberg* (The Magic Mountain, 1924), and *Doktor Faustus* (Doctor Faustus, 1947). Born on June 6, 1875, in Lübeck, Germany, Mann moved to Munich after his father's death in 1891. He remained there until 1933, working first in an insurance office and later as an editor on a weekly magazine. While at the magazine he began writing stories. His first novel, *Buddenbrooks*, was published in 1901. Many other novels followed, and in 1929 he won the Nobel Prize for Literature. In 1930 he began speaking out against Nazi policies in Germany. Three years later, while he was on vacation in Switzerland, family members warned him not to return home, fearing for his safety. He remained in Switzerland until 1938 when, after making several visits to the United States, he decided to move to America. He spent two years on the east coast before settling in southern California. By this time his native country had stripped him of his German citizenship, and in 1944 he became an American citizen. During the tumultuous period after leaving Germany, he wrote a series of novels based on the biblical story of Joseph, collectively called *Joseph und seine Brüder* (Joseph and His Brothers): *Die Geschichten Jaakobs* (The Tales of Jacob in the United Kingdom, Joseph and His Brothers in the United States, 1933), *Der junge Joseph* (Young Joseph, 1934), *Joseph in Ägypten* (Joseph in Egypt, 1936), and *Joseph der Ernahrer* (Joseph the Provider, 1943). Four years later he published *Doktor Faustus*, which relates the personal tragedy of a German composer to the destruction of Germany during World War II. Mann's last novel was a humorous work, *Die Bekenntnisse des Hochstaplers Felix Krull* (The Confessions of Felix Krull, Confidence Man, 1954). It was left unfinished at his death on August 12, 1955, near Zurich, Switzerland.

See also *Magic Mountain, The*

Manorialism

Manorialism was an economic and social system whereby members of the nobility allowed peasants to farm their land in exchange for money, goods, and services. It began in the fourth century, became widespread during the Middle Ages, and remained the prevalent economic system until the end of the sixteenth century, when it was largely replaced by capitalism. In Austria, however, manorialism remained until the eighteenth century, and in Russia it lasted until the revolution of 1917. In all countries injustices against peasants laboring under manorialism were rampant. Consequently, many authors called attention to the unfairness of the system, including Maria Edgeworth, Leo Tolstoi, and Ivan Turgenev. (Herlihy 1970)

> See also Capitalism; Edgeworth, Maria; Tolstoi, Leo; Turgenev, Ivan

"Man's a Man for a' That, A"

Written in Scottish dialect by poet Robert Burns, the poem "A Man's a Man for a' That" (1786) expresses the view that all men, however poor, are still human beings and that a person should be defined by his character rather than his income or social position. Burns (Sinclair, 1996, 163) writes: "The honest man, though e'er sae puir [ever so poor],/ Is king o' men for a' that." Conversely, a lord "what struts, and stares, and a' that" is not worthy of much respect (163).

> See also Burns, Robert; Class, Social; Poverty

Maqui, Rosendo

Mayor of the Indian village of Rumi in Ciro Alegría's 1941 novel *El mundo es ancho y ajeno* (Broad and Alien Is the World), Rosendo Maqui is an old man who has long been respected for his wisdom and his kindness. Nonetheless, as a result of the trickery of nonnative rancher Don Alvaro Amenabar, he is labeled a thief and thrown into prison, where he is beaten to death by the guards. However, government officials declare that he has died of a heart attack and bury his body in secret. (Alegría 1941)

> See also Alegría, Ciro; Amenabar, Don Alvaro; *Broad and Alien Is the World;* Castro, Benito; Justice

Markham, Edwin

Edwin Markham (originally Charles Edward Anson Markham) is best known for his 1899 social protest poem "The Man with the Hoe," which was his first published work. His poetry collections include *The Man with the Hoe and Other Poems* (1899), *Lincoln and Other Poems* (1901), and *Shoes of Happiness* (1915). Markham was born in Oregon City, Oregon, on April 23, 1852, and grew up in California. He died on March 7, 1940, in New York, New York. (Sinclair 1996)

> See also "Man with the Hoe, The"

Martin, Donald

Donald Martin is the innocent victim of a lynching in Walter Van Tilburg Clark's 1940 western novel *The Ox-Bow Incident*. After struggling to convince the lynching party that it is about to hang the wrong man, Martin accepts his fate with courageous resignation. He writes a loving farewell note to his wife and arranges for someone to help provide for her after his death. In an analysis of the novel's main characters, scholar Max Westbrook (1969, 67) calls Martin "an innocent, naïve in the affairs of the manly world, the natural prey of the mob-beast." (Westbrook 1969)

> See also Clark, Walter Van Tilberg; Croft, Art; Davies, Art; Justice; *Ox-Bow Incident, The;* Tetley, Gerald

Marx, Bernard

Bernard Marx is one of the main characters in Aldous Huxley's 1932 futuristic novel *Brave New World*. He lives in a society where people are created in test tubes and chemically altered to have different intellects and personalities. They are labeled from Alpha down to Epsilon according to their traits; Alphas have superior intellects, whereas Epsilons are drone workers. After being created as an Alpha fetus, Bernard is accidentally given a solution meant for a Beta. This makes him slightly different from others in his classification, and he does not feel comfortable among them. One day he goes on vacation to the Savage Reservation in New Mexico and discovers a misfit in its primitive culture. The young man, John, is the son of a woman from Bernard's society who got lost while visiting the reservation. When Bernard brings John home with him, he finally feels popular and important. He brags about his role as John's guardian and ignores the young man's unhappiness. But Bernard's position in his society is still tenuous, and when John speaks out against his new world, Bernard is blamed for the resulting trouble and exiled to an island of misfits. (Huxley 1989)

> See also *Brave New World;* Exiles; Huxley, Aldous

Marxism
See Communism; Socialism

"Masks, a Story"
"Masks, a Story" is a short story by Eloise Bibb Thompson, an African American who often wrote about racism in the United States. Originally published in *Opportunity* magazine in October 1927, the story tells of a black man, Aristile Blanchard, who believes that the way for black men to achieve greatness is to appear to be white. He begins making white masks, and after his death his granddaughter Julie takes over his work. She quickly realizes that no mask would be as realistic as natural skin, and she therefore decides that breeding is the only way for black people to appear white. She marries a black man who looks white, and when she becomes pregnant, she is certain that the baby will look white, too. When the child is born dark, Julie looks at her and dies. The epitaph on her tombstone reads, "Because she saw with the eyes of her grandfather, she died at the sight of her babe's face" (Roses and Randolph 1996, 38). This story is representative of much of Thompson's work, which concerns feelings of self-worth and pride. (Roses and Randolph 1996)

> See also Harlem Renaissance; Racism; Thompson, Eloise Bibb

Maslova, Katusha
In Leo Tolstoi's 1899 novel *Voskreseniye* (Resurrection), Katusha Maslova is an innocent peasant girl who becomes pregnant by a Russian nobleman. Her child dies en route to an orphanage, and she becomes a prostitute. Later she is sentenced to prison for murder, even though she is clearly innocent. One of the jurors at her trial is the same nobleman who seduced her, Prince Dmitri Ivanovitch Nekhludof. Feeling guilty for his sin, he works for her release and offers to marry her. She refuses, choosing instead to marry a member of her own social class. At the same time, through Nekhludof's attentions and her association with political prisoners who expose her to high ideals, Maslova regains her self-respect. (Tolstoy 1911)

> See also Nekhludof, Prince Dmitri Ivanovitch; *Resurrection;* Tolstoi, Leo

Materialism
See Capitalism

McCarthyism
The term *McCarthyism* refers to the anticommunist attitudes that existed during a period in U.S. history known as the McCarthy era. In 1950 Senator Joseph McCarthy began a campaign to expose Communists in the government, whom he believed were evil subversives. His accusations soon spread to include writers, artists, actors, and other prominent figures. Anyone suspected of being a Communist was attacked, and many lost their jobs as McCarthy's anticommunism hysteria spread throughout the country.

Social protest authors were particularly susceptible to charges of being subversives. Many of them, such as Tillie Olsen, belonged to the Communist Party or had attended its meetings. This automatically made them targets for persecution. In addition, when Arthur Miller protested the injustice of McCarthyism in his play *The Crucible,* he, too, was attacked for being a Communist sympathizer. Another playwright who experienced McCarthyism was Lillian Hellman, who depicted unfair persecution in her play *The*

Senator Joseph McCarthy with his two investigators, Roy Cohn and David Schine, during the House Un-American investigation (Archive Photos)

Children's Hour. The McCarthy era ended in 1954 after televised hearings exposed McCarthy as being irrational in his accusations. (Schrecker 1994, 1998)

See also Censorship; *Children's Hour, The;* Communism; *Crucible, The;* Hellman, Lillian; Miller, Arthur; Olsen, Tillie

McMurphy, Randall Patrick

Randall Patrick McMurphy is one of the main characters in Ken Kesey's 1962 novel *One Flew over the Cuckoo's Nest.* A gambler, a swindler, and a fighter, McMurphy feigns insanity to gain transfer from a prison work camp to a mental hospital, where he believes that life will be easier. However, he soon finds himself in a battle of wills with the head nurse, Nurse Ratched, a domineering woman who in some ways is less sane than her charges. McMurphy challenges her authority with humor and wit, and gradually the other patients come to share his strength of character. Then McMurphy learns that his six-month sentence, of which he had already served two months, is now an indefinite one; he cannot leave the hospital without Nurse Ratched's approval. He begins to conform to

her demands, but when the other patients quickly slip back into submission and insanity, he decides to sacrifice himself for the group. He escalates his opposition to Nurse Ratched's rules and in a fit of frustration and anger attacks her. This act helps the patients regain their sanity but ultimately brings about McMurphy's death. In this regard the novel uses Christ imagery to emphasize McMurphy's martyrdom. (Kesey 1964)

See also Kesey, Ken; *One Flew over the Cuckoo's Nest*

Mellama, Mauritas

In the 1980 novel *Bumi manusia* (This Earth of Mankind), by Pramoedya Ananta Toer, the character of Mauritas Mellama represents the arrogance of the Dutch rulers of Indonesia, who are prejudiced against native Javanese. Mauritas is the son of a Dutch colonialist, Herman Mellama, who abandoned his wife to move to the island of Java. Mauritas was raised by his mother in the Netherlands. As an adult he travels to Java on business and discovers that his father is living there with his concubine, Ontosoroh. He confronts Herman and castigates him for associating with native women. When Ontosoroh tries to defend her master, Mauritas does not even acknowledge her existence. Later, when Herman dies, he takes over the estate and throws the woman off the farm. He also separates her from her daughter, Annalies, whom he considers more European than native. He then dissolves Annelies's marriage to a native man and sends her to school in the Netherlands. (Toer 1996)

See also Ontosoroh; *This Earth of Mankind;* Toer, Pramoedya Ananta

Mellama, Robert

Robert Mellama appears in *Bumi manusia* (This Earth of Mankind) (1980), by Pramoedya Ananta Toer, which concerns the prejudice that Europeans have against native Javanese in Indonesia. Robert is the child of a native concubine and her Dutch master. However, he pretends to be fully European. He expresses hatred for all natives and threatens to kill his sister's native lover, Minke. He is consumed by anger, and on one occasion he rapes his own sister. When his father is poisoned, he disappears and is suspected of the crime. He visits his sister on her wedding day and tells her he is going to Europe, where he hopes to erase his past. (Toer 1996)

See also Minke; *This Earth of Mankind;* Toer, Pramoedya Ananta

Melvyn, Sybylla

First-person narrator of Miles Franklin's 1901 Australian novel *My Brilliant Career,* Sybylla Melvyn is a feminist at a time when women are encouraged to subjugate themselves in marriage. She often finds herself frustrated by her male relatives' patronizing treatment of women. Moreover, although she is poor, she breaks off her engagement to a wealthy, kind man because he does not view women as equal to men. (Franklin 1965)

See also Feminism; Franklin, Miles; *My Brilliant Career*

Meredith, Anthony

Anthony Meredith is the fictional scholar who provides the footnotes for Jack London's 1907 novel *The Iron Heel.* Meredith lives seven centuries in the future, after a series of revolts have created a truly socialistic American society, and he makes it clear that his world is far better than previous ones. For example, the society of the future has no theft, no bloodshed, and no poverty. Meredith's footnotes therefore allow London to comment on the problems within contemporary American society. (London 1924)

See also *Iron Heel, The;* London, Jack

Merou, Ulysse

Ulysse Merou is the first-person narrator of Pierre Boulle's 1963 science fiction novel *La Planète de singes* (Planet of the Apes). After traveling from Earth to a distant planet, he encounters a world where humans behave like apes and apes like humans. His observations on the prejudices and faulty reasoning within ape society are Boulle's way of commenting on the flaws within human society. (Boulle 1963)

See also Boulle, Pierre; *Planet of the Apes;* Science Fiction and Fantasy

Merridew, Jack

In William Golding's 1954 novel *Lord of the Flies,* the character of Jack Merridew symbolizes violence as a threat to civilization. He is one of several British schoolboys stranded on an island without adult supervision. As time passes, he becomes a cruel, primitive savage who enjoys hunting and killing pigs. Eventually he challenges the established order of the group and tries to kill its elected leader, Ralph. (Golding 1954)

See also Golding, William; *Lord of the Flies;* Ralph

Meursault, Monsieur

Narrator of Albert Camus's 1942 novel *L'Etranger* (The Stranger), Monsieur Meursault is a man who shows no outward emotion, even at his mother's funeral. When he kills a man in a moment of panic, the prosecutor condemns him for this lack of grief and accuses Meursault of displaying no remorse. Meursault admits: "I have never been able to truly feel remorse for anything. My mind was always on what was coming next, today or to-morrow" (Camus 1989, 100). According to Camus biographer Germaine Brée (1961, 112), Meursault is "a man content just to live and who asks no questions," and ultimately it is his apathy toward life that causes his death. (Bree 1961; Camus 1989)

See also Camus, Albert; Justice; *Stranger, The*

Mexican-American Literature

Although Mexican Americans have histori-cally experienced racism and social injustices similar to other nonwhite ethnic groups in the United States, they have not created a large body of book-length fiction to protest their circumstances. As Raymond A. Paredes ex-plains in a chapter on Mexican-American lit-erature in the *Columbia Literary History of the United States* (Elliott 1988, 800–801):

> In the second half of the nineteenth cen-tury, when a distinctly Mexican-American literature began to emerge, it followed a line of development common among frontier cultures. Historical and personal narratives predominated, many of them apologetic in tone. . . . Mexican Ameri-cans also produced a considerable volume of verse. . . . Oddly enough, so far as we now know, little sustained fiction was produced, perhaps because the harsh envi-ronment of the Southwestern frontier dis-couraged prolonged periods of creativity.

However, Paredes also reports that Mexi-can-American creativity did find one impor-tant outlet for expression: oral verse, most no-tably a type of ballad called the *corrido*. These *corridos* spoke of "economic struggle, legends of the [Mexican] revolution, and . . . the pain of immigration and acculturation" (803).

During the 1940s and 1950s Mexican-American authors also increasingly expressed themselves through written personal narra-tives and short stories. Once again, their liter-ature primarily dealt with acculturation into white society. But in the 1960s a new form of expression began to develop—the social protest drama. According to Paredes, a group

called the Teatro Campesino sprang up during the 1960s to support César Chávez's farm-workers' union and began to produce plays, or *actos*. Paredes (806) reports:

> Performed in open fields as well as univer-sity halls and theaters, the Teatro's *actos* at-tacked greedy farmers, dishonest labor con-tractors, brutal policemen—in short, all the enemies of the farmworkers' union—with deadly wit. More than any other develop-ment of the time, the Teatro Campesino demonstrated to Mexican Americans the manifold potential of literary expression.

Consequently, Mexican-American writing began to flourish, and new publishing compa-nies sprang up to produce Spanish-language books and magazines. Paredes (806–807) writes of one, Quinto Sol Publications, which was established in 1967:

> Quinto Sol Publications opened its doors in Berkeley [California] for the sole pur-posed of issuing Mexican-American writ-ing. Although diverse, the authors associ-ated with Quinto Sol shared certain assumptions and goals. They wanted to create a body of work that remained free of stereotypes while remaining faithful to their Mexican folk and belletristic tradi-tions; they wanted to find forms and tech-niques compatible with the social, politi-cal, and cultural needs of their people; and they wanted, like their predecessors, to confront the language issue and the questions of voice. In addition, however, they displayed new pride in their Indian heritage by evoking Aztec thought and culture. The notion of Aztlan, the ances-tral home of the Aztecs believed to be lo-cated in the American Southwest, became a controlling metaphor for many writers. Aztlan freed Mexican Americans from the onus of being recent, displaced immi-grants and provided them with a sense of place and continuity. With the concept of Aztlan, the Southwest became theirs again.

The most notable Mexican-American writers discovered by Quinto Sol Publications, according to Paredes, were Roland Hinojosa-Smith, who wrote sketches about Mexican Americans in Texas; Rudolfo Anaya, who wrote short stories about ethnic and economic issues; and Tomas Rivera, who wrote stories and sketches about Mexican-American farmworkers during the 1970s. Of these, only Anaya published in English, and as with earlier authors, they all preferred short forms.

Although Quinto Sol Publications no longer exists, short-form Mexican-American literature continues to thrive via Spanish-language magazines and newspapers. However, Paredes points out that the nature of this literature has changed. He (809) says: "Mexican-American writers no longer feel bound to the program of cultural preservation and political activism of the 1960s and early 1970s. Richard Rodriguez's autobiographical *Hunger of Memory* (1981), which accepts as inevitable—and deems ultimately desirable—the process of assimilation, makes this clear."

Paredes believes that modern Mexican-American authors are more concerned with "self-examination" (809), which they express primarily through poetry. Their protest literature increasingly concerns itself with problems within the Mexican-American community, such as poverty and violence, as opposed to struggles between Anglo and Mexican cultures. (Elliott 1988)

Miller, Arthur

Playwright Arthur Miller is the author of several dramas that criticize American society. His most famous works are *Death of a Salesman* (1949) and *The Crucible* (1953), for which he was persecuted by the U.S. government.

Born on October 17, 1915, in New York, New York, Miller grew up in a comfortable home as the son of a coat manufacturer. However, when he was 13, his father lost his business, and the family was forced to move into a poorer neighborhood in Brooklyn, New York. Miller graduated from high school there in 1932 and went to work in an auto parts warehouse. Each week he set aside part of his salary for college tuition; in 1934 he enrolled at the University of Michigan as a journalism student. Eighteen months later he started writing plays, and his first drama, *Honors at Dawn,* won a prestigious drama award. The following year another of his dramas, *No Villain,* won the same award.

After graduating from college in 1938, Miller worked at a variety of odd jobs, including delivery boy, dishwasher, waiter, and warehouse clerk. At the same time he wrote dramas for the Federal Theater Project and radio scripts for both the Columbia Workshop (CBS) and the Cavalcade of America (NBC). Although Miller appreciated the income from these scripts, he disliked the censorship he encountered among radio executives. He (Moss 1967, 25) later said: "There is so much you can't say on the radio that for a serious writer it presents a blank wall. . . . Radio today is in the hands of people most of whom have no taste, no will, no nothing but the primitive ability to spot a script that does not conform to the format."

With the onset of World War II, he began visiting army camps to collect material for a movie screenplay, *The Story of GI Joe.* He was exempt from serving in the military himself because of an old injury. In 1944 he published a journal of his experiences at the camps, entitled *Situation Normal,* and wrote more award-winning plays, as well as a novel, *Focus* (1945), about anti-Semitism. However, his work did not become widely known until 1947 when his drama *All My Sons* received the New York Drama Critics Award. Two years later his drama *Death of a Salesman* received several prestigious awards, including the Pulitzer Prize.

However, these awards did not protect him from attack after the publication of his play *The Crucible* in 1953. Set in 1692, the drama concerns witch-hunts in Salem, Massachusetts, but critics correctly interpreted it as being an attack on the anticommunist "witch-hunts" that were taking place at the time of the play's production. Miller was immediately labeled a Communist sympathizer, and on those grounds he was denied a passport to attend the play's

Belgian premiere in 1954. Two years later, in June 1956, he was called to testify before the House Committee on Un-American Activities, the anticommunist witch-hunting agency of the U.S. Congress. Forced to defend himself as a loyal American, he said that, although he once attended a few Communist-sponsored meetings for writers, he was no longer involved with such things. However, he refused to name the other writers at the meeting and was therefore indicted for contempt of court. He stood trial and on May 31, 1957, was found guilty and fined $500. The following year the U.S. Court of Appeals for the District of Columbia reversed the decision, clearing Miller's name.

During the period of his persecution and trial, Miller wrote little. Afterward, however, he returned to his work. His later plays include *After the Fall* (1964), *The Price* (1968), *The Archbishop's Ceiling* (1977), *The Ride Down Mount Morgan* (1991), and *The Last Yankee* (1991). He also wrote the screenplay for *The Misfits* (1961), which starred his second wife, actress Marilyn Monroe, as well as a collection of short stories, *I Don't Need You Any More* (1967), and an autobiography, *Timebends* (1987). Miller currently lives in the Connecticut countryside. (Moss 1967)

See also Censorship; *Crucible, The;* McCarthyism

Miller, Henry

The novels of American author Henry Miller were banned in the United States until the 1960s because of their sexual explicitness. He therefore became a symbol in the fight against censorship. He was also a social critic, and his 1945 nonfiction book *The Air-Conditioned Nightmare,* which includes poetry, is a harsh commentary on modern American life. Many of his works are a mixture of poetic fiction and autobiographical material.

Miller was born on December 26, 1891, in New York, New York. He grew up in Brooklyn but traveled to France in 1930. His most famous novel, *Tropic of Cancer,* is based on his experiences there. It was published in France in 1934 and the United States in 1961. *Tropic*

of Capricorn, published in France in 1939 and the United States in 1961, concerns Miller's earlier experiences in New York. Both books were the subject of a protracted court case; in 1964 the U.S. Supreme Court reversed a ruling that they were obscene. His other works include the novels *Black Spring* (1936) and *The Colossus of Maroussi* (1941) and the essay collections *The Cosmological Eye* (1939) and *The Wisdom of the Heart* (1941). In later years Miller lived in Big Sur, California. He died in Pacific Palisades, California, on June 7, 1980. (Widmer 1963)

See also *Air-Conditioned Nightmare, The;* Censorship

Milvain, Jasper

A character in George Gissing's 1891 novel *New Grub Street,* Jasper Milvain is a writer who does not care about his work's artistic merit. He writes strictly for money, saying: "I maintain that we people of brains are justified in supplying the mob with the food it likes. . . . If only I had the skill, I would produce novels out-trashing the trashiest that ever sold fifty thousand copies" (Gissing 1926, 10). But since he is unable to write novels, Milvain instead writes articles for newspapers and magazines, and eventually he becomes moderately successful. Then he breaks off his engagement to a poor woman to marry a rich one because he believes that "to have money is becoming of more and more importance in a literary career; principally because to have money is to have friends" (27). To Jasper Milvain, poverty "is the root of all social ills; its existence accounts even for the ills that arise from wealth. The poor man is a man labouring in fetters" (30). (Gissing 1926)

See also Gissing, George; *New Grub Street;* Reardon, Edwin

Minke

Minke is the main character in Pramoedya Ananta Toer's 1980 novel *This Earth of Mankind,* which concerns social and political injustices on the island of Java. A native, he attends a Dutch-run school and experiences a great deal of prejudice because of his race.

Students tease him for having no last name, which is what separates the natives from the Europeans. However, at a school assembly a teacher honors Minke by saying: "Students, having a family name is just a custom. Before Napoleon Bonaparte appeared on the stage of European history, not even our ancestors—not one of them—used family names. . . . It was through contact with other peoples that Europeans learned the importance of family names" (Toer 1996, 215). Moreover, she attacks racism by saying: "Europeans who feel themselves to be a hundred percent pure do not really know how much Asian blood flows in their veins. From your study of history, you will all know that hundreds of years ago, many different Asian armies attacked Europe, and left descendants" (215).

For raising such points, the teacher is fired. However, Minke continues to spread her views in his writings. He is an accomplished author and becomes a regular contributor to an Indonesian newspaper, addressing many important social and political issues. At the same time he becomes embroiled in a personal scandal that threatens to end his education and his writing career. When his lover's father is murdered, rumors spread regarding Minke's relationship to the girl and her family. He writes a passionate defense, and in the end many people rally to his side. He has shown his ability to influence public opinion and will undoubtedly be influential in Indonesia's political future. (Toer 1996)

See also *This Earth of Mankind;* Toer, Pramoedya Ananta

Misérables, Les

Les Misérables, by Victor Hugo, was published both in French and in English in 1862. The novel, which covers a period of approximately 18 years, comments on French politics, war, and history, discussing such events as the fall of Napoleon, the restoration of the monarchy, and the revolution of 1830. One of its most famous passages describes and analyzes the Battle of Waterloo. More importantly, however, the novel offers a portrait of French society and examines various aspects of human nature. For this reason, the book is often compared to the works of Charles Dickens and Fyodor Dostoyevsky, which portray English and Russian society, respectively.

The plot of *Les Misérables* centers around the life of Jean Valjean, who arrives at the home of Monsieur Charles-Francois-Bienvenu Myriel, the bishop of Digne, one evening in 1815. Valjean has just been released from prison, where he served 5 years for stealing a loaf of bread and 14 more for trying to escape. He explains to the bishop that the inns have all refused him lodging because of his criminal past, which is revealed through his specially marked passport, and the bishop does not hesitate to take him in. But despite the bishop's kindness, during the night Valjean steals his silver table settings and flees. When the police catch him with the silver, they bring him to the bishop, who insists that he gave his dishes to the man as a gift. The bishop then tells Valjean: "Do not forget, ever, that you have promised me to use this silver to become an honest man. . . . You no longer belong to evil but to good. It is your soul I am buying for you. I withdraw it from dark thoughts and from the spirit of perdition, and I give it to God!" (Hugo 1987, 106). Valjean leaves town with the silver, and shortly thereafter he steals a small boy's coin. Remembering the bishop's words, his conscience is troubled, and he realizes the depths to which he has sunk. He vows to reform.

Meanwhile a young Parisian girl named Fantine has been abandoned by her lover, with whom she has had a child, Cosette. Shortly thereafter she leaves her three-year-old daughter with the Thénardier family and sets off to the nearby city of Montreuil-sur-mer to find a job. Soon she is working at the factory of the mayor, Monsieur Madeleine, who has a mysterious past. Madeleine arrived in town as a stranger, but because he saved the lives of two little girls during a fire, he was immediately accepted into the community. He became rich after inventing a new manufacturing process, opened his factory, and began donating much of his profits to the poor. For his kindness the government awarded him the

Legion of Honor, but out of modesty he refused to accept it.

Fantine is pleased to be working at Madeleine's factory, but soon the overseer learns that she had a child out of wedlock and fires her. Now she has difficulty paying the Thénardiers for Cosette's upkeep, yet they continue to ask for more and more money. Fantine quickly descends into poverty, prostitution, and illness, blaming Madeleine for her fate. Her only comfort is that she believes her daughter is living a better life. She is unaware that the Thénardiers have turned Cosette into their slave even though the girl is only five years old; as the story's omniscient narrator points out, "social suffering can begin at any age" (157).

When Madeleine learns of Fantine's suffering, he takes her home, summons a doctor, and sends for Cosette. Meanwhile the town's police inspector, Javert, informs Madeleine that he once suspected Madeleine of being Jean Valjean, a convict who stole money from a little boy and was never caught. Javert then offers apologies and says that the real Jean Valjean has just been arrested for the crime. Madeleine wrestles with his conscience and finally interrupts the man's trial to announce that he is really Jean Valjean. He then goes home to await his arrest. Javert finds him in Fantine's sickroom and berates him, whereupon a shocked Fantine dies.

After Jean Valjean's arrest everyone in town forgets about his good deeds and excellent reputation. They condemn him as a convict and are glad to be rid of him. However, his former servants remain loyal to him, and when he escapes from jail, they help him leave town. He withdraws a large sum of money from the bank and hides it before being arrested again. He is sent to work on board a ship, where he saves a sailor's life, then falls into the sea and is believed drowned.

Shortly thereafter he rescues eight-year-old Cosette from the Thénardiers and takes her to Paris, where Javert discovers him and gives chase. Valjean escapes with the little girl to a convent, where he becomes the gardener's assistant under an assumed name. Cosette attends the convent school as his granddaughter. After she graduates, Valjean decides that she should see something of the world and takes her from the convent. He believes that no one will recognize him after so many years.

The two live together in a small house in Paris, where Valjean becomes involved in charitable causes. One day he answers the plea of a man named Monsieur Jondrette, who has written him for aid. When Valjean and Cosette bring them clothes and blankets, Jondrette recognizes them; he is actually Monsieur Thénardier, but Valjean and Cosette do not realize this. Meanwhile a young man is observing the scene through a crack in the wall. He is Jondrette's neighbor, Marius Pontmercy. Marius was raised by his maternal grandfather, Monsieur Gillenormand, who kept the young man from knowing his father because of the elder Pontmercy's political views. Upon his father's death Marius expressed support for those same views, and Gillenormand threw him out of the house. Marius then became a lawyer and a member of a revolutionary group.

Now Marius recognizes Cosette and Valjean as well, but not for the same reason. He has been in love with Cosette for some time, having seen her in the park from a distance. Shortly after they leave Jondrette's room, he overhears Jondrette telling his wife that when Valjean returns, he will ask the man for a lot of money and perhaps kill him. Marius reports this to Inspector Javert, who tells him to hide in his room and fire a pistol when the crime has begun, so that his officers will know when to rush in. Marius returns home, and soon Valjean arrives.

When Jondrette tells Valjean that he is Thénardier, Marius is shocked. In his last request before death his father had asked him to find Thénardier, who once saved his life in a battle, and honor him. As Thénardier talks, Marius realizes it is the same man, and he does not fire the pistol at the appropriate time. Nonetheless, the police arrive, and during the ensuing scuffle Valjean escapes through a window. Marius disappears, too, not willing to testify against Thénardier, and begins searching for Cosette. One day he finds her again, and the two fall in love.

Meanwhile Valjean has decided that he is no longer safe in France and decides to take Cosette to England. She tells Marius of their travel plans and asks him to accompany them, but Marius cannot afford to do so. He goes to his grandfather for help but finds none. Now certain that he will never marry Cosette, Marius joins his revolutionary friends in a riot. He sends Cosette a note to this effect, and when Valjean intercepts it, he rushes to keep the young man from harm. In the process he rescues Javert from revolutionaries who intend to kill him and carries a wounded, unconscious Marius to safety through the sewers of Paris. He then encounters Javert once more, and the two men take Marius to his grandfather's house. Afterward Javert lets Valjean go home to say good-bye to Cosette and realizes that he cannot arrest someone who saved his life. Feeling himself a failure as a police officer, he drowns himself in the Seine River.

When Marius recovers from his wounds, his grandfather tells him that he may marry Cosette. The day after the wedding Valjean confesses to Marius that he is a former convict. Marius is horrified and does not want Valjean in his home. For a time Valjean visits Cosette when Marius is away, but eventually he stops visiting altogether. Knowing nothing of what he has told Marius, she does not understand why he is staying away. Meanwhile Marius investigates Valjean's past and learns that the convict murdered a factory owner named Madeleine and stole his money and later killed Inspector Javert. Eventually he discovers that that these facts are wrong and that Valjean was the one who saved his life during the revolt. With Cosette, he rushes to Valjean's home and professes his love for the man. Valjean is happy, but he is also ill, and he dies shortly after the young couple's arrival. He is buried under a stone with no name.

In discussing his work, Hugo emphasizes its religious aspects, presenting the tale as the struggle between good and evil within each individual's soul. However, the novel also makes it clear that people are a product of their environment, influenced by society and experience. Valjean commits his first theft because his family is starving; he is redeemed by the kind treatment of a stranger, the bishop. However, Hugo recognizes that under some circumstances no act of charity can change a man's nature. For this reason, despite Valjean's generosity, Thénardier remains a thief and a murderer. (Hugo 1987; Swinburne 1970)

See also Cosette; Dickens, Charles; Dostoyevsky, Fyodor; Hugo, Victor; Javert; Pontmercy, Marius; Valjean, Jean

Modest Proposal, A

Written by Jonathan Swift, *A Modest Proposal* is a satirical pamphlet published in October 1729. It outlines a plan to reduce the number of Irish poor by allowing them to sell their children as food. In this way, according to Swift (Van Doren 1977, 555–556),

> the poorer tenants will have something valuable of their own. . . . It would increase the care and tenderness of mothers toward their children. . . . We should see an honest emulation among the married women, which of them could bring the fattest child to the market, men would become as fond of their wives, during the time of their pregnancy, as they are now of their mares in foal, their cows in calf, or sows when they are ready to farrow, nor offer to beat or kick them (as it is too frequent a practice) for fear of a miscarriage.

(Van Doren 1977)

See also Poverty; Swift, Jonathan

Monkey Wrench Gang, The

The Monkey Wrench Gang is a novel by environmental activist Edward Abbey. Published in 1975, it concerns the escapades of a band of activists who use ecological sabotage, or ecotage, to fight against development in the deserts of the American Southwest. The book inspired the environmental group Earth First! to adopt similar tactics in real life. Today these tactics, which include damaging roads, bridges, and industrial equipment, are called monkeywrenching.

The Monkey Wrench Gang begins with a fictional act of ecotage: the dynamiting of a new bridge across Glen Canyon, intended to connect Utah and Arizona. The novel then flashes back to an earlier episode: Dr. A. K. Sarvis and his assistant, Bonnie Abzzug, setting fire to billboards along a desert highway. Sarvis considers it one of his "nighttime highway beautification projects" (Abbey 1975, 47). Shortly thereafter Sarvis and Abzzug go on a river-rafting trip. Their guides are Joseph Fielding "Seldom Seen" Smith and his new assistant, a Vietnam veteran and former Green Beret named George Washington Hayduke. Both Smith and Hayduke believe that the government is destroying the desert. After Smith tells Sarvis and Abbzug that the Glen Canyon Dam has diminished the power of the Colorado River and ought to be dynamited, the group begins to discuss environmental activism. By the time the four of them leave the river, the Monkey Wrench Gang has been born.

Their first act of ecotage is against some bulldozers clearing a forest. After nightfall gang members use a variety of methods to damage the bulldozers' engines and succeed in delaying the clear-cutting project. Emboldened by this success, they undertake more difficult acts of ecotage. They move surveying stakes for a government road project, damage power lines and geological sensor devices, and blow up an electric train at a coal company, leaving behind clues that suggest a Native American activist group is responsible for the damage. Eventually, however, a local Mormon bishop named Love begins to suspect that Smith is involved in these activities. Bishop Love is the leader of a desert Search and Rescue Team, and after Hayduke and Smith drive an untended bulldozer off a cliff in broad daylight, he and his team chase them. The two monkeywrenchers escape, but afterward Love continues to look for them.

Pursued by Bishop Love and law enforcement officials, the gang temporarily splits up. Sarvis returns to work, Smith stays out of sight, and Hayduke and Abbzug head for a forest near the Grand Canyon to destroy clear-cutting equipment. Abbzug was once Sarvis's lover, but now she is in love with Hayduke. At the Grand Canyon the couple encounters another ecoteur, a masked horseman whom Hayduke calls the Lone Ranger. The man helps them destroy some bulldozers and rides off without telling them his name. Hayduke and Abbzug return to the desert, where they commit another act of ecotage, but two helicopter pilots catch Abbzug in the act. Hayduke rescues her and sets the helicopter on fire. Now Bishop Love increases his efforts to find the monkeywrenchers, and one night he discovers all four trying to blow up a bridge. He and his posse chase the gang into a desert wilderness area. The terrain is difficult, and the monkeywrenchers have little water. Nevertheless, they keep hiking until Bishop Love falls ill and his team calls on Dr. Sarvis for help. Unable to let Love die, Sarvis and Abbzug turn themselves in, but Hayduke and Smith keep going. Eventually the two men split up. Smith is captured when he tries to steal food from some campers. Hayduke is cornered at the edge of a cliff, and law enforcement officials shoot his body to pieces. Later Sarvis's lawyers manage to keep Sarvis, Abbzug, and Smith from serving time in prison.

The group settles along the Colorado River and appears to lead a quiet life. Then Hayduke and the Lone Ranger show up, and Hayduke explains that he fooled the lawmen by putting a dummy in his place. Hayduke accuses the monkeywrenchers of being responsible for blowing up the new bridge across Glen Canyon, but the book ends without the monkeywrenchers admitting their involvement.

Inspired by *The Monkey Wrench Gang,* Earth First! decided to stage its first major act of ecotage at the Glen Canyon Dam. Earth First!ers snuck on top of the dam and unfurled a plastic "crack" across its face, symbolically destroying the concrete. Abbey was present during the event. (Abbey 1975; McCann 1977)

See also Abbey, Edward; Environmentalism; Sarvis, Dr. A. K.

Montag, Guy

Guy Montag is the main character of Ray Bradbury's 1953 novel *Fahrenheit 451*. Montag lives in a future society where owning books is a crime, and as a fireman it is his job to burn them. One day he begins to wonder what is inside the books he burns. He steals some and reads them. After that he can no longer destroy them. He becomes a fugitive from society and lives among a hobo band of fellow book lovers, each of whom has memorized a different section of a text. Someday they hope to rewrite what has been lost. (Bradbury 1996)

See also Beatty, Captain; Bradbury, Ray; Censorship; *Fahrenheit 451*

Montage of a Dream Deferred

Montage of a Dream Deferred, by American poet Langston Hughes, is a collection of poetry devoted to the black experience in Harlem. In writing his verse, the author intends to imitate a cycle of jazz music or, as he once explained in a speech, to "put jazz into words" (Hughes 1958, 494). Published in 1951, *Montage* is organized into six sections and subtitles to address all aspects of Harlem life. Many of the poems also protest racism and the inequalities in American society. For example, "Children's Rhymes" points out that "what's written down / for white folks / ain't for us a-tall" (91) and notes that black children cannot hope to grow up to be president, and "Not a Movie" talks about a black man who is beaten for trying to vote in a southern election (91). The most famous poem in the collection, "Harlem," suggests that if a dream is deferred, it will either "dry up like a raisin in the sun," fester, and sicken or eventually explode (123). Author Lorraine Hansberry was inspired by Hughes in writing her social protest play *A Raisin in the Sun.* (Hughes 1958; Muller 1986; O'Daniel 1971)

See also Hansberry, Lorraine; Harlem Renaissance; Hughes, Langston; *Raisin in the Sun, A*

Moore, Daniel Vivaldo

Daniel Vivaldo Moore appears in James Baldwin's 1960 novel *Another Country.* Called Vivaldo by his friends, he is an Irish American who prefers the company of African Americans at a time when racism is prevalent in the United States. His best friend, Rufus Scott, is a black jazz drummer from Harlem, and his girlfriend is Scott's sister, Ida. When Rufus commits suicide, Vivaldo blames himself for not being friend enough to prevent it. But when Ida blames Vivaldo for being white, and therefore part of the reason for Rufus's suffering, Vivaldo says, "Suffering doesn't *have* a color" (Baldwin 1962, 417). He accuses her of being just as racist as the people she condemns, arguing: "What I've never understood is that you always accuse me of making a thing about your color, of penalizing you. But you do the same thing. You always make me feel white" (414). (Baldwin 1962)

See also *Another Country;* Baldwin, James; Jones, Eric; Racism; Scott, Ida and Rufus

Moreno, Señora

In Helen Hunt Jackson's 1885 novel *Ramona,* Señora Moreno is a wealthy Mexican woman living in Southern California during the late 1880s. She is extremely prejudiced against Native Americans, even though her adopted daughter, Ramona, is half Indian. Señora Moreno does not tell the girl of her heritage and refuses to let Ramona marry a full Indian named Alessandro. Moreover, Señora Moreno lies and tells the girl that her mother's will gave her the power to decide whom Ramona would wed. Distraught, Ramona and Alessandro run away to a life of poverty and hardship. Meanwhile Señora Moreno keeps the girl's dowry of precious jewels locked away, intending to give them to her church. She dies without repenting her lies and theft, whereupon her son finds the jewels and eventually returns them to Ramona. (Jackson 1988)

See also Alessandro; Jackson, Helen Hunt; *Ramona*

Morrison, Arthur

British author Arthur Morrison wrote novels that called attention to the plight of the poor in England's slums. As a result of his work, the

British government changed its housing laws to improve living conditions there.

The son of an engine fitter, Morrison was born in Popular, Kent, England, on November 1, 1863. He worked first as a clerk and then as a journalist, writing stories for several London journals, including the *National Observer*. His first book was a collection of these stories, *Tales of Mean Streets* (1894). His most important work was a novel, *A Child of the Jago*. Published in 1896, it depicted the desperate plight of the poor in a London slum called the Jago and eventually led to the area's cleanup. Morrison also wrote a novel entitled *A Hole in the Wall* (1902), a series of detective stories, and a book about Japanese art entitled *Painters of Japan* (1911). He died on December 4, 1945, in Chalfont St. Peter, Buckinghamshire, England. (Morrison 1995)

See also *Child of the Jago, A;* Poverty

Morrison, Toni

American author Toni Morrison writes novels from a black feminist perspective. In 1988 she received the Pulitzer Prize for her novel *Beloved,* which concerns black slavery during the Civil War, and in 1993 she was awarded the Nobel Prize in literature.

Morrison was born Chloe Anthony Wofford on February 18, 1931, in Lorain, Ohio, and attended both Howard University and Cornell University. After graduation she became a university professor, teaching first at Texas Southern University, then at Howard University, and finally at the State University of New York, where in 1965 she also began working as a senior editor at Random House, a large publishing company. Her first novel, *The Bluest Eye,* appeared in 1970, and her second, *Sula,* in 1973. Both novels deal with black issues from a woman's perspective. She continues to write novels today. Her other works include *The Song of Solomon* (1977), *Tar Baby* (1981), and *Jazz* (1992). In addition, she has written several critical essays and articles. (Gates and Appiah 1993c; McKay 1988; Samuels 1990)

See also *Beloved; Bluest Eye, The;* Feminism; Racism; *Sula*

Mukhtaar

Mukhtaar is a character in Nuruddin Farah's 1983 novel *Close Sesame,* which protests certain social and political practices in modern Somalia. After he attempts to assassinate the leader of the country, his father beats him to death. Later the incident is deemed a suicide because Mukhtaar's father is a member of the ruling clan. However, even if Mukhtaar's death had been judged a murder, his murderer would not have stood trial. As another character in the novel explains: "A father can beat his son to madness in full public view and the son is expected not to raise a hand but to receive the beating in total silence. The son is not allowed to question the wisdom of his parent's statements, must never answer back, never raise his voice or head. . . . Nothing would happen to avenge Mukhtaar's life and his father would not be submitted to questioning: after all, it is the prerogative of a parent what to do with the life and property of an offspring" (Farah 1992, 120–121). (Farah 1992)

See also *Close Sesame;* Farah, Nuruddin

Toni Morrison, 1994 (Horst Tappe/Archive Photos)

Mursal

Mursal is a character in Nuruddin Farah's 1983 novel *Close Sesame*. Opposed to the corrupt, oppressive dictatorship of his native country of Somalia, he becomes involved in a plot to assassinate the ruling general. The plot fails, and one by one each of the four men who helped plan the assassination are murdered. Mursal is last on the list, and before he can be arrested, he tries to blow up the general. Mursal fails and is later killed. After his death his widow tries to decide whether to stay in the country. She was born in the United States and does not understand the Somali language or culture very well. (Farah 1992)

See also *Close Sesame;* Farah, Nuruddin

My Brilliant Career

The 1901 novel *My Brilliant Career,* by Miles Franklin, concerns an educated but tomboyish Australian girl, Sybylla Melvyn, who has been reduced to poverty through her father's alcoholism and bad investments. While visiting wealthy relatives, she meets a rich landowner, and he falls in love with her. He is a good man, and they become secretly engaged. However, she soon realizes that as his wife she would always be under his control; he is the kind of man who would never consider a woman to be his equal. Therefore, she breaks off their engagement and determines to make her own way in life. Sybylla's decision reflects the feminism of the author, who was a journalist active in the women's rights movement. (Franklin 1965)

See also Feminism; Franklin, Miles

N

Naranjo, Huberto

A guerrilla fighter in Isabel Allende's 1987 novel *Eva Luna,* Huberto Naranjo leads a revolutionary group in the mountains of South America. Also known as Comandante Rogelio, he moves people not by persuasive oration but "by the force of his courage" (Allende 1988, 182). He instills great loyalty in his men and succeeds in freeing political prisoners from a supposedly impenetrable prison. (Allende 1988)

See also Allende, Isabel; Carle, Lukas; Carle, Rolf; *Eva Luna;* Rodríguez, Colonel Tolomeo

Native American Issues

The first social protest literature to deal with Native American issues was written by non-Native Americans. Perhaps the most famous of these is Helen Hunt Jackson's 1885 novel *Ramona,* which deals with prejudice against Native Americans in California. This work influenced public opinion and helped create new government policies toward Indian management.

Another novel that raised public awareness of Native American issues was Thomas Berger's novel *Little Big Man.* It was published in 1964 at a time when Native Americans were beginning to become active politically. Therefore, although *Little Big Man* depicts injustices that were perpetrated against Native Americans during the 1800s, the book did much to further the modern Native American rights movement of the 1960s and 1970s.

Little Big Man shows the forced relocation of Native Americans to Indian reservations owned and controlled by the U.S. government. The first reservations were established in 1815, and they still exist today. However, they are now owned by the Native Americans themselves. During the transition from government to tribal ownership, many reservations fell into poverty and alcoholism rose among their residents. These problems continue to be a part of modern reservation life, and they are the main concern of Native American social protest authors, including James Welch and nila northSun. Such authors also depict the difficulties experienced by Native Americans who leave the reservation to live in large cities. However, like Asian-American and Mexican-American authors, their primary means of expression is through poetry or nonfiction, and much of their work is ignored by major publishers. (Grossman 1996)

See also Asian-American Literature; Berger, Thomas; Jackson, Helen Hunt; *Little Big Man;* Mexican-American Literature; northSun, nila; *Ramona;* Welch, James

First and second graders during their singing lesson at the Carlisle Indian School, 1901 (Cumberland County Historical Society)

Native Son

The 1940 novel *Native Son,* by Richard Wright, addresses the problem of racism in the United States by showing both the injustice of oppression and the anger of the oppressed. In writing about the novel, Wright (1993a, 523) categorizes its main character, a 20-year-old black man named Bigger Thomas, as "resentful toward whites, sullen, angry, ignorant, emotionally unstable, depressed and unaccountably elated at times, and unable even, because of his own lack of inner organization which American oppression has fostered in him, to unite with the members of his own race." He reports that he hesitated to write about such an angry, bitter character for fear that it would upset blacks and whites alike. However, he had met people like Bigger and felt it was important to acknowledge their existence in American society.

According to scholar Arnold Rampersad (xi), writing in a 1993 introduction to *Native Son,* Wright wanted to dispel misperceptions about blacks and whites and their relationship with each other:

> Wright believed that few Americans, black or white, were prepared to face squarely and honestly the most profound consequences of more than two centuries of the enslavement and segregation of blacks in North America. . . . Wright knew, black and whites alike continued to cling to a range of fantasies about the true nature of the relationship between the two races even as the nation lurched inexorably toward a possible collapse over the fundamental question of justice for the despised African American minority.

Moreover, Rampersad (xii) believes that Wright was concerned with showing black men's "sometimes unconscious but powerful identification of violence against other human beings as the most appropriate response to the disastrous conditions of their lives. Within the confines of the black world, this violence was easily directed at fellow blacks; but increasingly, Wright warned his readers, this violence would be aimed at whites.

At first Bigger Thomas takes out his anger on other blacks, bullying and robbing them at will. He does not dare rob a white store because he and his friends believe that such an act "would be a violation of ultimate taboo; it would be a trespassing into territory where the full wrath of an alien white world would be turned loose upon them; in short, it would be a symbolic challenge of the white world's rule over them; a challenge which they yearned to make, but were afraid to" (14). Bigger also avoids contact with the white world. Then he is offered a job as a chauffeur to a white millionaire, Mr. Dalton, who is a prominent citizen in Chicago. Bigger decides to take the job because

> his mother had always told him that rich white people liked Negroes better than they did poor whites. He felt that if he were a poor white and did not get his share of the money, then he would deserve to be kicked. Poor white people were stupid. It was the rich white people who were smart and knew how to treat people. He remembered hearing somebody tell a story of a Negro chauffeur who had married a rich white girl and the girl's family had shipped the couple out of the country and had supplied them with money. (37)

When around Mr. Dalton, Bigger immediately falls into a subservient role and hates himself for doing so. He also hates Mr. Dalton's daughter, Mary, whom he has heard is a Communist. His first night on the job, Bigger is ordered to drive Mary to a university lecture. However, once they are in the car, she asks Bigger to pick up her radical boyfriend, Jan Erlone, and take them to a black restaurant, making him promise not to tell her father about it later. Bigger is uncomfortable with the situation. Moreover, he is angry at the couple for treating him as an equal. He

does not want to go into the restaurant with the two of them, but they insist.

Once inside, all of Bigger's friends stare at him. Meanwhile Jan and Mary tell him about communism. They also have a lot to drink, and by the time Bigger gets Mary home, she can barely walk. He helps her to her room, but after he puts her into bed, her mother walks in. Mrs. Dalton is blind but has sharp ears. When Mary starts to mumble, Bigger is afraid she will give his presence away, and he is frightened at what will happen if he is found in a white girl's bedroom. He covers Mary's face with a pillow until Mrs. Dalton leaves. To his horror, he then discovers that he has inadvertently killed the young woman. Bigger knows he must cover up his crime. He puts the body in a trunk, carries it to the furnace, and burns it. Later he thinks about his intent when he killed Mary and realizes that,

> though he had killed by accident, not once did he feel the need to tell himself that it had been an accident. He was black and he had been alone in a room where a white girl had been killed; therefore he had killed her. That was what everybody would say anyhow, no matter what he said. And in a certain sense he knew that the girl's death had not been accidental. He had killed many times before, only on those other times there had been no handy victim or circumstance to make visible or dramatic his will to kill. His crime seemed natural; he felt that all of his life had been leading to something like this. It was no longer a matter of dumb wonder as to what would happen to him and his black skin; he knew now. The hidden meaning of his life—a meaning which others did not see and which he had always tried to hide—had spilled out. No; it was no accident, and he would never say that it was. There was in him a kind of terrified pride in feeling and thinking that some day he would be able to say publicly that he had done it. It was as though he had an obscure but deep debt to fulfil to himself in accepting the deed. (119)

In this scene from the 1950 movie Native Son, *Bigger Thomas (played by author Richard Wright) appeals to his girlfriend, Bessie Mears, for help. (The Museum of Modern Art Film Stills Archive)*

At first Bigger thinks he is going to get away with his crime. Mary's parents think she has just run off. But later they begin to suspect foul play and hire a private investigator. This man questions Bigger, who intentionally casts suspicion on Jan. Later Jan asks Bigger what he has done to deserve the young man's accusations. Bigger grows frightened and pulls a gun on him, and Jan runs away. Suddenly Bigger decides to take an action that he has long been considering. He writes a ransom note that makes it seem as though Mary has been kidnapped by the Communist Party, demanding payment of $10,000 for her release. The Daltons take the note seriously, while Jan believes that Mr. Dalton has set up a fake kidnapping to increase public opposition to the Communist Party. Then someone finds one of Mary's bones and an earring in the Dalton's furnace ashes. Bigger sneaks away from the house and goes to his girlfriend, Bessie, for help. But after he confesses his crime, he realizes that he cannot let her live. He kills her and runs.

On the streets he sees newspaper headlines that suggest he not only killed Mary but also raped her. The public is incensed. Violent acts against innocent blacks increase, and many are fired from their jobs without cause. A massive manhunt takes place, and eventually Bigger is caught. He refuses to speak. Then Jan visits him in jail and tells him that he understands why Bigger hates white people and that he wants to help Bigger with his defense. Jan brings in an attorney, Max, who works for the Communist Party. After some resistance Bigger realizes that Jan and Max are his friends. Later, when police try to get him to say that the Communists were involved in Mary's death, Bigger refuses to comply. Instead, he dictates an honest confession, explaining that Mary's death was an accident. Shortly thereafter the court holds an inquest to determine whether Bigger should stand trial for the crime, and it quickly becomes apparent that the coroner and prosecutor are racist and anticommunist.

Max fights back by exposing Mr. Dalton, who is involved in black charities, as a hypocrite; the millionaire owns many rental properties and charges blacks an exorbitant rate to live in them. But the inquest turns sensational when Bessie's battered body is displayed for all to see. Now Max realizes that no jury will view Mary's death as accidental. He decides to change Bigger's plea from not guilty to guilty, so that the sentence will be determined by a judge. Max hopes that the judge will recognize Bigger's innocence and give him a merciful sentence. The lawyer offers an eloquent argument in this regard, discussing slavery, racism, and black anger and fear. Nonetheless, Bigger is sentenced to death in the electric chair. He awaits his execution with a bitter smile.

Native Son is a powerful novel, and it became a best-seller shortly after its publication. It was also nominated for several major literary awards. However, according to scholar Kenneth Kinnamon in his essay "How *Native Son* Was Born" (Gates and Appiah 1993b, 126), "literary America was not yet ready to award a black writer a major prize in fiction," and the novel was passed over for the Pulitzer Prize. Kinnamon adds that aside from its literary merits, *Native Son* had an immediate impact on American society. He (126–127) says:

Several journalists and sociologists cited *Native Son* in discussions of poor housing in Chicago and elsewhere. Others drew parallels between Bigger Thomas and actual living individuals. A writer in the denominational organ of the Disciples of Christ suggested that *Native Son* "would be a good book for all judges, police officers, and prosecutors who have to do with a Negro to read." Irving Howe once wrote that "the day *Native Son* appeared, American culture was changed forever." The change was not basic or profound, but it was real. The several hundred thousand readers of the work could no longer see racial issues in quite the same way. *Native Son* did not start a war, as Lincoln claimed *Uncle Tom's Cabin* did, or directly bring about legislation, as *The Jungle* did, but it

did alter the social as well as literary sensibilities of many of its readers.

(Gates and Appiah 1993b; Wright 1993a)

See also Communism; Erlone, Jan; *Jungle, The;* Racism; Thomas, Bigger; *Uncle Tom's Cabin;* Wright, Richard

Nekhludof, Prince Dmitri Ivanovitch

Prince Dmitri Ivanovitch Nekhludof is one of the main characters in *Voskreseniye* (Resurrection, 1899), by Leo Tolstoi. A member of the Russian nobility, the prince begins the novel as an arrogant spendthrift who seduces a young girl without concern for her feelings. Later he discovers that this seduction ruined her life; she became pregnant, descended into prostitution, and ended up in prison for murder even though she was innocent of the crime. Feeling guilty for his sin, Nekhludof works for her release. He also asks her to marry him, but she refuses. Nonetheless, he visits her often in prison, where he learns that many other innocent people have been jailed. He begins to question the justice of the Russian prison system and to consider the causes of crime among the lower classes. Consequently, he visits the peasants who farm his estate and for the first time sees their poverty. He gives them his land, vowing to live more modestly himself. In addition, he studies the Bible and decides that oppression, imprisonment, and capital punishment are against its teachings. He condemns the Russian church for supporting such activities. (Tolstoy 1911)

See also *Resurrection;* Tolstoi, Leo

New Grub Street

Published in 1891, *New Grub Street,* by George Gissing, concerns the London literary scene. Its plot centers on the lives of two authors: Edwin Reardon, who writes for artistic reasons, and Jasper Milvain, who writes for money. The former soon finds himself penniless, whereas the latter becomes extremely successful. After Reardon's wife begs him to write something more commercial and he fails, he decides to abandon the writing trade, and she leaves him. He dies alone, and a few months later she marries Milvain.

New Grub Street criticizes many aspects of the literary establishment, including book reviewers who base their comments on whether they like a writer's personality. But the novel also offers broader social protest commentary on the plight of the poor. Gissing (1926, 251) depicts a London of uncaring rich, describing one character as a woman who "would shed tears over a pitiful story of want, and without shadow of hypocrisy. It was hard, it was cruel; such things oughtn't to be allowed in a world where there were so many rich people. The next day she would argue with her charwoman about halfpence, and end by paying the poor creature what she knew was inadequate and unjust." Through Reardon, the author bemoans a world that "has no pity on a man who can't do or produce something it thinks worth money. You may be a divine poet, and if some good fellow doesn't take pity on you you will starve by the roadside. Society is as blind and brutal as fate" (209). (Coustillas 1968; Gissing 1926; Goode 1979)

See also Gissing, George; Milvain, Jasper; Poverty; Reardon, Edwin

1984

Published in 1949, George Orwell's novel *1984* is the author's antiutopian vision of the future. It is set in the aftermath of a global war in a society where people's thoughts and actions are under the complete control of their government. Orwell wrote the novel as a commentary on the totalitarian dictatorships of his time, but he also intended it to be a cautionary tale, fearing that one day his vision would become a reality. The book's tone is pessimistic and was written while the author was dying of a fatal illness.

The novel's main character is 39-year-old Winston Smith. Separated from his wife, he lives in Oceania and works at the Ministry of Truth. His job is to rewrite historical records, making it seem as though the government's predictions are always accurate and its stated goals always met. One day while on his lunch break he unconsciously doodles a slogan

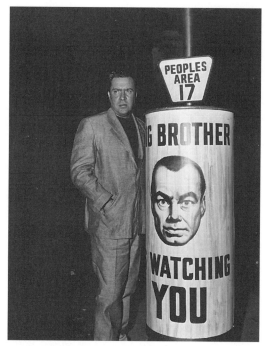

Winston Smith fears the watchful eye of Big Brother in this scene from the 1956 film 1984. *(Hulton Deutsch Collection/Corbis)*

against Big Brother, the symbol of the all-watching party that controls the government. Big Brother keeps an eye on the citizens of Oceania through two-way telescreens and other means. The government also uses telescreens during a daily two-minute hate period, showing a picture of one of its enemies and rousing the viewers to hate him.

As Winston goes about his daily routine, he notices that a young woman is often nearby. He becomes afraid that she is a member of the thought police. He considers killing her, until she leaves him a note saying she loves him. Consequently, the two begin having an affair, and Winston rents a room over an antique shop where they can meet in privacy. The room appears to have no telescreen; however, Winston and Julia eventually discover a hidden one. By this time they have become involved with a man named O'Brien, who purports to be part of a conspiracy to overthrow the government. He gives Winston and Julia a book about the conspiracy. While the couple is reading it aloud in the room, police rush into the room to arrest both of them. Winston realizes that the owner of the antique shop is a member of the thought police. Later he learns that O'Brien is actually working for the government, too, and that the book was created by the government to catch would-be conspirators. Because he has fallen into O'Brien's trap, Winston is severely tortured for several days. Eventually he says whatever they want him to say. The narrator explains:

> His sole concern was to find out what they wanted him to confess, and then confess it quickly, before the bullying started anew. He confessed to the assassination of eminent party members, the distribution of seditious pamphlets, embezzlement of public funds, sale of military secrets, sabotage of every kind. . . . He confessed that he was a religious believer, an admirer of capitalism, and a sexual pervert. . . . He confessed that for years he had been . . . a member of an underground organization which had included almost every human being he had ever known. It was easier to confess everything and implicate everybody. (Orwell 1961, 200)

Eventually Winston's torturers break his spirit, and he renounces his love for Julia. He is released from jail and returns to an ordinary life. On one occasion he meets Julia, and she confirms what Winston's captors once told him: under torture she, too, betrayed their love. Their relationship is over, and Winston has no one to love. In the end he begins to love Big Brother because there is nothing else. (Orwell 1961; Williams 1974)

See also Orwell, George; Science Fiction and Fantasy; Smith, Winston

Norris, Frank

Frank Norris is the author of one of the most famous social protest novels ever written. Entitled *The Octopus* and published in 1901, it concerns political corruption and immoral business practices as they relate to the wheat industry in the United States.

Norris was born Benjamin Franklin Norris in Chicago, Illinois, on March 5, 1870. He originally planned to be an artist, but he later decided on a career in journalism, working as a newspaper reporter for the San Francisco *Chronicle* from 1895 to 1896. His first novel was published in 1899. Entitled *McTeague,* it concerns the destructive force of materialism, which eventually leads a man to murder his wife over money and jealousy. Norris's subsequent novel, *The Octopus,* was the first in a trilogy collectively called *The Epic of the Wheat.* Its second volume is *The Pit* (1903), but its third remained unfinished upon Norris's death in San Francisco on October 25, 1902. At that time another of his novels, *Vandover and the Brute,* was still unpublished. It was then lost during the 1906 San Francisco earthquake but rediscovered and published in 1914. (Dillingham 1969; Graham 1978; McElrath 1992; Norris 1901; Pizer 1966)

See also Labor Issues; *Octopus, The*

northSun, nila

Born in Nevada in 1951, nila northSun is a Native American poet who uses her work to comment on the social and economic hardships of her people. Her mother is Shoshone, and her father is Chippewa. northSun's poetry collections include *Small Bones, Little Eyes* (1982), which was written with Jim Sagel, and *A Snake in Her Mouth: Poems 1974–96* (1997). (Velie 1991)

See also Native American Issues; "up & out"

Octopus, The

Set in the San Joaquin Valley of Central California, the 1901 novel *The Octopus,* by Frank Norris, focuses on moral corruption within the wheat and railroad industries. Its title refers to the railroad engine, a Cyclopean monster "with tentacles of steel clutching into the soil" (Norris 1901, 48).

Norris intended *The Octopus* to be the first volume of a trilogy entitled *The Epic of the Wheat.* In 1889 he (Pizer 1966, 113) wrote, "My Idea is to write three novels around the one subject of Wheat. First, a study of California (the producer), second, a study of Chicago (the distributor), third, a study of Europe (the consumer) and in each to keep to the idea of this huge, Niagara of wheat rolling from West to East." The trilogy's second volume, *The Pit,* was published posthumously in 1903, but Norris died before writing his third volume, *The Wolf.*

The Octopus, subtitled *The Story of California* and divided into Books 1 and 2, has three central characters: Presley, Annixter, and Vanamee. Each of these young men struggles with a particular obsession. Vanamee, a rootless shepherd, cannot forget his deceased girlfriend; he tries to use psychic powers to bring her back from the grave. Annixter, a wealthy rancher, is in love with his milkmaid, but to marry her, he must replace self-absorption with altruism. Presley, an idealistic poet, is fixated on writing the perfect epic. He rejects this idea once he develops a social protest conscience.

At the beginning of the novel Presley is a guest of the Derrick family at its vast wheat ranch, El Rancho de los Muertos, where he admires the beauty of the wheat but has little concern for those who steward it. When Hooven, a German tenant on Los Muertos, begs Presley to ask the Derricks not to evict their tenants, Presley refuses to help. He does not want to get involved because "these uncouth brutes of farmhands and petty ranchers, grimed with the soil they worked upon, [are] odious to him beyond words. Never could he feel in sympathy with them, nor with their lives, their ways, their marriages, deaths, bickerings, and all the monotonous round of their sordid existence" (Norris 1901, 3).

But Presley soon finds himself drawn into a dispute between the wheat ranchers and the railroad executives. The railroad, through its local representative, S. Behrman, has raised the freight rate for wheat, leaving the ranchers with little possibility of making a profit on their harvest. Behrman later hikes the price for freighting hops when a hops farmer, Dyke, boasts that he will actually profit from his crop. Financially ruined, Dyke turns to crime and eventually ends up in prison.

When Presley learns of such unjust tariffs, he is "roused to a pitch of exaltation . . . [and] a mighty spirit of revolt heaved tumultuous within him" (85). He abandons his idea for a romantic epic and instead writes a poem of social protest called "The Toilers." His friend Vanamee urges him to publish it in the daily press rather than in a literary magazine because the poem "must be read *by* the Toilers. It *must* be common; it must be vulgarized. You must not stand upon your dignity with the People if you are to reach them" (91). Vanamee warns Presley not to be as insincere as "the social reformer [who] writes a book on the iniquity of the possession of land, and out of the proceeds, buys a corner lot. The economist who laments the hardships of the poor, [but] allows himself to grow rich upon the sale of his book" (91).

Presley does publish his poem in the daily press, and it brings him some measure of fame, but it does not bring about social reform. In fact, the situation in the valley grows worse. The railroad industry, which owns most of the land there, has reneged on a promise to sell it at a reasonable price. The wheat growers had settled on the land and improved it based on its previously advertised price, and when the amount is raised, they are incensed. They take legal action against the railroad and in the process become as morally corrupt as the railroad men themselves.

When the wheat growers lose their legal battle, a group of railroad representatives arrives to evict them from their land. A gunfight breaks out, and several men are killed, including Annixter, Hooven, and a member of the Derrick family. Now destitute, Hooven's wife travels to San Francisco, where she and her youngest daughter starve to death in the streets outside a lavish railroad-sponsored charity banquet.

Meanwhile grief-stricken by Annixter's death, Presley throws a bomb into Behrman's home. Behrman survives the blast, and Presley realizes that he cannot embrace violence as a means of social protest. He leaves the valley and arranges passage on a ship that carries wheat to the starving poor in India. Ironically, Behrman visits the ship before it sails and accidentally falls into the hold of wheat. There he drowns beneath waves of grain and remains unnoticed.

The Octopus ends with a reminder that "greed, cruelty, selfishness, and inhumanity are short-lived; the individual suffers, but the race goes on. Annixter dies, but in a far-distant corner of the world a thousand lives are saved. The larger view always and through all shams, all wickednesses, discovers the Truth that will, in the end, prevail, and all things, surely, inevitably, resistlessly work together for good" (361).

Frank Norris's preoccupation with truth and realism has led some scholars to compare him with author Émile Zola, whose writings Norris often discussed. In creating *The Octopus,* Norris

drew upon Zola for such matters as the metaphor of the railroad engine as an animal. . . . He also borrowed an entire plot from Zola, that of the symbolic conquest of the grave by the "return" of a girl many years after her death. . . . Most important of all, however, Norris derived from *Germinal* and *La Terre,* Zola's most successful panoramic novels, two of the unifying structural devices of *The Octopus. Germinal,* which deals with a dispute between miners and their employers, suggested to Norris the technique (also used in *La Terre* to a lesser degree) of introducing an outsider into an economic struggle and of using his innocence as a means both for exposition and for the gradual crystallization of an attitude towards the dispute. (126)

Norris was also influenced by historical events. The climactic gun battle of *The Octopus* was based on the Mussel Slough massacre of 1880, which broke out when agents of the Southern Pacific Railroad attempted to evict wheat growers from their land. Other events in the novel were also drawn from real life, in particular the 1894 Mid-Winter Fair in San

Francisco and the 1897 famine in India. Similarly, the characters of Presley, Annixter, and Vanamee were loosely based on Norris and his friends Seymour Waterhouse and Bruce Porter. Presley's poem "The Toiler" was a reference to Edwin Markham's poem "The Man with the Hoe," which was published in the *San Francisco Examiner* on January 15, 1899.

As for Norris's own views regarding social protest, some scholars believe that he was not really interested in reform; he merely used social protest issues as a literary device. Others believe Norris did seek social reform. They call *The Octopus* "an early, prime example of Progressive Era muckraking art" that uniquely depicts immorality on *both* sides of a conflict (McElrath 1992, 92).

Donald Pizer (1966, 120), in discussing the issue of Norris's social consciousness, acknowledges that Norris did indeed use the Mussel Slough massacre "less [for] the opportunity it offered for the depiction of social injustice than [for] its literary usefulness." But he argues that Norris was nonetheless interested in social reform and intended to protest a larger target than just the railroad trusts.

Pizer (152) believes that Norris's goal was to use *The Octopus* to portray "some of the principal social problems and injustices caused by the growth of corporate wealth and power." The novel is therefore still relevant to modern society because, "although trusts no longer plague us as they once did, many of our social problems still arise out of the relationship between the individual and vast corporate and state powers which seem inexorably to control his life" (153). (Dillingham 1969; Graham 1978; McElrath 1992; Norris 1901; Pizer 1966)

See also Capitalism; Justice; Labor Issues; "Man with the Hoe, The"; Markham, Edwin; Norris, Frank; Poverty; Zola, Émile

Offred

The narrator of Margaret Atwood's futuristic novel *The Handmaid's Tale* (1985), Offred tells the story of her life under the regime of Gilead, run by religious fundamentalists. Gilead's government assigns women to spe-

cific roles within society. For example, women who work as household servants are called Marthas and must wear brown, whereas Wives of government leaders wear blue and spend most of their time socializing with other Wives. Offred is a Handmaid and must wear red. As a fertile woman her job is to bear children for the Wives, who are sterile. She performs this duty against her will, struggling to maintain her sanity while remembering the way life used to be when she was free. Her story serves as a cautionary tale for women who take their own freedoms for granted. (Atwood 1986; McCombs 1988)

See also Atwood, Margaret; Feminism; *Handmaid's Tale, The;* Joy, Serena

Old Lodge Skins

In *Little Big Man,* Thomas Berger's 1964 novel about the mistreatment of Native Americans during the 1800s, Old Lodge Skins is peace chief of a Cheyenne tribe. According to the story's narrator, Jack Crabbe, this means that he advises his people on daily matters but does not lead them into battle. Fighting is the duty of the war chief. Old Lodge Skins is a wise and thoughtful man. His people do not call themselves Cheyenne, which is a white man's term, but rather Tsistsistas, which means "the human beings." However, white soldiers do not consider them human beings and want to exterminate them. They systematically set out to destroy their villages and put them in compounds with other Native Americans. Eventually the tribal leaders fight back, slaughtering General George Armstrong Custer's troops at the Battle of the Little Big Horn.

After the battle Old Lodge Skins, who is nearly blind, sees a great deal, and he realizes that his people and white men have different philosophies regarding battles. He says that for the Cheyenne, who enjoy a good fight, after the Little Big Horn

it would now be the turn of the other side to try to whip *us*. We would fight as hard as ever, and perhaps win again, but they would definitely start with an advantage, because that is the *right* way. There is no permanent winning or losing when things move, as they should, in a circle. For is not life continuous? And though I shall die, shall I not also continue to live in everything that *is*? . . . But white men, who live in straight lines and squares, do not believe as I do. With them it is rather everything or nothing. . . . And because of their strange beliefs, they are very persistent. They will even fight at night or in bad weather. But they hate the fighting itself. Winning is all they care about, and if they can do that by scratching a pen across paper or saying something into the wind, they are much happier. . . . For killing is a part of living, but they hate life. They hate war. (Berger 1964, 433–434)

Old Lodge Skins then decides that he has lived too long. He prays and gives thanks to the Everywhere Spirit who made all people, sings a death song, and dies. (Berger 1964)

See also Berger, Thomas; Crabbe, Jack; *Little Big Man;* Racism

Olenska, Countess Ellen

In Edith Wharton's 1920 novel *The Age of Innocence,* Countess Ellen Olenska is an unconventional woman who lives in a conventional age. During the 1870s she leaves her Polish husband and moves in with her relatives in New York, where she discovers a rigid set of social codes. She has difficulty fitting into this society; her untraditional clothing, friends, and behavior bring her much criticism. She also finds herself attracted to her cousin's husband, and when he asks her to run away with him, she realizes that he would be unhappy living outside of his society. In the end she leaves him and moves to Paris, where she believes that her bohemian lifestyle will be more acceptable. (Wharton 1993)

See also *Age of Innocence, The;* Exiles; Feminism; Wharton, Edith

Olsen, Tillie

A political activist during the Great Depression, Tillie Olsen is the author of the unfinished novel *Yonnondio: From the Thirties* (1974). She was born January 14, 1913, on a Nebraska tenant farm. Her parents, Samuel and Ida Lerner, were socialist Russian Jews who emigrated to the United States after the failed 1905 revolution in their homeland. In 1917 they took their six children to Omaha, Nebraska, where Olsen's father found work at the local meatpacking house. This setting features prominently in *Yonnondio,* which is partly autobiographical.

In Omaha Olsen was exposed to many socialist ideas. Her father was active in the Socialist Party and had many guests in his home, including workers who wanted to organize themselves and fight unfair labor practices. During her high school years, Olsen herself became a worker, shelling almonds at a local processing plant. She also joined the Young People's Socialist League.

In 1929 when the Depression began, Olsen quit high school and took a series of low-paying jobs. Over the next four years she moved several times, from Nebraska to California, then to the Kansas-Missouri area, Minnesota, and back to California again. She also started writing both poetry and novels and became involved in the Communist Party. While in the Kansas-Missouri area, she was arrested briefly for passing out leaflets to packing house workers. While in Minnesota, her first daughter was born.

In 1934 she settled in San Francisco, California, where she became romantically involved with a leader of the Young Communist League, Jack Olsen. He had a job in a waterfront warehouse and encouraged Tillie to help him organize the workers there. She wrote and passed out leaflets and was consequently arrested during a general strike. Shortly thereafter she published several poems and short pieces in support of workers' rights, as well as the short story "The Iron Throat," which was actually the first chapter of her novel *Yonnondio.*

Over the next several years she continued to be involved in workers' rights. In 1939 she joined the Congress of Industrial Organizations and soon became its California director.

By this time her second daughter had been born, and, in 1943, after giving birth to a third, she married Jack Olsen. The following year she worked to establish San Francisco's first child care center. Her fourth daughter was born in 1948, whereupon Tillie became involved in bettering public schools and libraries. She was also an antinuclear activist. However, the pressure of raising four children and working odd jobs to help support the family kept her from producing fiction.

In the 1950s, however, she once again began to write. During this period Senator Joseph McCarthy was persecuting American members of the Communist Party, and Olsen and her husband were labeled subversives. Forced to quit job after job, Olsen enrolled in a creative writing course, and in 1955 she published a short story, "I Stand Here Ironing." The following year she received a Stanford University Creative Writing Center Fellowship. In 1960, her novella "Tell Me a Riddle" won the O. Henry Award for Best Story of the Year. In 1964 this novella was published along with three short stories as a book entitled *Tell Me a Riddle*. Her novel *Yonnondio*, although unfinished, was published in 1974.

Olsen received a great deal of public recognition for both books. She became a writing professor, and over the next two decades she taught at several prominent universities, including Stanford University, Amherst College, Radcliffe, the University of Massachusetts in Boston, and the University of California at Los Angeles. She also received many prestigious writing awards and honorary degrees. In 1979 she published a nonfiction book about creativity entitled *Silences*. During the 1980s she wrote several essays, and today she continues to lecture about writing at various conferences throughout the United States, including the 1998 Festival of Books at the University of California at Los Angeles. (Nelson and Huse 1994; Olsen 1980; Pearlman and Werlock 1991)

See also Feminism; Labor Issues; *Yonnondio: From the Thirties*

One Day in the Life of Ivan Denisovich

The novel *Odin den iz zhizni Ivana Denisovicha* (One Day in the Life of Ivan Denisovich) was written by Aleksandr Solzhenitsyn, who opposed the prison camps that existed in the Soviet Union under Stalin's regime. Published in Russian in 1962 and in English in 1963, the novel presents a day in the life of a prisoner, Ivan Denisovich Shukhov, who was once a carpenter in a small village. During World War II he was captured by the Germans and escaped. His government then sent him to a forced-labor camp for having associated with the enemy. Now it is 1951 and Shukhov doubts he will ever be set free. Nonetheless, he does not submit to despair. As one of the best workers in the camp, he takes pride in his job skills and in his ability to stay alive under difficult living conditions. However, as he struggles to stay warm and get enough to eat, he reflects that he still has 3,655 days left to his sentence.

One Day in the Life of Ivan Denisovich was based on Solzhenitsyn's own experiences in Soviet labor camps; he spent eight years in forced labor for criticizing Joseph Stalin's policies. Its 1962 publication, initially in an issue of a Soviet magazine, was personally approved by Soviet president Nikita Khrushchev, who saw it only as a condemnation of an earlier era. Other people, however, quickly realized that that the novel was intended to criticize problems in Soviet society. In a 1963 introduction to the book, scholars Max Hayward and Leopold Labedz (ix) explain:

Solzhenitsyn goes far beyond the bounds of what had hitherto been permissible in public discussions about the past. He shows that the camps were not an isolated feature in an otherwise admirable society—the unfortunate result of a temporary "infringement of socialist legality"—but that they were, in fact, microcosms of that society as a whole. The novel draws an implicit parallel between life "inside" and "outside" the camp: A day in the life of an ordinary Soviet citizen had much in common with that of his unfortunate fellow countrymen behind barbed wire. We now see that on both sides of the fence it was the same story of material and spiritual squalor, corruption, frustration, and terror.

As a result of his honesty, Solzhenitsyn eventually got into more trouble with government authorities, and his subsequent works were not published in the Soviet Union. However, he continued to campaign for human rights, and in 1974 he was officially exiled from the country. (Carter 1977; Solzhenitsyn 1972)

See also Exiles; Prison Reform; Shukhov, Ivan Denisovich; Solzhenitsyn, Aleksandr

One Flew over the Cuckoo's Nest

One Flew over the Cuckoo's Nest (1962), by Ken Kesey, concerns conformity to social norms and questions society's definitions of insanity. Its narrator, Chief Bromden, is an inmate at an Oregon mental hospital. A Native American from a tribe on the Columbia River, he is an extremely tall, strong man but has been made to feel weak by white society. As a boy he became used to having his opinions ignored; now he pretends to be a deaf-mute and endures verbal abuse without complaint. Moreover, because he has been given medication and shock treatments to control his behavior, he sometimes imagines himself in a thick fog and believes that the hospital is part of a mechanized combine that uses mysterious technological devices to control people. In discussing the head nurse, Nurse Ratched, he says:

Practice has steadied and strengthened her until now she wields a sure power that extends in all directions on hairlike wires too small for anybody's eye but mine; I see her sit in the center of this web of wires like a watchful robot, tend her network with mechanical insect skill, know every second which wire runs where and just what current to send up to get the results she wants. . . . What she dreams of there in the center of those wires is a world of precision efficiency and tidiness like a pocket

watch with a glass back, a place where the schedule is unbreakable and all the patients who aren't . . . obedient under her beam . . . [sit in wheelchairs] with catheter tubes run direct from every pant-leg to the sewer under the floor. (Kesey 1964, 26–27)

For several years Nurse Ratched has had complete control over every person on her ward, patient or staff member. But at the opening of the novel a new inmate, Randall Patrick McMurphy, arrives to threaten her dominance. McMurphy feigned insanity to get himself transferred out of a prison work camp. He is a powerful, charismatic leader who brags about his sexual conquests, and the other inmates are immediately in awe of him. A gambler and a hustler with a strong sense of humor, he immediately begins challenging Nurse Ratched's rules through manipulative teasing and joking rather than violent confrontation. He convinces the ward's attending physician, Dr. Spivey, to allow the patients to use a spare room for card games and Monopoly and tries to gain permission to watch the World Series. When Nurse Ratched blocks his attempts to see the baseball game, McMurphy sits in front of the blank television screen and pretends he is watching anyway. The other inmates soon join him. Under McMurphy's spell, they have begun to share his strength of character and disrespect for authority, and Bromden believes that McMurphy has the power to make them all stronger not just in an emotional sense but in a physical sense as well. After McMurphy touches his hand, Bromden says: "I remember the fingers were thick and strong closing over mine, and my hand commenced to feel peculiar and went to swelling up out there on my stick of an arm, like he was transmitting his own blood into it. It rang with blood and power. It blowed up near as big as his, I remember" (23–24).

But one day McMurphy learns that because he was involuntarily committed to the hospital, Nurse Ratched holds the power to keep him there forever, whereas most of the other patients were self-committed and are therefore

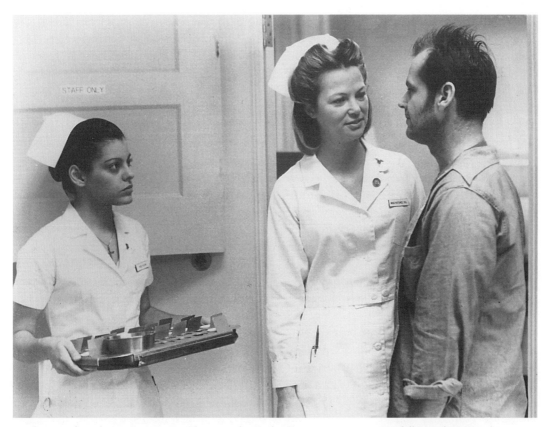

In this scene from the 1975 movie One Flew over the Cuckoo's Nest, *new inmate Randall Patrick McMurphy challenges the authority of Nurse Ratched. (United Artists/The Museum of Modern Art Film Stills Archive)*

free to leave at any time. He feels betrayed and decides to cooperate with the nurse, who quickly reestablishes her dictatorial control. When she closes the card-playing room and no one complains, McMurphy realizes that the others will not learn to stand up to her without his help. He "accidentally" puts his fist through her glass window and again becomes her opponent. Nurse Ratched quickly appears to accept defeat, but Bromden knows that she is only waiting for a chance to bring McMurphy down. Her chance arrives after McMurphy arranges for several of the patients to go on a fishing trip with Dr. Spivey. During the trip the patients grow much stronger, while McMurphy seems to be growing weaker and more tired. When they return home, an orderly goads McMurphy into getting into a fistfight with him, and he loses control. After Chief Bromden joins the fight, both inmates are taken away for shock treatment.

This is the turning point for Bromden.

Whereas before he allowed the treatments to propel him further into madness, this time he struggles toward sanity. When he returns to the ward, he is able to talk to the other men with confidence. McMurphy seems unchanged, but several of the inmates realize that their friend is not the same. They help him plan an escape, which will take place after a secret, middle-of-the-night party designed to help Billy Bibbett lose his virginity. McMurphy smuggles in a prostitute for Billy and himself, and the women bring alcohol. Everyone gets drunk and falls asleep, and McMurphy fails to make his escape. In the morning Nurse Ratched discovers what has happened, and she ridicules Billy Bibbett so cruelly that he later slits his throat. When the nurse blames McMurphy for this death, McMurphy loses control and attacks her. He is sent to another floor to have a lobotomy.

Meanwhile most of the other patients realize that they are no less sane than their keepers and check themselves out of the hospital. Shortly thereafter McMurphy returns to the ward as a "vegetable" on a gurney. That night Bromden kills McMurphy by smothering him with a pillow, then throws a heavy control panel through a window and escapes. He hitches a ride north toward his former home, clearly competent to face life in the outside world.

In analyzing *One Flew over the Cuckoo's Nest*, many scholars believe that Chief Bromden is the protagonist of the story because he has taken an almost mythic journey from insanity to sanity. Others, however, argue that the protagonist is actually McMurphy, an archetypal hero battling against an oppressive society as represented by Nurse Ratched. Bromden often comments on this society and on its ability to pressure people into submitting to conformity. For example, after seeing a train disgorge its passengers, "a string of full-grown men in mirrored suits and machined hats . . . a hatch of identical insects," he notes that they enter "five thousand houses punched out identical by a machine and strung across the hills outside of town," and he says:

All that five thousand kids lived in those five thousand houses, owned by those guys that got off the train. The houses looked so much alike that, time and again, the kids went home by mistake to different houses and different families. Nobody ever noticed. They ate and went to bed. The only one they noticed was the little kid at the end of the whip. He'd always be so scuffed and bruised that he'd show up out of place wherever he went. He wasn't able to open up and laugh either. It's a hard thing to laugh if you can feel the pressure of those beams coming from every new car that passes, or every new house you pass. (227–228)

The novel suggests that in fighting this conformity, McMurphy is a Christ figure who redeems men while sacrificing himself. There is a great deal of Christ imagery in the novel.

For example, when McMurphy is being prepared for shock treatment on a "crucifix-shaped table" he says, "Do I get a crown of thorns?" (270). His death gives Bromden a clear mind that allows him to break free of oppression.

However, despite the novel's strong social protest message and the fact that its narrator is a Native American, *One Flew over the Cuckoo's Nest* has been criticized for being a racist and sexist novel. Nurse Ratched and most other female characters in the book are depicted as evil emasculators, and the orderlies, all of whom are African American, as lazy, cruel, and cowardly. But Bromden's narration suggests that these traits do not apply to society as a whole because Nurse Ratched has skewed her staff in accordance with her own view of the world. He says:

Year by year she accumulates her ideal staff. . . . Her three daytime black boys she acquires after more years of testing and rejecting thousands. They come at her in a long black row of sulky, big-nosed masks, hating her and her chalk doll whiteness from the first look they get. She appraises them and their hate for a month or so, then lets them go because they don't hate enough. When she finally gets the three she wants . . . she's damn positive they hate enough to be capable. (27–28)

Moreover, the novel was published in 1962, when African Americans were typically relegated to menial jobs such as orderly or janitor and women who held positions of power were often seen as threatening. The 1960s were also a time when struggles against authority figures were becoming more common. Therefore, the book was very successful, as was a film version of the novel. Released in 1975, it was the first movie in 41 years to win all five top Academy Awards: Best Picture, Best Director, Best Screenplay, Best Actor, and Best Actress. (Kesey 1964)

See also Bibbett, Billy; Bromden, Chief; Kesey, Ken; McMurphy, Randall Patrick; Ratched, Nurse

O'Neill, Eugene

Eugene O'Neill was an American playwright who won the Nobel Prize in literature in 1936. He was deeply interested in the family relationships, and many of his plays concern broader social issues as well. Born on October 16, 1888, in New York, New York, O'Neill was the son of Irish immigrants. His father moved from poverty to wealth by becoming a famous actor. Consequently, O'Neill attended a Catholic boarding school, and in 1906 he enrolled in Princeton University. He was suspended a year later for bad behavior. After a series of odd jobs he shipped off to sea, but in 1912 he returned to New York and became an alcoholic vagrant. Shortly thereafter he tried to commit suicide. He then briefly held a job as a reporter, but in 1913 he was diagnosed as having tuberculosis and went to the Gaylord Farm Sanatorium in Wallingford, Connecticut. There he began to write plays. Between 1920 and 1943 he produced more than 20 works, only one of which, *Ah Wilderness!* (1933), was a comedy. His first major success was a play called *Beyond the Horizon;* it won the Pulitzer Prize and was produced on the Broadway stage in 1920. He also won Pulitzer Prizes for *Anna Christie* (1921), *Strange Interlude* (1928), and *Long Day's Journey into Night* (1956). However, many critics consider *The Iceman Cometh* to be his best work. Written in 1939 and published and performed in 1946, this four-act drama deals with self-deception and questions the motives of a social reformer. During the late 1940s O'Neill developed serious health problems. No longer able to write, he became a recluse. He died in Boston, Massachusetts, on November 27, 1953. (Clark 1947)

See also *Iceman Cometh, The*

Ontosoroh

The character of Ontosoroh appears in Pramoedya Ananta Toer's 1980 Javanese novel *Bumi manusia* (This Earth of Mankind). As a girl, Ontosoroh's native father gives her to a Dutch colonialist in exchange for a better job. She becomes the man's concubine and bears two children. In the beginning her husband, Herman Mellama, treats her well. He teaches her to read, write, and speak Dutch and trains her to run the family farm. She becomes a shrewd businesswoman. Then Herman is visited by his oldest son, Mauritas Mellama, whose mother lives in the Netherlands. The young man scorns his father for associating with natives and makes him feel ashamed. Consequently, Herman becomes a drunkard and begins associating with prostitutes at a nearby pleasure palace. Now Ontosoroh must run the farm by herself. She does a good job, but after Herman dies, Mauritas takes it over and throws her out. He also becomes guardian of Ontosoroh's half-European daughter, and the law recognizes Mauritas's right to separate Ontosoroh from her child. Nonetheless, she plans to continue fighting for her rights. (Toer 1996)

See also Mellama, Mauritas; *This Earth of Mankind;* Toer, Pramoedya Ananta

Oroonoko

Oroonoko: or, The Royal Slave, by Aphra Behn, criticizes the treatment of blacks by whites during the seventeenth century. Published as a novel in 1688 and presented as a play in 1694, it tells the story of Oroonoko, an African prince who always behaves honorably and is incapable of lying. As a young man he is tutored in French and English, and he proves himself a great soldier in battle.

One day he falls in love with a beautiful woman named Imoinda and asks her to marry him. She agrees, but before the wedding the king, Oroonoko's grandfather, hears of Imoinda's many virtues and forces her to become his wife instead. Oroonoko is upset but is determined not to go against his king. However, when he visits Imoinda at the palace, his passion overtakes him. Discovering that her marriage has not yet been consummated, he makes love to her. Later the king hears about this and sells Imoinda into slavery, but he tells Oroonoko she is dead.

Oroonoko grieves deeply for his lost bride. Then he and some of his friends are invited to a sumptuous dinner on a European ship. They become drunk, and the captain imprisons them before setting sail for Surinam, a

European colony in South America. Oroonoko rails against such trickery; among his own people, slaves are only those who have been captured nobly in battle. He therefore resolves to starve himself to death. However, the captain apologizes for what has happened and tells him that he will set him free at the next land they come to. He releases Oroonoko from his bonds on the promise that the prince will eat and behave well while on board. Despite this promise, Oroonoko is chained and sold as a slave as soon as they reach Surinam, where his regal bearing earns him the respect and admiration of everyone at the colony, including his master, Trefry.

Trefry has bought Oroonoko in the name of Surinam's lord-governor, who is off on a voyage, but Trefry promises that he will do everything possible to return the prince to Africa as soon as possible. Meanwhile Oroonoko, who has been renamed Caesar, discovers that Imoinda, now named Clemene, is at the colony. The two marry and she immediately becomes pregnant. Wanting his child to be born free, Oroonoko becomes even more eager to return to Africa.

> He was every day treating with Trefry for his and Clemene's Liberty, and offer'd either Gold, or a vast quantity of Slaves, which should be paid before they let him go, provided he could have any Security that he should go when his Ransom was paid. They fed him from day to day with Promises, and delay'd him till the Lord-Governour should come; so that he began to suspect them of Falshood, and that they would delay him till the time of his Wife's Delivery, and make a Slave of that too: for all the Breed is theirs to whom the Parents belong. (Behn 1973, 45)

Consequently, Oroonoko goes to the other slaves and entreats them to rise up against their masters, saying:

> And why . . . should we be Slaves to an unknown People? Have they vanquished us nobly in Fight? Have they won us in Honourable Battle? And are we by the Chance of War become their Slaves? This wou'd not anger a noble Heart; this would not animate a Soldier's Soul: no, but we are bought and sold like Apes or Monkeys, to be the sport of Women, Fools and Cowards; and the Support of Rogues and Runagades, that have abandoned their own Countries. . . . And shall we render Obedience to such a degenerate Race, who have no one human Vertue left, to distinguish them from the vilest Creatures? (61)

The slaves follow him into the jungle, and when their escape is discovered, they are pursued by the Europeans. There is a fierce battle, during which the other slaves desert Oroonoko. He continues to fight until Trefry convinces him to surrender on the promise that he and his wife will be returned to Africa. Afterward, however, the governor orders him whipped and tortured. When he recovers from his wounds, he vows to revenge himself on his captors. But first, afraid that Imoinda will be tortured for his deeds, he kills her and their unborn child. This act causes him such grief that he collapses and is unable to attack his captors. When they discover Imoinda's body, they try to arrest Oroonoko; he slices his own stomach in an attempt to kill himself. They chain him, heal him, and then publicly dismember him while he is still alive, hoping to make him an example to other rebellious slaves.

Author Aphra Behn points out that Oroonoko's behavior is more honorable than that of his Christian captors. She had an opportunity to witness such cruelties firsthand. *Oroonoko* was written while she was living in Surinam, and she introduces the novel as though it were a true story. (Behn 1973)

See also Behn, Aphra; Imoinda; Racism; Slavery

Orwell, George

George Orwell is the pseudonym of Eric Arthur Blair, an English novelist and essayist who often wrote against political and social oppression in his work. Born in India in

1903, Orwell attended Eton School in England. After graduation he traveled to Burma (now Myanmar), where he became a member of the Indian Imperial Police. He stayed in that position for five years. Eventually, however, he grew discouraged over the race and class distinctions in Burma. In 1927 he decided to travel through England and live among the poor. He dressed as a beggar to discover what it was like to be a social outcast and subsequently published a book about his experiences entitled *Down and Out in Paris and London* (1933). His first novel, *Burmese Days,* was published the next year. It, too, addressed the issue of social oppression, and there were elements of social protest in the two comic novels that followed it. Orwell began to identify himself as an independent socialist, and in 1937 he published a political treatise, *The Road to Wigan Pier,* to express some of his views. He also traveled to Spain to become involved in the Spanish Civil War, first as a reporter and then as a volunteer for Republican militia. In 1938 he published a book about his experiences, *Homage to Catalonia* (1938). It expressed his opposition to Communist oppression and totalitarian governments, a theme that would recur in his subsequent works. Orwell also worked as a journalist during World War II, and in 1945 he published the novel *Animal Farm,* which brought him international fame. His equally popular novel *1984* was published in 1949. Orwell died on January 21, 1950, in London, England. (Crick 1980)

See also *Animal Farm; 1984;* Science Fiction and Fantasy

Outsider, The

First published in 1953, *The Outsider,* by Richard Wright, examines racism in terms of the personal identity of blacks in the United States. Many scholars have compared it to Ralph Ellison's *Invisible Man* because both novels concern black men who try to use communism to become a part of the white world, but remain outsiders nonetheless.

The main character of *The Outsider* is a black man named Cross Damon, an intellectual who works as a postal clerk in Chicago. Unhappy with his life, he drinks heavily and abandons his wife and three children. When his underaged girlfriend becomes pregnant, she threatens to sue him for rape unless he marries her. Unfortunately, his wife not only refuses to give Damon a divorce, but also tells him that unless he pays her $800, she will turn him in to the authorities herself. Damon reluctantly takes out a loan from his employers. On the way home he is in a subway wreck, and the police mistakenly identify him as one of the dead. Now free of his past, he changes his name and makes plans to leave town. However, before he can escape, he runs into an old friend, who is shocked to see him alive. Damon kills the man.

Damon then takes a train to New York. En route he meets Ely Houston, the district attorney of New York City. Houston is curious about the black race, and the two men talk about the psychology of what Houston calls "excluded people" (Wright 1993b, 162). Houston is impressed with Damon's intelligence. Meanwhile Damon is feeling guilty and nervous about his fake identity. Shortly after Damon reaches New York, he realizes that he will need a birth certificate in order to get a job. He goes to a black cemetery and chooses yet another new name, this time of someone only three days dead. Damon knows that it will take far longer for officials in the Office of Public Records to learn of the man's death, and indeed he easily obtains a duplicate of "his" birth certificate. Damon is now Lionel Lane.

As Lionel he tracks down a black man he met on the train and through him meets Gilbert Blount, a white man who is in the upper levels of the Communist Party. Gilbert and his wife, Eva, are impressed with Damon. They mistakenly believe that he is in hiding from a crime against white injustice and view him as sympathetic to their cause. They ask him to come live with them, so that he can study communism. As Damon considers their offer, the story's third-person narrator explains: "He had no desire whatsoever to join the Communist Party, but he knew that he would feel somewhat at home with Communists, for they, like he, were outsiders. Would not Communism be the best temporary camouflage behind which he could hide from the law? Would not his secret past make the Communists think that he was anxious for their help? To be with them was not at all a bad way of ending his isolation and loneliness" (223).

Damon goes to live with the Blounts. When he arrives, they explain that they have invited him in order to make a political point. Their landlord, Herndon, is a racist fascist, and the Blounts know that the man will object to Damon living in his building. However, Damon's being there is legal. The Blounts hope to provoke some kind of incident with Herndon in order to make a point about racism in the United States. Unfortunately, this plan soon turns disastrous. Herndon demands to see Gil, and the two get into a horrible fight in the fascist's apartment. Damon walks in to find both of them bloody and battered. He grabs a table leg and smashes both of their heads, making it look as though they killed each other. He then goes out and makes the door lock behind him. When the police arrive, they believe as Damon had hoped. For a moment, however, Damon is afraid that the district attorney, whom he met earlier on the train, will realize that his name has changed. But Houston only recalls their pleasant conversation and treats Damon as a friend.

Meanwhile the Communist Party, in the person of a man named Hilton, is trying to use Gil's death to advantage. The Communists want Damon to say that he saw Herndon kill Gill before dying of his own wounds. Damon has admitted being in the apartment but says he was chased outside by Herndon before the two men died. In trying to convince Damon to support the Communist position, Hilton says:

> You are a Negro and you've an instinct for this sort of thing. I don't mean a racial instinct; it's a socially conditioned instinct for dissimulation which white Americans have bred in you, and you've had to practice it in order to survive. Watching and

coping with the racially charged behavior of white Americans are a part of your learning how to live in this country. Look, every day in this land some white man is cussing out some defenseless Negro. But that white bastard is too stupid in intelligence and deficient in imagination to realize that his actions are being duplicated a million times in a million other spots by other whites who feel hatred for Negroes just like he does; therefore, he is too blind to see that this daily wave of a million tiny assaults acts to build up a vast reservoir of resentment in Negroes. At night at home Negroes discuss this bitterly. But the next morning, smiling, they show up on their jobs, swearing that they love white people. . . . Why? You know the answer. They have to live, eat, have a roof over their heads. . . . So they collaborate with people who they feel are their sworn enemies. . . . White America has built upon something in you that can help the Party now. . . . If you are honest in your heart, you cannot deny the Party. (330–331)

Once again Damon does not accept the party's position, but he decides to cooperate nonetheless. Later he learns that Hilton has discovered evidence that Damon killed Gil and is planning to use it to control him. Damon then kills Hilton, too. Now the party is suspicious of Damon. Their members investigate his background, uncover his true name, and turn it over to the police. When Gil's wife, Eva, learns of Damon's deception, she kills herself; by this time she has fallen in love with him. Houston quickly realizes that Damon is a murderer but does not have enough evidence to arrest him. The two men talk, discussing lawlessness, racism, and the nature of outsiders. Finally Houston says:

> I'm pretty certain you're finished with this killing phase. . . . So, I'm going to let you go. . . . I'm going to let you keep this in your heart 'til the end of your days! Sleep with it, eat with it, brood over it, make love with it. . . . You are going to punish

yourself, see? You are your own law, so you'll be your own judge. . . . I wouldn't *help* you by taking you to jail. . . . I've very little concrete evidence. . . . And I'll not give you the satisfaction of sitting in a court of law with those tight lips of yours and gloating at me or any jury while we try to prove the impossible. . . . I'll not give you the chance to make that kind of fool out of me, Damon! (571–572)

But once Damon is out on the street, he realizes how alone he is. When a party member sneaks up on him and shoots him, he is almost glad to die. With his last breaths, he tells Houston: "I wish I had some way to give the meaning of my life to others . . . to make a bridge from man to man. . . . Starting from scratch every time is . . . is no good. Tell them not to come down this road. . . . Men hate themselves and it makes them hate others. . . . We must find some way of being good to ourselves. . . . Man is all we've got. . . . I wish I could ask men to meet themselves. . . . We're different from what we seem . . . maybe worse, maybe better . . . but certainly different. . . . We're strangers to ourselves" (585).

Earlier Cross's mother told him that he was named for Jesus' death on the cross. Therefore, according to scholar Maryemma Graham in a 1993 introduction to the work (xxviii), "because of the death-rebirth symbolism and the moral tone which Cross adopts, many critics have chosen to read this story as Wright's attempt to reinscribe a politically corrupt world with a moral message. Just as Cross Damon, himself demonic, is born again, so too must the ideas of humankind be grounded in morality." However, Graham believes that more emphasis should be placed on the work as "a cautionary tale about the excesses of individuality and the dangers of human alienation" (xxviii). She adds: "By demonstrating the consequences of human alienation—irrational, irresponsible murder and death—in a racist society, Wright highlights the inadequacy of interpretations which privilege individualism, even at the risk of being self-critical. Cross's fatal flaw is ultimately

his individualism. When carried to its logical conclusion, he has nothing left" (xxviii-xxix). (Gates and Appiah 1993b; Webb 1968; Wright 1993b)

See also Blount, Gil; Communism; Damon, Cross; Ellison, Ralph; Houston, Ely; *Invisible Man;* Racism; Wright, Richard

Ox-Bow Incident, The

The western novel *The Ox-Bow Incident,* by Walter Van Tilburg Clark, is about an American lynching. However, when it was published in 1940, many people believed its deeper meaning concerned the fascism of Nazi Germany, even though, as scholar Max Westbrook (1969, 11) points out, the Nazi parallel "ignores the fact that no one in the novel uses Nazi techniques, believes in Nazi values, or works for Nazi aims."

In an afterword to a 1960 edition of *The Ox-bow Incident,* Walter Prescott Webb (223) quotes author Clark as explaining: "The book was written in 1937 and '38, when the whole world was getting increasingly worried about Hitler and the Nazis. . . . A number of the reviewers . . . saw it as something approaching an allegory of the unscrupulous and brutal Nazi methods, and as a warning against the dangers of temporizing and of hoping to oppose such a force with reason, argument, and the democratic approach." But Clark (224) says that it was actually "a kind of American Naziism that I was talking about. I had the parallel in mind, all right, but what I was most afraid of was not the German Nazis . . . but that ever-present element in any society which can always be led to act the same way, to use authoritarian methods to oppose authoritarian methods."

Westbrook (1969, 67) believes that the book can be interpreted even more broadly, as an "archetypal ethic" representing the reality that "man does not achieve his real self in idea or office or emotion, but as an individual part of a larger whole. Man's only hope is to act from a sense of the integrity of that larger entity, and his most shocking failure is to murder innocent men on behalf of his own dedication to a severed piece of man called the

The cowboys prepare for a lynching in this scene from the 1943 movie The Ox-Bow Incident, *which depicts how mob mentality can lead to violence. (Twentieth Century Fox/Archive Photos)*

male ego." Westbrook (67) concludes that "the subject of *The Ox-Bow Incident* is not a plea for legal procedure. The subject is man's mutilation of himself, man's sometimes trivial, sometimes large failures to get beyond the narrow images of his own ego."

On the surface the novel is the first-person narrative of Art Croft, a cowboy who rides into the town of Bridger's Wells with his partner, Gil Carter. The two men have just spent a winter together on the range. Extremely irritable, they decide to get drunk at Canby's saloon, where they hear some disturbing news: someone has been rustling cattle from the valley, and everyone is a suspect, including Art and Gil. Therefore, the atmosphere in the bar is tense. When Art and Gil join a poker game, another cowboy, Farnley, implies that Gil is cheating. A fight breaks out between the two men; Canby ends it by hitting Gil over the head with a bottle.

After Gil recovers, a young cowboy, Greene, rushes in to report that the rustlers have killed Farnley's friend Kinkaid and stolen his cattle. Farnley declares that he is going to hunt the killers down. Other cowboys agree to go with him, declaring they will hang the rustlers as soon as they are found. Osgood, a minister, and Davies, who owns the town's only store, try to convince them to let the sheriff handle the situation. However, an old rancher, Bartlett, delivers a powerful speech convincing the group to take action. Bartlett criticizes the legal system, saying: "They don't wait for that kind of justice in Texas anymore, do they? No, they don't. They know they can pick a rustler as quick as any fee-gouging lawyer that ever took his time in any courtroom. They go and get the man, and they string him up" (Clark 1960, 35). While the men rush to find a rope, Davies asks Art to find the sheriff. Art discovers that the sheriff has gone out of town for the day and has left his deputy, Mapes, in charge. Mapes is eager to join the lynching party, as is Major Tetley, a prominent rancher.

After much discussion and argument, a posse of 28 men finally rides out after the killers. This group includes Davies and Sparks, a former minister, who want to convince everyone to return home; Sparks is the town's only African American, and he once saw his own brother lynched because of racism. Another reluctant participant is Tetley's son Gerald. Gerald tells Art that his father made him come along, explaining, "I'm here because I'm weak and my father's not" (106). Gerald believes that most of the other members of the group do not really want to be there either. He compares the men of the lynching party to a pack of wolves or coyotes and says: "We're doing it because we're afraid not to be in the pack. We don't dare show our pack weakness; we don't dare resist the pack" (106). Gerald then offers a scathing criticism of human nature, and Art becomes uncomfortable at his outburst. Art knows that he and Gil have joined the posse not because they believe it to be right but because they want to fit in with the other cowboys. As Westbrook (1969, 59) explains: "Both give in to society's divisive value system which associates virtue with a willingness to join the he-man lynch mob. Repeatedly, Art and Gil show themselves ready to fight with fists or with guns in order to show their allegiance to a cause in which they do not believe."

The two men often question their decision to be a part of the posse. Nonetheless, they continue forward. Along the way, tracks and witnesses reveal that three men and a herd of cattle are heading for the Ox-Bow, a small valley between high peaks. The posse follows their trail, even after heavy snow and darkness begin to fall. Finally it is so dark that the men do not see an approaching stagecoach until it almost runs them down. They yell, and the stagecoach drivers, thinking they are bandits, fire several shots into the crowd before stopping the coach. Art is hit in the shoulder but refuses to take the stagecoach back to town, partly because its passengers include Gil's girlfriend, Rose Mapen, and Rose's new husband,

who treats Gil badly. Art endures the painful bandaging of his wound and remounts his horse.

Finally the posse comes across three sleeping men: a cowboy named Donald Martin and his employees, a confused old man and a Mexican who at first pretends to speak no English. The Mexican has Kinkaid's gun, and nearby is a herd of cattle, marked with the brand of a local rancher named Drew. The posse concludes that the cattle are stolen and that these men killed Kinkaid. Martin insists that he bought the cattle from Drew, who let him take them without a receipt, and that the Mexican found the gun on the road. He says he is taking the herd to his new ranch in nearby Pike's Hole, where his wife and small children are waiting for him. The posse does not believe him. Major Tetley, who is now in charge, tells Martin that he and his friends must hang.

Martin begs the men to send someone to check out his story with Drew. No one is willing to do this, and after much arguing Martin finally resigns himself to his fate. He writes a farewell letter to his wife and gives it to Davies, who reads it and realizes that Martin is innocent. Davies tries to convince the posse not to go through with the lynching, but Major Tetley orders the hangings to proceed. Gerald does not want to participate because he finds lynching morally repugnant. Earlier he confessed to Art: "I tell you I won't go on living and remembering I saw a thing like this; was part of it myself. I couldn't. I'd go really crazy" (107). Major Tetley scorns his son's feelings and places him in charge of Martin's hanging. Gerald botches the job, so that Martin does not die. Major Tetley orders Farnley to shoot the dangling, choking man.

With the lynching over, the posse rides back to town. On the way the men encounter Drew, the sheriff, and Kinkaid, who had not been murdered after all. Now they know that Martin was telling the truth; the posse killed three innocent men. This mistake troubles everyone involved, particularly Gerald, Major Tetley, and Davies. Gerald tries to kill himself on the way back to town, and later he hangs himself in his barn. Shortly afterward his father commits suicide in his library. Davies is also tortured by guilt. He tells Art that he knew Martin was innocent and that he should have shot Major Tetley because it would have stopped the hangings. Art agrees that this would have been the only solution. Davies berates himself for lacking the courage to shoot, and it is clear that he will never forgive himself. In the end Art and Gil are glad to leave town and return to their range. (Clark 1960; Westbrook 1969)

See also Clark, Walter Van Tilburg; Croft, Art; Davies, Art; Fascism; Justice; Martin, Donald; Tetley, Gerald

P

Pardiggle, Mrs.

The character Mrs. Pardiggle appears in Charles Dickens's novel *Bleak House,* which was first published in serialized form between 1852 and 1853. She is a social worker whose own children are extremely unhappy and resent her activities. Moreover, she offers the poor her opinions but does nothing to ease their miseries. When she barges into one house to ask its owner questions and preach cleanliness, he says:

> I wants a end of these liberties took with my place. I wants a end of being drawed like a badger. Now you're a-going to poll-pry and question according to custom—I know what you're a-going to be up to. Well! You haven't got no occasion to be up to it. I'll save you the trouble. Is my daughter a-washin? Yes, she *is* a-washin. Look at the water. Smell it! That's wot we drinks. How do you like it, and what do you think of gin, instead! An't my place dirty? Yes, it is dirty—it's nat'rally dirty, and it's nat'rally onwholesome; and we've had five dirty and onwholesome children, as is all dead infants, and so much the better for them, and for us besides. Have I read the little book wot you left? No, I an't read the little book wot you left. There an't nobody here as knows how to read it; and if there wos, it wouldn't be suitable to me. It's a book fit for a babby, and I'm not a babby. If you was to leave me a doll, I shouldn't nuss it. How have I been conducting of myself? Why, I've been drunk for three days; and I'd a been drunk four, if I'd a had the money. Don't I never mean for to go to church? No, I don't never mean for to go to church. I shouldn't be expected there, if I did; the beadle's too gen-teel for me. And how did my wife get that black eye? Why, I giv' it her; and if she says I didn't, she's a Lie! (Dickens 1987a, 107)

Mrs. Pardiggle's response is to pull out a religious tract and begin reading it to him. She completely misunderstands the poor and seems to have become a charity worker for her own self-aggrandizement rather than for the good of the downtrodden. (Dickens 1987a)

See also *Bleak House;* Dickens, Charles; Poverty; Religion

Paris in the Twentieth Century

The novel *Paris au XXe Siècle* (Paris in the Twentieth Century) was written in 1863 by French science fiction author Jules Verne, but it was not published in France until 1994; an

English version first appeared in 1996. The original manuscript had been rejected for publication and was tucked away in a household safe. It was rediscovered by the author's great-grandson upon the sale of the Verne family home in 1989.

Set in the future (specifically, 1960), the novel concerns a young classical poet, Michel Dufrenoy, who cannot practice his art because society has become completely dedicated to science and technology. The only poets who succeed are ones who write about the glories of industrialism; people are uninterested in literature from earlier times. They also do not care for classical music, preferring a chaotic modern form that represents the dissonance of machinery. In this world Michel struggles to earn a living. He works at a bank until he is fired and then tries his hand at writing drama. However, dramatic works are written in collaborative groups according to a pre-scribed format, and Michel finds he cannot work this way. He values originality too much. He therefore decides to quit his job and write a book of poetry, but after much effort he realizes he will never get it published. Meanwhile he has fallen in love with the daughter of a classics professor who loses his job. One day in deep winter Michel goes to visit her and discovers that she and her father have been evicted. He cannot find them and believes that they will freeze to death on the cold Paris streets. In despair he goes to a graveyard and collapses on the snow.

Scholar Eugen Weber, in a 1996 introduction to the novel, explains that Michel's plight reflects the difference between this book and the other works of Jules Verne. Weber (xii) says: "In classic Jules Verne adventures the environment is there to be mastered; in twentieth century Paris it can only be suffered, and the narrative offers less entertaining descrip-tion than cultural criticism." In discussing this criticism, Weber compares the novel to Aldous Huxley's *Brave New World* and George Orwell's *1984,* both of which depict a bleak future of conformity and government control. He also likens one character in *Paris in the Twentieth Century,* a man who is trying to save great literature of the past, to the book-savers in Ray Bradbury's *Fahrenheit 451.*

Interestingly, Weber also points out that Verne predicted many of today's modern con-veniences long before they were invented. For example, the novel mentions automobiles, el-evated railways and subways, electric musical instruments, the electric chair, fax machines, copy machines, and calculators. It also men-tions many social problems that did not yet exist, such as the corruption of the French language by American phrases, the weakening of marriage as an institution, and the increas-ing acceptability of illegitimate births. Nonetheless, Verne's publisher, Pierre-Jules Hetzel, rejected the manuscript as implausi-ble, saying, "No one today will believe your prophecy" (xxv). (Verne 1996)

See also Bradbury, Ray; *Brave New World;* Dufrenoy, Michel; *Fahrenheit 451;* Huxley, Aldous; *1984;* Orwell, George; Science Fiction and Fantasy; Verne, Jules

"Parish Workhouse, The"

The 1807 poem "The Parish Workhouse," by George Crabbe, concerns itself with a poor-house housing children and their parents, along with widows, unmarried women, the handicapped, the insane, and the chronically ill. It is a place of grief and toil, in sharp con-trast to life among the rich. The poet criticizes those more fortunate who complain of imagi-nary pains, lying on a "downy couch" and ask-ing their doctor "to name the nameless ever-new disease" when there is real suffering in the world (Sinclair 1996, 99). He asks such com-plainers: "How would ye bear in real pain to lie, / Despised, neglected, left alone to die?" (99). (Sinclair 1996)

See also Crabbe, George; Poverty

Path of Thunder, The

Written by South African author Peter Abra-hams, this novel addresses the issue of interra-cial marriage in South Africa. It was published in the United States in 1948, just one year prior to South Africa's passage of the Prohibi-tion of Mixed Marriages Act, which made such unions illegal. *The Path of Thunder* was therefore banned for publication and distribution in Abrahams's native country.

In the novel Abrahams (1975, 29) explains that there are three classes of people in South Africa: whites, blacks, and coloureds, who are "neither white nor black; neither Europeans nor native Africans but a blending of the two that was at once different from both white and black, and lived neither in the one world nor in the other, but precariously between the two." These three races exist on a "colour bar" that ranks racial superiority, with whites at the top, coloureds in the middle, and blacks at the bottom. Therefore, the novel's main character, a coloured teacher named Lanny Swartz, thinks himself better than Mako, the Zulu teacher from a neighboring black village.

Lanny has returned to his hometown, Stilleveld, after earning his teacher's certificate and arts degree in Capetown, South Africa. Now that he is an educated man, Lanny finds himself emotionally distant from his people. The only person he can talk to about his feelings is Isaac Finkelberg, the well-educated son of a Jewish shopkeeper. He and Isaac have long conversations that often include Isaac's friend Mako. He believes in black nationalism and criticizes the coloureds for feeling superior because they have white blood in them. He says that "they try to grade toward the white man because he has power. They accept the inferior position and try to escape it by trying to become white themselves. You see, it is a slavery of the mind and that is even worse than the slavery of the body" (91). He also applies this attitude toward interracial marriages, arguing: "If it is compensation for not being white then I will fight it with all my strength. If it is the business of a man and a woman who love and have stepped above and beyond color then it is their business" (91).

Nonetheless, when Lanny falls in love with Sarie Villier, a young white woman from a prominent family, Mako tries to convince him to give up the affair. Sarie is related by adoption to a prominent white landowner, Gert Villier, and Mako knows that this will bring Lanny trouble. He tells Lanny:

If our country were a free country where people lived freely and not like slaves it would be only your business and her business. In a world that is sane I would wish you luck, and you two, coloured boy and white girl, would be married and would be happy. But it is not so. Here the black people are like slaves. The white people here fear the very idea of equality between you and that girl and when they find out, there will be trouble for you, you know that, and there will be trouble for her too. It will lead only to unhappiness and pain. (232)

Lanny refuses to listen, even after he learns that another villager, a crippled, mentally disturbed person called "Mad Sam," once a normal young man named Sam Du Plessis, was in love with a white woman related to Gert Villier. When this love was discovered, Gert beat Sam nearly to death, and soon thereafter the young woman died under mysterious circumstances. Now Sam works for Gert. According to scholar Robert Ensor (1992, 174), Sam symbolizes "alienated manhood, deformed and literally rendered impotent by white male dominance."

Similarly, Gert tries to emasculate Lanny. When the teacher first comes to Capetown, the white man threatens him, saying: "You are proud. You feel as good as any man. . . . You have forgotten your place! . . . *We* don't like that sort of spirit here" (63). Gert expresses nothing but hatred for Lanny, who eventually discovers that he and Gert are actually half brothers. This relationship means nothing to Gert. When he finds out that Lanny and Sarie are planning to run away together to Portuguese East Africa, where interracial mingling is allowed, Gert lies in wait for Lanny. He beats the young man until Mad Sam intervenes. Sam and Gert struggle, and in the end both die of knife wounds. Lanny then flees to Sarie's house, and the two try to hold off Gert's friends. A gunfight breaks out, and the next day the newspaper reports that "a young coloured teacher . . . had run amok, killed a prominent farmer, Mr. Gert Villier, and then been chased into the house of Mr. Villier. Alone in the house was Miss Sarie Villier. He had found a gun, shot her, and then turned the gun on his pursuers. In the ensuing battle three other people had been killed before Swartz had finally been shot down" (279).

Ensor (1992, 128) reports that Lanny and Sarie's "unity in death is not in itself a conclusion to the struggle for equality as it does not penetrate into the consciousness of the dominant white community." However, he (128) adds that "their short-lived relationship . . . serves as an example, pointing ahead to a future liberation and opens up the possibility of interracial love." In fact, at one point in *The Path of Thunder* Mako suggests that Lanny think more about the future than the present, saying that he should not only give up Sarie but "go away from here, live in another place and fight till your people are no longer slaves so that one day in the future if another coloured man loves another white woman they will be free to love openly and it will not be a crime. That is a good thing to do for your people. And in the fight you will find forgetfulness and your pain will be less. . . . For [our generation] there is no time for love. There is only the fight to live and be men instead of slaves" (Abrahams 1975, 232). However, Mad Sam disagrees with this position. He argues that "love is the only thing that can kill hate, nothing else. You see, hate destroys and that's why love is stronger. It builds. There is hope for all the coloured people in this country while one white woman can love one coloured man" (177).

Abrahams relates Lanny and Sarie's love to a relationship expressed in the poem "Tableau," by Countee Cullen, which he quotes in the novel. This poem describes a moment when "the black boy and the white" can walk together "locked arm in arm" along a "path of thunder," despite the censure of their communities (241). Cullen was a black American poet and one of the leaders of a black literary movement called the Harlem Renaissance. According to Ensor, Abrahams's work was heavily influenced by this movement, as well as by the work of social protest author Richard Wright. Ensor compares the

structure of *The Path of Thunder*, which is divided into three sections entitled "Home," "Love," and "Hate," to the structure of Wright's novel *Native Son*, which is divided into three sections entitled "Fear," "Flight," and "Fate." (Abrahams 1975; Ensor 1992)

See also Abrahams, Peter; Apartheid; Cullen, Countee; Finkelberg, Isaac; Mako; *Native Son;* Racism; Swartz, Lanny; Wright, Richard

Paton, Alan

Alan Stewart Paton was a prominent South African writer whose novel *Cry, the Beloved Country* (1948) brought international attention to his country's policies regarding racial discrimination and segregation. Born January 11, 1903, in Pietermaritzburg, Natal, South Africa, he attended the University of Natal and became a teacher and then a principal. He worked for reforms at his school, and in 1953 he helped form the Liberal Party of South Africa, which sought to end apartheid. That same year he published the novel *Too Late the Phalarope.* He subsequently wrote a short story collection and two collections of articles and speeches, as well as novels, biographies, memoirs, and a newspaper column. He died on April 12, 1988, near Natal. (Callan 1982)

See also Apartheid; *Cry, the Beloved Country;* Racism

Peace

Peace, by Aristophanes, is the second play in a series of three comedies about the Peloponnesian War (431–404 B.C.) between the rival Greek city-states of Athens and Sparta. First performed in 422 B.C., it was preceded by *The Archanians* in 426 B.C. and followed by *Lysistrata* in 411 B.C. It concerns a patriot named Trygaeus who trains a dung-beetle to fly him to the home of the god Zeus on Mount Olympus. Trygaeus wants to convince Zeus to end the war, but at Olympus he finds that Zeus has given his house to the god War and that the goddess Peace is now War's prisoner in a distant pit. After some difficulty Trygaeus frees Peace and restores her to her honored place on earth. (Aristophanes 1930; Murray 1933)

See also *Archanians, The;* Aristophanes; *Lysistrata;* Peace

Peace

Peace appears as the main theme in many works of social protest. One early example is the play *Peace,* by Aristophanes. Later examples include the antiwar novels *Stalingrad,* by Theodor Plevier, and *Catch-22,* by Joseph Heller. Science fiction novels such as *Brave New World,* by Aldous Huxley; *Looking Backward, 2000–1887,* by Edward Bellamy; *1984,* by George Orwell; *Planet of the Apes,* by Pierre Boulle; and *Player Piano,* by Kurt Vonnegut deal with the issue of peace by showing how futuristic societies deal with conflict. Works that discuss socialist revolutions and fascism also talk about conflict; however, they often advocate war rather than peace. (Cohen 1962; Hook 1959)

> See also Aristophanes; Bellamy, Edward; Boulle, Pierre; *Brave New World; Catch-22;* Fascism; Heller, Joseph; Huxley, Aldous; *Looking Backward, 2000–1887; 1984;* Orwell, George; *Peace; Planet of the Apes; Player Piano;* Plevier, Theodor; Socialism; *Stalingrad;* Vonnegut, Kurt

Peace, Sula

Sula Peace is the main character of Toni Morrison's 1973 novel *Sula.* Restless because she has no outlet for her creative energies, she behaves contrary to the morals of her black community. Her neighbors therefore ostracize her. After her death, however, her former best friend, Nel Wright, recognizes the value of Sula's individuality and vitality. (Gates and Appiah 1993c; Morrison 1974)

> See also Feminism; Morrison, Toni; *Sula;* Wright, Nel

Penochkin, Arkady Pavlych

Russian landowner Arkady Pavlych Penochkin appears in the short story "Bailiff," which is part of an 1852 collection entitled *Zapiski okhotnika* (A Sportsman's Sketches). Written by Ivan Turgenev, this collection emphasizes the unfair treatment of the peasants by the landed gentry, and "Bailiff" is perhaps its harshest story. In it, Penochkin treats his peasants poorly and feeds them very little, a fact that causes the first-person narrator of the story to say:

> A strange kind of unease seizes hold of you in his house; even the comforts of it evoke no pleasure, and each evening, when the frizzle-haired lackey appears before you . . . and proceeds deferentially to pull off your boots, you feel that if only in place of his lean and hungry figure there were suddenly presented to you . . . a strapping lad just brought in from the plough by the master of house . . . you would be indescribably pleased and would willingly submit to the danger of losing, along with your boot, the whole of your leg right up to the thigh. (Turgenev 1983, 101–102)

(Lloyd 1972; Turgenev 1983)

> See also *Sportsman's Sketches, A;* Turgenev, Ivan

Piggy

In the microcosm of society represented in William Golding's 1954 novel *Lord of the Flies,* the character "Piggy" has the role of scapegoat. He is a bright but overweight child stranded on an island with a group of British schoolboys. With no adults present, Piggy endures teasing, yet continues to make suggestions that help the boys survive. He is an important member of the group, and his eyeglasses are the only way the children can light fires. Nonetheless, his intelligence separates him from the rest of his society. In fact, one of the boys, Jack Merridew, hates Piggy so much that he convinces the rest to steal his glasses, which by then are cracked, and kill him. (Golding 1954)

> See also Golding, William; *Lord of the Flies;* Merridew, Jack

Pittman, Jane Brown

Jane Brown Pittman is the first-person narrator of Ernest J. Gaines's 1971 novel *The Autobiography of Miss Jane Pittman.* An African-American woman over 100 years old, she describes her life in Louisiana from the time of the Civil War to the beginning of the civil rights movement. She is an intelligent, perceptive, strong-willed character who represents an indomitable spirit in the fight against racism. (Gaines 1971)

> See also *Autobiography of Miss Jane Pittman, The;* Gaines, Ernest J.

Planet of the Apes

Published in 1963, the science fiction novel *La Planète des singes* (Planet of the Apes), by Pierre Boulle, depicts racism and rigid thinking in a simian society on the planet Soror. Its first-person narrator, a French journalist named Ulysse Merou, travels there from Earth in the year 2500 in the company of a brilliant scientist, Professor Antelle, and his protégé, Arthur Levain. The three men take a small craft from their spaceship to the planet's surface, where they encounter a primitive tribe of humans who attack them simply to destroy their clothes and equipment. Merou notes that these people are apparently unintelligent and unable to smile or talk. He finds one young woman, whom he names Nova, particularly attractive.

The scientists spend the night in the humans' camp, and the next morning they are awakened by shouts and gunshots. They flee the sounds with the rest of the humans, but Professor Antelle cannot keep up and is left behind. Meanwhile Merou and Levain soon find themselves surrounded by hunters. To Merou's horror, these hunters are not humans but gorillas. He is astonished to see them wearing clothes, firing guns, and shouting orders to their assistants, who are chimpanzees. Merou hides in the brush, but Arthur Levain panics and bursts into the clearing, where he is shot dead. While his killer is reloading, Merou runs away but is snared in a net. He is then taken to a research laboratory, where he speaks to his guards. They are astonished by his vocalizations but do not understand his language. They call one of the scientists, a female chimpanzee named Zira, who suspects that Merou might have some form of intelligence. She reports this to her superior, an

orangutan named Zaius, but he refuses to listen, believing that Merou was once an ape's pet who has been taught some simple tricks. He continues to treat Merou as an ignorant animal and gives him Nova, who has also been captured, as a mate.

Meanwhile Zira meets with Merou in secret to teach him her language. In return, he teaches her French. Together the two discuss his journey from Earth and the differences between Earth and Soror. Zira introduces Merou to her fiancé, Cornelius, who arranges for the man to appear at a scientific gathering. The assembled guests believe that Merou is there to do some tricks. Instead, he delivers a speech about his journey from Earth and the wonders of technology he can show them.

The apes decide to release him to work with Cornelius. One day the two travel to an archaeological dig, where they discover evidence that an advanced human culture existed on the planet over 10,000 years ago. Back at the laboratory, Cornelius manipulates human brains to extract collective memories of the race and discovers that humans were once masters over apes. Gradually the apes learned to mimic their oppressors and took over the planet. The humans then descended into a primitive state. Cornelius has proof that men can easily revert to a savage state; a few weeks earlier Merou discovered Professor Antelle in the zoo, and the scientist had forgotten how to talk or behave in a civilized manner. Despite Merou's efforts to rehabilitate him, Antelle remains savage and stupid.

Cornelius's discoveries about ape evolution are revolutionary, and he is afraid to reveal them to his superiors. At the same time the government has decided that Merou is a threat to the ape way of life. Nova has given birth to his child, and the boy has demonstrated intelligence and an ability for speech. Fearing that the family could create a new race of clever humans, government officials plot to kill Merou and Nova and imprison their baby in a research institution. Before this can happen, Zira and Cornelius switch the family with three humans who are to be sent into space on an experimental satellite. Merou then pilots the satellite to his spaceship and takes off for Earth. When he arrives there, he discovers that gorillas are running the airport. He takes off again, planning to find a safe planet somewhere. Meanwhile he places his story in a sealed bottle and jettisons it into space.

The main plot of *Planet of the Apes* is framed by the discovery of the bottle by a young couple, Phyllis and Jinn, who are taking a holiday in space. They are not from Earth, but because Jinn once went to school there, he can read the manuscript. At the end of the novel they express disbelief over Merou's story, and the reader learns that they are chimpanzees.

Planet of the Apes blames the deterioration of the human race on its loss of interest in mental pursuits. In the section describing the collective memory of the race, Merou quotes one woman as saying: "What is happening could have been foreseen. A cerebral laziness has taken hold of us. No more books; even detective novels have now become too great an intellectual effort. No more games; at the most a hand or two of cards. Even the childish motion picture does not tempt us any more. Meanwhile the apes are meditating in silence. Their brain is developing in solitary reflection" (Boulle 1963, 116).

Similarly, in discussing how easy it was for apes to take over human activities, Merou says:

What is it that characterizes a civilization? . . . Let us concede that it is principally the arts, and first and foremost, literature. Is the latter really beyond the reach of our higher apes, if it is admitted that they are capable of stringing words together? Of what is our literature made? Masterpieces? . . . But once an original book has been written—and no more than one or two appear in a century—men of letters *imitate* it, in other words, they copy it so that hundreds of thousands of books are published on exactly the same theme, with slightly different titles and modified phraseology. This should be able to be achieved by apes, who are essentially imi-

tators, provided, of course, that they are able to make use of language. (100)

In fact, the orangutans in Soror's ape society are prolific authors, writing countless derivative works. They are rigid thinkers incapable of seeing reason. They are given control of the scientific community, even though the chimpanzees make most of the scientific and technical discoveries. Meanwhile the gorillas are masters at exploiting those discoveries and making them profitable. In this way each type of ape fulfills a designated role in society, exhibiting racism toward those unlike itself.

By showing the flaws in this fictional ape society, *Planet of the Apes* is actually criticizing real-life human society. However, many aspects of this criticism were missing from a movie version of the novel released in 1968. The movie attributed humanity's downfall not to a loss of intellectualism but to a nuclear war. The film is set entirely on Earth, although this is not revealed until the end of the story. (Boulle 1963; Frackman 1996)

See also Boulle, Pierre; Merou, Ulysse; Science Fiction and Fantasy; Zaius

Player Piano

The 1952 science fiction novel *Player Piano*, which was reissued as *Utopia 14* in 1954, is author Kurt Vonnegut's vision of a future where people are oppressed because of technology. A modern industrial revolution has occurred in the United States, and machines have replaced a large percentage of the nation's workers. Engineers, scientists, and managers who can care for machines have become an elite class. Meanwhile those people whose jobs have been replaced by machines must join either the army or the Reconstruction and Reclamation Corps, which performs menial jobs such as road repair.

The novel's main character, Dr. Paul Proteus, is a member of the elite class. He is in charge of the machines in Ilium, New York, but his wife hopes he will be promoted to the Pittsburgh division. Paul, however, is not seeking a promotion and is vaguely unhappy with his current job. He has been visiting the nonelite section of town and has realized that machines have increased unemployment, which in turn has increased a variety of social ills. In discussing the dispossessed workers, he tells his wife: "In order to get what we've got, . . . we have, in effect, traded these people out of what was the most important thing on earth to them—the feeling of being needed and useful, the foundation of self-respect" (Vonnegut 1980, 151).

Paul's friend Ed Finnerty has come to the same conclusion. One day he quits his job as an act of rebellion. Later he becomes involved in a revolutionary group, the Ghost Shirts, which intends to smash the machines and overturn the government. Because of Paul's continuing friendship with Ed, Paul's superiors pretend to fire him, so that he can join the Ghost Shirts as a spy. What they do not understand is that Paul shares the philosophy of the revolutionaries and soon becomes a true member of their group. He is arrested and put on trial, but he escapes when the Ghost Shirts begin their nationwide revolution. It is a failure everywhere but Ilium. However, after the machines are smashed, the working-class people begin fixing them again. Paul and his associates realize that human nature will not allow an end to technology, and they surrender to authorities.

Player Piano alternates Paul's story with chapters concerning a Middle Eastern shah who is visiting the United States. The shah's guide, an American diplomat named Ewing J. Halyard, keeps referring to the American people as "citizens." The shah insists on using the word *slave*. The shah is an astute judge of the nation's flaws, and Ewing's defense of U.S. society is weak. By the end of the novel Ewing has lost his job because of a technicality, and he realizes that the work policies of the United States are unjust. (Schatt 1976; Vonnegut 1980)

See also Proteus, Paul; Science Fiction and Fantasy; Vonnegut, Kurt

Plevier, Theodor

German novelist Theodor Plevier, who also used the pseudonym Plivier, protested Nazi political and social policies in his work. The German government banned his books in 1933 and expelled him from the country in 1934. Born in Berlin, Germany, on February 12, 1892, Plevier served in his country's navy during World War I. In 1918 while the government was discussing the terms of its surrender, he participated in a mutiny of the German fleet in Kiel, Germany. Afterward he became a Communist and was involved in liberal causes. He began writing articles and novels to express his views. His best-known work is a trilogy of novels concerning World War II, *Stalingrad* (1945), *Moskau* (Moscow, 1952), and *Berlin* (1954). Plevier died in Avegno, Switzerland, on March 12, 1955. (Plevier 1948)

See also Peace; *Stalingrad*

Ponderevo, George

George Ponderevo is the first-person narrator of *Tono-Bungay* (1908), by H. G. Wells. A successful British boat builder, Ponderevo reflects on a time in his life when he made money through less honest means. His uncle Edward, a chemist, created a worthless medicine called Tono-Bungay, and the two men used clever advertising to promote it. Soon they were rich, but George's conscience was troubled. Meanwhile his uncle squandered their fortune, turned to forgery, and died a ruined man. George now realizes how easily greed can corrupt people's morals. He also criticizes British society for creating the conditions under which greed can spread. (Wells 1935)

See also Quap; *Tono-Bungay*; Wells, H. G.

Pontmercy, Marius

Marius Pontmercy is a French revolutionary in Victor Hugo's 1862 novel *Les Misérables*. He was raised by his grandfather, a royalist, but becomes estranged from him when he expresses his support for the politics of his deceased father, who was one of Napoleon's soldiers. After leaving his grandfather's house, Marius becomes involved with a revolutionary group and participates in a citizen uprising in June 1832, during which he is seriously wounded. When he recovers, he reconciles with his grandfather and marries a beautiful young woman named Cosette. (Hugo 1987)

See also Cosette; Hugo, Victor; *Misérables, Les*

Possessed, The

Published in two volumes between 1870 and 1872, the novel *Besy* (The Possessed), by Fyodor Dostoyevsky, concerns social and political turmoil in Russia during the 1860s. At that time Russian liberalism was being supplanted by Russian radicalism, which sought to overthrow governments and undermine spiritual and moral beliefs. *The Possessed* criticizes this revolutionary movement, portraying its leaders as godless men who do not care about individual worth.

In a foreword to a 1936 edition of the book, scholar Avrahm Yarmolinsky (v) says that "Dostoyevsky's avowed intention in writing it was to drive home certain convictions of his, regardless of whether or not he met the requirements of the art of fiction. He wanted to deal a body blow to the rebels who threatened what he considered to be the foundations of Russian life." Consequently, the novel is "a tangled skein of many threads" with an intricate plot that presents the author's beliefs on a wide variety of political and social issues (vii). In particular, it highlights Dostoyevsky's belief that only through Christianity can humanity better itself. The novel's two main characters, Pyotr Stepanovitch Verhovensky and Nikolay Vsyevolodovitch Stavrogin, are both atheists who use people to their own advantage, Verhovensky on a political level and Stavrogin on a personal one.

Verhovensky is the son of eccentric writer and professor Stepan Trofimovich Verhovensky, whose friend, Mr. G—v, narrates the story. Stepan Verhovensky's patroness, Vavara Petrovna Stavrogin, is a member of the wealthy elite, and Pyotr Verhovensky uses this connection to Vavara to gain stature in the community for himself. At the same time he forms a small, secret revolutionary group whose intention is to sow discord throughout the area, "to bring about the downfall of everything—both the government and its moral standards" (617). To this aim, Verhovensky

Fyodor Dostoyevsky (Popperfoto/Archive Photos)

exhorts his followers to "organize to control public opinion; it's shameful not to snatch at anything that lies idle and gaping at us" (617). He has them print manifestos, which he then secretly distributes throughout the town in hope of inciting riots.

Verhovensky's ultimate plan is to use Vavara's son, Nikolay Vsyevolodovitch Stavrogin, to help him gain power once the government is overthrown. Verhovensky believes that Stavrogin, because he is nobly born, will be accepted as the new ruler of postrevolutionary Russia and that through Stavrogin Verhovensky's group will control the government. However, Stavrogin does not want to participate in the plan. He is a man troubled by guilt and a desire for self-punishment. The reason for Stavrogin's guilt is explained in a chapter entitled "At Tihon's," which the novel's original editor refused to print and which remained unknown until its publication in 1927. In it Stavrogin confesses to a monk named Tihon that he once sexually abused a 12-year-old girl, who then committed suicide.

This act has led Stavrogin to want to believe in the Devil, although he professes not to believe in God; therefore he is struggling with the issue of religious faith.

Because of this struggle, Avrahm Yarmolinsky (vii) calls Stavrogin "the real protagonist of the tale." He explains that Dostoyevsky originally planned to write a novel concerning the "Life of a Great Sinner" and that he incorporated parts of that work into *The Possessed*. Stavrogin represents Dostoyevsky's sinner, a man "unable to distinguish between good and evil, or to give himself in love, without attachment to his people and so without religious faith" and therefore "beyond the pale of the living" (viii).

Stavrogin becomes involved with several women during the course of *The Possessed*, and because he is incapable of love, he ultimately ruins them all. But he feels particularly guilty over the death of Marya Timofyevna, a mentally imbalanced girl whom he married out of his desire for self-punishment. Verhovensky ordered a convict named Fedka to kill the girl because she was not a suitable wife for Stavrogin and therefore would have interfered with his image of the new ruler of Russia. At the same time Fedka murdered Marya's brother, Captain Lebyadkin, for threatening to expose the secret organization.

But while Stavrogin's conscience is tortured by these deaths, Verhovensky feels no remorse over them. He is an atheist who does not believe in a punishing God, and he remains confident that his revolutionary group will succeed in taking over the government. When his followers start to doubt him, he falsely tells them that he is connected to hundreds of similar groups throughout Russia, implying that their organization is powerful. Nonetheless, Verhovensky's control over his group soon weakens. He argues with Fedka and later kills him. He also kills Shatov, who announced he was planning to leave the organization, and dumps the body in a remote lake.

Shatov's murder is actually based on a true event. In 1869 a Russian revolutionary group led by Sergey Nechayev killed one of its members and abandoned his body in a pond at the Moscow Agricultural Academy. According to Yarmolinsky, Dostoyevsky based *The Possessed* on this event, much in the way Theodore Dreiser based his social protest novel, *An American Tragedy*, on a real murder. However, Yarmolinsky also notes that, whereas Nechayev was born of peasants, Dostoyevsky chose to make Verhovensky the son of a professor and gentleman, a European sophisticate. Yarmolinsky says Dostoyevsky made this choice because he "hated the liberals who would Europeanize Russia, and considered them the begetters of revolution" (vi).

Moreover, in the end Verhovensky proves himself to be an ineffectual revolutionary. He convinces a troubled man, Kirillov, to confess to the murders in writing and then kill himself. Once Kirillov is dead, Verhovensky leaves town and disappears. Shortly thereafter the members of his group begin informing on one another. At the same time Stavrogin's guilt overwhelms him, and he hangs himself. Verhovensky's father also dies after an illness caused by disillusionment and grief; just before his death he questions his own atheism and begins to accept God. (Dostoyevsky 1936; Dostoyevsky 1968)

See also *American Tragedy, An;* Dostoyevsky, Fyodor; Dreiser, Theodore; Religion; Shatov; Stavrogin, Nikolay Vsyevolodovitch; Verhovensky, Pyotr Stepanovitch

"Poverty"

The short social protest poem "Poverty" is one of the few surviving works of the Greek poet Alcaeus, who lived from approximately 620 to 580 B.C. Published in the second century B.C., it was included in one of ten books of Alcaeus's poetry, along with other social and political protest poems, hymns, drinking songs, and love poetry. Describing a society where "wealth makes the man," it calls penury "the worst of ills" (Sinclair 1996, 283) and speaks of the desolation of the poor. (Sinclair 1996)

See also Alcaeus; Poverty

Poverty

Poverty is perhaps the most common problem depicted in social protest literature throughout the world. It appears in ancient writings, such as the poems of Alcaeus, as well as in modern novels, such as Kurt Vonnegut's *Player Piano*. Times of economic hardship inspire the largest amount of antipoverty literature. For example, George Crabbe, Charles Dickens, and Arthur Morrison wrote about poverty during the Industrial Revolution, and Rebecca Harding Davis, Tillie Olsen, Upton Sinclair, and John Steinbeck addressed the issue during the Depression. Poverty also appears in literature that addresses labor issues, socialism, capitalism, and a rigid class structure. In many works, such as Theodore Dreiser's *An American Tragedy*, George Gissing's *New Grub Street*, and Frank Norris's *The Octopus*, a desire for wealth leads to moral corruption, and the poor are depicted as more honorable than the rich. (Marris and Rein 1967)

See also Alcaeus; *American Tragedy, An;* Capitalism; Class, Social; Crabbe, George; Davis, Rebecca Harding; Dickens, Charles; Dreiser, Theodore; Gissing, George; Great Depression; Labor Issues; Morrison, Arthur; *New Grub Street;* Norris, Frank; *Octopus, The;* Olsen, Tillie; *Player Piano;* Sinclair, Upton; Socialism; Steinbeck, John; Vonnegut, Kurt

Power and the Glory, The

Published in 1940, *The Power and the Glory*, by Graham Greene, concerns religious persecution in Mexico during the late 1930s. The novel is set in the state of Tabasco, where Catholic priests are forbidden to practice their faith. In fact, unless a priest openly forsakes his religious beliefs by getting married, he is executed. As a result, at the beginning of the novel only one practicing priest still lives in the area.

The Power and the Glory traces this man's attempts to avoid capture while he continues to perform his duties. It also depicts his struggles to come to terms with his sins. He is an alcoholic who once fathered a child out of wedlock and therefore does not believe himself worthy of the priesthood. Nonetheless, he perseveres under deplorable conditions. He has little to eat and must run from one village to another to escape the police. His main pur-

suer, a police lieutenant, is a good man who is as passionate about communism as the priest is about Catholicism.

Finally the priest decides to leave Tabasco. He is almost to safety when someone comes to tell him that a dying man has requested his services. The priest recognizes the messenger as a police informant but still decides to go with him. Consequently, the priest is caught and sentenced to die. Just before his execution he becomes reconciled to his sins, and the day of his death another priest arrives in town to take his place.

Of the work Greene (1962, xiii) says, "I think *The Power and the Glory* is the only novel I have written to a thesis," which is that the power of the Catholic Church will remain despite human corruption and persecution. However, Greene's other novels are also set in oppressive world regions, including Cuba, Haiti, Czechoslovakia, Poland, Indo-China, Africa. (Greene 1962)

See also Greene, Graham; Religion

Prison Reform

Social protest authors often raise public awareness of prison conditions, and sometimes this has led to prison reforms. For example, John Galsworthy's play *Justice* brought about changes in England's prison system, and Charles Dickens's depiction of debtor's prison in *Little Dorrit* hastened its already impending demise. Leo Tolstoi and Aleksandr Solzhenitsyn called attention to problems within the Russian prison system. Authors Julia Ward Howe and Oscar Wilde were prison-reform activists, and writers concerned with the issue of justice, such as Victor Hugo and Ursula Le Guin, often discussed prisons in their work.

See also Dickens, Charles; Galsworthy, John; Howe, Julia Ward; Hugo, Victor; Justice; Le Guin, Ursula; *Little Dorrit;* Solzhenitsyn, Aleksandr; Tolstoi, Leo; Wilde, Oscar

Proteus, Paul

Dr. Paul Proteus is the main character in Kurt Vonnegut's 1940 science fiction novel *Player Piano*. Proteus's father was one of the leaders of an industrial revolution that made an American society almost completely dependent on machines. As a result of this revolution, many workers became unemployed, and society's middle class descended into poverty and dissatisfaction. Paul gradually realizes that mechanization is killing men's souls. He joins a revolutionary group, the Ghost Shirts, dedicated to destroying technology and overturning the government. In the process he loses his job, his wife, and his privileged status in society. At the same time he inspires others to revolt against society. But in the end the revolution fails, and Vonnegut suggests that this was inevitable because it is human nature to love machines. (Vonnegut 1980)

See also *Player Piano;* Vonnegut, Kurt

Q

Quap

A fictional radioactive substance, Quap appears in H. G. Wells's 1908 novel *Tono-Bungay* as a symbol of moral decay. It is part of a get-rich-quick scheme; the novel's main character, George Ponderevo, intends to steal the quap from an African island and sell it in England. Unfortunately, his journey is a failure. Everyone who handles the quap breaks out in sores, and George ends up shooting a native to keep the man from reporting the theft. In fact, George admits, "I hated all humanity during the time that the quap was near me" (Wells 1935, 339). When the crime is discovered, George barely escapes from the island. However, while at sea the quap destroys the cargo hold of his ship, and the vessel sinks. (Wells 1935)

See also Ponderevo, George; *Tono-Bungay;* Wells, H. G.

Quest, Martha

Martha Quest is the main character in Doris Lessing's five-novel series *Children of Violence.* The series explores her awakening to various social problems, including racism and anti-Semitism, as well as her interest in socialism and her struggle against a society that wants to see her as a wife and mother rather than an individual. In the end she discovers that she has psychic abilities and that the power to change society resides within herself. (Lessing 1964)

See also *Children of Violence;* Lessing, Doris

Quirk, Thady

First-person narrator of Maria Edgeworth's 1800 novel *Castle Rackrent,* Thady Quirk is an Irish servant devoted to the Rackrent family. In fact, he is so devoted that he excuses all of the Rackrents' faults, which are many. For example, when one of his masters, a drunkard, goes into debt by throwing lavish parties, Thady praises the man for being so merry and generous. He is therefore considered an unreliable narrator, and as such he is a device for Edgeworth's ironic criticisms of the Irish feudal system. (Edgeworth 1992)

See also *Castle Rackrent;* Edgeworth, Maria

R

Racism

The term *racism* refers to any prejudice against a person based on her or his inherited ethnic group or race. This prejudice is often based on an easily identified physical characteristic, such as skin color, or a behavior, such as a religious practice.

Racism against blacks in the United States is addressed in the works of James Baldwin, Ralph Ellison, Alice Walker, Richard Wright, and the authors of the Harlem Renaissance. It is also the subject of antislavery literature such as Harriet Beecher Stowe's novel *Uncle Tom's Cabin*. Racism in South Africa is the focus of antiapartheid writings such as Alan Paton's *Cry, the Beloved Country*. Racism against Jews, or anti-Semitism, is featured prominently in the novel *Children of the Ghetto* by Israel Zangwill.

Other groups have also experienced racism. For example, in *This Earth of Mankind*, Ananta Pramaodya Toer protests racism against native Javanese; in *Broad and Alien Is the World*, Ciro Alegría shows the persecution of Peruvian Indians; and in *Untouchable*, Mulk Raj Anand deals with the racism inherent in India's caste system. However, the most widely read and influential of works depicting racism against Native Americans, such as Thomas Berger's *Little Big Man* and Helen Hunt Jackson's *Ramona*, have been written not by Native Americans, but by whites; Native American authors more often protest racism through nonfiction or poetry. (Feldstein 1972; Frederickson 1997; Moss 1978; Witt and Steiner 1972)

See also Alegría, Ciro; Anand, Mulk Raj; Apartheid; Baldwin, James; Berger, Thomas; *Broad and Alien Is the World; Children of the Ghetto; Cry, the Beloved Country;* Ellison, Ralph; Harlem Renaissance; Jackson, Helen Hunt; *Little Big Man;* Native American Issues; Paton, Alan; *Ramona;* Stowe, Harriet Beecher; *This Earth of Mankind;* Toer, Ananta Pramaodya; *Uncle Tom's Cabin; Untouchable;* Walker, Alice; Wright, Richard; Zangwill, Israel

Radley, Arthur ("Boo")

The character Arthur "Boo" Radley appears in *To Kill a Mockingbird,* by Harper Lee (1960). He never leaves his house and is rumored to be crazy and dangerous. One day he saves the life of a little girl, proving himself to be a kind, compassionate man. Through this act the girl, who is also the narrator of the story, learns not to judge people by outward appearances or rumors. (Lee 1993)

See also Lee, Harper; *To Kill a Mockingbird*

Raisin in the Sun, A

The three-act play *A Raisin in the Sun,* by Lorraine Hansberry, was produced in 1959. It is credited with being the first drama by a black woman ever performed on Broadway, and is considered important for its statements on racism and a black family's pride in its African heritage.

However, audiences of the time were eager to dismiss the black pride elements of the story, remarking on how much the central characters, the Youngers, resembled white people. In an article about the play, one of its actors, Ossie Davis, explains:

> One of the biggest selling points about *Raisin*—filling the grapevine, . . . laying the foundation for its wide, wide acceptance—was how much the Younger family was just like any other American family. Some people were ecstatic to find that "it didn't really have to be about Negroes at all!" It was, rather, a walking, talking, living demonstration of our mythic conviction that, underneath, all of us Americans, *color-ain't-got-nothing-to-do-with-it,* are pretty much alike. People are just people, whoever they are; and all they want is a chance to be like other people. This uncritical assumption . . . made any other questions about the Youngers, and what living in the slums of Southside Chicago had done to them, not only irrelevant and impertinent, but also disloyal . . . because everybody who walked into the theater saw in Lena Younger . . . his own great American Mama. (Hansberry 1988, 9)

Lena is the head of her household, which includes her daughter, Beneatha; her son, Walter; his wife, Ruth; and his son, Travis. The family lives in a cramped ghetto apartment. At the beginning of the play Lena is awaiting the arrival of a check for $10,000, the insurance payment on the death of her husband. Walter wants to use the money to start a liquor business because he hates his current job as a white man's chauffeur. Meanwhile Beneatha argues that the money should

be used to send her to college. She is interested in her black heritage and wants to become a doctor, perhaps in Africa.

Lena decides to pay for Beneatha's schooling, but she refuses to let Walter buy his business. As a result, he becomes despondent, and his mood darkens further when Ruth tells him she's pregnant. The two discuss abortion, and when Lena finds out, she is horrified. Wanting to give her family hope for the future, she uses part of her money as down payment on a new home in an all-white neighborhood. This upsets Walter so much that he refuses to go to work anymore.

Finally Lena gives her son what is left of her money, telling him to spend part of it on the liquor business and put the rest in the bank for Beneatha. Instead, he gives all of it to his business partner, who promptly disappears. Now his dreams as well as Beneatha's have been destroyed, and when the white home owners' committee offers to pay the family not to move into the neighborhood, he considers taking the offer. Then he realizes that his pride and self-respect are more important than money. He turns down the offer just as the moving van arrives.

With this resolution, *A Raisin in the Sun* emphasizes the importance of dreams and hope. It also does this through its title, which was taken from the poem "Harlem," by black poet Langston Hughes. Hughes suggests that "a dream deferred" can "dry up / like a raisin in the sun" (Hansberry 1988, 3). (Cheney 1984; Hansberry 1994)

See also Hughes, Langston; Racism; *Raisin in the Sun, A;* Younger Family

Ralph

In William Golding's 1954 novel *Lord of the Flies,* Ralph symbolizes authority and civilized society. He is the elected leader of a group of British schoolboys stranded on an island without adults. Although he establishes rules and tries to maintain order, he eventually loses control of the group, and the boys begin to follow Jack, a primitive savage. Eventually Jack convinces his tribe to hunt and kill Ralph. Before they can catch him, however, he is rescued by the arrival of a British naval officer, the representative of an even stronger civilization. (Golding 1954)

See also Golding, William; *Lord of the Flies;* Merridew, Jack

Ramona

Published in 1885, *Ramona,* by Helen Hunt Jackson, changed public opinion about the American Indian. In a 1988 introduction to the work, Native American author Michael Dorris points out that it was Jackson's portrayal of her characters, as well as her criticisms about oppressive society policy, that made the work so effective. He explains: "By peopling these communities with [Native American] characters who exemplified the highest American attitudes and behaviors, Mrs. Jackson invited her readers to empathize with Native Americans whom the public had been educated—by a century of U.S. dishonor and conquest—to disdain. According to *Ramona* . . . [they] were paragons of industry, gentle creatures who were hard-working, law-abiding, and devout" (Jackson 1988, xvii).

For this reason, Dorris calls the novel propaganda and reports that it helped bring about the passage of the Dawes Act in 1887. This piece of legislation was intended to promote Indian homesteading by decreeing that tribal lands be divided into individual land grants. In actuality, however, the Dawes Act made it easier for white settlers to move into Indian Territory.

The year after the novel's publication, the *North American Review* compared *Ramona* with Harriet Beecher Stowe's 1852 novel *Uncle Tom's Cabin,* which created sympathy for black slaves and furthered the antislavery, or abolitionist, movement. According to Dorris (v), the magazine classified the two works as the greatest "ethical novels" of the century. But *Ramona* is also a love story. Set in California, its main character, Ramona, is the daughter of an Irish man and a Native American woman. She has blue eyes and does not look Indian. As an infant she is given to a wealthy but childless Mexican landowner to raise, and when the woman dies, her sister,

Señora Moreno, takes Ramona in. The girl does not know her ancestry, but because Señora Moreno knows Ramona's race, she cannot love her. Consequently, she treats the girl far worse than her own son, Señor Felipe.

One day Ramona falls in love with an Indian named Alessandro, and the two plan to be married. When Señora Moreno finds out, she is furious. She refuses to let Ramona marry an Indian and threatens to send her to a convent. Felipe, who loves Ramona himself, tries to convince his mother to change her mind. He wants Ramona to be happy. But although Señora Moreno agrees not to send the young woman away, she still refuses to sanction the marriage. As a result, Ramona and Alessandro are forced to run away together.

By this time Alessandro's people have been driven from their village by greedy white men, and the young couple must travel south to San Diego to find work. Eventually he earns enough money to start his own farm. When some white homesteaders take it away, the young couple must again travel to another town to start over. Along the way Ramona and Alessandro meet a kindly white woman, Aunt Ri' Hyer, who becomes like a mother to Ramona. Nevertheless, the hardships continue. Their firstborn child falls ill, and when Alessandro goes to a government doctor for help, the man refuses to see the little girl. Instead, he gives Alessandro some medication to take home. The tonic proves fatal. Saddened and hearing rumors that whites want to take over the new town, Alessandro and Ramona decide to move up into the mountains, where Ramona gives birth to another child. All goes well until Alessandro accidentally takes the wrong horse home from a nearby village. Before he can return it, the owner finds him and shoots him for horse thieving. Grief-stricken, Ramona falls unconscious and is too ill to testify at the man's trial. He is found innocent.

Meanwhile Señora Moreno has died and Felipe has been searching for Ramona. He finds her right after the trial and helps nurse her back to health. He also threatens to kill Alessandro's murderer, and the man flees the country. When Ramona recovers, Felipe takes her and her daughter home. Eventually he marries her, and the family moves to Mexico. Greedy Americans have begun taking away the land of the Mexicans in California, and Felipe knows he will not find justice there. (Jackson 1988; Mathes 1990)

> See also Alessandro; Hyer, Aunt Ri'; Jackson, Helen Hunt; Moreno, Señora; Native American Issues; Racism; Slavery

Rand, Ayn

American novelist Ayn Rand, in her writings, promotes selfishness, extols the virtues of capitalism, and opposes the oppressive nature of governments. She was born in St. Petersburg, Russia, as Alice or Alissa Rosenbaum on February 2, 1905. In 1926 she moved to the United States, where she worked as a Hollywood screenwriter. Her first novel, *We the Living* (1936), concerns a Russian career woman who struggles against government oppression. She followed it with *The Fountainhead* (1943), which addresses issues of creativity and nonconformity, and *Atlas Shrugged* (1957), which emphasizes the benefits of capitalism in furthering the interests of the individual. Rand also wrote nonfiction books and

Ayn Rand, 1957 (The New York Times Company/ Archive Photos)

journals related to her views. They include *The Virtue of Selfishness* (1964), *Capitalism: The Unknown Ideal* (1967), and *The Ayn Rand Letter* (1971–1976). She died on March 6, 1982, in New York, New York. (Baker 1987)

> See also *Atlas Shrugged;* Capitalism

Ransom, Basil

Basil Ransom is one of the main characters in Henry James's 1886 novel *The Bostonians.* A chauvinistic southern gentleman who practices law in New York, he falls in love with a speaker for the suffragette movement, Verena Tarrant. Throughout the course of the novel he tries to convince Verena that her feminist views are foolish. He expresses his own convictions with passion, and in the end he convinces her to marry him and abandon her cause. (James 1956)

> See also *Bostonians, The;* James, Henry; Tarrant, Verena

Ras the Destroyer

A character from Ralph Ellison's 1952 novel *Invisible Man,* Ras the Destroyer proselytizes black separatism on street corners in Harlem, New York, during the late 1940s. He berates blacks who join a Communist organization called the Brotherhood because the group is run by white men. He is eventually killed during a race riot incited by the Brotherhood. (Ellison 1952)

> See also Communism; Ellison, Ralph; *Invisible Man*

Ratched, Nurse

Nurse Ratched is the antagonist in Ken Kesey's 1962 novel *One Flew over the Cuckoo's Nest.* The head nurse in a mental hospital, she represents social conformity, rigid control, and the suppression of sexuality. She cannot stand to have her authority challenged or her femininity pointed out, and as she tries to emasculate the men in her care, she becomes increasingly cruel. This behavior calls into question society's definition of sanity. (Kesey 1964)

> See also Kesey, Ken; *One Flew over the Cuckoo's Nest*

Reardon, Edwin

Edwin Reardon is a character in George Gissing's 1891 novel *New Grub Street* who dies in poverty despite a once-promising career as a novelist. Marriage was his undoing; whereas he was able to support himself by writing books, he could not bring in enough income to provide for his wife and newborn son. Another character, Jasper Milvain, points out that Edwin Reardon could have maintained his literary career if only he had remained single, saying: "As a bachelor, he might possibly have got into the right circles. . . . But as a married man, without means, the situation was hopeless. Once married, you must live up to the standard of the society you frequent; you can't be entertained without entertaining in return" (Gissing 1926, 28). Milvain believes that Reardon should have at least married a rich woman, as he himself did. (Gissing 1926)

See also Gissing, George; Milvain, Jasper; *New Grub Street*

Reardon, Hank

In Ayn Rand's 1957 novel *Atlas Shrugged,* Hank Reardon is an industrialist who invents a new kind of metal. The material proves incredibly profitable, but Reardon's family makes him feel guilty for the wealth it brings him. Moreover, the government wants to take away his exclusive rights to manufacture the material. The novel presents a United States that takes from the rich and gives to the poor. It punishes Reardon for his inventiveness, and in the end he decides to join a group dedicated to ending the current regime. (Rand 1992)

See also *Atlas Shrugged;* Rand, Ayn

Reisling, Paul

A character in the 1922 novel *Babbitt,* by Sinclair Lewis, Paul Reisling struggles to conform to the expectations of American middle-class society but fails in the attempt. In his youth he wants to be a violinist, but after marrying he must become a roofing salesman to support his wife, Zilla. She proves to be a terrible nag, making him feel like a failure in life. He hates his job and grows despondent. Eventu-

ally he begins having an affair, but this only increases his misery. One day, in response to his wife's nagging, he shoots her. She recovers from her injury, but he is sent to prison. (Grebstein 1962; Lewis 1950)

See also *Babbitt;* Doane, Seneca; Lewis, Sinclair

Religion

When social protest authors criticize religion, they often do so on the basis of hypocrisy, arguing that a church's members often do not adhere to its rules. For example, in *Elmer Gantry* Sinclair Lewis exposes the transgressions of Protestant ministers. In *Major Barbara,* George Bernard Shaw shows how greed corrupts Salvation Army Christians.

In other cases social protest authors question theology and examine issues of faith. For example, Björnstjerne Björnson's play *Beyond Our Power* considers religious superstition. Graham Greene's *The Power and The Glory* deals with religious persecution in Mexico and the subsequent loss of faith among its Catholic priests. Shūsaku Endō examines the difficulties of adapting Catholicism to the Japanese way of thinking in the novel *Silence,* which also depicts religious persecution. (Commons 1967)

See also *Beyond Our Power;* Björnson, Björnstjerne Martinius; *Elmer Gantry;* Endō, Shūsaku; Greene, Graham; Lewis, Sinclair; *Major Barbara; Power and the Glory, The;* Shaw, George Bernard; *Silence*

Resurrection

The novel *Voskreseniye* (Resurrection), by Leo Tolstoi, protests the Russian prison system and questions whether capital punishment is an effective deterrent to crime. Published in 1899, the novel concerns a domestic servant, Katusha Maslova, who becomes pregnant by a member of the Russian nobility, Prince Dmitri Ivanovitch Nekhludof. The young man does not learn of Maslova's predicament until years later when, while serving on a jury, he recognizes her as the defendant. She is now a prostitute and has been accused of helping someone else poison and rob one of her clients. She insists that she is innocent, having believed that the poison was actually a harmless sleeping poison.

Nekhludof is convinced that she is innocent of the crime. The other jury members concur. However, they fill out the verdict form incorrectly, and as a result she is sentenced to several years of hard labor in Siberia. Nekhludof protests the decision, but the judge says he can do nothing to remedy the situation. Nekhludof hires a lawyer to begin an appeal. The prince visits Maslova in jail to atone for his sins. He tells her that he will marry her and follow her to Siberia. She refuses his offer, hating him for ruining her life, but he continues to visit her. Gradually he becomes aware of injustices within the prison system. He asks himself:

> What right have some men to imprison, torture, exile, flog, and kill other men, when they themselves are just like those they torture, flog, and kill? And he was answered by discussions as to whether man has a free will or not? Whether a man can be proved a criminal by the measurements of his skull, etc.? What part does heredity play in crime? Is there such a thing as natural depravity? What is morality? What is insanity? What is degeneration? What is temperament? How do climate, food, ignorance, imitativeness, hypnotism, and passions affect crime? What is society? What are its duties, etc.? (Tolstoi 1911, 117)

Eventually Nekhludof begins to reexamine his own role in the oppression of others. He decides that he has no right to own land, believing that much of the peasants' misfortunes were due to their enslaving by landowners. In discussing Nekhludof's reasoning, the omniscient narrator says:

> Nobody could deny that infants and old people died for want of milk; the reason they had no milk was because they had no pastures for their cattle, no land for raising bread-stuffs, no hay-fields. It is perfectly plain that all the people's misery, or at least the greater part of it, arises from the fact that they do not own the land which ought to support them, this same land being in the hands of men who take advantage of their ownership to exact the utmost amount of labor from the tillers of the soil. The peasants, reduced to the depths of poverty, actually dying for want of enough land to support them, go on toiling in order that the landowners may have crops to sell in foreign lands, and buy all the hats and canes, carriages and bronzes, that their hearts desire. (274–275)

After much thought, Nekhludof realizes why the peasants do not protest this arrangement. The narrator says:

> At this moment everything seemed so clear to him that he could never cease wondering why others couldn't see it, too. . . . The people are dying out; and they have really become so accustomed to the perishing process, that they have unconsciously come to accept as inevitable the untimely deaths of the children, the overwork of the women, and the insufficient nourishment, particularly for the old people. And this state of affairs has been of a growth so gradual, that the peasants have not realized the full horror of it, neither have they lifted up their voices to complain. (274)

Consequently, Nekhludof decides that "the only sure remedy for the uplifting of the masses . . . is to return to them the land which has been taken from them and which they so much need" (275). He gives his land to local peasants, not as individual plots but as a single estate whose profits will be shared by all. He also donates cash to the poorest of the villagers. Then he follows Maslova to Siberia while continuing to use his political contacts to obtain her release. During this process he learns that many other prisoners besides Maslova are actually innocent. He realizes that

Russian officials have a backward approach to justice: "In this way not only was that rule neglected which enjoins forgiveness of ten guilty men sooner than one innocent man should suffer, but quite the contrary. . . . They removed ten innocent persons in order to get rid of one guilty person" (101). Therefore, he wonders whether "all this talk about God, justice, religion, kindness, and the law, were only words that concealed the most brutal cupidity and cruelty" (102).

Nekhludof is a harsh critic of the Russian church, believing it to be hypocritical. When he witnesses a prison church service, the narrator says:

> And not one among those who were present . . . seemed to be aware that this same Jesus whom the priest had lauded . . . had expressly forbidden all that had been going on here; not only the senseless volubility and the blasphemous incantations of the priest over the wine and the bread, but had most positively forbidden one man to call another master, had forbidden all worship in temples, commanding every man to pray in solitude, had forbidden the very temples themselves . . . but above all the rest, he had forbidden human judgments and the imprisonment of men, or their subjection to the shame, torture, or death which was visited on them in this place. He had forbidden violence in all its forms and had proclaimed that he set the captive free. (171)

In the final chapter of the novel Nekhludof reads the Bible and decides that the church has distorted its message. He vows to begin a new life using its tenets as his guide. By this time his efforts have led to Maslova's release from prison, and she has decided to marry a man in her own social class even though she now loves Nekhludof. She and Nekhludof both recognize that Russian society would never accept their union.

Because of the novel's denunciation of the church, its author was excommunicated in 1901. *Resurrection* was his last full-length novel. He contributed much of his profits from the work to the Dukhobors, a peasant religious sect that rejected both church and government authority. The group emigrated to western Canada in 1898. Tolstoi remained in Russia, where he continued to criticize his society. (Tolstoi 1911)

See also Class, Social; Maslova, Katusha; Nekhludof, Prince Dmitri Ivanovitch; Poverty; Prison Reform; Tolstoi, Leo

Rivers, Clementine ("Tish")

Tish Rivers is the first-person narrator of James Baldwin's 1974 novel *If Beale Street Could Talk*. A pregnant, 19-year-old black woman, she is engaged to Alonzo "Fonny" Hunt, a 22-year-old sculptor who is awaiting trial for a crime he did not commit. Tish's love for Fonny is strong, and according to Baldwin biographer David Leeming (1994, 325), "when Tish cries for Fonny and longs for his freedom, she is the Baldwin voice expressing his life's search for a lover free of the bondage of society's taboos." (Baldwin 1988; Leeming 1994)

See also Baldwin, James; Hunt, Alonzo ("Fonny"); *If Beale Street Could Talk;* Racism

Roberts, David

David Roberts appears in the three-act play *Strife* (1909), by John Galsworthy. Roberts represents the factory workers in a labor dispute, encouraging them to remain out on strike despite severe hardships. When the labor union tries to get the men to accept a compromise position, he fights against it. In this respect he is just as rigid as his opposition. However, whereas the people who control the factory are wealthy and can weather a strike, Roberts and his men truly suffer for their beliefs. In fact, Roberts's wife falls ill and dies because her home lacks heat and good food. (Galsworthy 1928)

See also Galsworthy, John; *Strife*

Rodrigues, Sebastian

Sebastian Rodrigues appears in the 1969 novel *Chimmoku* (Silence), by Shūsaku Endō. A Portuguese priest, Sebastian goes to Japan trying to find his mentor, Father Christovao Ferreira, whom he has heard renounced his faith. In Japan Rodrigues is forced to hide from the Japanese authorities, who have been torturing and killing Christians in order to stamp out the religion. Eventually he is captured, and during his imprisonment he meets often with officials to discuss and defend Christianity. In the end, however, he, too, recants his faith, having been convinced by his mentor Ferreira that the lives he will save through his sacrifice are ultimately more important than his religious convictions. (Endō 1980)

See also Endō, Shūsaku; Ferreira, Christovao; *Silence*

Rodríguez, Colonel Tolomeo

A South American military leader in Isabel Allende's 1987 novel *Eva Luna,* Colonel Tolomeo Rodríguez is feared by everyone but the novel's main character, Eva Luna. When the colonel asks her to become his mistress, Eva refuses, believing it would be dangerous for her. Tolomeo respects her refusal; however, he also warns her that her relationship with guerrilla leader Huberto Naranjo is dangerous. (Allende 1988)

See also Allende, Isabel; Carlé, Lukas; Carlé, Rolf; *Eva Luna;* Naranjo, Huberto

Rougon-Macquart Cycle

The *Rougon-Macquart cycle* is a term used for a series of 20 novels by the French author Émile Zola. The first title in the series, *La Fortune des Rougon* (The Fortune of the Rougons) was published in 1871, and the last, *Le Docteur Pascal* (Doctor Pascal) was published in 1893. Collectively, these works are subtitled *The Natural and Social History of a Family under the Second Empire.* They depict several generations of a family that has split into two branches: the Rougons, who are legitimate, and the Macquarts, who are illegitimate and lower class. Through their lives, Zola comments on many aspects of French society. For example, the 1877 novel *L'Assommoir* (The Drunkard) deals with alcoholism among working-class people, the 1885 novel *Germinal* shows the struggle of laborers in a mining community, and the 1887 novel *La Terre* (The Earth) concerns peasants who want to own land. (Grant 1966)

See also Zola, Émile

Rudkus, Jurgis and Ona

Jurgis Rudkus is the main character of Upton Sinclair's 1906 novel *The Jungle,* which exposes injustices and unsanitary conditions in the U.S. meatpacking industry during the early twentieth century. A Lithuanian immigrant, Jurgis and his fiancée, Ona, come to Chicago hoping to make their fortune working in a stockyard factory. At first things go well, and they save enough to afford a festive wedding. Later, however, Jurgis is injured and loses his job. Meanwhile Ona's boss forces her to become his mistress in order to save her job. Jurgis finds out, attacks the boss, and is jailed. Without her husband's income and love, Ona falls into malnourishment and despair; she eventually dies in childbirth. Jurgis then works at a series of jobs, but while living as a beggar and thief, he discovers socialism. A socialist hotel keeper gives him a job, and he experiences much better treatment in life. In the end he believes that socialism will save others as well. (Sinclair 1972)

See also *Jungle, The;* Sinclair, Upton; Socialism

S

Sartre, Jean-Paul

French philosopher and author Jean-Paul Sartre believed that with freedom comes social responsibility. He expressed this view in many of his novels, plays, and essays. Born in Paris, France, on June 2, 1905, he graduated from the École Normale Supérieure in 1929 and became a teacher, working at various schools from 1931 to 1945. He also spent a year in Germany studying philosophy. His first published works were articles on literature, and his first novel, *Le Nausée* (Nausea), appeared in 1938. The following year he joined the French army to fight in World War II, only to be taken captive by the Germans in 1940. After nine months of imprisonment he escaped and went to Paris to join an underground Resistance movement. His play *Les Mouches* (The Flies, 1943) was written during this period to express his views on freedom, responsibility, and resistance to oppression.

Sartre produced many plays during his career, including *Le Diable et le bon dieu* (The Devil and the Lord, 1951), which concerns political activism, and *Les Séquestrés d'Altona* (The Condemned of Altona, 1959), which deals with a Nazi obsessed with his past crimes. He also edited a monthly review with writer Simone de Beauvoir, with whom he had a lifelong romantic relationship. His es-

Jean-Paul Sartre, October 23, 1964 (Archive France/ Archive Photos)

says from this period were later included in a collection entitled *Situations*, a ten-volume series published from 1947 to 1972. Of his novels, perhaps his most widely read is *L'Âge de raison* (The Age of Reason), which was published in 1945. Part of a trilogy known as *Les Chemins de la liberté* (The Roads to Freedom), it depicts a philosopher who has trouble putting his beliefs into practice. Sartre also wrote biographies, memoirs, and other non-fiction books. He received the Nobel Prize in literature in 1964 but declined it, believing that no honor was necessary for his work. His last work, the third volume of a biography of Gustave Flaubert, was published in 1972. He subsequently went blind and was unable to write anymore. He died on April 15, 1980, in Paris, France. (Brustein 1964; Madsen 1977)

See also *Age of Reason, The;* Beauvoir, Simone de

Sarvis, Dr. A. K.

In Edward Abbey's 1975 novel *The Monkey Wrench Gang,* Dr. A. K. Sarvis is a wealthy surgeon who funds an environmental group that engages in acts of ecological sabotage. Its members destroy bulldozers and other equipment used by road builders and developers. Sarvis's motives for participating in such activities concern the public health. The narrator remarks:

The Southwest had once been the place where Eastern physicians sent their more serious respiratory cases. No more; the developers—bankers, industrialists, subdividers, freeway builders and public utility chiefs—had succeeded with less than thirty years' effort in bringing the air of Southwestern cities "up to the standard," that is, as foul as any other.

Doc thought he knew where the poison came from that had attacked the boy's lungs, the same poison eating into the mucous membranes of several million other citizens including himself. From poor visibility to eye irritation, from allergies to asthma to emphysema to general asthenia, the path lay straight ahead, pathogenic all the way. They were already having afternoons right here in Albuquerque when schoolchildren were forbidden to play outside in the "open" air, heavy breathing being more dangerous than child molesters. (Abbey 1975, 203)

An older man, Sarvis himself is physically weak, and Abbey uses him to show why all people should be involved in environmental activism. (Abbey 1975)

See also Abbey, Edward; Environmentalism; *Monkey Wrench Gang, The*

Schreiner, Olive

An ardent feminist, Olive Schreiner was a nineteenth-century novelist who wrote about women's rights at a time when men considered themselves superior to women. She was born in South Africa in 1855, the daughter of a German Methodist missionary and his English wife. Schreiner's first novel, *The Story of an African Farm,* was based on her childhood experiences; it was published when she was only 28 years old under the pseudonym Ralph Irons. Her subsequent works include *Women and Labour* (1911), a sociological study that advocated equality between men and women; *Trooper Peter Halkett of Mashonaland* (1897), an allegorical discussion of British politics in South Africa; and the feminist novels *From Man to Man* (1927) and *Undine* (1929), both published posthumously. In *From Man to Man,* Schreiner writes about a feminist who marries, bears a child, and becomes an unhappy housewife; Schreiner herself did not marry until the age of 39, and she was, according to scholar Dan Jacobson in a 1970 essay accompanying the work (Schreiner 1970, 18), a "desperately unhappy woman." She insisted that her husband, S. P. Cronwright, change his last name to Cronwright-Schreiner. In 1924, four years after her death, he published a biography of his wife entitled *The Life of Olive Schreiner.* (Clayton 1997; Schreiner 1970)

See also Feminism; *Story of an African Farm, The*

Science Fiction and Fantasy

The science fiction and fantasy genre offers authors an opportunity to criticize contemporary society by showing how problems might evolve or be resolved in the future. Anthony Burgess, Ursula Le Guin, Jack London, George Orwell, Jules Verne, Kurt Vonnegut, and H. G. Wells have all taken advantage of this opportunity. Their novels depict fictional societies that highlight flaws in the real world. (Ketterer 1974)

See also Burgess, Anthony; Le Guin, Ursula; London, Jack; Orwell, George; Verne, Jules; Vonnegut, Kurt; Wells, H. G.

Scott, Ida and Rufus

Sister and brother, Ida and Rufus Scott are two African-American characters from James Baldwin's 1960 novel *Another Country*. Both encounter racism when they begin dating white people. Both also become angry at their situations and take that anger out on their loving partners. Rufus beats and berates his girlfriend, Leona; Ida cheats on her boyfriend, Vivaldo.

Eventually Rufus feels ashamed of his cruelty. According to Baldwin biographer David Leeming (1994, 201), Rufus represents someone who is "too broken to accept love or to give it. Society has taken away his freedom to find *his* individual identity and in so doing has removed the self-respect and respect for human life that, for Baldwin, make love possible. Rufus can only assume the worst even of those who mean well." Isolated from society, he commits suicide by jumping off New York City's George Washington Bridge.

Rufus's death increases Ida's own sense of isolation. She tells a white woman, "*You* don't know, and there's no way in the world for you to find out, what it's like to be a black girl in this world" (Baldwin 1962, 347). Moreover, her brother's suicide increases her anger at society and at Vivaldo. According to Leeming (1994, 201), "Ida's love for Vivaldo is marred by a deep need to avenge what she considers her brother's murder at the hands of white racism." At one point she says, "Some days, honey, I wish I could turn myself into one big fist and grind this miserable country to powder. Some days, I don't believe it has a right to exist" (Baldwin 1962, 351).

Leeming (1994, 201) quotes author Baldwin as explaining that the main action in *Another Country* was "the journey of Ida and Vivaldo toward some kind of coherence." At the book's conclusion Ida sets aside her anger, ends her affair, and confesses her infidelity to Vivaldo, who still loves her. (Baldwin 1962; Leeming 1994)

See also *Another Country;* Baldwin, James; Jones, Eric; Moore, Daniel Vivaldo; Poverty; Racism

Sears, Louis

Louis Sears is a character in *The Ugly American* (1958), by William J. Lederer and Eugene Burdick. At the beginning of the novel Sears is the U.S. ambassador in Sarkhan, a small country in Southeast Asia. He has little interest in his job, having taken the position merely to improve his chances of being appointed a U.S. judge. He spends a great deal of his time at diplomatic parties and is appallingly ignorant of Asian culture. In an epilogue to the novel the authors explain that, even though Sears is a fictional character, he is based on his real-life counterparts. Lederer and Burdick (1958, 272) say: "Ambassador Sears . . . does not exist. But there have been more than one of him in Asia during recent years. He is portrayed as a political warhorse, comfortably stabled by his party while he awaits a judgeship. . . . The roster of our ambassadors throughout the world bears out the fact that too often personal wealth, political loyalty, and the ability to stay out of trouble are qualities which outweigh training in the selection of ambassadors." (Lederer and Burdick 1958)

See also Burdick, Eugene; Lederer, William J.; *Ugly American, The*

Season in Paradise, A

The book *'n Seisoen in die Paradys* (A Season in Paradise), by poet Breyten Breytenbach, chronicles a visit he made to South Africa after being exiled from that country for his antiapartheid stance. Published in 1980, it is primarily a work of nonfiction, but it includes some of the author's social protest poetry translated from Afrikaans. Of this writing Breytenbach (1980, 160) says:

> To write is to communicate, to eat together, to have intercourse, a communion, all of our blood, all of our flesh. We are

men, writing for men about men, and therefore about relationships between men.. . . . I want to write for *here,* for *now.* I want to come as close as I can in my work to the temporal—not the infinite; that has always been around. . . . I think that by taking cognizance of the nature of the struggle we are involved in and share, by making that struggle clearer—and even more: by taking a stand based on this knowledge—we expand our humanity and our language.

Breytenbach uses his poetry to comment on the injustices perpetrated against his country and his people and argues that a writer has a "social responsibility" to speak out for the freedom of all people (155). (Breytenbach 1994; Jolly 1996)

See also Apartheid; Breytenbach, Breyten; Exiles

Sereno, Daniel

Daniel Sereno appears in Jean-Paul Sartre's 1945 novel *L'Âge de raison* (The Age of Reason). A homosexual filled with self-loathing, he hides his lifestyle from all of his friends. When he learns that an acquaintance has become pregnant by a man who will not marry her, he decides to marry her himself. He does not love her, but he desperately wants to live an "acceptable" life as a husband and father. (Sartre 1947)

See also *Age of Reason, The;* Sartre, Jean-Paul

Sethe

The main character of Toni Morrison's 1987 novel *Beloved,* Sethe must come to terms with a difficult past. Before the Civil War she was a black slave who ran away from a cruel master. Upon recapture she killed her child to save her from being enslaved, too. The novel begins 18 years later. The ghost of Sethe's daughter, now a 21-year-old woman, arrives in the flesh to haunt her, and in the end, with the help of friends, Sethe must free herself from her torment. (Gates and Appiah 1993c; Morrison 1987)

See also *Beloved;* Morrison, Toni

Settembrini, Ludovico

The character Ludovico Settembrini appears in Thomas Mann's 1924 novel *Der Zauberberg* (The Magic Mountain). An Italian humanist and nationalist, he tries to convince the main character, Hans Castorp, to share his point of view on various philosophical, social, and political issues. He is opposed in these discussions by a converted Catholic, Leo Naphta, who defends a rigid spiritual, authoritarian, medieval approach to life. The two men quarrel passionately over their beliefs and eventually decide to duel with pistols. But when the moment comes, Settembrini refuses to shoot the Jesuit. Naphta then cannot honorably shoot the Italian, but he also cannot forget their quarrel; he shoots himself instead. Naphta's death troubles Settembrini, who descends deeper into his illness. At the same time he begins to question his beliefs, especially after war breaks out in Europe. As the novel explains, in Settembrini "the boldness of the eagle was gradually outbidding the mildness of the dove" (Mann 1972, 710). (Mann 1972)

See also Castorp, Hans; *Magic Mountain, The;* Mann, Thomas

Sexism

See Feminism

Shallard, Frank

Frank Shallard, a character in the novel *Elmer Gantry* (1927), reflects author Sinclair Lewis's opposition to organized religion. Frank becomes a minister because his father wants him to be one, yet he is an atheist. He is also the most moral character in Lewis's novel. Shallard lives an otherwise ethical life and helps his parishioners in many important ways. Yet when church leaders discover that he is not a true believer, they force him to leave the pulpit in disgrace. Meanwhile the novel's main character, the highly immoral Elmer Gantry, is lauded as an exemplary man of God. (Lewis 1970)

See also *Elmer Gantry;* Lewis, Sinclair

Shatov

Shatov is the member of a Russian revolutionary organization in Fyodor Dostoyevsky's novel *Besy* (The Possessed) published in two volumes between 1871 and 1872. Shatov struggles with his religious and political beliefs and eventually decides to leave the radical group. He believes that "socialism is . . . an atheistic organization of society . . . [that] intends to establish itself exclusively on the elements of science and reason" and that as such it cannot succeed because "there never has been a nation without a religion, that is, without an idea of good and evil. . . . Reason has never had the power to define good and evil, or even to distinguish between good and evil. . . . It has always mixed them up in a disgraceful and pitiful way" (Dostoyevsky 1936, 253–254). But the leader of the group, Pyotr Stepanovitch Verhovensky, does not want Shatov to leave because he fears the man might become a police informant. Verhovensky therefore lures Shatov to a dark, secluded place and murders him. Shatov's death is modeled after a real-life incident, the murder of a young revolutionary in Russia in November 1869. (Dostoyevsky 1936; Wasiolek 1964)

See also Dostoyevsky, Fyodor; *Possessed, The;* Stavrogin, Nikolay Vsyevolodovitch; Verhovensky, Pyotr Stepanovitch

Shaw, George Bernard

Born on July 26, 1856, in Dublin, Ireland, George Bernard Shaw wrote five unsuccessful socialist novels before becoming a book, art, music, and theater critic in 1885. He then decided to try promoting his socialist views through plays. Unfortunately, he could find no one willing to produce his first works, some of which had been banned by government censors. In 1898 he published them in a collection entitled *Plays Pleasant and Unpleasant.* The book includes a lengthy preface for each play, a practice Shaw was to continue in later collections of his work. As a result of this publication, Shaw's works began to be performed in the United States and Europe. However, they did not appear in England until 1907 when a play about Irish-English conflict, *John*

Bull's Other Island (1904), was performed in London. That same year Shaw published his play *Major Barbara,* an important work that criticizes English attitudes toward poverty and religion. In subsequent years he published the plays *The Doctor's Dilemma* (1911), *Pygmalion* (1914), *Androcles and the Lion* (1916), and *Heartbreak House* (1919), all of which deal with social issues. He also began to become involved in politics, helping to found a socialist group called the Fabian Society in 1883. In addition, he wrote political essays, antiwar speeches and pamphlets, and a political tract entitled *The Intelligent Woman's Guide to Socialism and Capitalism* (1928). He died on November 2, 1950, in Ayot St. Lawrence, Hertfordshire, England. (Hill 1978; McCabe 1974)

See also *Major Barbara;* Socialism

Shelby, George

George Shelby is the son of a plantation owner in Harriet Beecher Stowe's 1852 novel *Uncle Tom's Cabin.* When Shelby's father sells one of his trusted slaves, Uncle Tom, the young George vows that one day he will buy him back. Eventually he is ready to fulfill his promise, but he discovers that Tom has been beaten to death by a cruel owner. George helps two other slaves escape the man's plantation and returns home to free his own slaves after his father's death. (Stowe 1960)

See also Stowe, Harriet Beecher; Tom, Uncle; *Uncle Tom's Cabin*

Shukhov, Ivan Denisovich

Ivan Denisovich Shukhov is the main character in Aleksandr Solzhenitsyn's 1962 novel *Odin den iz zhizni Ivana Denisovicha* (One Day in the Life of Ivan Denisovich). Ivan has been unjustly sentenced to several years in a forced-labor camp, and it is a struggle for him to survive. The camp is bitterly cold, his clothing and food are inadequate, he is seriously overworked, and some of the other prisoners are dangerous. Nonetheless, he wonders whether life outside the camp would be just as bad. (Solzhenitsyn 1972)

See also *One Day in the Life of Ivan Denisovich;* Solzhenitsyn, Aleksandr

Silence

Chimmoku (Silence), by Japanese writer Shūsaku Endō, is a historical novel concerning the persecution of Japanese Christians during the late 1500s and early 1600s. However, when it was published in Japan in 1969, it was received as a criticism of contemporary anti-Christian sentiments in that country. Scholar William Johnson (xiv–xv) points this out in a 1980 introduction to the work, adding that "one is left with the impression that the novel is in some way the expression of a conflict between [the author's] Japanese sensibility and the Hellenistic Christianity that has been given to him." The novel's theme concerns whether Christianity is a suitable religion for the Japanese people. In this regard Johnson (xviii) explains that *Silence* has been controversial with both non-Christian and Christian Japanese and suggests that this indicates the country is "not indifferent to Christianity but looking for that form of Christianity that will suit its national character."

The novel's main character is a Portuguese priest, Sebastian Rodrigues, who decides to travel to Japan to find his missing mentor, Father Christovao Ferreira. Portuguese authorities have heard that Ferreira renounced his faith, or apostatized, after being tortured by the Japanese. Rodrigues cannot believe that such a pious man would ever abandon his faith. The first four chapters of the novel are letters from Rodrigues to Portugal concerning his travel to Japan and attempts to remain hidden from authorities there. Japan has banned Catholicism and has a policy of killing all known Catholics unless they are willing to apostatize. Eventually Rodrigues is captured, too, and his letters end.

The rest of the novel relates his experiences at the hands of his Japanese persecutors. The Japanese want him to step on a picture of Jesus Christ and renounce him. When Rodrigues refuses, he is forced to watch the torture and execution of innocent people. At first he remains firm in his resolve to honor his faith. Then the authorities bring Ferreira to talk to him. Ferreira is now living as a Japanese, having indeed apostatized in order to save

lives. He convinces Rodrigues that Jesus Christ would have done the same thing because He would have considered a man's life more important than a mere ritual. Ferreira urges Rodrigues to step on the picture as a formality, without changing what is in his heart. Rodrigues does so, but he realizes that his heart is changed nonetheless. He is no longer a Christian. He and Ferreira live out the rest of their lives as Japanese, dying of old age on foreign soil.

Interestingly, throughout the novel various characters discuss the relationship of Christianity to the Japanese in terms of a soil metaphor. Christianity is called a tree that has been transplanted in Japan only to wither and die. Rodrigues believes that the tree's death has been caused by a lack of nurturing, by not having fertilizer applied. In other words, Japanese authorities have not encouraged it to grow, and so it has not. But other characters, such as Ferreira and a Japanese official, argue that the tree has died because it is not suited to the climate or soil of the foreign country. They believe that no nurturing can change its suitability, and therefore it should be left to die.

According to Johnson, when the novel was published, some Japanese Christians pointed out that the people who died as martyrs when Rodrigues refused to apostatize do indeed prove that Christianity can exist in Japan even without nurturing. He (xvii–xviii) quotes one of them as saying: "Obviously the belief of Ferreira . . . that Japan is a swamp which cannot absorb Christianity is not a reason for apostasy. It was because he lost his faith that Ferreira began to think in this way. . . . In that Christian era there were many Japanese who sincerely believed in Christ, and there are many who do so today. No Christian will believe that Christianity cannot take root in Japan."

Because *Silence* had engendered so much discussion regarding the nature of Christianity and its appropriateness in a particular society, Johnson compares the work to the writing of Graham Greene. Greene wrote not only about Christianity but also about religious persecution, and his novel *The Power and the Glory* has many similarities to *Silence*. (Endō 1980)

See also Endō, Shūsaku; Ferreira, Christovao; Greene, Graham; *Power and the Glory, The;* Religion; Rodrigues, Sebastian

Sinclair, Upton

Born on September 20, 1878, in Baltimore Maryland, Upton Beall Sinclair is perhaps best known for his best-selling social protest novel *The Jungle,* which brought public attention to poor working and sanitary conditions at slaughterhouses. Its publication in 1906 led Congress to pass the Pure Food and Drug Act that same year. The novel was originally printed at Sinclair's expense after several publishers rejected the manuscript. At the time he was working as a journalist and had investigated the meatpacking industry as part of a newspaper assignment. After *The Jungle* became a success, however, he left journalism to write more novels, including *Oil!* (1927) and *Boston* (1928). The former was based on the Teapot Dome Scandal of the 1920s and the latter on the case of Sacco and Vanzetti, whom many people believe were tried and executed for murder not because they were guilty but because they were avowed anarchists.

As a socialist Sinclair often wrote about social and political issues. He also edited a collection of social protest literature entitled *Cry for Justice* (1915). In addition, he was politically active. With the money he received from sales of *The Jungle,* he founded a short-lived cooperative housing project, the Helicon Home Colony, in Englewood, New Jersey. He then moved to California, where he organized a socialist reform group called End Poverty in California (EPIC). In 1934 he ran for governor of California using the EPIC platform and nearly won the election. In later years he became increasingly interested in international politics, and his writings reflect this interest. Starting in 1940, he wrote a series of 11 novels featuring an antifascist who fights against injustice and tyranny. He also wrote nonfiction books and an autobiography. Sinclair died on November 25, 1968, in Bound Brook, New Jersey. (Bloodworth 1977)

See also Anarchism; Fascism; *Jungle, The;* Labor Issues; Socialism

Slavery

Slavery is the ownership and exploitation of one human being by another. It has occurred throughout the world from ancient times, and writers have always protested the practice. The most extensive antislavery literature, however, concerns black slavery in the United States, which began when the country was founded and lasted until 1865. During this period an antislavery activist, or abolitionist, named Harriet Beecher Stowe produced one of the most influential works of literature in history, *Uncle Tom's Cabin.* This novel increased antislavery sentiment in the United States, and some scholars credit it with hastening slavery's demise. *The Biglow Papers,* by abolitionist James Russell Lowell, similarly furthered the abolitionist cause, as did *Oroonoko,* by Aphra Behn. American slavery is also an issue in modern works concerning racism against blacks, such as the novel *Sula,* by Toni Morrison. (Filler 1960; Mathews 1972; Thomas 1965)

See also Behn, Aphra; *Biglow Papers, The;* Lowell, James Russell; Morrison, Toni; *Oroonoko;* Racism; Stowe, Harriet Beecher; *Sula; Uncle Tom's Cabin*

Smith, Winston

The main character of George Orwell's 1949 novel *1984,* Winston Smith lives in a society of the future where the government controls people's thoughts and actions. He tries to obey its wishes but finds himself disobeying several rules. He keeps a secret journal, has an affair with a woman even though he is married, and is eventually drawn into a revolutionary group. The group proves to be a government trap, and Winston is arrested. He is then tortured for his crimes and betrays his mistress. Their love destroyed, he later gives his love to the government. (Orwell 1961)

See also *1984;* Orwell, George

Socialism

Socialism is an ideology that advocates equality and the abolishment of class structure and capitalism. Socialists believe that the people, in the form of the state, should control all property and production of goods. Many forms of modern socialism have developed since the concept originated in the late eighteenth century. Two of these, Marxism and Leninism, are the foundation of communism.

During the nineteenth century the socialist movement became powerful throughout Europe and England, where playwright George Bernard Shaw helped create the Fabian Society. The Fabian Society promoted a more democratic version of socialism, arguing that men of science and wisdom, rather than the state, should control property and production. During the twentieth century the differences between British and Soviet socialism grew more pronounced, and in 1945 British author George Orwell offered an unflattering portrayal of Soviet socialism in his novel *Animal Farm.*

Socialism never gained much credence in the United States. However, a few authors, such as Edward Bellamy, Jack London, and Upton Sinclair, did promote its doctrines. Authors in other parts of the world also examined socialist issues in their work. These include Doris Lessing in South Africa, Sibilla Aleramo in Italy, and Mulk Raj Anand in India. (Cohen 1962; Egbert 1967; Shaw 1984)

> **See also** Aleramo, Sibilla; Anand, Mulk Raj; *Animal Farm;* Bellamy, Edward; Lessing, Doris; London, Jack; Orwell, George; Shaw, George Bernard; Sinclair, Upton

Solzhenitsyn, Aleksandr

Russian novelist and historian Aleksandr Tsayevich Solzhenitsyn protested social and political policies in the Soviet Union. He was expelled from his country in 1974. Born on December 11, 1918, in Kislovodsk, Russia, he was awarded a degree in mathematics from the University of Rostov-na-Donu. He then joined the military but was arrested after criticizing Joseph Stalin. Solzhenitsyn was imprisoned and worked in forced-labor camps before being released as rehabilitated in 1956. His first novel, *Odin den iz zhizni Ivana*

Soviet author Aleksandr Solzhenitsyn takes notes at Stanford University Library. (UPI/Corbis-Bettmann)

Denisovicha (One Day in the Life of Ivan Denisovich, 1962), was based on his experiences as a prisoner. It was very successful and led to the appearance of several short stories in a Soviet magazine followed by a collection of short stories published in 1963.

These stories displeased the Soviet government, however, and his subsequent works were banned for publication in his own country. He was also ousted from the Soviet Writers Union for his efforts to oppose censorship. Nonetheless, Solzhenitsyn had several novels, including *Rakovy Korpus* (Cancer Ward, 1968) and *Avgust 1914* (August 1914, 1971), published abroad, and in 1970 he was awarded the Nobel Prize in literature. By this time his relationship with the government was extremely poor, and in 1973 he was arrested for writing *Arkhipelag Gulag* (The Gulag Archipelago), which criticized many aspects of Soviet history and policy. Solzhenitsyn was subsequently convicted of treason and forced into exile. He eventually settled in the United States, in Cavendish, Vermont, and wrote several more books. In 1989 the Soviet Union finally began publishing Solzhenitsyn's work, including *The Gulag Archipelago,* and in 1990 the government restored the author's citizenship. He returned to his country in 1994 to live in Moscow, where he recently completed a collection of essays that have not yet been published. (Moody 1975)

> See also Exiles; *One Day in the Life of Ivan Denisovich;* Prison Reform

"Song of the Shirt, The"

Published in 1825, the poem "The Song of the Shirt," by English author Thomas Hood, is considered one of the most important social protest poems ever written. It brought attention to the plight of poor women who labor at piecemeal work, sewing shirts "till the brain begins to swim . . . till the eyes are heavy and dim" (Sinclair 1996, 46) in exchange for meager wages and deplorable living conditions. (Sinclair 1996)

> See also Hood, Thomas; Labor Issues; Poverty

"Song of the Stormy Petrel"

"Pesnya o burevestnike" (Song of the Stormy Petrel) is a revolutionary poem by Russian novelist, short-story writer, and poet Maxim Gorky. Its publication in 1901 led to the author's arrest. The phrase "Stormy Petrel" refers both to the *Stormy Petrel,* a Russian anarchist periodical, and to a type of bird, the storm petrel. The storm-petrel always flies ahead of a storm, thereby warning of its approach. (Levin 1965)

> See also Anarchism; Gorky, Maxim

Sorde, Itale

Itale Sorde is one of the main characters in Ursula Le Guin's 1979 novel *Malafrena.* The heir to a large estate in the Austrian-controlled country of Orsinia, Sorde values his political beliefs more than his family responsibilities. He leaves home, becomes involved in a revolutionary group, and gains prominence for his political writings and speeches. He is eventually arrested by the Austrian police and spends two years in prison, an experience that damages both his health and his spirit. However, he soon recovers his passion for revolution and continues the fight for his country's freedom from oppression. (Le Guin 1979)

> See also Le Guin, Ursula; *Malafrena*

South Africans
See Apartheid

Sportsman's Sketches, A

The collection of stories *Zapiski okhotnika* (A Sportsman's Sketches), by Russian author Ivan Turgenev, was first published in the Russian journal *The Contemporary* between 1847 and 1851. Their 1852 appearance in book form, in a collection of the same name, led to their author's arrest and exile. During this time Turgenev continued to write new stories; he eventually produced a total of 25. Collections in English have been published in varying numbers under different titles, including *Sketches from a Hunter's Album, A Sportsman's Notebook,* and, simply, *Sketches.*

Turgenev's stories primarily concern the relationship between Russian peasants and the landed gentry prior to the 1861 emancipation of the serfs. Their fictional first-person narrator is a member of the nobility who expresses sympathy for the peasants he encounters during his hunting trips. He also expresses contempt for those who exploit the serfs or treat them cruelly. Perhaps the harshest story in this regard is "Bailiff," which concerns a young landowner, Arkady Pavlych Penochkin, and the overseer of his estate, Sofron Yakovlich. Penochkin tells the narrator that the way to deal with peasants is to "treat them like children" (Turgenev 1983, 100). When an extremely poor peasant approaches him to protest Yakovlich's cruelty and injustice, Penochkin shouts: "Be quiet, I'm telling you! Be quiet! Oh, my God, this is quite simply rebellion. No, my friend, I don't advise you to try being rebellious on my property" (115). Later the narrator learns from another peasant that the overseer will surely punish the protester for his temerity. The peasant says that Yakovlich is "just that kind of a cur, a dog . . . that he knows who to get his teeth into. The old men what are richer and with bigger families, them he doesn't touch" (117). Because of such portraits, Turgenev's work increased public awareness of the harsh realities of peasant life, thereby fueling the movement to emancipate Russia's serfs. (Lloyd 1972; Turgenev 1983)

See also Class, Social; Penochkin, Arkady Pavlych; Poverty; Turgenev, Ivan; Yakovlich, Sofron

Stalingrad

The 1948 novel *Stalingrad*, by Theodor Plevier, is primarily a war story, but it has elements of social protest. In portraying the battle between the German and Red Armies near Stalingrad, Russia, the book not only exposes the difficulties that soldiers must endure in the field but also shows the attitudes that cause these difficulties. For example, in discussing why the dying soldiers do not receive more compassion, one German soldier says: "The strong eat up the weak; the weak fall; the sick lie and are left behind. It's all logical. If a man is sick and can no longer crawl to the feed trough, it shows poor breeding, inferior racial stock. But those who steal from others and fill their own bellies will live a few minutes longer and are therefore of superior stock" (Plevier 1948, 122).

The novel also criticizes Germany's war policies and, like all of the author's works, was banned from that country. Plevier was exiled from his native Germany in 1934 for criticizing the government's social and political policies. (Plevier 1948)

See also Peace; Plevier, Theodor

Stark, Joe

Joe Stark appears in the 1937 black feminist novel *Their Eyes Were Watching God,* by Zora Neale Hurston. After Joe marries the story's main character, Janie Crawford, he tries to make her into his ideal wife. Conscious of his social standing in the community, he tells her how to dress, where to go, what to do, and whom to talk to. At the same time he does not allow Janie to criticize his own behavior. Eventually he falls ill, and on his deathbed his wife scolds him for treating her so badly when they could have had a wonderful life together. (Hemenway 1977; Hurston 1990)

See also Crawford, Janie; Hurston, Zora Neale; *Their Eyes Were Watching God*

Stavrogin, Nikolay Vsyevolodovitch

Son of a Russian nobleman in Fyodor Dostoyevsky's novel *Besy* (The Possessed), which was published in two volumes between 1871 and 1872, Nikolay Vsyevolodovitch Stavrogin is an atheist who is incapable of loving anyone, even himself. He damages every woman with whom he comes in contact. He enjoys perverse sexual behavior until his abuse of a 12-year-old girl causes her to commit suicide, at which point he begins to feel guilt. Eventually this guilt expands to include other misdeeds in his life, and he commits suicide. In struggling with his lack of religious faith, Stavrogin represents Dostoyevsky's belief that without God, humanity is doomed. (Dostoyevsky 1936; Dostoyevsky 1968)

See also Dostoyevsky, Fyodor; *Possessed, The;* Shatov; Verhovensky, Pyotr Stepanovitch

Steinbeck, John

American novelist John Steinbeck received the Nobel Prize in literature in 1962. He is perhaps best known for his social protest novel *The Grapes of Wrath* (1939), about the struggle of a poor Oklahoma farm family against harsh environmental and economic conditions.

Steinbeck was born in Salinas, California, on February 27, 1902. In 1920 he enrolled at Stanford University as an English major, but his attendance was sporadic, and he left in 1925 without his degree. He then began working for a New York newspaper called the *American*. In 1929 he published his first novel, *Cup of Gold*. It was unsuccessful, as were his next two novels, *The Pastures of Heaven* (1932) and *To a God Unknown* (1933). His third novel, *Tortilla Flats* (1935), and a collection of stories entitled *The Red Pony* (1937) were more popular. However, it was not until the 1937 publication of the novel *Of Mice and Men* that Steinbeck became truly successful. *Of Mice and Men* earned him many prestigious awards, both as a novel and as a play adaptation, and two years later he received the Pulitzer Prize and the National Book Award for *The Grapes of Wrath*, which was the top best-seller of 1939.

Shortly thereafter Steinbeck became interested in documentary films. He traveled to Mexico to do a movie on its mountain villages, and during World War II he wrote propaganda films and literature for the U.S. government. The most significant of this work is a novel entitled *The Moon Is Down* (1942), about Nazi oppression in Norway. After the war he continued writing best-selling novels, including *Cannery Row* (1945), *The Pearl* (1947), and *East of Eden* (1952), as well as movie adaptations of his work. He also wrote nonfiction books, such as *Travels with Charley in Search of America* (1962), which documents a three-month trip through the United States with his poodle Charley. Steinbeck died on December 20, 1968, in New York, New York. (Fontenrose 1964; French 1975; Lisca 1958)

See also *Grapes of Wrath, The;* Great Depression

Steppenwolf

Steppenwolf (1927), by Hermann Hesse, depicts a man struggling to repress his natural human urges in order to fit in with modern society. The novel's main character, Harry Haller, considers himself half man, half wolf, although he has been told that this view of himself as a duality is too simplistic. As he goes about his daily life, the "wolf" side of him frequently breaks through his civilized veneer, and at first he despairs of ever being able to control its cruelty. In fact, he sees all of life's efforts as futile, saying:

> Just as I dress and go out to visit the professor and exchange a few more or less insincere compliments with him, without really wanting to at all, so it is with the majority of men day by day and hour by hour in their daily lives and affairs. Without really wanting to at all, they pay calls and carry on conversations, sit out their hours at desks and on office chairs; and it is all compulsory, mechanical and against the grain, and it could all be done or left undone just as well by machines; and indeed it is this never-ceasing machinery that prevents their being, like me, the critics of their own lives and recognising the stupidity and shallowness, the hopeless tragedy and waste of the lives they lead, and the awful ambiguity grinning over it all. (Hesse 1963, 86)

Eventually Harry rejects this sense of hopelessness and allows himself to enjoy sensory experiences, such as dancing and making love. However, when he discovers happiness, he grows uneasy, saying: "My happiness fills me with content and I can bear it for a long while yet. But sometimes when happiness leaves a moment's leisure to look about me and long for things, the longing I have is not to keep this happiness forever, but to suffer once again, only more beautifully and less meanly than before. I long for the sufferings that make me ready and willing to die" (168).

Later he attends a mysterious performance called The Magic Theater, which leads him to an alternate reality in which chaos reigns. After watching and participating in several strange events, he meets the German composer Mozart, who tells him: "You are to live and to learn to laugh. You are to listen to life's radio music and to reverence the spirit behind it and to laugh at the bim-bim in it" (244). In the end Harry realizes that life is a game he has been taking too seriously. Like Hesse's other works, *Steppenwolf* relies heavily on symbolism to tell the story of a man's inner conflicts and personal growth. It also includes criticism of those who support a political position without understanding or questioning it. (Hesse 1963; Ziolkowski 1965)

See also Haller, Harry; Hesse, Hermann

Story of an African Farm, The

The Story of an African Farm, by Olive Schreiner, was first published in 1883 under the pseudonym Ralph Iron. According to scholar Dan Jacobson in his introduction to a 1970 edition of the book, it was the first work of fiction ever set in colonial South Africa. However, he (21) points out that the novel is "far from being the novel of 'race relations' which many people have come to expect every South African novel to be," because the story concerns "the white people on the farm, not the black. . . . The black people in it are merely extras, supernumeraries, part of the background."

Therefore, *The Story of an African Farm* does not concern itself with racism. Instead, it deals with feminist issues at a time when British and Dutch white males considered themselves superior to other members of their society. Its main character, Lyndall, is a young Englishwoman who values her independence and decides to live with a man rather than marry him. The novel's editors tried to convince its author to change this aspect of the plot, so that Lyndall marries her lover, but Schreiner refused.

The story begins with Lyndall's childhood. She is the orphaned cousin of a girl named Em, with whom she lives on an African farm. Em's parents are also dead; the girls are both under the care of Em's stepmother, an un-

pleasant Boer woman named 'Tant Sannie who treats them badly. In a separate building on the farm lives the overseer, a kindly German man, and his son, Waldo. He is much like Lyndall; both yearn for knowledge and want to leave the farm someday.

Into this setting comes an unscrupulous drifter named Bonaparte Blenkins. He convinces 'Tant Sannie that he is related to nobility and will someday inherit a small fortune. After he gains her trust, he tells her that her overseer has been stealing sheep from her. She throws the old man out, but the morning he is to leave the farm, they find that he has died in his sleep. Blenkins now takes over his possessions and his job. He treats Waldo cruelly, ridiculing and beating him. On one occasion, after Em gives Waldo one of her late father's books, Blenkins berates the boy, then calls the book evil and burns it. The narrator says that Blenkins's philosophy was "whenever you come into contact with any book, person, or opinion of which you absolutely comprehend nothing, declare that book, person, or opinion to be immoral. Bespatter it, vituperate against it, strongly insist that any man or woman harbouring it is a fool or a knave, or both. Carefully abstain from studying it. Do all that in you lies to annihilate that book, person, or opinion" (Schreiner 1970, 112).

Eventually, however, 'Tant Sannie discovers that Bonaparte Blenkins is a rogue and throws him out of the house. By that time, however, Lyndall has gone away to school. She returns when Em writes that she is planning to be married to a farmer named Gregory Rose. Em has followed the traditional path for a woman, becoming a dutiful housekeeper and striving for nothing more than a husband. But Lyndall says, "I am not in so great a hurry to put my neck beneath any man's foot; and I do not so greatly admire the crying of babies" (184). She then enters into a long discussion with Em about the role of women in a society that values their beauty more than their intelligence. Lyndall is far more beautiful than Em; therefore it does not surprise either of them when Gregory Rose decides he would rather marry Lyndall.

Lyndall rejects Gregory, but he becomes obsessed with her, even after she runs off with a secret lover. Gregory follows her, and after a long search he discovers that she gave birth to a child who lived only three days, then fell ill and sent her lover away. Now she is alone on her deathbed. Gregory disguises himself as a nurse and tends to her needs until she dies. Then he returns to the farm to marry Em. Meanwhile Waldo has left the farm to travel. He comes back shortly after Lyndall's death, and Em offers him money to go away to school. Waldo refuses it, saying that he no longer wants to learn about the world. He leaves her to sit and contemplate the pleasures of the farm, and apparently drifts into death.

Jacobson (20) notes the similarity between the fates of Lyndall and Waldo, saying, "Those who seek and strive are killed off; the others survive." He explains that this has relevancy to Schreiner's own life. Her novel was semiautobiographical; she grew up in South Africa as a missionary's daughter, was jilted by a lover when she was 16, and ended up in an unsatisfying job as a governess. After marrying at age 39, she became, according to Jacobson (18), a "desperately unhappy woman" who suffered from a variety of psychosomatic ailments. A devout feminist, she wrote in favor of women's rights, and during World War I she also advocated pacifism. Schreiner died on December 11, 1920, in Cape Town, South Africa. (Clayton 1997; Schreiner 1986)

See also Feminism; Schreiner, Olive

Stowe, Harriet Beecher

Harriet Beecher Stowe is best known for writing *Uncle Tom's Cabin,* an 1852 novel that protested American slavery. Born on June 14, 1811, in Litchfield, Connecticut, she was the daughter of a famous clergyman, Lyman Beecher. In 1824 she began attending the Connecticut Female Seminary at Hartford, and eight years later she started working as a schoolteacher in Cincinnati, Ohio, where she sometimes encountered slaves who had escaped across the Ohio River. She would later incorporate this knowledge into *Uncle Tom's*

Harriet Beecher Stowe (Library of Congress)

Cabin. Meanwhile Stowe wrote stories for local publications, and in 1834 she won a short story competition with a work entitled *A New England Sketch.* That same year she published her first book, entitled *The Mayflower; or, Sketches of Scenes and Characters among the Descendants of the Pilgrims.*

In 1836 Stowe married a theological professor, and in 1850 the couple settled in Brunswick, Maine. After the appearance of *Uncle Tom's Cabin* in 1852, Stowe became famous and went on a European tour. She continued to write articles and novels for the rest of her life, although none of them brought her the same acclaim as *Uncle Tom's Cabin* did. Her novels include *Dred: A Tale of the Great Dismal Swamp* (1856), which also concerns slavery; *The Minister's Wooing* (1859), which deals with religion; and a series based on her husband's New England childhood that includes the books *The Pearl of Orr's Island* (1862), *Old-Town Folks* (1869), and *Poganuc People* (1878). She is also noted for her series of articles on the English poet Lord Byron (1869). Stowe died on July 1, 1896, in Hartford, Connecticut. (Stowe 1960)

See also Slavery; *Uncle Tom's Cabin*

Stranger, The

The Stranger was originally published in 1942 in French as *L'Etranger* and in English as *The Outsider*. Written by Algerian author Albert Camus, it offers the first-person narrative of Monsieur Meursault, who is ultimately condemned to death for not conforming to society's expectations of how a loving son should behave.

The Stranger opens with Meursault traveling to attend his mother's funeral at an old person's home near Algiers. He does not know the exact day she died, or her correct age, and he displays no emotion over her death. Of the funeral he says, "Everything happened so fast, so deliberately, so naturally that I don't remember any of it anymore" (Camus 1989, 17). When he returns home, he sleeps for 12 hours, then goes for a swim at the beach, where he runs into Marie Cardona, a former coworker. The two of them go to the movies, and Marie stays overnight with Meursault. Shortly thereafter the two become engaged.

Meursault begins to spend time with his neighbor Raymond Sintes, whose girlfriend has been cheating on him. Sintes asks Meursault to write a letter to her, "one with a punch and also some things in it to make her sorry for what she's done" (32). Meursault obliges, and consequently the woman shows up at Sintes's apartment. Sintes beats her until the police arrive, and afterward he asks Meursault to be a witness at his trial.

Meursault also spends time with another neighbor, Salamano, who is distraught because his dog has run away. The old man says that Meursault must be sad about the death of his mother, adding that many people think he was wrong to send her to the old people's home. Meursault replies simply that he did not have enough money to care for her in his apartment anymore and that she was bored living with him. He does not say that he is saddened by her death.

One day Meursault, Marie, and Sintes take the bus to a friend's beach house. Meursault has already testified on Sintes's behalf regarding the beating, and the two men notice that the victim's brother is following them. At the beach they encounter the man and a group of his friends. A fight breaks out, and Sintes is slightly wounded. After a doctor attends to the injury, Meursault and Sintes, who now has a gun, return to the beach. This time the man appears unarmed; Meursault convinces Sintes to give him the gun to make the fight fair. But the man does not want to fight, so Meursault and Sintes return to the beach house.

Minutes later Meursault decides to go for a walk alone, and once more he sees the man. This time Meursault panics. He pulls out Sintes's gun and shoots the man five times. He is arrested for murder, and at his trial the prosecutor portrays him as a ruthless killer without a soul, emphasizing that Meursault went on a date the day after his mother's death. Witnesses confirm that Meursault did not grieve properly for his mother, and in the end the jury sentences him to the guillotine.

Meursault cannot believe that "men who change their underwear" can actually order someone to die (109). He wants to "reform the penal code" (111) so that a condemned man has a one in ten chance to escape his fate. What bothers him is that "it was an open-and-shut case, a fixed arrangement, a tacit agreement that there was no question of going back on" (111). He rails against the unfairness of society but finally realizes that nothing matters because all people are condemned to death. He accepts "the gentle indifference of the world," which reminds him of his own indifference toward life (122).

Meursault's plight shows, as scholar René Girard (Bloom 1989, 88) explains, that *The Stranger* "was not written for pure art's sake, nor was it written to vindicate the victims of persecution everywhere. Camus set out to prove that the hero . . . will necessarily be persecuted by society. He set out to prove, in other words, that 'the judges are always in the wrong.'" Girard (80) points out that Camus also depicts judges as flawed in his subsequent novel, *La Chute* (The Fall), wherein the main character, a lawyer, seeks "not to save his clients but to prove his moral superiority by discrediting the judges." These judges are, according to Girard (102), "the middle class who [are Camus's] sole potential readers." Camus's ultimate intent is not just to criticize the legal system but to criticize the judgmental nature of his society and to explore the relationship between that society and the individual.

However, Girard (102) reports that "instead of rejecting the book as the author had half hoped, half feared, [his] bourgeois readers showered it with praise. The 'judges,' obviously, did not recognize their portrait when they saw it. They, too, cursed the iniquitous judges and howled for clemency. They, too, identified with the innocent victim." (Bloom 1989; Camus 1958, 1989)

See also Camus, Albert; *Fall, The;* Meursault, Monsieur

Strife

A three-act drama, by John Galsworthy, *Strife* concerns a strike at the Trenartha Tin Plate Works factory around the turn of the century. The play was written in 1909. When it opens, it is February, and the workers have been off the job since October. The company's board of directors is ready to settle the strike, but the chair of the board, John Anthony, is firmly against it. He believes that the workers will return to their jobs once their wives and children begin to starve to death. Moreover, he thinks that giving in to strikers is bad for the country. He says: "I have been accused of being a domineering tyrant, thinking only of my pride—I am thinking of the future of this country, threatened with the black waters of confusion, threatened with mob government, threatened with what I cannot see. If by any conduct of mine I help to bring this on us, I shall be ashamed to look my fellows in the face" (Galsworthy 1928, 101–102).

Meanwhile the leader of the workers' committee, an engineer and inventor named David Roberts, believes that the strike is "the fight o' the country's body and blood against a blood-sucker. The fight of those that spend themselves with every blow they strike and every breath they draw, against a thing that fattens on them . . . a thing that buys the sweat o' men's brows and the tortures o' their brains, at its own price" (92). Roberts is sup-porting the men with his own savings and refuses to compromise the workers' demands, even when his men ask him to. Soon it becomes clear that the battle between the two groups is really a personal struggle between Anthony and Roberts.

In the middle of these two men is trade union official Simon Harness. He has been suggesting a compromise position since the beginning of the strike. The union believes that the men's demands are excessive and will not support them; at the same time the union believes that the company's directors are being unfair. Also caught in the middle is Anthony's daughter, Enid Underwood. Her former maid, Annie, is Robert's wife. Enid knows that Annie is ill and needs money for medical care, heat, and good food. However, the Roberts will not accept her charity, so Enid tries to convince David Roberts to end the strike. He refuses. Later while at a workers' meeting he receives word that his wife has died. He rushes from the room, and in his absence the workers vote to accept the union's compromise position. The company's board then votes to accept it, too, and an infuriated Anthony resigns. In the end both men have lost everything, and the workers have gained very little of what they were asking for.

Strife shows the difficulties inherent in reaching a compromise on labor issues, but it also expresses some hope for future generations. Anthony's son, Edgar, is a very different man from his father. During discussions of the strike he suggests that employers need to take more responsibility for the suffering of their employees, and after Annie Roberts dies, he accuses the company of murdering her. Ultimately even Anthony acknowledges that things are changing, but he criticizes the new sensibility, saying: "There is only one way of treating 'men'—with *the iron hand.* This half and half business, the half and half manners of this generation has brought all this upon us. Sentiment and softness, and what this young man, no doubt, would call his social policy. You can't eat cake and have it! This middle-class sentiment, or socialism, or whatever it may be, is rotten. Masters are masters, men are men! Yield one demand, and they will make it six" (101). Anthony's position is unyielding, as is Robert's. This rigidity of thinking makes them obsolete in a world of change and compromise. (Barker 1969; Galsworthy 1928)

See also Anthony, John; Galsworthy, John; Labor Issues; Roberts, David

Suffragist Movement
See Feminism

Sula

Written in 1973, *Sula,* by Toni Morrison, is the story of two women, Sula Peace and Nel Wright, who grow up together in a black neighborhood called the Bottom on the outskirts of Medallion, Ohio. The novel begins in 1920, when Nel is ten years old. Both she and Sula come from fatherless homes, but their personalities are very different. Nel is well mannered and conservative, whereas Sula is rebellious and promiscuous. Nonetheless, their friendship remains strong until Nel's wedding day, when Sula leaves town. She returns ten years later and soon seduces Nel's husband. Later she tells Nel that she did not see anything wrong with sharing a man with her friend.

Sula often fails to follow the moral guidelines of her community. For example, when her mother's skirt catches fire, Sula watches her burn to death rather than run for help, and when her grandmother accuses her of behaving badly, Sula sends her to a nursing home noted for its poor management. Her neighbors also accuse her of what they consider to be the ultimate sin—sleeping with white men. As their dislike of Sula grows, they begin to shun her. They call her a witch or a devil and keep their children away from her. In fact, their hatred of Sula unifies the community. When she dies of a prolonged illness, people consider it God's punishment and no one mourns her death. However, the community loses its unity and strength, and some time later Nel realizes that Sula's passing was a terrible loss. She begins to mourn her friend's death.

In discussing *Sula,* scholar Roberta Rubenstein says that the community is one of the main characters of the novel. In her essay "Pariahs and the Community," she (Gates and Appiah 1993c, 148) explains that it is "a kind of collective conscience that arbitrates the social and moral norms of its members. Functioning as a life-sustaining structure for its members, it tolerates certain kinds of eccentricity. . . . Yet it is also punitive to those who step absolutely outside the boundaries of the communally acceptable." She (148) quotes Morrison as saying: "In the black community where I grew up, there were eccentricity and freedom, less conformity in individual habits—but close conformity in terms of the survival of the village, of the tribe." Through the lives of Nel and Sula, the novel shows both the positive and negative aspects of such conformity.

Sula also presents the idea that every woman should have a purpose in life. In "A Hateful Passion, a Lost Love," scholar Hortense J. Spillers (Gates and Appiah 1993c, 212–213) explains that it is a feminist novel in which the main character's faults "are directly traceable to the absence of a discursive/imaginative project—some *thing* to do, some object-subject relationship which establishes the identify in time and space. We do not see Sula in relationship to an 'oppressor,' a 'whitey,' a male, a dominant and dominating being outside the self. . . . Instead, Sula emerges as an embodiment of a metaphysical chaos in pursuit of an activity both proper and sufficient to herself." When Sula's grandmother suggests that having a baby will settle her down, Sula replies: "I don't want to make somebody else. I want to make myself" (Morrison 1974, 92). And in describing the source of Sula's unhappiness and rebellion, the narrator remarks: "Had she paints, or clay, or knew the discipline of the dance, or strings; had she anything to engage her tremendous curiosity and her gift for metaphor, she might have exchanged the restlessness and preoccupation with whim for an activity that provided her with all she yearned for. And like any artist with no art form, she became dangerous" (121).

Morrison's work is therefore similar to another feminist novel, *A Woman,* by Sibilla

Aleramo, in which the main character must express her creativity or go insane. Many scholars have also compared *Sula* to Zora Neale Hurston's novel *Their Eyes Were Watching God* and to Jean Toomer's novel *Cane,* both of which are set within the black community and show characters ostracized by their neighbors. (Gates and Appiah 1993c; McKay 1988; Morrison 1974; Samuels 1990)

> See also *Cane;* Feminism; Hurston, Zora Neale; Morrison, Toni; Peace, Sula; Racism; *Their Eyes Were Watching God;* Toomer, Jean; Wright, Nel

"Surviving"

"Surviving" is a poem by Native American author James Welch. Originally published in a 1971 collection entitled *Riding the Earthboy 40,* it depicts a group of Native Americans huddled around a stove on a cold day. They tell stories of better times and bemoan all they have lost because "to stay alive this way, it's hard" (Turner 1974, 597). (Turner 1974)

> See also Native American Issues; Poverty; Welch, James

Swartz, Lanny

As the main character in Peter Abrahams's 1948 novel *The Path of Thunder,* Lanny is a South African coloured man who returns to his rural village after receiving a good education in the nearby city of Capetown. He opens a school and, according to scholar Robert Ensor (1992, 273), "sets an example of essential equality, self-respect and assertiveness for the community." Ensor (237) sees Lanny as "the black representative of a European-based liberal humanism" who only wants to "liberate and educate" his people. However, before

Lanny can accomplish these goals, he falls in love with a white woman named Sarie Villiers. Since intermingling of the races is forbidden in South Africa, Lanny and Sarie try to flee to the more liberal Portuguese East Africa. Before they can escape, white landowners kill them both. (Abrahams 1975; Ensor 1992)

> See also Abrahams, Peter; Finkelberg, Isaac; Mako; *Path of Thunder, The;* Racism

Swift, Jonathan

Born on November 30, 1667, Jonathan Swift is best known for two works, an essay entitled *A Modest Proposal* (1729) and a novel entitled *Gulliver's Travels* (1726). Both of them use satire to criticize English society. Swift's parents were English, but they lived in Dublin, Ireland, and Swift attended Trinity College there. In 1689, amid anti-Catholic sentiment in his country, he left for England as secretary to a retired politician. He soon became interested in politics himself and considered becoming a politician. However, in 1694 during a visit to Ireland Swift was ordained a minister, and his first published work, *Tale of a Tub* (1794), is a satire of religious extremists. Swift continued writing essays about religion and politics, and in 1710 he became editor of a journal, the *Examiner,* that was the voice of the Tory political party. He remained in this position until the Tories lost control of the government in 1714. At this point Swift became dean of Saint Patrick's Cathedral in Dublin. He soon began to write about the poor treatment of the Irish people by the English and produced his two greatest works. A national hero, Swift died in Dublin on October 19, 1745. (Murry 1967)

> See also *Gulliver's Travels; Modest Proposal, A*

T

Tachibana, Akiko

One of the main characters of Sawako Ariyoshi's novel *The Twilight Years*, Akiko Tachibana must care for her senile father-in-law with almost no help from her husband. A modern, working woman, she nonetheless accepts the traditional Japanese role of wife and mother at home. She worries over what to cook for her family, which dislikes easy-to-prepare frozen foods, and is obsessed with keeping her house immaculate. Given the extra responsibility of her father-in-law's care, she quickly becomes overwhelmed. She is angry at her husband for making her deal with the situation alone, yet she has trouble expressing that anger. Even when she does tell him how she feels, he appears to ignore her, and she wonders how their life together will be when they grow old. (Ariyoshi 1987)

See also Ageism; Ariyoshi, Sawako; Feminism; Tachibana, Nobutoshi; *Twilight Years, The*

Tachibana, Nobutoshi

This character from Sawako Ariyoshi's 1972 novel *Kokotso no hito* (The Twilight Years) represents the traditional Japanese male in his fifties. He refuses to help his working wife, Akiko, with any household chores or with the care of his own father, who has become senile. He views Akiko's pleas for help as nagging and does not consider her work outside the home important. As the narrator explains: "The younger generation probably had different views about the role of women, but the feudalistic attitude among men of Nobutoshi's age could not easily be brushed aside. Men of his generation did not acknowledge the fact that a family's financial situation was vastly improved when the wife worked. They gave the impression that they were simply letting their wives do as they pleased and put up with their neglect of their household duties with tolerance and patience" (Ariyoshi 1987, 69). (Ariyoshi 1987)

See also Ariyoshi, Sawako; Feminism; *Twilight Years, The*

Taggert, Dagny

Dagny Taggert is the main character in Ayn Rand's 1957 novel *Atlas Shrugged*. In charge of a railroad company, Taggert Transcontinental, Taggert embodies capitalism. She is intelligent, creative, strong-willed, and beautiful, yet masculine. When the government tries to destroy her business through a variety of socialistic laws, she fights back and tries to save it. In the end, however, she is forced to walk away from her company in order to save society instead. (Rand 1992)

See also *Atlas Shrugged*; Rand, Ayn

Tarrant, Verena

Verena Tarrant is a speaker for the suffragette movement in Henry James's 1886 novel *The Bostonians*. Although she has a powerful speaking voice, she is a weak-willed woman easily swayed by others' opinions. At first she is ruled by her parents. Then she falls under the control of a feminist named Olive Chancellor and gradually accepts Olive's ideas as her own. Later, however, Verena is wooed by a chauvinistic southern gentleman, Basil Ransom, who convinces her not to listen to the opinions of Olive or her parents. Instead, he talks her into leaving the suffragette cause to marry him. Verena therefore represents a social reformer who lacks conviction. (James 1956)

See also *Bostonians, The;* Chancellor, Olive;
Feminism; James, Henry; Ransom, Basil

Tea Cake

Tea Cake appears in Zora Neale Hurston's black feminist novel *Their Eyes Were Watching God* (1937). After he marries Janie Crawford, he teaches her to enjoy life, not just as a woman but as a human being. Tea Cake does not worry about social conformity; he values Janie's individuality. Moreover, he ultimately sacrifices his own life to save hers by protecting her from a rabid dog. After he contracts rabies and goes mad, Janie is forced to shoot him. (Hemenway 1977; Hurston 1990)

See also Crawford, Janie; Hurston, Zora
Neale; *Their Eyes Were Watching God*

Temple of My Familiar, The

Published in 1989, *The Temple of My Familiar*, by Alice Walker, includes some of the characters from the author's best-known novel, *The Color Purple*. Both books address issues of racism and oppression, particularly as they relate to women. *The Temple of My Familiar* primarily concerns the lives of two women, a South American native named Zede and a black woman named Lizzie, and all of the people who are important to them. Some of these people existed thousands of years ago because Lizzie has been reincarnated many times and can remember all of her past lives. She has experienced human life in all its forms and was once even a lion.

As an old woman Lizzie tells her stories to a young man named Suwelo, who in return tells her of his problematic marriage with Fanny Nzingha. Fanny is the daughter of Olivia, who appeared in *The Color Purple*. One day she and her mother decide to go to Africa so that Fanny can meet her father, a political activist known as Ola. During the trip Fanny and her parents discuss the history of racism against their people. For example, on one occasion her mother says:

> [The white man] was all-powerful. In fear and dread we watched him from our compounds the world over. Some of us were greedy. We believed, as he seemed to, that he was bringing something better than we had. This *never* happened. Always, we were left poorer, with a lowered opinion of ourselves. He blocked the view between us and our ancestors, us and our ways; not all of them good ways, but needing to be changed according to our own light. He needed to keep us terrorized and desperately poor, in order to feel powerful. No one who was secure in himself as a person would put such emphasis on the nonpersonhood and unworthiness of another. (Walker 1990, 307)

Other characters in the novel also discuss racism and share tales of historical figures, both real and fictional, who have suffered from oppression in Africa and the Americas. In addition, characters refer to the work of black feminist social protest authors such as Zora Neale Hurston and Nella Larsen. After Ola dies, Fanny decides to become a protest author, writing plays with her half sister Nzingha in memory of her father's political activism. At the same time Fanny decides to return to the United States to work things out with Suwelo.

Suwelo has become involved with Zeda's daughter, Carlotta, but when Fanny returns he drops Carlotta. Then the two women become friends, and they begin talking about their mothers with Suwelo and Carlotta's husband, Arveyda, who is a musician and somewhat of a mystic. Zeda was a teacher in South America when the government arrested her for being too progressive. Later she escaped to the United States, where she raised Carlotta and had an affair with her daughter's husband. Zeda and Arveyda then went to South America together. He eventually returned to live with Carlotta, while Zeda remained behind to find her own mother. Zeda was successful, and the two women now live in Mexico. After hearing this story, Suwelo reveals that both of his parents were killed in a car accident. Suwelo's father often drove drunk and forced his wife to sit beside him. Suwelo now realizes the fear his mother must have experienced.

By this point Lizzie has died and left Suwelo a tape recording about her life as a lion. He goes to share it with her friend, a man who never understood all of what Lizzie was. Meanwhile Arveyda and Fanny make love and pronounce themselves of one spirit and one flesh. (Walker 1990)

See also Feminism; Hurston, Zora Neale; Larsen, Nella; Racism; Walker, Alice

Tereza

A character in the 1984 novel *Nesnesitelna lehkost byti* (The Unbearable Lightness of Being), by Milan Kundera, Tereza documents political oppression through photography. Of her work, the unnamed narrator of the story says:

All previous crimes of the Russian empire had been committed under the cover of a discreet shadow. . . . Sooner or later they will therefore be proclaimed as fabrications. Not so the 1968 invasion of Czechoslovakia, of which both stills and motion pictures are stored in archives throughout the world. Czech photographers and cameramen were acutely aware that they were the ones who could best do the only thing left to do: preserve the face of violence for the distant future. . . . Seven days in a row, Tereza roamed the streets, photographing Russian soldiers and officers in compromising situations. . . . Many of her photographs turned up in the Western press. They were pictures of tanks, of threatening fists, of houses destroyed, of corpses covered with bloodstained red-white-and-blue Czech flags. (Kundera 1984, 67)

But despite the importance of her work, Tereza abandons it to concentrate on her lover, who eventually becomes her husband. Other characters in the novel make choices between personal relationships and political awareness and/or activism. In Tereza's case, she justifies her decision by convincing herself that her photographs actually advanced the Soviet cause by providing the Communists with pictures of rebels. (Kundera 1984)

See also Communism; Kundera, Milan; *Unbearable Lightness of Being, The*

Tetley, Gerald

Gerald Tetley participates in a lynching party in Walter Van Tilburg Clark's western novel *The Ox-bow Incident* (1940). He is only a part of the group because he is afraid to oppose its leader: his father, Major Tetley. To other people, Gerald voices his disgust for the mob's actions. Scholar Max Westbrook (1969, 56) has therefore called him an "articulate spokesman for morality." But Westbrook (56) also points out that Gerald's arguments against lynching, which are made in an overly emotional manner, make him appear "so weak that he is disgusting to Art Croft, the narrator." Moreover, after the lynching takes place and the men discover they have killed three innocent men, this weak nature leads Gerald to suffer such guilt that he hangs himself in the family barn. His father commits suicide shortly thereafter. (Clark 1960; Westbrook 1969)

See also Clark, Walter Van Tilberg; Croft, Art; Davies, Art; Justice; Martin, Donald; *Ox-Bow Incident, The*

Tewce, Ainsley

A character in Margaret Atwood's 1969 novel *The Edible Woman*, Ainsley Tewce professes to be a feminist, yet cannot shake off conventionality. Feeling unfulfilled, she decides to get pregnant and looks for a suitable sperm donor. She has no intention of marrying, believing it will be easy to raise the child on her own. But during her pregnancy, after she reads an article on the importance of fathers in a child's upbringing, she asks her baby's father to marry her. When he refuses, she convinces another man to marry her instead. (Atwood 1996)

See also Atwood, Margaret; *Edible Woman, The;* Feminism

Their Eyes Were Watching God

Their Eyes Were Watching God, by Zora Neale Hurston, is the story of a black woman's search for independence and love in a black community where men have all the power. In an afterword to the novel, scholar Henry Louis Gates Jr. (187) calls it a "bold feminist novel, the first to be explicitly so in the Afro-American tradition."

However, when the novel was published in 1937, it was criticized by both white and black reviewers. Scholar Mary Helen Washington reports that white men had difficulty believing black people could have so much power, whereas black men did not think the novel was an accurate depiction of life in the rural American South. In a foreword to the novel, Washington (viii) explains that Hurston was chastised for not following the "protest tradition" among black writers, which required a harsh portrayal of racism, and adds:

> The most damaging critique of all came from the most well-known and influential black writer of the day, Richard Wright. Writing for the leftist magazine *New Masses,* Wright excoriated *Their Eyes* as a novel that did for literature what the minstrel shows did for theater, that is, make white folks laugh. The novel, he said, "carries no theme, no message, no thought," but exploited those "quaint" aspects of Negro life that satisfied the tastes of a white audience. By the end of the forties, a decade dominated by Wright and by the stormy fiction of social realism, the quieter voice of a woman searching for self-realization could not, or would not, be heard.

As a result of such criticism, the book went out of print and remained so for almost 30 years. Hurston herself died in poverty in 1960. Shortly thereafter the American feminist movement began, and used copies of *Their Eyes Were Watching God* became popular among women everywhere. The book was reissued in a limited quantity, and university professors such as noted author Alice Walker began featuring the novel in their literature classes. Nonetheless, *Their Eyes* was often out of print until 1978, when scholars finally encouraged publishers to make it permanently available.

Today *Their Eyes Were Watching God* is considered one of the most important feminist works in African-American literature. Its significance lies in the voice of its main character, Janie Crawford, who tells the story of her three marriages to her best friend, Pheoby. Janie's first husband, Logan Killicks, is chosen for her by her grandmother. Janie does not love Logan, but her grandmother tells her to serve him nonetheless, saying: "Honey, de white man is de ruler of everything as fur as Ah been able tuh find out. . . . So de white man throw down de load and tell de nigger man tuh pick it up. He pick it up because he have to, but he don't tote it. He hand it to his womenfolks. De nigger woman is de mule uh de world so fur as Ah can see" (14).

But Janie has trouble obeying Logan, and one day she runs off with Joe Stark, an older man who is on his way to a black-run town in Florida. She imagines a life with him of love and freedom. But after Joe becomes the town mayor and builds his own general store, he becomes as controlling as Janie's first husband. He tells her what to do and does not allow her to socialize with most of the townspeople, who call her "Mrs. Mayor Stark." She quickly loses her own identity, and when Joe contracts a fatal illness, she tells him: "You gointuh listen tuh me one time befo' you die. . . . Ah run off tuh keep house with you in uh wonderful way. But you wasn't satisfied wid me de way Ah was. Naw! Mah own mind had tuh be squeezed and crowded out tuh make room for yours in me. . . . All dis bowin' down, all dis obedience under yo' voice—dat ain't whut Ah rushed off down de road tuh find out about you" (82).

After Joe's death she meets Tea Cake, a younger man who encourages her to enjoy life. He takes her hunting, fishing, and picnicking. The townspeople believe she is making a fool of herself; only Pheoby believes that

Janie can make her own decisions. Eventually Tea Cake marries her, and the two leave town to take a job picking beans on a plantation. Their love remains strong, and Janie is finally her own person. Her only aggravation is a local black woman, Mrs. Turner, who believes that light-skinned blacks like Janie are superior to dark-skinned ones like Tea Cake.

Then one day a violent hurricane hits the plantation. While Janie and Tea Cake are running for higher ground, a mad dog bites Tea Cake in the face. He contracts rabies, goes mad, and attacks Janie, who is forced to shoot him. The white townspeople put her on trial for murder. After she testifies, she is acquitted and returns to her former home to tell Pheoby her story.

Interestingly, the novel does not offer Janie's speech to the white jury. Mary Helen Washington reports that this aspect of *Their Eyes* has engendered much debate among scholars. She (xi) says that in 1979 Robert Stepto of Yale University first "raised the issue that has become one of the most highly controversial aspects of the novel: whether or not Janie is able to achieve her voice." She (xi-xii) explains:

> What concerned Stepto was the courtroom scene in which Janie is called on not only to preserve her own life and liberty but also to make the jury, as well as all of us who hear her tale, understand the meaning of her life with Tea Cake. Stepto found Janie curiously silent in this scene, with Hurston telling the story in omniscient third person so that we do not hear Janie speak—at least not in her own first-person voice. Stepto was quite convinced . . . that the frame story in which Janie speaks to Pheoby creates only the illusion that Janie has found her voice. . . . [However,] Alice Walker . . . [insists] passionately that women did not have to speak when men thought they should, that they would choose when and where they wish to speak because while many women *had* found their own voices, they also knew when it was better not to use it.

Washington (xii) believes that this argument reflects "the earliest feminist reading of voice in *Their Eyes*." The novel has many references to oral tradition, perhaps because Hurston was not only a novelist but also a folklorist. In addition, Gates (187) believes that it powerfully shows "language as an instrument of injury and salvation, of selfhood and empowerment." (Hemenway 1977; Hurston 1990)

See also Crawford, Janie; Feminism; Hurston, Zora Neale; Racism; Stark, Joe; Tea Cake; Walker, Alice; Wright, Richard

This Earth of Mankind

The book *Bumi Manusia* (This Earth of Mankind), by Javanese author Pramoedya Ananta Toer, concerns racism and sexism on the Dutch-controlled island of Java. Written while Toer was in prison for his political writings, it was published in 1980, a year after his release. He followed this book with three sequels, *Anak semua bangsa* (Child of All Nations), *Jejak langkah* (Footsteps), and *Ruma kaca* (House of Glass), also composed while he was in prison. Together these books are known as the Buru Quartet. All of them have been banned in Indonesia.

This Earth of Mankind begins in 1898, when its main character, Minke, is 18. He is one of the few natives in Java to attend a prestigious Dutch-run school there. An excellent student gifted in several languages, he is expected to become a government official. However, he would rather be a journalist. He writes articles and stories for local publications about his people and their culture, and these are well received by the public. Meanwhile, the leaders of the Dutch school are unhappy that he, a native, has proved himself to be superior to the European students there, and no one applauds when he is recognized as the institution's top scholar.

One day a friend takes him to visit a beautiful young woman, Annalies Mellema. Annalies is the daughter of a European's concubine, or *nyai*, named Ontosoroh. Although native women are usually uneducated, Ontosoroh is intelligent and has taught herself to read well. Her Dutch master, Herman Mellama, is a drunkard who cannot manage their farm, so she successfully runs it herself. Minke is drawn to her and her half-European daughter. However, he is frightened by Annalies's brother, Robert Mellema, who pretends to be a full European and hates all natives. After Minke accepts Ontosoroh's invitation to move in with the family, Robert threatens his life. Nonetheless, Minke becomes romantically involved with Annalies, who grows ill every time he leaves her side.

Rumors about Minke's relationship with the girl and her mother spread throughout the town. They grow worse after Annalies's father is poisoned while in a pleasure palace. During the investigation into his death authorities uncover the fact that Minke has been sleeping with Annalies, and he is expelled from school. However, because he has become an influential writer, many people rise to his defense, and he is reinstated. Meanwhile Robert Mellama has disappeared, so the court delays its verdict on the death until his capture.

Shortly thereafter Minke marries Annalies to quell the rumors. His marriage does not last. With Herman Mellama dead, the estate passes into the hands of Annalies's half brother, Mauritas Mellama. The son of Herman Mellama and his lawful Dutch wife, Mauritas becomes Annalies's legal guardian and convinces a European court to annul the marriage because she is underage and did not have her father's permission to wed. Minke and Ontosoroh try to fight the court's decision. Several religious groups come to their aid, saying that under Islamic law the marriage cannot be annulled. Nonetheless, Mauritas eventually takes custody of Annalies and sends her to the Netherlands. Minke is dejected over his defeat, but Ontosoroh reminds him that at least they tried to fight their oppressors.

This Earth of Mankind emphasizes the importance of struggling against injustice. Many characters stand up for their rights, typically with success. For example, Minke defends himself in print against ugly rumors and is reinstated in school. Ontosoroh stands up to her drunken husband and expels him from her house. Minke's friends frighten away a man sent to kill Minke. Annalies fights off her brother Robert while he is raping her and fires a gun at him as he flees.

The novel also compares the unfairness of racism with that of sexism. Throughout the story Minke is persecuted for being a native, but Ontosoroh is persecuted far worse for being a native woman. Minke is allowed to attend school, and when he distinguishes himself through his writing, he is considered an important person. Ontosoroh, who became a concubine against her will, cannot attend school, and when she becomes an accomplished businesswoman, her farm is taken away, as is her daughter. European law does not even honor her role as a mother. *This Earth of Mankind* harshly criticizes European law and Dutch colonialism. In addition, it provides enough information about Javanese history to show that, even though the Dutch have modernized the island, they have also destroyed many important aspects of Javanese culture. (Toer 1996)

See also Censorship; Class, Social; Feminism; Mellama, Mauritas; Mellama, Robert; Minke; Ontosoroh; Racism; Toer, Pramoedya Ananta

Thomas, Bigger

Bigger Thomas is the main character of the 1940 novel *Native Son,* by Richard Wright. An angry black man emasculated by white society, he commits acts of violence against other blacks. Then he accidentally kills a white woman and experiences the full wrath of the white community. Despite the best efforts of his Communist lawyer, he is tried and sentenced to death without receiving true justice.

In writing about Bigger Thomas, Richard Wright relates him to angry victims of oppression in other parts of the world. He (1993a, 519) says that before writing the novel, "I read every account of the Fascist movement in Germany I could lay my hands on, and from page to page I encountered and recognized familiar emotional patterns." Eventually he (521–522) came to a conclusion:

I felt that Bigger, an American product, a native son of this land, carried within him the potentialities of either Communism or

Fascism. I don't mean to say that the Negro boy I depicted in *Native Son* is either a Communist or a Fascist. He is not either. But he is a product of a dislocated society; he is a dispossessed and disinherited man; he is all of this, and he lives amid the greatest possible plenty on earth and he is looking and feeling for a way out. Whether he'll follow some gaudy, hysterical leader who'll promise rashly to fill the void in him, or whether he'll come to an understanding with the millions of his kindred fellow workers under trade-union or revolutionary guidance depends upon the future drift of events in America. But, granting the emotional state, the tensity, the fear, the hate, the impatience, the sense of exclusion, the ache for violent action, the emotional and cultural hunger, Bigger Thomas, conditioned as his organism is, will not become an ardent, or even a lukewarm, supporter of the *status quo*.

(Wright 1993a)

See also Communism; Fascism; *Native Son;* Wright, Richard

Thompson, Eloise Bibb

Born in 1878, Eloise Bibb Thompson was a black poet, playwright, and short story author who wrote about racism and black pride. Her first book, *Poems,* appeared in 1895. She attended Howard University in Washington, D.C., and graduated from its Teacher's College in 1908. Shortly thereafter she moved to Los Angeles, where she began writing for newspapers. Many of her short stories were published in a magazine called *Opportunity,* but her plays were largely unpublished. One 1915 drama, however, did attract a great deal of attention. Entitled *A Reply to the Clansman,* it was a criticism of a racist group called the Ku Klux Klan. But although the rights to make it into a movie were bought by two noted filmmakers, Cecil B. DeMille and D. W. Griffith, the play was never produced. Thompson died in 1928. (Roses and Randolph 1996)

See also Harlem Renaissance; *Masks, a Story*

Titorelli

Titorelli appears in Franz Kafka's 1925 novel *Der Prozess* (The Trial). He is a portrait painter for a mysterious court that operates outside the traditional legal system. Titorelli inherited his position from his father, and he must adhere to strict rules regarding the poses and settings he uses in his paintings. However, his close connection with the court also provides him with a chance to influence its judges. When an accused man, Joseph K., comes to ask for his help, Titorelli explains the types of verdicts the man can expect and offers to prolong his trial indefinitely, explaining that no one is ever deemed innocent. In return, Joseph K. is expected to buy Titorelli's landscapes, which all depict the same bleak scene. (Kafka 1964)

See also Joseph K.; Kafka, Franz; *Trial, The*

To Kill a Mockingbird

To Kill a Mockingbird was published in 1960, a time of racial segregation in the southeastern United States. The novel depicts racial prejudice and moral courage in Alabama during the 1930s. The book's author, Harper Lee, won a Pulitzer Prize for the novel, which is narrated in the first-person by Jean Louise "Scout" Finch, a woman recalling the events of her childhood from ages six to nine. Scout lives in the fictional town of Maycomb, Alabama, with her brother, Jem; black housekeeper, Calpurnia; and widowed father, Atticus, an attorney. Scout's story begins when she meets six-year-old Charles Barker "Dill" Harris, who dares Scout and Jem to run up and touch Arthur "Boo" Radley's house. Boo developed psychological problems as a boy, and rather than send him to a mental institution, his family has kept him cloistered at home for years. The children have never seen him but imagine that he is a monster.

After Jem suppresses his fear of Boo and takes the dare, he becomes fascinated with the Radley house. He tries to leave Boo a note asking him to come out, but his father catches him and tells him never to bother Boo again. Jem finds it hard to obey, and in a nearby tree he sometimes finds little gifts, such as chewing gum or a coin, that he believes have been left there by Boo.

Atticus Finch defends Tom Robinson in this courtroom scene from the 1962 movie To Kill a Mockingbird, *which depicts racial injustice in the segregated southern United States. (United Artists/The Museum of Modern Art Film Stills Archive)*

Time passes, and Scout describes other, seemingly minor events in her life. These incidents reveal a great deal about the moral character of the town. Some of the people of Maycomb are good and courageous, whereas others are evil and cowardly, but most are a mixture of both good and bad. Scout learns this more fully when Atticus is appointed to defend Tom Robinson, a black man accused of battering and raping a white woman, Mayell Ewell. The night before the trial, a group of men show up at the jail to lynch Tom. Atticus tries to stop them, and soon it appears that they will hurt him, too. Then Scout recognizes the father of one of her friends in the crowd. She calls out to him, asks him about his boy, and tries to carry on a pleasant conversation with him. Reminded of his child and his humanity, the man grows embarrassed and leaves; the crowd disperses.

At the trial the next day Atticus proves that Tom could not have committed the crime. The assailant was clearly left-handed, and

Tom's left hand was crippled when he was a boy. Atticus points out that Mayell's father, Bob Ewell, is left-handed, and it soon becomes clear that the man beat up his daughter when he saw her with a black man. However, because the members of the jury are racially prejudiced, they convict Tom despite the facts. He is sentenced to death and is later shot while trying to escape from prison. Scout overhears talk of racial tension in the town, and she and Jem cannot understand why all people are not treated the same.

Meanwhile Bob Ewell has vowed revenge on Atticus for the way he defended Tom. Ewell is too cowardly to attack Atticus directly, so one night he follows Scout and Jem home from a school pageant and attacks them with a knife. Boo Radley saves the children's lives, killing Bob Ewell during the struggle. There are no witnesses to the crime, and the sheriff decides that Ewell killed himself by falling on his own knife. He does not want to expose the sheltered Boo to fame. It would be like killing a mockingbird, a creature that harms no one, or like causing the death of an innocent man.

By the end of the novel, Scout's view of the world has broadened. As scholar Timothy Healy (304) explains in a 1993 afterword to the book:

> Scout's understanding of life gradually widens as the story progresses. She begins with the street, the neighbor's houses, the small world of people who live within sight of her front porch. . . . As the trial begins, Scout enters the larger world of Maycomb itself. She learns about juries, the kind of people who make them up, and about the larger issues of justice and prejudice. In the last part of the book, though it is only hinted at, Scout discovers the world beyond Maycomb and Alabama. There are discussions of national events . . . and the bad times that make people unable to pay their taxes. Finally the whole wide world itself breaks into the schoolroom as . . . the children talk about Adolf Hitler and his racial hatred.

This discussion relates Hitler's persecution of the Jews to racial prejudice in the United States and is perhaps the most powerful passage of social protest in the book. Scout's teacher says that she cannot understand why Hitler does not like the Jews because "they contribute to every society they live in, and most of all, they are a deeply religious people," adding that their story is horrible because they "have been persecuted since the beginning of history, even driven out of their own country" (259). The comparison with African Americans is obvious. Yet Scout observes that her teacher is one of the most racially prejudiced people in town.

Because of such passages, when *To Kill a Mockingbird* was published, some people criticized it for being more of a sermon than a story. Nonetheless, the book was a best-seller and was made into a successful motion picture in 1962. Both the book and the movie increased awareness of racial issues at a time when the civil rights movement in the United States was just beginning to come to public awareness. (Lee 1993)

See also Ewell, Bob; Finch, Jean Louise ("Scout"); Justice; Lee, Harper; Racism; Radley, Arthur ("Boo")

Toer, Pramoedya Ananta

Born on the island of Java in 1925, Pramoedya Ananta Toer has written about racism, sexism, and colonialism in Indonesia. His father was the headmaster of a nationalist school in Blora, Java, and a prominent political figure. However, the young Toer was a poor scholar and took ten years to complete a seven-year elementary school course at his father's school. Afterward, using money he earned from trading rice, he went to the city of Surabaya to attend the Dutch-run Radio-vakschool (Radio Vocational School). The Dutch had been in control of Indonesia for hundreds of years, and Toer was soon forced to join the radiotelegraph section of the Stadswacht (City Civil Defense). He fled the city and returned home, where he remained until his mother's death. He then moved to Jakarta, became a newspaper editor, and joined a movement to make Indonesia independent. In 1947 he was arrested by the Dutch Colonial Army for his activities. He spent two years in prison, where he wrote a short story collection, *Percikan Revolusi,* and a novel, *Perburuan.* After his release he started teaching history and journalism. In 1949 Indonesia at last became independent. Toer became active in political and social reform groups and often spoke in favor of social protest writing. He severely criticized novels that ignored his country's problems.

In 1965 he was again arrested. The Communists had attempted to take over the government, and in the aftermath the anticommunist rulers arrested anyone involved in a left-wing political group. An estimated 500,000 people were killed during this purge, and Toer was imprisoned on Buru Island from 1965 to 1979. During this time he told stories to the other prisoners, and after eight years he was allowed to use paper to write them down. After his release this material was published as four novels, *Bumi manusia* (This Earth of Mankind), *anak semua bangsa* (Child of All

Nations), *Jejak langkah* (Footsteps), and *Rumah kaca* (House of Glass). They are collectively known as the Buru Quartet. All of Toer's works have been banned in Indonesia, and Toer himself cannot leave Jakarta to travel overseas. Moreover, the translator of the Buru Quartet, a secretary in the Australian Embassy in Jakarta, was forced to leave the city in 1981 because of his work on the novels.

In 1988 Toer was awarded the PEN Freedom-to-Write Award and in 1995 the Raymond Magsaysay Award. In 1996 he filed suit to have his home returned to him; it had been confiscated by the Indonesian government in 1966, and all of his books, papers, and manuscripts had been burned. However, the court refused to return Toer's property, and the verdict is currently being appealed. (Toer 1996)

See also Censorship; Racism; *This Earth of Mankind*

Leo Tolstoi (Corbis-Bettmann)

Tolstoi, Leo

Leo Tolstoi is considered one of the world's greatest novelists. His works criticize various aspects of Russian society and human nature. The son of a nobleman, Tolstoi was born on September 9, 1828, just south of Moscow, in Yasnaya Polyana, Tula province, Russia. His mother died when he was a year old, and when he was nine his father died as well. He and his three brothers were subsequently raised by their aunts. In 1844 Tolstoi enrolled in the University of Kazan, but he was unhappy there and returned home in 1847. In 1851 he traveled to the Caucasus Mountains, where he joined the army and fought in several battles.

The next year he published the first part of an autobiographical trilogy. Entitled *Detstvo* (Childhood), it was followed by Otrochestvo (Boyhood) in 1854 and *Yunost* (Youth) in 1857, and depicted life on Tolstoi's estate. In 1854 during the Crimean War the army transferred him to the city of Sevastopol, and Tolstoi wrote several stories there. Three of them, known collectively as *Sevastopolskiye rasskazy* (Sevastopol Sketches) and published between 1855 and 1856, brought him recognition as a short story writer.

Tolstoi's first novel, *Kazaki* (The Cossacks),

was published in 1863, but it was two subsequent novels, *Voyna i mir* (War and Peace, 1865–1869) and *Anna Karenina* (1875–1877), that made him famous as a novelist. *War and Peace* concerns Napoleon's invasion of Russia in 1812, and *Anna Karenina* is the story of an adulterous affair with tragic consequences. Tolstoi's later works, which include short stories, plays, novels, and essays, show his increasing concern for social and moral problems. For example, *Voskreseniye* (Resurrection, 1899) depicts a young nobleman's awakening to the need for social reform. Tolstoi himself was a social reformer. He was involved in a variety of causes and publicly condemned capitalism, private property laws, and the labor system. In November 1910 he decided to retire to a monastery, but he died at a train station along the way. (Tolstoy 1911)

See also Capitalism; Labor Issues; *Resurrection*

Tom, Uncle

The main character in Harriet Beecher Stowe's 1852 novel *Uncle Tom's Cabin,* Uncle Tom is an African-American slave whose owner, Mr. Shelby, describes him as a "good, steady, sensible, pious fellow," adding: "I've trusted him . . . with everything I have,—

money, house, horses,—and let him come and go round the country; and I always found him true and square in everything" (Stowe 1960, 14). Nonetheless, when Shelby falls into debt, he sells Tom to a slave trader. Eventually Tom becomes the property of an evil plantation owner, Simon Legree, who beats him to death. (Stowe 1960)

See also Stowe, Harriet Beecher; *Uncle Tom's Cabin*

Tomas

One of the main characters in Milan Kundera's 1984 novel *Nesnesitelná lehkost bytí* (The Unbearable Lightness of Being), Tomas is a Czechoslovakian physician with several mistresses; even after he marries, he continues to see other women. Then he writes a political essay and his life changes. The government asks him to write a retraction to the essay, but he refuses and eventually loses his job. He becomes a window washer and later a farmer, gives up his mistresses, and eventually attains happiness. However, his wife notes that in doing so, he has given up his power, and she dreams that he has turned into a rabbit pursued by hunters from the government. Shortly thereafter Tomas and his wife are reported to have died in a car crash. (Kundera 1984)

See also Kundera, Milan; Tereza; *Unbearable Lightness of Being, The*

Tono-Bungay

The 1908 novel *Tono-Bungay* was first published in serialized form in the *English Review*. Written by H. G. Wells, it criticizes British society for clinging to outmoded traditions and class distinctions. The novel also suggests that people are too easily duped by clever marketing strategies. The first-person narrator of the story, George Ponderevo, is the son of a housekeeper. He goes to college to better himself, but his studies are difficult and he is impatient. When his uncle Edward, a chemist, invents a "miracle medicine" called Tono-Bungay, George leaves school to help him sell it. In actuality, Tono-Bungay is worthless, but through a clever advertising campaign the Ponderevos convince the public that it can cure almost any ailment. Edward and George

soon become wealthy. Edward spends his money freely, buying his way into the upper classes.

Meanwhile George longs to give society something of value. He studies aerodynamics and experiments with gliders and hot-air balloons in an attempt to invent an airplane. At the same time he falls in love with Beatrice Normandy, the mistress of a wealthy man. Then George learns that Edward has mismanaged their company's finances. In an attempt to save his fortune, George sails for Africa to acquire a rare, valuable, highly radioactive substance called quap. But before he can return it to England for trade, it eats away at the wood in his ship and the vessel sinks. When George is rescued, he discovers that he and Edward are bankrupt. Moreover, Edward is wanted for forgery. George helps him escape to France in a hot-air balloon, but the journey makes the old man ill.

After Edward dies, George returns to England and asks Beatrice to marry him despite his poverty. She refuses, explaining that she has been spoiled by money and that "people can be ruined by wealth just as much as by poverty" (Wells 1935, 388). After she returns to her lover, George becomes a boat builder and develops a new perception of England. He sees it as a place of "greedy trade, base profit-seeking, [and] bold advertisement" and says that despite its ruling classes, "kingship and chivalry . . . are dead" (394).

Wells uses the metaphor of quap to show the destructive power of greed. The radioactive substance eats away at the ship and at the hands of the men who handle it, and George becomes sick in his soul during his journey to find it. He even shoots a man in the back rather than have him interfere with the success of the adventure. Similarly, as Edward becomes rich, the quality of his once-loving marriage deteriorates. He becomes estranged from his wife and his health suffers.

Meanwhile George criticizes the institutions of marriage and religion and tries to find something to replace them. An atheist, he considers joining a socialist group but decides that its members are not his sort of people. However, he continues to believe in socialism as a theory. When he sees the ruin of the mansion his uncle was constructing before his death, George says, "For this the armies drilled, for this the Law was administered and the prisons did their duty, for this the millions toiled and perished in suffering, in order that a few of us should build palaces we never finished, . . . run imbecile walls round irrational estates, scorch about the world in motor-cars, devise flying-machines, play golf and a dozen such foolish games of ball, crowd into chattering dinner parties, gamble and make our lives one vast, dismal spectacle of witless waste!" (356).

In the end, however, George realizes that all things change and suggests that England's "feudal scheme" will eventually crumble (296). He builds a destroyer, which he considers a symbol of progress, and sails it down the Thames River, reflecting on England as it passes by. (Wells 1935)

See also Capitalism; Ponderevo, George; Quap; Wells, H. G.

Toomer, Jean

Nathan Eugene Toomer is the author of *Cane,* a collection of short stories and poems about the black experience in the United States during the 1920s. Born on December 26, 1894, Toomer was a mixed-race child: his paternal grandfather was a wealthy white plantation owner, and his maternal grandfather was a prominent black politician and activist. Toomer identified with both races. He spent his childhood with his mother's family in Washington, D.C., his father having disappeared shortly after his birth. In 1914 Toomer enrolled in the University of Wisconsin as an agricultural student. He was unhappy there and soon left to enroll in the American College of Physical Training in Chicago, where he planned to become a gym teacher. Then he decided to change careers. In 1916 he enrolled in the University of Chicago as a biology major, intending to become a doctor. Shortly thereafter he began studying socialism and decided to become a scholar. In 1917 he enrolled in New York University as a sociology major, but soon changed course again, studying history and psychology at the City

College of New York. Finally he quit school altogether.

After a short period as a salesman, he began teaching physical education. Meanwhile he continued to study literature on his own time. In 1920 he decided to become a writer himself. He began producing stories and poems, and in 1923 his famous collection, *Cane,* was published. All of his subsequent books were rejected for publication, and Toomer grew frustrated. Even though his stories had been published in magazines, eventually he abandoned fiction writing entirely. However, he continued to write poetry, essays, and autobiographical works, and in 1931 he self-published a book of sayings entitled *Essentials.* In addition, he lectured on writing and on a meditational philosophy that he learned in France. In his later years he experimented with communal living and various Eastern religions. Toomer died on March 30, 1967.

(Benson and Dillard 1980)

See also *Cane;* Harlem Renaissance

Trial, The

The Trial, by Franz Kafka, was published in German as *Der Prozess* in 1925, a year after the Austrian author's death. Some of its chapters were left unfinished, and it was Kafka's last wish that the entire manuscript be destroyed, but the executor of his will refused to honor this request. The novel was translated into English in 1937 and was one of the most widely read books of the period.

Written in the third person, the story is told from the point of view of Joseph K., who is placed under arrest on the morning of his thirtieth birthday. The two arresting officers represent a mysterious court that operates outside of the traditional legal system. They will not tell him why he is under arrest, nor will they provide him with any information about court procedures. However, they say that he can continue his daily routine as a bank clerk until the matter is settled. At first Joseph considers his arrest a practical joke and refuses to take it seriously, but eventually he decides it is real. He complies with a summons to attend a court interrogation in a seedy tenement, where he finds an evasive, hostile crowd that leaves him more confused than before. He gives an indignant speech to the assembly and walks out. The next day he returns to the tenement to try to learn more about the court. When his efforts prove useless, he decides to take his uncle's advice and hire a lawyer who specializes in such cases. But the lawyer does little and tells him nothing, and finally Joseph decides to handle his own defense. When he goes to the lawyer's house to fire him, he meets another of the man's clients, a tradesman named Block. His case has been ongoing for over five years, and he paints a bleak picture of Joseph's future.

Shortly thereafter Joseph hears about a portrait painter, Titorelli, who is known for influencing the court's decisions. He visits the man and learns that the judges are corrupt, vain, and loath to admit that anyone can be innocent. Titorelli gives Joseph little hope of being acquitted but says that he might be able to postpone the case indefinitely. Joseph cannot decide what to do. Then he encounters the court chaplain, who implies that Joseph's conviction is certain. In the end Joseph does nothing to advance his case, and on the night before his thirty-first birthday two men arrive to escort him from the city. At a distant site they plunge a knife into Joseph's heart.

Scholars have long debated the meaning of Kafka's story. Some believe that the mysterious court represents a totalitarian regime. Others suggest that it symbolizes religious oppression. However, the novel offers no certainties. Its readers remain as confused as Joseph K., who accepts his fate without understanding it. (Kafka 1964)

See also Block; Joseph K.; Kafka, Franz; Titorelli

Trueba, Esteban

In Isabel Allende's 1982 novel *La casa de los espíritus* (The House of the Spirits), Esteban Trueba is a senator from the Conservative Party in an unnamed South American country who vocally opposes communism, Marxism, and socialism. He believes that the poor are incapable of governing themselves because "they need someone to do their thinking for them, someone around to make decisions" (Allende 1985, 241). He criticizes his wife, Clare; his children, Jaime, Nicolás, and Blanca; and his granddaughter, Alba, for supporting charitable causes because "charity, like Socialism, is an invention of the weak to exploit the strong and bring them to their knees" (252). However, after he encourages a military dictatorship that brings about Nicolás's death and Alba's arrest and torture, Esteban realizes the error of his beliefs. (Allende 1985)

See also Allende, Isabel; Capitalism; De Satigny, Alba Trueba; Del Valle, Clara; Garcia, Esteban; Garcia, Pedro Tecero; *House of the Spirits, The;* Socialism

Turgenev, Ivan

Born on November 9, 1818, in Orel province, Russia, Ivan Turgenev wrote about the relationship between peasants and nobility in his native country. His collection of short stories, *Zapiski okhotnika* (A Sportsman's Sketches, 1847–1852), is credited with hastening Russia's emancipation of the serfs, which occurred in 1861. Turgenev graduated from the University of St. Petersburg and subsequently studied at the University of Berlin in Germany. There he became involved with a group of Russian students who discussed philosophical and political issues. When he returned to Russia in 1841, he sought out similar friends. He also obtained a job in the civil service. In 1843 he met the woman who was to be his life-long lover, a married singer named Pauline Viardot-Garcia. He wrote part of *A Sportsman's Sketches* while visiting her estate.

In 1850 Turgenev inherited his family's wealth, and he was able to begin writing full-time. He associated with many of the most important authors of his time, including Fyodor Dostoyevsky and Leo Tolstoi, and wrote several more novels. These works include *Nakanune* (On the Eve, 1860), whose main character fights against social injustice, and *Ottsy i deti* (Fathers and Sons, 1862), which depicts conflict between aristocrats and a new generation of intelligentsia. The latter provoked so much criticism that Turgenev decided to leave Russia. He lived first in Germany, then London, and then Paris. However, he continued to write about his native country; his last novel,

Nov (Virgin Soil, 1877), concerns Russian revolutionaries. In his later years Turgenev developed cancer of the spine and began making short visits to Russia. He died in France on August 23, 1883. (Lloyd 1972; Turgenev 1973)

See also Dostoyevsky, Fyodor; *Sportsman's Sketches, A;* Tolstoi, Leo

Twilight Years, The

Published in 1972, *Kokotsu no hito* (The Twilight Years), by Sawako Ariyoshi, focuses on the problem of ageism in Japan. The novel's main character, Akiko Tachibana, is forced to deal with the advancing senility of her father-in-law, Shigezō, when her mother-in-law dies suddenly. Akiko's husband, Nobutoshi, is a traditional Japanese man who does not offer any help in the household, despite the fact that his wife works full-time as a secretary in a law firm and Akiko's son, Satoshi, is busy studying for his college entrance exams. In addition to doing the cooking, the cleaning, and the laundry, Akiko must take care of her father-in-law herself.

At first things go fairly well. Akiko and Nobutoshi move Shigezō into their home, and a neighbor takes him to a senior citizen's center each day; Satoshi picks him up at night. But soon Shigezō's mental condition grows worse. He becomes less communicative, has trouble recognizing people, and wakes the family up every night to insist there are burglars in the house. He also occasionally runs away from home, and the police have to bring him back. Finally Akiko decides to put him in a nursing home; however, when she speaks to a government social worker, she learns that Shigezō does not qualify for nursing home care. The only facility that will accept him is a mental institution. Moreover, the social worker explains that there is a long waiting list for all types of elderly care in Japan. When Nobutoshi researches the subject himself, he learns that "the percentage of senior citizens had increased dramatically in Japan in recent years, and that very few measures had been taken to deal with the aged

even in the advanced countries of the West. The more he investigated, the more he appreciated the gravity of each aspect of the problem—the psychological as well as the medical" (Ariyoshi 1987, 166).

As Nobutoshi and Akiko watch Shigezō deteriorate both physically and mentally, they begin to confront their own fears about aging. They talk to friends, family, colleagues, and geriatric experts about the problems associated with old age and with a society that "by about the year 2000" will have "more than 30 million people over sixty" and therefore be a "nation of senior citizens" (167). Several people tell them that "the young are no longer taught to respect the elderly" (118), even though the aged have great wisdom to share. At the same time Akiko and Nobutoshi are concerned about student unrest at the universities and worry that their own son might become involved in such "defiance" (193).

Nonetheless, they hire two of the student protesters, a young married couple, to look after Shigezō during the day. The arrangement allows Akiko to continue working three days a week. By now Shigezō is behaving like an infant. He must wear diapers, and when Akiko leaves him alone in the bath, he almost drowns. Finally he becomes ill, and he dies peacefully at home. Akiko handles the funeral arrangements calmly and expertly, having learned the traditional customs for burying the dead when her mother-in-law passed away. At that time she marveled about the high cost of funerals and "wondered how a family with only one breadwinner could make ends meet in these times of rampant inflation. Since both she and her husband worked, they had somehow managed up till now, but their end-of-year bonuses had been used up on the funeral expenses" of Nobutoshi's mother (48). Such criticisms of Japan's economy as it relates to the elderly and their health care appear frequently throughout *The Twilight Years*. (Ariyoshi 1987)

See also Ageism; Ariyoshi, Sawako; Tachibana, Akiko; Tachibana, Nobutoshi

U

Ugly American, The

The Ugly American, by William J. Lederer and Eugene Burdick, concerns the spread of communism in Southeastern Asia during the 1950s. Published in 1958 and set primarily in the fictional country of Sarkhan near Vietnam, the novel has little plot. Instead, it presents several characters and shows their successes or failures in dealing with the Asian people. In this regard, the novel depicts most of the American and French politicians and military leaders as appallingly ignorant of Asian customs and beliefs, whereas the Russians know much about the Asian culture. Moreover, whereas the Americans refuse to learn Sarkhanese, the Russians are fluent in Asian languages. Lederer and Burdick (1958; 275) discuss this difference in an epilogue to their novel, saying: "Think, for a moment, what it costs us whenever an official American representative demands that the native speak English, or not be heard. The Russians make no such mistake. The sign on the Russian Embassy in Ceylon, for example, identified it in Sinhalese, Tamil, English, and Russian. The American Embassy is identified only in English." The authors (275–276) also quote an American politician, John Foster Dulles, who says: "Interpreters are no substitute. It is not possible to understand what is in the minds of other people without understanding their language, and without understanding their language it is impossible to be sure that they understand what is on our minds."

Many characters in *The Ugly American* cause diplomatic problems because of their inability to understand Sarkhanese. They also behave in ways that offend the Asians, throwing lavish parties and refusing to socialize with the natives. These characters do not understand the needs of the lower classes or recognize the appeal of communism among the poor. The few Americans who are knowledgeable about such things are treated badly by the U.S. government. For example, when an engineer brought to Asia to help plan the construction of dams and military roads recommends that the money be spent instead on local projects such as brick factories and canning plants, the U.S. and French governments dismiss his advice as worthless. Similarly, an agricultural expert is ridiculed for suggesting that money be spent on chickens instead of a new canal. According to Lederer and Burdick (281), these characters were created "to point out the fact that we spend billions on the wrong aid projects while overlooking the almost costless and far more helpful ones."

In fact, *The Ugly American* illustrated so many deficiencies in the way the U.S. government was dealing with the Asians that the book created an uproar among the American

Tomas with his wife, Tereza, in a scene from the 1987 movie The Unbearable Lightness of Being, *which explores political and moral corruption. (Technicolor/The Museum of Modern Art Film Stills Archive)*

public. Eventually this led Congress to review its policies and change some of its practices regarding foreign aid. In addition, the term *ugly American* passed into the common language; it refers to Americans abroad who display insensitivity and ignorance regarding other cultures. (Lederer and Burdick 1958)

> See also Atkins, Homer; Brown, Jonathan; Burdick, Eugene; Communism; Lederer, William J.; MacWhite, Gilbert; Sears, Louis; *Ugly American, The*

Unbearable Lightness of Being, The

The Unbearable Lightness of Being, by Czechoslovakian author Milan Kundera, was published in English and French in 1984 and in its original language as *Nesnesitelná lehkost byti* in 1985, but it was banned in Czechoslovakia until 1989. The novel primarily concerns love and personal choices, but it is set against a background of political unrest and has elements of social protest. The main character, Tomas, is a Czechoslovakian physician who becomes involved in one love affair after another while remaining detached from his

country's political troubles. One day in 1968, however, he writes a letter to a newspaper criticizing those who do nothing to stop Communist abuses of power. For him, ignorance is no excuse. He believes that "whether they knew or didn't know is not the main issue; the main issue is whether a man is innocent because he didn't know. . . . When Tomas heard Communists shouting in defense of their inner purity, he said to himself, As a result of your 'not knowing,' this country has lost its freedom, lost it for centuries, perhaps, and you shout that you feel no guilt? How can you stand the sight of what you've done? How is it you aren't horrified?" (Kundera 1984, 177).

The government pressures Tomas to retract his letter, and when he refuses, he is forced out of his job. Eventually he becomes a window washer. Meanwhile his wife, Tereza, worries that government agents have been spying on her. She was once a photographer who took pictures of political unrest to document her people's struggles for freedom, but she allowed her love for Tomas to pull her away from her work. At her urging Tomas abandons his many mistresses, and the couple moves to the country. Shortly thereafter both are reported killed in a car crash. (Kundera 1984)

See also Censorship; Kundera, Milan; Tereza; Tomas

Uncle Tom's Cabin

Uncle Tom's Cabin: Or, Life Among the Lowly, by Harriet Beecher Stowe, was published in serialized form in the *National Era,* a Washington, D.C., antislavery newspaper, from 1851 to 1852 and as a book in 1852. The novel offers a powerful protest of the institution of slavery, humanizing its African-American characters and presenting them in a positive light. As a result, many scholars believe that the book's publication and subsequent popularity hastened the onset of the U.S. Civil War.

The story's protagonist is an African-American man named Uncle Tom, who is owned by a white man named Mr. Shelby. Shelby treats his slaves well and does not want to sell any of them. However, when he falls into debt, he changes his mind. Despite protests from his wife and son George, he sells Tom and a young boy, Harry, to a slave dealer named Haley. Before the dealer can take him away, Harry's mother, Eliza, hears of this and escapes with her child across the Ohio River. Haley sends two slave catchers in pursuit. They encounter her in a Quaker settlement, but they are unable to capture her because by this time Eliza's husband, George, has also escaped and is there to defend her. George fights with the slave catchers; one of them is wounded, and the other flees.

Meanwhile Haley has shackled Tom and taken him on a boat bound for New Orleans. On route Tom saves the life of a young girl, Eva St. Clare, and her grateful father buys him. Tom becomes head coachman for the St. Clare family. For a while he is happy, but when Eva dies of an illness and her father is accidentally killed during a knife fight, Tom is sent to the slave market. This time he is bought by a cruel plantation owner named Simon Legree. Tom tries to please his new master, but when he is ordered to whip a woman

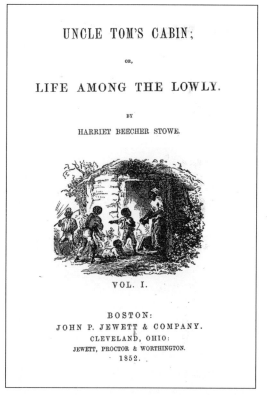

Frontispiece from the first edition of Uncle Tom's Cabin *by Harriet Beecher Stowe, 1852 (Library of Congress/ Rare Book Division)*

who did nothing wrong, he refuses and is himself flogged. Later he is flogged again when two female slaves turn up missing and Legree decides that Tom knows where they are. This beating is extremely harsh, and two days later Tom dies from his wounds. Just before his death George Shelby, the son of Tom's former owner, arrives to buy him back.

Seeing what has happened to Tom, George threatens to have Legree tried for murder, and when Legree laughs, George hits him. George then finds the two missing slaves, who have been hiding in an attic, and helps them escape the plantation. The two women eventually go to Canada, where Eliza and her husband, George, are now living with their son, Harry. Back on the plantation, George Shelby's father dies, and the young man frees all of his father's slaves in the name of Uncle Tom.

At the end of the novel its author offers a chapter of concluding remarks concerning her abolitionist views. Stowe (1960, 511) explains that her novel "has given only a faint shadow, a dim picture, of the anguish and despair that are, at this very moment, riving thousands of hearts, shattering thousands of families, and driving a helpless and sensitive race to frenzy and despair." She calls for an end to slavery, reminding her audience of their Christian beliefs, and she argues that the newly freed slaves should not be returned to Africa. Instead, she suggests that the United States has the obligation to provide former slaves with an education and chance to improve their lives in the United States. (Stowe 1960)

See also Shelby, George; Slavery; Stowe, Harriet Beecher; Tom, Uncle

Undershaft, Andrew

Andrew Undershaft is one of the main characters in George Bernard Shaw's 1904 play *Major Barbara*. A wealthy munitions manufacturer, Undershaft is called immoral for making weapons of war. He counters his critics by pointing out that he is also providing the common people with a way to fight their oppressors and better themselves. At one point he says:

> I hate poverty and slavery worse than any other crimes whatsoever. And let me tell you this. Poverty and slavery have stood up for centuries to your sermons and . . . articles: they will not stand up to my machine guns. . . . Killing . . . is the final test of conviction, the only lever strong enough to overturn a social system, the only way of saying Must. . . . Whatever can blow men up can blow society up. The history of the world is the history of those who had courage enough to embrace this truth. (Shaw 1962, 436)

In the end the other characters in the play are persuaded to accept Undershaft's point of view. (Shaw 1962)

See also *Major Barbara;* Shaw, George Bernard

Untouchable

Indian author Mulk Raj Anand wrote *Untouchable* in 1935 to publish the plight of the Untouchables in his native country. Responsible for cleaning latrines and sweeping dung, the Untouchables are the lowest caste in Hindu society. As such, they are forbidden to touch other human beings, and anything else they touch, such as a doorstep or a coin, must be ritually washed before anyone else can handle it.

According to Anand, as quoted by scholar Margaret Berry (1971, 40), his novel derives its conflict from "the anal-erotic complex of the puritan upper caste Hindus against whom [an Untouchable] is constrained to say: 'They think we are dung, because we clean their dung.' [This Untouchable] can't put it like a Professor of Psychology, but he says it in his own naïve manner. And his insights about the joy of the upper castes in seeing the outcasts condemned to do the business of cleaning at the same time as they express disgust against the untouchable reflects the paradox of the puritan temperament, unified for generations into ritualistic orthodoxy."

Berry (47–48) explains that "Anand's depiction of caste shows . . . that no one is ever so low that someone else is not lower, that snobbery flourishes everywhere. Among the untouchables, washermen hold themselves higher than leatherworkers; leatherworkers insist on preceding the sweepers." Moreover, the novel's main character, an Untouchable 18-year-old named Bakha who chafes at his restraints and longs for a classless society, "himself despises the beggars, a congeries of many castes" (48).

Untouchable depicts one day in Bakha's life. It begins well, with Bakha cheerfully going about his duties, cleaning latrines and streets, and playing field hockey with neighbor boys who ignore the fact that he is an Untouchable. However, when his father sends him on an errand and Bakha accidentally touches an adult, he is berated by an angry mob. From that moment on nothing seems the same to him. He is despondent about his position in life and is drawn to the temple, but as an Untouchable he is not allowed inside. He creeps up the steps anyway, and once again he finds himself berated by an angry mob. After several smaller indignities he returns home dejected and quarrels with his father.

Running away to sulk, Bakha comes upon a Salvation Army missionary who tries to convert him to Christianity. Bakha does not understand the man's teachings, so he goes instead to hear Mahatma Gandhi speak. Gandhi says that India's attitude toward the Untouchables is "the greatest blot on Hinduism" because "while we are asking for freedom from the grip of [the British], we have ourselves, for centuries, trampled underfoot millions of human beings without feeling the slightest remorse for our iniquity" (Anand 1940, 146). Gandhi believes that the Untouchables should no longer be oppressed.

This cheers Bakha, but he is more interested in a remark heard after Gandhi's speech, when a noted poet comments that "caste is now mainly governed by profession. When the sweepers change their profession, they will no longer remain Untouchables. And they can do that soon, for the first thing we will do . . . will be to introduce the machine which clears dung without anyone having to handle it—the flush system. Then the sweepers can be free from the stigma of untouchability and assume the dignity of status that is their right as useful members of a casteless and classless society" (155). Bakha is intrigued by the idea of such a machine and thinks about it all the way home.

Author E. M. Forster (vii-viii), writing in an introduction to the novel, finds this solution "prosaic, straightforward, and considered in the light of what has gone before in the book, it is very convincing. No god is needed to rescue the Untouchables, no vows of self-sacrifice and abnegation on the part of more fortunate Indians, but simply and solely—the flush system. Introduce water-closets and main-drainage throughout India, and all this wicked rubbish about untouchability will disappear." However, Berry (1971, 63) points out that the novel also deals with broader issues; it promotes socialism and "calls for a casteless and classless society." (Anand 1940; Berry 1971)

See also Anand, Mulk Raj; Bakha; Class, Social; Poverty; Socialism

"up & out"

The poem "up & out" first appeared in a collection entitled *Small Bones, Little Eyes*, by Native American poet nila northSun. It is typical of her work, which protests the social and economic hardships endured by her people. The poem speaks of Native Americans who try to better themselves by moving off the reservation and into cities, where they can make more money. But although they get good jobs, they soon discover that their cost of living is higher. The poem explains: "We made better money but it / got sucked up" (Velie 1991, 291). Therefore, they feel poorer than ever before. (Velie 1991)

See also Native American Issues; northSun, nila

V

Valjean, Jean

Jean Valjean is the main character in Victor Hugo's 1862 novel *Les Misérables*, which concerns poverty, morality, and injustice. Sentenced to 5 years in prison for stealing a loaf of bread for his sister's starving family, Valjean serves 19 because of several escape attempts. This experience hardens him. After his release he steals a bishop's silver and a small boy's coin, but his conscience is troubled, and he decides to change his life. He takes a new name, moves to a small town, and eventually becomes a man of good standing in the community. Highly respected by all, he donates large sums of money to the poor. Nonetheless, when his true identity is uncovered, he is sentenced to life in prison for theft. Later he escapes and, under another assumed name, again lives a good and charitable life. But because he is afraid of capture, he does not truly live a free life. (Hugo 1987)

See also Hugo, Victor; *Misérables, Les*

Valtoskar, Piera

One of the main characters in Ursula Le Guin's 1979 novel *Malafrena,* Piera Valtoskar lives in Europe during the early nineteenth century. As a young girl she is concerned about nothing but marriage, but as she matures, she realizes that other things in life are more im-portant. She breaks tradition and takes over the management of her father's estate when he becomes ill, proving herself as competent as any man. In the end she doubts whether she will ever take a husband, saying: "I don't understand what love is, or what it's supposed to be. Why is it supposed to be my whole life?" (Le Guin 1979, 268). (Le Guin 1979)

See also Le Guin, Ursula; *Malafrena*

Verhaeren, Émile

Born on May 21, 1855, in Saint Amand lez-Puers, Belgium, Émile Verhaeren was a poet who often wrote about social problems. His most well-known works in this regard are "Les Villages illusoires" (The Illusory Villages) and "Les Villes tentaculaires" (The Tentacled Cities). Both poems were published in 1895 and concern the decline of peasant life. Verhaeren believed in socialism and bemoaned the loss of rural communities. As a young man he studied law but became involved in a Brussels literary group and decided to write. His first book was published in 1883. A collection of poems entitled *Les Flamandes,* it praised peasant life and was very popular. Verhaeren produced more than 30 volumes of poetry over the ensuing years. His works include *Les Moines* (The Monks, 1886), *Les Campagnes hallucinées* (The Moonstruck

Jean Valjean attempts to defend himself in an illustration from Les Misérables, *which explores the conditions that led to the French Revolution of 1830. (North Wind Picture Archive)*

Countryside, 1893), and a trilogy of love poems to his wife entitled *Les Heures claires* (The Sunlit Hours, 1896), *Les Heures d'apres-midi* (The Afternoon Hours, 1905), and *Les Heures du soir* (The Evening Hours, 1918). He also wrote short stories, plays, and books on art. Verhaeren died on November 27, 1916, in Rouen, France.

See also Class, Social; Poverty

Verhovensky, Pyotr Stepanovitch

Leader of a Russian revolutionary group in Dostoyevsky's novel *Besy* (The Possessed), which was published in two volumes between 1871 and 1872, Pyotr Verhovensky manipulates people to gain social and political advantage. An avowed atheist, he has no conscience. He hires a convict named Fedka to kill two people because they threaten the secrecy of his group, and after the murders, when Fedka argues with him, Verhovensky decides to kill him, too. Verhovensky also kills a member of his group, Shatov, who wants to leave the organization, and he encourages another man, Kirillov, to take the blame for the murder and commit suicide. In the end Verhovensky escapes to Petersburg, leaving his followers to suffer for his crimes. (Dostoyevsky 1936; Dostoyevsky 1968)

See also Dostoyevsky, Fyodor; *Possessed, The;* Shatov; Stavrogin, Nikolay Vsyevolodovitch

Verne, Jules

Jules Verne is the author of several famous science fiction novels. One of them, the futuristic *Paris au XXe Siècle* (Paris in the Twentieth Century), is an important work of social protest, but the manuscript was rejected for publication in Verne's time and did not resurface until 1994. Verne was born on February 8, 1828, in Nantes, France. He studied law but later chose to become a playwright. His first success in this regard was *Les Pailles rompues* (The Broken Straws), which was produced at the Theatre Historique in 1850. He worked as a secretary for that theater from 1852 to 1854. He subsequently became a stockbroker but continued to write.

His first novel, *Voyages extraordinaires—Cinq semaines en ballon* (Five Weeks in a Balloon), was published in 1863, followed by *Le Voyage au centre de la Terre* (Journey to the Center of the Earth) in 1864, *De la Terre à la Lune* (From the Earth to the Moon) in 1865, *Vingt Mille Lieus sous les mer* (Twenty Thousand Leagues under the Sea) in 1869, *Le Tour du mond en quatre-vingt jour* (Around the World in Eighty Days) in 1873, and *L'Île mystérieuse* (The Mysterious Island) in 1874. All of Verne's works were extremely popular, and they uncannily predicted many future inventions. Verne died on March 24, 1905, in Amiens, France. (Quackenbush 1985)

See also *Paris in the Twentieth Century;* Science Fiction and Fantasy

Vonnegut, Kurt

Kurt Vonnegut is a novelist who uses science fiction and satire to criticize various aspects of modern society. Born on November 11, 1922, in Indianapolis, Indiana, he worked for an electric company until 1950, when he became a freelance writer and began selling his short stories to science fiction magazines. His first novel was published in 1952. Entitled *Player Piano*, it depicts a futuristic United States in which the workers have been replaced by machines and society is beginning to crumble. Vonnegut's best-known novels are *Cat's Cradle* (1963) and *Slaughterhouse Five* (1969), which concern war and global destruction. He continues to write novels, plays, short stories, articles, and autobiographical works. His most recent novels include *Galapagos* (1985), *Bluebeard* (1987), and *Hocus Pocus* (1990). (Schatt 1976)

See also *Player Piano;* Science Fiction and Fantasy

W

Walker, Alice

Alice Walker writes primarily about black feminist issues in the United States. Born on February 9, 1944, in Eatonton, Georgia, she participated in the civil rights movement in the 1960s, and her first published writings were poetry collections. They include *Once* (1968) and *Revolutionary Petunias* (1973). Her first novel was *The Third Life of Grange Copeland* (1970), which concerns racism among black sharecroppers. She has written several more novels, poems, and short stories dealing with issues of racism and feminism but is perhaps best known for *The Color Purple*. This 1982 novel received the Pulitzer Prize and was made into a highly successful motion picture in 1985. In 1989 Walker published a sequel to the work, *The Temple of My Familiar,* which includes some of the same characters but addresses new themes. Her most recent works include the novels *Possessing the Secret of Joy* (1992), *Everyday Use* (1994), and *By the Light of My Father's Smile* (1998), a collection of essays entitled *In Search of Our Mother's Gardens* (1983), and the nonfiction book *Warrior Marks: Female Genital Mutilation and the Sexual Blinding of Women* (1993). (Gates and Appiah 1993a; Winchell 1992)

See also *Color Purple, The;* Feminism; Racism; *Temple of My Familiar, The*

Alice Walker, 1991 (F. Capri/Saga/Archive Photos)

Watch on the Rhine

The three-act drama *Watch on the Rhine,* by American playwright Lillian Hellman, was first performed in April 1941. It concerns an antifascist freedom fighter, Kurt Muller, who eventually commits murder to protect his family. Muller is visiting his wife's relatives in the United States when another houseguest, Teck de Brancovis, discovers his true identity and antifascist activities. Brancovis threatens to turn Muller in to his enemies, so Muller murders him and makes plans to return to Europe. Before he leaves, he compares his situation to that of a character in a novel, saying:

> Do you remember when we read "*Les Misérables*"? . . . Well, he stole bread. The world is out of shape we said, when there are hungry men. And until it gets in shape, men will steal and lie and— . . . kill. But for whatever reason it is done, and whoever does it—you understand me—it is all bad. I want you to remember that. Whoever does it, it is bad. . . . But you will live to see the day when it will not have to be. All over the world, in every place and every town, there are men who are going to make sure it will not have to be. They want what I want: a childhood for every child. For my children, and I for theirs. . . . In every town and every village and every mud hut in the world, there is always a man who loves children and will fight to make a good world for them. (Hellman 1979, 299)

(Hellman 1979)

See also Fascism; Hellman, Lillian; *Misérables, Les*

Welch, James

Born in 1940 in Browning, Montana, James Welch is a Native American poet and novelist who writes about the history and experiences of his people. He grew up on reservations and attended the University of Montana. A collection of his poetry entitled *Riding the Earthboy 40* was published in 1971. Its poems, which include "Surviving" and "Harlem, Montana: Just Off the Reservation," depict reservation life, as does his first novel, *Winter in the Blood*, which was published in 1974. His other novels include *The Death of Jim Loney* (1979),

Fools Crow (1986), and *The Indian Lawyer* (1990). (Velie 1991)

See also "Harlem, Montana: Just Off the Reservation"; Native American Issues; "Surviving"

Wells, H. G.

Writing in the late nineteenth and early twentieth centuries, English novelist Herbert George Wells correctly predicted many future inventions. At one point he believed that science would solve humanity's problems, but later he decided that society's overdependence on technology would eventually destroy it. He also used his works to criticize various aspects of capitalism and class structure.

Wells was born on September 21, 1866, in Bromley, Kent, England. The son of a maid and a shopkeeper, he received a scholarship to the Normal School of Science in London, and after graduation he attended London University on a grant. The university awarded him a degree in biology in 1890. Shortly thereafter he decided to become a freelance writer.

At first he wrote articles and short stories, but later he turned to novels. His first book, *The Time Machine,* was published 1895 to immediate success. It is considered one of the first works of science fiction but is also a commentary on the class structure, depicting a futuristic London society that has split into two races: the materialistic, flighty Eloi and the laboring Moloch who care for them in order to eat them.

Wells's subsequent works include *The Invisible Man* (1897), *The War of the Worlds* (1898), and *Tono-Bungay* (1908), which criticizes many aspects of London society. He also wrote a nonfiction work on social issues, *Anticipations* (1901). Shortly thereafter he joined a socialist group called the Fabian Society, whose founders include George Bernard Shaw, but Wells left over a philosophical disagreement. Throughout his life he continued to write nonfiction books outlining his position on social problems. These include *A Modern Utopia* (1906), *New Worlds for Old* (1908), *The Shape of Things to Come* (1933), and *The Work, Wealth, and Happiness of*

Mankind (1931), which he coauthored. Wells also wrote a one-volume history of humanity entitled *Outline of History,* which was published in 1920 and revised in 1931. He died in London, England, on August 13, 1946. (Scheick and Cox 1988)

See also Science Fiction and Fantasy; Shaw, George Bernard; Socialism; *Tono-Bungay*

West, Julian

Julian West is the fictional narrator of Edward Bellamy's 1887 novel *Looking Backward, 2000–1887.* Born in Boston on December 26, 1857, by the age of 30 West has developed terrible insomnia, and after a hypnotist helps him fall asleep, he accidentally wakes up 113 years later, in the year 2000. Subsequently, from his perspective as an inhabitant of two very different societies, West reports on the contrasts between the nineteenth century, with its labor struggles and poverty, and the twentieth century, which he views as a utopia of equality and justice. He eventually becomes a historian and marries Edith Leete, who is the great-granddaughter of a woman he loved in his previous life. (Bellamy 1982)

See also Bellamy, Edward; Capitalism; Leete, Edith; *Looking Backward, 2000–1887;* Poverty; Socialism

Wharton, Edith

Edith Wharton was born Edith Jones on January 24, 1862, in New York, New York, and married Boston banker Edward Wharton in 1885. A member of upper-class society, she wrote about her world and criticized its rigid attitudes and customs. Her work has often been compared to that of another critic of social norms, Henry James, with whom she was acquainted. Wharton's first successful writing was a book entitled *The Decoration of Houses* (1897), an attack on upper-class interior decorating. Later she incorporated her interest in decorating and architecture in her fiction, using detailed settings and commenting on the order or disorder in her characters' homes and lives.

Wharton's first story collection was *The Greater Inclination* (1899) and her first novel *The Valley of Decision* (1902). Her first successful book was *The House of Mirth* (1905), the story of a woman who descends from the upper classes into poverty. Two years after its publication Wharton began having an affair, and six years after that she divorced her husband. She moved to France and remained there for the rest of her life, receiving the French Legion of Honor award in 1916 for her volunteer work with war refugees during World War I. In addition to this work, she continued to write. Her novels include *Ethan Frome* (1911), *The Reef* (1912), *The Custom of the Country* (1913), and *The Age of Innocence* (1920), which won her the Pulitzer Prize in 1921. She was the first woman to receive this honor. Wharton also wrote short stories, poetry, an autobiography, and several nonfiction books, including *The Writing of Fiction* (1925). Her last novel, *The Buccaneers* (1938), was published posthumously. Wharton died on August 11, 1937, in St.-Brice-sous-Foret, France. (Howe 1962)

See also *Age of Innocence, The;* Feminism; James, Henry

Wilde, Oscar

Oscar Wilde is considered one of Ireland's greatest writers. He wrote poetry, plays, essays, and a novel, *The Picture of Dorian Gray* (1891). Several of his plays, including *The Importance of Being Earnest* (1895), reveal flaws within Victorian society, and his most important poem, "The Ballad of Reading Gaol" (1898), protests inhumane prison conditions.

Wilde was born on October 16, 1854, in Dublin, Ireland, and attended Trinity College there. In 1881 he published his first volume of poetry, and he toured the United States and Canada in 1882 to lecture on writing. In 1884 he married and had two children, but in 1891 he became romantically involved with Lord Alfred Douglas. Because of his relationship with this man, Wilde was eventually sentenced to two years of hard labor. It was this experience that prompted him to write "The Ballad of Reading Gaol." After his release Wilde found himself bankrupt. He moved to

Paris, France, where he died on November 30, 1900. (Aldington 1946; Ellman 1969)

See also "Ballad of Reading Gaol, The"; Prison Reform

Woman, A

Published in Italy as *Una Donna* in 1906, *A Woman,* by Sibilla Aleramo, concerns the plight of Italian women during the early 1900s. At that time they were under the complete control of their fathers and husbands, with no rights under the law. Therefore, the novel's publication engendered great controversy, particularly after it was translated into English in 1908, and it has since been hailed as one of the most important feminist works in world literature.

Written in the first person, *A Woman* is largely autobiographical, describing Aleramo's own struggles to free herself from an abusive husband. Like Aleramo, the narrator of the story was raped at the age of 15 and forced to marry her rapist to maintain her honor. Despite her husband's brutal nature, she tries to be a dutiful wife and, later, a good mother to her son. Nonetheless, her life is miserable, and eventually she tries to commit suicide. After her attempt fails, she begins to write to maintain her sanity. Her articles appear in many Italian magazines, and she is offered an editing job in Rome. When her husband loses his job, he allows her to accept the position, and they move to the city.

Now the narrator experiences a new sense of freedom and begins fighting with her husband. When he decides to move back to his small town, she asks him for a separation. After some argument he agrees, but he tells her she will never see her son again. She remains in Rome thinking that the law will help her gain custody of her child. However, she soon finds she has no rights in that regard. Left with no way to tell her son why she left him, she writes a novel for him to read when he is older.

In addition to offering this story, *A Woman* comments on the role of women in Italian society. For example, the narrator speaks of the way mothers sacrifice their identities for their children, saying: "Who gave us this inhuman idea that mothers should negate their own wishes and desires? The acceptance of servitude has been handed down from mother to daughter for so many centuries that it is now a monstrous chain which fetters them. . . . What if mothers refused to deny their womanhood and gave their children instead an example of a life lived according to the needs of self-respect?"(Aleramo 1983, 193–194).

The narrator also criticizes poets who praise only women who are "unattainable," yet fail to mention "the women they lived with, who bore their children! They idolised one set of women in verse, while the prosaic reality of their lives was that even if they married them they turned the women they lived with into domestic servants" (156). She speaks often of women as slaves, as mere sexual objects whose sole duty is to satisfy their husbands or be beaten for their defiance. In addition, the narrator mentions the beginnings of socialism in Italy, expressing her desire to see all people live decent lives. In fact, at the end of *A Woman* the narrator satisfies her longing for her own child by helping other children at a clinic for the poor. (Aleramo 1983)

See also Aleramo, Sibilla; Feminism

Women's Rights

See Feminism

Working Conditions

See Labor Issues

Wright, Nel

Nel Wright is the childhood friend of Sula Peace, the main character in Toni Morrison's 1973 novel *Sula*. Whereas Sula is rebellious and promiscuous, Nel conforms to the expectations of the black community in which she lives. She marries but separates from her husband when he and Sula have an affair. At this point Nel ends her friendship with Sula. Afterward her life is colorless, and when Sula dies, Nel realizes how much she missed by losing her friend. (Gates and Appiah 1993c; Morrison 1974)

See also Feminism; Morrison, Toni; Peace, Sula; *Sula*

Wright, Richard

Richard Wright has written novels and short stories protesting racism in the United States during the 1940s and 50s. Born near Natchez, Mississippi, on September 4, 1908, he was the grandson of southern slaves and grew up in poverty. He held a variety of jobs before joining the Federal Writers' Project during the Depression, first in Chicago and then in New York. In 1932 he joined the Communist Party and began writing for Communist publications. He became the Harlem editor of the *Daily Worker* in 1937. The following year he gained recognition with the publication of *Uncle Tom's Children*, a volume of novellas. His first novel, *Native Son* (1940), only increased his fame. It was extremely popular and triggered a great deal of discussion about the nature and causes of racism in the United States.

In subsequent works Wright continued to write about racism, and eventually he decided that American society would never consider blacks equal to whites. Consequently, in 1945 he moved to Paris, France. By this time he had become dissatisfied with the Communist Party and broken his ties to it. His novel *The Outsider* (1953) reflects this dissatisfaction. Wright's other works include an autobiograph-

Richard Wright, 1950 (Archive Photos)

ical novel, *Black Boy* (1945), a nonfiction book entitled *Black Power* (1954), and a posthumously published collection of short stories, *Eight Men* (1961). Wright died on November 28, 1960, in Paris, France. (Webb 1968)

See also *Native Son; Outsider, The;* Racism

Y

Yakovlich, Sofron

Sofron Yakovlich is a cruel overseer in the short story "Bailiff," from a collection by Ivan Turgenev entitled *Zapiski okhotnika* (A Sportsman's Sketches). Yakovlich exploits the serfs under his control, manipulating the serf system in order to make himself rich at the peasants' expense. When they protest, he makes their situation worse or beats them into compliance. In describing Yakovlich, one peasant says: "Clever, awful clever he is, and rich, too, the varmint! What's bad about him is—he's always knocking someone about. A wild beast, not a man. I tell you he's a dog, a cur, a real cur if ever there was one" (Turgenev 1983, 116). (Turgenev 1983)

See also *Sportsman's Sketches, A;* Turgenev, Ivan

Yellow Horse

In *Little Big Man,* Thomas Berger's 1964 novel about the mistreatment of Native Americans during the 1800s, Yellow Horse is a gay man whose Cheyenne tribe not only tolerates him but also appreciates him. The narrator of the story explains: "If a Cheyenne don't believe he can stand a man's life, he ain't forced to. He can become a heemaneh, which is to say half-man, half-woman. There are uses for these fellows and everybody likes them. They are sometimes chemists, specializing in the making of love-potions, and generally good entertainers. They wear women's clothes and can get married to another man, if such be his taste" (Berger 1964, 76–77). Throughout the novel the Cheyenne are shown to be loving, accepting people, in contrast to the whites, who have many prejudices. (Berger 1964; Landon 1989)

See also Berger, Thomas; Crabbe, Jack; Gay and Lesbian Issues; *Little Big Man;* Old Lodge Skins; Racism

Yevtushenko, Yevgeny

During the 1950s and 1960s Russian poet Yevgeny Aleksandrovich Yevtushenko (also spelled Evgenii Evtushenko) was an outspoken critic of the way the Soviet government sought to limit artistic freedom. A gifted speaker, he was popular with the public and spread his message through poetry readings in Europe, the United States, and Australia. Born on July 18, 1933, Yevtushenko was a descendent of Ukrainians exiled to Siberia. He studied at the Gorky Institute of World Literature in Moscow and produced a large body of work during his lifetime. He is perhaps best known for the 1961 poem "Babii Yar" (also spelled "Baby Yar" or "Babi Yar"), which criticizes anti-Semitism in the Soviet Union. In 1963 he published his *A Precocious Autobiog-*

raphy in English without prior approval of Soviet censors. This led the Soviet government to recall him from one of his reading tours and revoke many of his privileges. Eventually his rights were restored, and for a time he continued to live and write in Russia. His later works include a novel, *Yagodnyye mesta* (Wild Berries, 1981), and *The Collected Poems, 1952–1990* (1991). In writing about his work, Yevtushenko (1989) once said that he intended his poems to promote "liberation from the tyranny of censorship, from the tyranny of the observing eye of Orwell's Big Brother." Today Yevtushenko lives in the United States. In 1996 he was appointed a professor of Russian literature at Queen's College in New York, where in 1966 he gave his first American poetry reading. (Yevtushenko 1989)

> See also Anti-Semitism; "Babii Yar"; Censorship; Orwell, George

Yonnondio: From the Thirties

The title of this unfinished novel, *Yonnondio,* is a Native American word meaning "lament for the lost." Its story focuses on the hardships of working-class Americans during the 1920s. Although the novel was not published until 1974, the first chapter of *Yonnondio* appeared as a short story, "The Iron Throat," in a 1934 issue of the radical journal the *Partisan Review.* During the Great Depression, author Tillie Olsen was a political activist involved in labor and feminist issues.

Yonnondio follows two and a half years in the life of the Holbrook family: Jim Holbrook; his wife, Anna; and his children, Mazie, Will, Ben, Jim Junior, and Bess, who is born during the course of the story. At first Jim is a miner in a Wyoming mining town. Every day he risks lung damage from mine dust or death from a cave-in, while his wife and children endure poor living conditions and have little hope of bettering themselves. Finally he decides to become a tenant farmer, and the family travels to the Dakotas, where the children have good food and start going to school. However, at the end of the year Jim discovers that he is in debt to his landlord and must give up his livestock and some of his possessions.

The family leaves the farm and moves to a rental house in a midwestern city. Jim is soon hired to dig sewer ditches, but in this job, too, he finds it difficult to get ahead. Eventually he quits and gets a position at the local meatpacking house. There his pay is better, but the working conditions are horrible. The packing house bosses want the employees to work as quickly as possible and to take few breaks. During a heat wave, temperatures inside the packing house reach 108 degrees, but workers are still not allowed to slow down. As a result, one suffers a heart attack, and others are scalded when a steam pipe breaks.

Tillie Olsen knew about such labor abuses firsthand. Shortly before beginning to write *Yonnondio,* she was jailed for helping to organize workers in the Kansas City meatpacking industry. Later, in 1934, she became involved in a longshoreman's strike and various other forms of union activity. She was particularly concerned with the plight of female workers, whom she believed were doubly oppressed because of their gender. A feminist, Olsen uses the characters of Anna and her daughter Mazie to show how society conditions women to accept a subservient role.

It is Jim, not Anna, who makes the decisions in the family. Although he appears to love her, he ignores her opinions about where they should live and what they should do. Moreover, he treats many of her concerns as foolish, and on one occasion when she refuses to make love to him, he rapes her. But Anna does not teach her daughter to expect better, and when Mazie expresses an interest in male activities, Anna tells her that girls do not do such things.

Anna eventually suffers for her oppression. She has a miscarriage, becomes ill, and begins to lose touch with reality. Had Olsen finished the novel, Anna's fate was to have been far worse. Deborah Rosenfelt, who studied Olsen's papers and notes, says in her essay "From the Thirties: Tillie Olsen and the Radical Tradition" (Nelson and Huse 1994, 72):

> What we have today is only the beginning of the novel that was to have been. In

Olsen's initial plan, Jim Holbrook was to have become involved in a strike in the packing houses, a strike that would draw out the inner strength and courage of his wife Anna, politicize the older children as well, and involve some of the women in the packing plant as strike leaders in the essential collective action. Embittered by the length of the strike and its lack of clear initial success, humiliated by his inability to support his family, Jim Holbrook was finally to have abandoned them. Anna was to die trying to give herself an abortion. Will and Mazie were to go West to the Imperial Valley in California, where they would themselves become organizers. Mazie was to grow up to become an artist, a writer who could tell the experiences of her people, her mother especially living in her memory.

Many scholars have noted that the character of Mazie is partly autobiographical. Olsen experienced many of the same events as Mazie, including her family's move to the meatpacking town of Omaha. In addition, her father was a member of the Socialist Party who actively supported the unionization of American workers. (Nelson and Huse 1994; Olsen 1980)

See also Feminism; Holbrook Family; Labor Issues; Olsen, Tillie

Yossarian, Captain John

As the main character in Joseph Heller's 1961 novel *Catch-22*, Captain John Yossarian points out the absurdities of war. He is a bombardier stationed in Italy during World War II who feigns insanity to try to get out of flying. However, because the air force considers the desire to avoid warfare sane, Yossarian is judged fit for service. Tired of the death and corruption he sees all around him, he eventually escapes to neutral Sweden. (Heller 1994)

See also *Catch-22;* Heller, Joseph

Younger Family

The Youngers are the main characters in Lorraine Hansberry's three-act play *A Raisin in the Sun* (1959). Lena Younger, the head of the household, is a strong-willed matriarch who works as a domestic servant. Her daughter-in-law, Ruth, also cleans white people's houses, and her son, Walter, is a white man's chauffeur. Lena's daughter, Beneatha, is in school and wants to become a doctor. Her grandson, Travis, does not know what he wants to become, but he says he would be happy driving a bus. This makes his father mad.

The family lives together in a roach-infested ghetto apartment, sharing the bathroom with another family. The Youngers are discouraged but gain strength from one another and from pride in their African heritage. At the end of the play they are in the process of moving to a new home in an all-white neighborhood, where they will clearly not be welcome. (Hansberry 1994)

See also Hansberry, Lorraine; Racism; *Raisin in the Sun, A*

Z

Zaius

Zaius is an orangutan who appears in the 1963 science fiction novel *La Planète des singes* (Planet of the Apes), by Pierre Boulle. Zaius lives on a planet where apes behave like humans and humans like apes. A leading scientist, he is extremely narrow-minded, refusing to accept facts that counter his opinions. In fact, when he is presented with a human who acts like an ape, he wants to destroy him. (Boulle 1963)

See also Boulle, Pierre; *Planet of the Apes*

Zakeya

Zakeya is the main character in the 1974 Egyptian feminist novel *Mawt al-rajul al-wahid 'ala 'l-ard* (God Dies by the Nile), by Nawal El Saadawi. At the beginning of the novel Zakeya is hoeing crops and trying to forget her hard life. Then her brother, Kafrawi, comes to tell her that his daughter Nefissa has run away. Nefissa had been a servant in the house of the village mayor, who is a cruel tyrant. Now the mayor wants her younger sister, Zeinab, to take over the job. When she refuses, the mayor contrives to have Kafrawi arrested for a crime he did not commit. Shortly thereafter Zeinab marries Galal, and the mayor arranges for him to be arrested, too. Zeinab runs away, and Zakeya realizes

that the mayor raped both of her nieces. She takes up her hoe and bludgeons him to death. (El Saadawi 1990)

See also El Saadawi, Nawal; Feminism; *God Dies by the Nile*

Zangwill, Israel

Novelist and playwright Israel Zangwill wrote about the lives of Jewish immigrants in London ghettos. Born on February 14, 1864, in London, England, he was himself the son of immigrants and eventually became a Zionist leader. His best-known work is the novel *Children of the Ghetto* (1892), which shows the struggles of Jews trying to maintain their spirituality in a Christian culture. Zangwill wrote not only novels but also plays on immigrant culture, as well as a collection of essays on famous Jews. He died on August 1, 1926, in Midhurst, West Sussex, England. (Leftwich 1957)

See also Anti-Semitism; *Children of the Ghetto*; Poverty

Zeinab

Zeinab is a young peasant woman in Nawal El Saadawi's 1974 feminist novel *Mawt al-rajul al-wahid 'ala 'l-ard* (God Dies by the Nile). Beautiful and kind, she is the object of the village mayor's lust. He forces her to be his mistress, and when she marries and refuses to see him anymore, he has her husband arrested on a false charge. Nonetheless, Zeinab remains firm in rejecting the mayor. She leaves the village to visit her husband in jail but is waylaid by a man who wants her sexual favors. She is never seen again. (El Saadawi 1990)

See also El Saadawi, Nawal; *God Dies by the Nile*

Ziemssen, Joachim

A character in Thomas Mann's 1924 novel *Der Zauberberg* (The Magic Mountain), Joachim Ziemssen is a single-minded, practical soldier. He is therefore very unlike his cousin, Hans Castorp, an intellectual who allows other people to influence his decisions. Both men live in a mountain sanitorium, but whereas Hans revels in his illness and remains under a doctor's care even after he is pronounced well, Joachim denies his illness and leaves the sanitorium to further his military career. He spends several enjoyable months reveling in life, then returns to the sanitorium to die. (Mann 1972)

See also Castorp, Hans; *Magic Mountain, The;* Mann, Thomas

Zola, Émile

French novelist Émile Zola often wrote about the relationship between social conditions and evil. In this regard he created a sequence of 20 novels known collectively as the Rougon-Macquart Cycle (1871–1893), which depict such social ills as alcoholism among the labor classes and covetousness among peasants. Zola was born in Paris, France, on April 2, 1840. After failing his university examinations, he was unemployed for two years. Then he became a clerk in a shipping company and later worked for a publishing company. There he was encouraged to write, and in 1864 his first work, a collection of short stories entitled

Émile Zola (Library of Congress/Corbis)

Contes à Ninon, was published. His other works include *La Confession de Claude* (1865) and *Thérèse Raquin* (1867).

In later years Zola became involved in a famous court case involving anti-Semitism. He and many other French writers, including Anatole France, protested the unfair conviction of a Jewish army officer accused of treason. To bring the case to public attention, Zola wrote a letter, "J'Accuse" (I Accuse), which accused the French military of being prejudiced and deceitful. This letter was published in the January 13, 1898, edition of the newspaper *L'Aurore,* and the following month Zola was convicted of libel, fined 3,000 francs, and sentenced to one year in prison. He fled to London, where he remained until he was pardoned in 1899. He died in Paris, France, on September 28, 1902. (Grant 1966)

See also France, Anatole; Rougon-Macquart Cycle

REFERENCES

Aaron, Daniel. 1961. *Writers on the Left: Episodes in American Literary Communism.* New York: Harcourt, Brace and World.

Abbey Edward. 1975. *The Monkey Wrench Gang.* Philadelphia: Lippincott.

Abrahams, Peter. 1975. *The Path of Thunder.* Chatham, NJ: Chatham Bookseller.

Aji, Aron (ed.). 1992. *Milan Kundera and the Art of Fiction: Critical Essays.* New York: Garland.

Aldington, Richard (ed.). 1946. *The Portable Oscar Wilde.* New York: Viking Press.

Alegría, Ciro. 1941. *Broad and Alien Is the World.* New York: Farrar and Rinehart.

Aleramo, Sibilla. 1983. *A Woman.* Berkeley and Los Angeles: University of California Press.

Allende, Isabel. 1985. *The House of the Spirits.* New York: Knopf.

———. 1988. *Eva Luna.* New York: Bantam Books.

Anand, Mulk Raj. 1940. *Untouchable.* New York: Penguin Books.

Angelou, Maya. 1994. *The Complete Collected Poems of Maya Angelou.* New York: Random House.

Aristophanes. 1930. *Aristophanes: The Eleven Comedies.* New York: Horace Liveright.

Ariyoshi, Sawako. 1987. *The Twilight Years.* Trans. Mildred Tahara. New York: Kodansha America.

Atkins, John. 1968. *Aldous Huxley: A Literary Study.* New York: Orion Press.

Atwood, Margaret. 1986. *The Handmaid's Tale.* Boston: Houghton Mifflin.

———. 1996. *The Edible Woman.* New York: Bantam Books.

Babb, Valerie Melissa. 1991. *Ernest Gaines.* Boston: Twayne.

Baker, James R. 1965. *William Golding: A Critical Study.* New York: St. Martin's Press.

Baker, James Thomas. 1987. *Ayn Rand.* Boston: Twayne.

Baldwin, James. 1962. *Another Country.* New York: Dial Press.

———. 1988. *If Beale Street Could Talk.* New York: Dell.

Banning, Evelyn I. 1973. *Helen Hunt Jackson.* New York: Vanguard Press.

Barker, Dudley. 1969. *The Man of Principle: A Biography of John Galsworthy.* New York: Stein and Day.

Barnard, Marjorie Faith. 1967. *Miles Franklin.* New York: Twayne.

Barrow, Georgia M. 1979. *Ageing, Ageism, and Society.* St. Paul, MN: West.

Behn, Aphra. 1973. *Oroonoko: or, The Royal Slave.* New York: Norton.

Bellamy, Edward. 1951. *Looking Backward, 2000–1887.* Introduction by Robert Shurter. New York: Modern Library.

———. 1982. *Looking Backward, 2000–1887.* Introduction by Cecelia Tichi. New York: Penguin Books.

Benson, Brian Joseph, and Mabel Mayle Dillard. 1980. *Jean Toomer.* Boston: Twayne.

Berger, Thomas. 1964. *Little Big Man.* New York: Dial Press.

Berry, Margaret. 1971. *Mulk Raj Anand: The Man and the Novelist*. Amsterdam: Oriental Press.

Björnson, Björnstjerne. 1916. *Plays by Björnson Björnstjerne*. Trans. Edwin Björkman. New York: Scribner's.

Bloodworth, William A. 1977. *Upton Sinclair*. Boston: Twayne.

Bloom, Harold (ed.). 1989. *Modern Critical Views: Albert Camus*. New York: Chelsea House.

Boulle, Pierre. 1963. *Planet of the Apes*. New York: Signet.

Bowman, Sylvia. 1962. *Edward Bellamy Abroad: An American Prophet's Influence*. New York: Twayne.

———. 1979. *The Year 2000: A Critical Biography of Edward Bellamy*. New York: Octagon Books.

———. 1986. *Edward Bellamy*. Boston: Twayne.

Boyer, Paul S. 1968. *Purity in Print: The Vice-Society Movement and Book Censorship in America*. New York: Scribner's.

Bradbury, Ray. 1996. *Fahrenheit 451*. New York: Ballantine Books.

Brander, Lawrence. 1970. *Aldous Huxley: A Critical Study*. London: Hart-Davis.

Brée, Germaine. 1961. *Camus*. New Brunswick, NJ: Rutgers University Press.

Brewster, Dorothy. 1965. *Doris Lessing*. New York: Twayne.

Breytenbach, Breyten. 1994. *A Season in Paradise*. San Diego: Harcourt, Brace.

Brustein, Robert. 1964. *The Theatre of Revolt*. Boston: Little, Brown.

Burgess, Anthony. 1986. *A Clockwork Orange*. New York: Norton.

Butler, Marilyn. 1972. *Maria Edgeworth: A Literary Biography*. Oxford: Clarendon Press.

Butler, Ronnie. 1983. *Balzac and the French Revolution*. Totowa, NJ: Barnes and Noble Books.

Callan, Edward. 1982. *Alan Paton*. Boston: Twayne.

Camus, Albert. 1958. *The Fall*. Trans. Justin O'Brien. New York: Knopf.

———. 1989. *The Stranger*. Trans. Matthew Ward. New York: Vintage Books.

Carter, April. 1971. *The Political Theory of Anarchism*. New York: Harper and Row.

Carter, Stephen. 1977. *The Politics of Solzhenitsyn*. New York: Holmes & Meier.

Chamberlain, Robert Lyall. 1965. *George Crabbe*. New York: Twayne.

Cheney, Anne. 1984. *Lorraine Hansberry*. Boston: Twayne.

Cherkovski, Neeli. 1979. *Ferlinghetti: A Biography*. Garden City, NY: Doubleday.

Clark, Barrett Harper. 1947. *Eugene O'Neill: The Man and His Plays*. New York: Dover.

Clark, Walter Van Tilburg. 1960. *The Ox-Bow Incident*. New York: Penguin Books.

Clayton, Cherry. 1997. *Olive Schreiner*. New York: Twayne.

Cleugh, James. 1968. *Thomas Mann: A Study*. New York: Russell and Russell.

Clifford, Deborah Pickman. 1979. *Mine Eyes Have Seen the Glory: A Biography of Julia Ward Howe*. Boston: Little, Brown.

Cohen, Carl. 1962. *Communism, Fascism, and Democracy: The Theoretical Foundations*. New York: Random House.

Cole, George Douglas Howard. 1976. *Studies in Class Structure*. Westport, CT: Greenwood Press.

Commons, John Rogers. 1967. *Social Reform and the Church*. New York: Kelley.

Copper, Baba. 1988. *Over the Hill: Reflections on Ageism between Women*. Freedom, CA: Crossing Press.

Corrigan, Robert Willoughby (ed.). 1969. *Arthur Miller: A Collection of Critical Essays*. Englewood Cliffs, NJ: Prentice-Hall.

Coustillas, Pierre (comp.). 1968. *Collected Articles on George Gissing*. New York: Barnes and Noble Books.

Crick, Bernard R. 1980. *George Orwell: A Life*. Boston: Little, Brown.

Crompton, Rosemary, and Jon Gubbay. 1978. *Economy and Class Structure*. New York: St. Martin's Press.

Cruikshank, Robert James. 1949. *Charles Dickens and Early Victorian England*. London: Pitman.

Cullen, Countee. 1991. *My Soul's High Song: The Collected Writings of Countee Cullen*. New York: Doubleday.

Daiches, David. 1966. *Robert Burns*. New York: Macmillan.

Davidson, Arnold E., and Cathy N. Davidson (eds.). 1981. *The Art of Margaret Atwood: Essays in Criticism*. Toronto: Anansi Press.

Davis, Thadious M. 1994. *Nella Larsen, Novelist of the Harlem Renaissance: A Woman's Life Unveiled*. Baton Rouge: Louisiana State University Press.

De Vitis, A. A. 1964. *Graham Greene*. New York: Twayne.

———. 1972. *Anthony Burgess*. New York: Twayne.

Dick, Bernard F. 1967. *William Golding.* New York: Twayne.

Dickens, Charles. 1963. *Great Expectations.* New York: Signet Books.

———. 1966. *Hard Times.* New York: Norton.

———. 1987a. *Bleak House.* Oxford: Oxford University Press.

———. 1987b. *Little Dorrit.* Introduction by Lionel Trilling. Oxford: Oxford University Press.

Dillingham, William B. 1969. *Frank Norris: Instinct and Art.* Lincoln: University of Nebraska Press.

Dostoyevsky, Fyodor. 1936. *The Possessed.* New York: Modern Library.

———. 1968. *The Notebooks for The Possessed.* Ed. by Edward Wasiolek. Chicago: University of Chicago Press.

Dreiser, Theodore. 1964. *An American Tragedy.* New York: Signet Books.

Duberman, Martin B. 1966. *James Russell Lowell.* Boston: Houghton Mifflin.

Early, Eileen. 1980. *Joy in Exile: Ciro Alegria's Narrative Art.* Washington, DC: University Press of America.

Eckman, Fern Marja. 1966. *The Furious Passage of James Baldwin.* New York: Evans.

Edel, Leon. 1963. *Henry James: A Collection of Critical Essays.* Englewood Cliff, NJ: Prentice-Hall.

Edgeworth, Maria. 1992. *Castle Rackrent and Ennui.* New York: Penguin Books.

Egbert, Donald Drew. 1967. *Socialism and American Art in the Light of European Utopianism, Marxism, and Anarchism.* Princeton, NJ: Princeton University Press.

El Saadawi, Nawal. 1990. *God Dies By the Nile.* London: Zed Books Ltd.

Elliot, Jeffrey M. (ed.). 1989. *Conversations with Maya Angelou.* Jackson: University Press of Mississippi.

Elliott, Emory (ed.). 1988. *Columbia Literary History of the United States.* New York: Columbia University Press.

Ellison, Ralph. 1952. *Invisible Man.* New York: Random House.

Ellman, Richard (ed.). 1969. *Oscar Wilde: A Collection of Critical Essays.* Englewood Cliffs, NJ: Prentice-Hall.

Emanuel, James A. 1967. *Langston Hughes.* New York: Twayne.

Endō, Shūsaku. 1980. *Silence.* New York: Taplinger.

Ensor, Robert. 1992. *The Novels of Peter Abrahams and the Rise of Nationalism in Africa.* Essen, Germany: Verlag die Blaue Eule.

Estes, David C. (ed.). 1994. *Critical Reflections of the Fiction of Ernest Gaines.* Athens: University of Georgia Press.

Farah, Nuruddin. 1992. *Close Sesame.* St. Paul, MN: Graywolf Press.

Faris, Wendy B. 1983. *Carlos Fuentes.* New York: Ungar.

Farrison, William Edward. 1969. *William Wells Brown: Author and Reformer.* Chicago: University of Chicago Press.

Feldstein, Stanley. 1972. *The Poisoned Tongue: A Documentary History of American Racism and Prejudice.* New York: Morrow.

Ferguson, Blanche F. 1966. *Countee Cullen and the Negro Renaissance.* New York: Dodd, Mead.

Ferlinghetti, Lawrence. 1958. *A Coney Island of the Mind.* New York: New Directions.

Ferres, John H. (ed.). 1972. *Twentieth-Century Interpretations of* The Crucible. Englewood Cliffs, NJ: Prentice-Hall.

Fielding, K. J. 1958. *Charles Dickens: A Critical Introduction.* London: Longmans, Green.

Filler, Louis. 1960. *The Crusade against Slavery.* New York: Harper.

Flannery, Edward H. 1965. *The Anguish of the Jews: Twenty-Three Centuries of Anti-Semitism.* New York: Macmillan.

Fontenrose, Joseph Eddy. 1964. *John Steinbeck: An Introduction and Interpretation.* New York: Barnes and Noble Books.

Frackman, Lucille. 1996. *Pierre Boulle.* New York: Twayne.

Franklin, Miles. 1965. *My Brilliant Career.* Sydney: Angus and Robertson.

Fredrickson, George M. 1997. *The Comparative Imagination: On the History of Racism, Nationalism, and Social Movements.* Berkeley and Los Angeles: University of California Press.

French, Warren G. 1975. *John Steinbeck.* Boston: Twayne.

Friedman, Lenemaja. 1975. *Shirley Jackson.* Boston: Twayne.

Fuentes, Carlos. 1964. *The Death of Artemio Cruz.* Trans. Sam Hileman. New York: Farrar, Straus.

———. 1978. *The Hydra Head.* Trans. Margaret Sayers Peden. New York: Farrar Straus Giroux.

Gaines, Ernest J. 1972. *The Autobiography of Miss Jane Pittman.* New York: Bantam Books.

Galloway, David, and Christian Sabish (eds.). 1982. *Calamus: Male Homosexuality in*

Twentieth-Century Literature—An International Anthology. New York: Morrow.

Galsworthy, John. 1928. *Plays by John Galsworthy.* New York: Scribner's.

Gates, Henry Louis, Jr. (ed.). 1990. *Three Classic African-American Novels.* New York: Vintage Books.

Gates, Henry Louis, Jr., and K. A. Appiah (eds.). 1993a. *Alice Walker: Critical Perspectives Past and Present.* New York: Amistad.

Gates, Henry Louis, Jr., and K. A. Appiah (eds.). 1993b. *Richard Wright: Critical Perspectives Past and Present.* New York: Amistad.

Gates, Henry Louis, Jr., and K. A. Appiah (eds.). 1993c. *Toni Morrison: Critical Perspectives Past and Present.* New York: Amistad.

Geismar, Maxwell David. 1953. *Rebels and Ancestors: The American Novel 1890–1915: Frank Norris, Stephen Crane, Jack London, Ellen Glasgow, Theodore Dreiser.* Boston: Houghton Mifflin.

Gerber, Philip L. 1964. *Theodore Dreiser.* New York: Twayne.

Gissing, George. 1924. *Critical Studies of the Works of Charles Dickens.* New York: Greenberg.

———. 1926. *New Grub Street.* New York: Modern Library.

Godwin, Parke. 1967. *A Biography of William Cullen Bryant, with Extracts from His Private Correspondence.* New York: Russell and Russell.

Golding, William. 1954. *Lord of the Flies.* New York: Perigee Books.

Goode, John. 1979. *George Gissing: Ideology and Fiction.* New York: Barnes and Noble Books.

Goreau, Angeline. 1980. *Reconstructing Aphra: A Biography of Aphra Behn.* New York: Dial Press.

Grace, Sherrill. 1980. *Violent Duality: A Study of Margaret Atwood.* Montreal: Vehicule Press.

Graham, Don. 1978. *The Fiction of Frank Norris: The Aesthetic Context.* Columbia: University of Missouri Press.

Grant, Eliott M. 1966. *Emile Zola.* New York: Twayne.

Grebstein, Sheldon Norman. 1962. *Sinclair Lewis.* New York: Twayne.

Greene, Graham. 1962. *The Power and the Glory.* New York: Time.

Grossman, Mark. 1996. *The ABC-CLIO Companion to the Native American Rights Movement.* Santa Barbara, CA: ABC-CLIO.

Hagen, Lyman B. 1996. *Heart of a Woman, Mind of a Writer, and Soul of a Poet: A Critical Analysis of the Writings of Maya Angelou.* Lanham, MD: University Press of America.

Hamalian, Leo (comp.). 1974. *Franz Kafka: A Collection of Criticism.* New York: McGraw-Hill.

Hansberry, Lorraine. 1994. *A Raisin in the Sun.* New York: Vintage Books.

Harris, Sharon M. 1991. *Rebecca Harding Davis and American Realism.* Philadelphia: University of Pennsylvania Press.

Hart, Patricia. 1989. *Narrative Magic in the Fiction of Isabel Allende.* Rutherford, NJ: Fairleigh Dickinson University Press.

Hatfield, Henry Caraway (ed.). 1964. *Thomas Mann: A Collection of Critical Essays.* Englewood Cliffs, NJ: Prentice-Hall.

Haugen, Eva Lund, and Einar Haugen (eds.). 1978. *Land of the Free: Björnstjerne Björnson's American Letters, 1880–1881.* Northfield, MN: Norwegian-American Historical Association.

Heller, Joseph. 1994. *Catch-22.* New York: Simon and Schuster.

Hellman, Lillian. 1979. *Six Plays by Lillian Hellman.* New York: Vintage Books.

Hemenway, Robert E. 1977. *Zora Neale Hurston: A Literary Biography.* Chicago: University of Illinois Press.

Herlihy, David (comp.). 1970. *The History of Feudalism.* New York: Harper and Row.

Hersey, John (ed.). 1974. *Ralph Ellison: A Collection of Critical Essays.* Englewood Cliffs, NJ: Prentice-Hall.

Hesse, Hermann. 1963. *Steppenwolf.* New York: Modern Library.

———. 1986. *Magister Ludi.* New York: Bantam Books.

Hibbert, Christopher. 1967. *The Making of Charles Dickens.* New York: Harper and Row.

Hickey, Morgen. 1990. *The Bohemian Register: An Annotated Bibliography of the Beat Literary Movement.* Metuchen, NJ: Scarecrow Press.

Hill, Eldon C. 1978. *George Bernard Shaw.* Boston: Twayne.

Hook, Sidney. 1959. *Political Power and Personal Freedom: Critical Studies in Democracy, Communism, and Civil Rights.* New York: Criterion Books.

Houston, John Porter. 1975. *Victor Hugo.* New York: Twayne.

Howe, Irving (ed.). 1962. *Edith Wharton: A Collection of Critical Essays.* Englewood Cliffs, NJ: Prentice-Hall.

Huggins, Irvin. 1971. *Harlem Renaissance.* New York: Oxford University Press.

Hughes, Langston. 1958. *The Langston Hughes Reader.* New York: Braziller.

Hugo, Victor. 1987. *Les Misérables.* New York: Signet Classic.

Hurston, Zora Neale. 1990. *Their Eyes Were Watching God.* New York: HarperPerennial.

Huxley, Aldous. 1989. *Brave New World.* New York: HarperPerennial.

Hynes, Samuel Lynn. 1964. *William Golding.* New York: Columbia University Press.

Ibsen, Henrik. 1978. *Eleven Plays of Henrick Ibsen.* Ed. by H. L. Mencken. New York: Modern Library/Random House.

Jackson, Helen Hunt. 1988. *Ramona.* New York: Signet Books.

James, Henry. 1956. *The Bostonians.* New York: Modern Library.

Jenness, Linda (ed.). 1972. *Feminism and Socialism.* New York: Pathfinder Press.

Johnson, James Weldon. 1990. *The Autobiography of an Ex-Colored Man.* New York: Penguin Books.

Jolly, Rosemary Jane. 1996. *Colonization, Violence, and Narration in South African Writing: Andre Brink, Breyten Bretenbach, and J. M. Coetzee.* Athens: Ohio University Press.

Kafka, Franz. 1964. *The Trial.* New York: Modern Library.

Kazin, Alfred, and Charles Shapiro (eds.). 1955. *The Stature of Theodore Dreiser: A Critical Survey of the Man and His Work.* Bloomington: Indiana University Press.

Kesey, Ken. 1964. *One Flew over the Cuckoo's Nest.* New York: Viking Press.

Ketterer, David. 1974. *New Worlds for Old: The Apocalyptic Imagination, Science Fiction, and American Literature.* Garden City, NY: Anchor Books.

Kundera, Milan. 1984. *The Unbearable Lightness of Being.* New York: Harper and Row.

La Guma, Alex. 1972. *Apartheid: A Collection of Writings on South African Racism by South Africans.* London: Lawrence and Wishart.

Landes, David S. (ed.). 1966. *The Rise of Capitalism.* New York: Macmillan.

Landon, Brooks. 1989. *Thomas Berger.* Boston: Twayne.

Larsen, Nella. 1992. *An Intimation of Things Distant.* New York: Anchor Books.

Larson, Charles R. 1993. *Invisible Darkness: Jean Toomer and Nella Larsen.* Iowa City: University of Iowa Press.

Larson, Harold. 1944. *Björnstjerne Björnson: A Study in Norwegian Nationalism.* New York: King's Crown Press.

Le Guin, Ursula. 1979. *Malafrena.* New York: Putnam's.

Lederer, Katherine. 1979. *Lillian Hellman.* Boston: Twayne.

Lederer, William J., and Eugene Burdick. 1958. *The Ugly American.* New York: Norton.

Lee, Harper. 1993. *To Kill a Mockingbird.* Pleasantville, NY: Reader's Digest.

Leeming, David. 1994. *James Baldwin: A Biography.* New York: Knopf.

Leftwich, Joseph. 1957. *Israel Zangwill.* New York: Yoseloff.

Lessing, Doris. 1964. *Children of Violence.* Vols. 1 and 2. New York: Simon and Schuster.

———. 1969. *The Four-Gated City.* New York: Knopf.

Levin, Dan. 1965. *Stormy Petrel: The Life and Work of Maxim Gorky.* New York: Appleton-Century.

Levy, Eugene D. 1973. *James Weldon Johnson: Black Leader, Black Voice.* Chicago: University of Chicago Press.

Lewis, Sinclair. 1950. *Babbitt.* New York: Harcourt, Brace, and World.

———. 1970. *Elmer Gantry.* New York: Signet Books.

Light, Martin. 1975. *The Quixotic Vision of Sinclair Lewis.* West Lafayette, IN: Purdue University Press.

Link, Frederick M. 1968. *Aphra Behn.* New York: Twayne.

Lipow, Arthur. 1982. *Authoritarian Socialism in America: Edward Bellamy and the Nationalist Movement.* Berkeley and Los Angeles: University of California Press.

Lisca, Peter. 1958. *The Wide World of John Steinbeck.* New Brunswick, NJ: Rutgers University Press.

Lloyd, John Arthur Thomas. 1972. *Ivan Turgenev.* Port Washington, NY: Kennikat Press.

London, Jack. 1924. *The Iron Heel.* New York: McKinlay, Stone, and MacKenzie.

Lyons, Mary E. 1990. *Sorrow's Kitchen: The Life and Folklore of Zora Neale Hurston.* New York: Scribner's.

Macebuh, Stanley. 1973. *James Baldwin: A Critical Study.* New York: Third Press.

Madsen, Axel. 1977. *Hearts and Minds: The Common Journey of Simone de Beauvoir and Jean-Paul Sartre.* New York: Morrow.

Malti-Douglas, Fedwa. 1995. *Men, Women, and God(s): Nawal El Saadawi and Arab Feminist*

Poetics. Berkeley and Los Angeles: University of California Press.

Mann, Thomas. 1972. *The Magic Mountain.* New York: Knopf.

Marceau, Felicien. 1966. *Balzac and His World.* Trans. Derek Coltman. New York: Orion Press.

Marris, Peter, and Martin Rein. 1967. *Dilemmas of Social Reform: Poverty and Community Action in the United States.* London: Routledge.

Martin, Hubert. 1972. *Alcaeus.* New York: Twayne.

Mathes, Valerie Sherer. 1990. *Helen Hunt Jackson and Her Indian Reform Legacy.* Austin: University of Texas Press.

Mathews, Donald G. (ed.). 1972. *Agitation for Freedom: The Abolitionist Movement.* New York: Wiley.

May, J. Lewis. 1970. *Anatole France: The Man and His Work.* Port Washington, NY: Kennikat Press.

McCabe, Joseph. 1974. *George Bernard Shaw: A Critical Study.* New York: Haskell House.

McCann, Garth. 1977. *Edward Abbey.* Boise, ID: Boise State University.

McCombs, Judith (ed.). 1988. *Critical Essays on Margaret Atwood.* Boston: Hall.

McElderry, Bruce R., Jr. 1965. *Henry James.* New York: Twayne.

McElrath, Joseph R., Jr. 1992. *Frank Norris Revisited.* New York: Twayne.

McKay, Nellie Y. (ed.). 1988. *Critical Essays on Toni Morrison.* Boston: Hall.

McLean, Albert, Jr. 1964. *William Cullen Bryant.* New York: Twayne.

McPherson, Dolly Aimee. 1990. *Order Out of Chaos: The Autobiographical Works of Maya Angelou.* New York: Lang.

McWilliams, Carey. 1948. *A Mask for Privilege: Anti-Semitism in America.* Boston: Little, Brown.

Merrill, Robert. 1987. *Joseph Heller.* Boston: Twayne.

Merrill, Thomas F. 1969. *Allen Ginsberg.* New York: Twayne.

Miles, Barry (ed.). 1995. *Allen Ginsberg: Howl.* New York: HarperPerennial.

Miller, Arthur. 1954. *The Crucible.* New York: Viking Press.

Miller, Henry. 1970. *The Air-Conditioned Nightmare.* Vol. 1. New York: New Directions Books.

Moers, Ellen. 1969. *Two Dreisers.* New York: Viking Press.

Moody, Christopher. 1975. *Solzhenitsyn.* New York: Harper and Row.

Mookerjee, Rabindra Nath. 1988. *Art for Social Justice: The Major Novels of Upton Sinclair.* Metuchen, NJ: Scarecrow Press.

Moore, Harry Thornton. 1968. *The Novels of John Steinbeck: A First Critical Study.* Port Washington, NY: Kennikat Press.

Morrison, Arthur. 1995. *A Child of the Jago.* Chicago: Academy Publications.

Morrison, Toni. 1974. *Sula.* New York: Knopf.

———. 1987. *Beloved.* New York: Knopf.

———. 1993. *The Bluest Eye.* New York: Plume.

Moss, George L. 1978. *Toward the Final Solution: A History of European Racism.* New York: Fertig.

Moss, Leonard. 1967. *Arthur Miller.* Boston: Twayne.

Muller, Edward J. (ed.). 1986. *Critical Essays on Langston Hughes.* Boston: Hall.

Murray, Gilbert. 1933. *Aristophanes: A Study.* Oxford: Clarendon Press.

Murry, John Middleton. 1967. *Jonathan Swift: A Critical Biography.* New York: Farrar, Straus and Giroux.

Nagel, James (ed.). 1984. *Critical Essays on Joseph Heller.* Boston: Hall.

Nelson, Kay Hoyle, and Nancy Huse (eds.). 1994. *The Critical Response to Tillie Olsen.* Westport, CT: Greenwood Press.

Nolan, William F. 1975. *The Ray Bradbury Companion.* Detroit: Gale Research.

Norris, Frank. 1901. *The Octopus.* New York: Doubleday.

O'Connor, Richard. 1964. *Jack London: A Biography.* Boston: Little, Brown.

O'Daniel, Therman B. (ed.). 1971. *Langston Hughes, Black Genius: A Critical Evaluation.* New York: Morrow.

Oliver, Edward James. 1965. *Honoré de Balzac.* London: Weidenfeld and Nicholson.

Olsen, Tillie. 1980. *Yonnondio: From the Thirties.* London: Virago.

O'Neill, Eugene. 1967. *Selected Plays of Eugene O'Neill.* New York: Random House.

Orwell, George. 1961. *1984.* New York: Signet Books.

———. 1996. *Animal Farm.* New York: Signet Books.

Paton, Alan. 1987. *Cry, the Beloved Country.* New York: Collier Books.

Pearlman, Mickey, and Abby H.P. Werlock. 1991. *Tillie Olsen.* Boston: Twayne.

Pizer, Donald (ed.). 1966. *The Novels of Frank Norris.* Bloomington: Indiana University Press.

Plevier, Theodor. 1948. *Stalingrad.* Trans. Richard

and Clara Winston. New York: Appleton-Century-Crofts.

Price, Kenneth M., and Lawrence J. Oliver (eds.). 1997. *Critical Essays on James Weldon Johnson.* New York: Hall.

Pruden, Durward. 1968. *Democracy, Capitalism, and Communism.* New York: Oxford Book Company.

Pryce-Jones, David. 1968. *Graham Greene.* New York: Barnes and Noble Books.

Pulzer, Peter G.J. 1964. *The Rise of Political Anti-Semitism in Germany and Austria.* New York: Wiley.

Quackenbush, Robert M. 1985. *Who Said There's No Man on the Moon?: A Story of Jules Verne.* Englewood Cliffs, NJ: Prentice-Hall.

Ramelson, Marian. 1967. *The Petticoat Rebellion: A Century of Struggle for Women's Rights.* London: Lawrence and Wishart.

Rand, Ayn. 1992. *Atlas Shrugged.* New York: Signet Books.

Read, Herbert Edward. 1947. *Poetry and Anarchism.* London: Freedom Press.

Richardson, Joanna. 1976. *Victor Hugo.* New York: St. Martin's Press.

Roberts, R. Ellis. 1974. *Henrik Ibsen: A Critical Study.* New York: Haskell House.

Roderick, Colin Arthur. 1982. *Miles Franklin: Her Brilliant Career.* Adelaide, Australia: Rigby.

Rogers, Samuel. 1953. *Balzac and the Novel.* Madison: University of Wisconsin Press.

Rojas, Sonia Riquelme, and Edna Aguirre Rehbein (eds.). 1991. *Critical Approaches to Isabel Allende's Novels.* New York: Lang.

Rollyson, Carl E. 1988. *Lillian Hellman: Her Legend and Legacy.* New York: St. Martin's Press.

Rose, Henry. 1973. *Henrik Ibsen: Poet, Mystic, and Moralist.* New York: Haskell House.

Rose, Jane Atteridge. 1993. *Rebecca Harding Davis.* New York: Twayne.

Rosenberg, Jerome H. 1984. *Margaret Atwood.* Boston: Twayne.

Roses, Lorraine Elena, and Ruth Elizabeth Randolph (eds.). 1996. *Harlem's Glory: Black Women Writing, 1900–1950.* Cambridge, MA: Harvard University Press.

Ruhle, Jurgen. 1969. *Literature and Revolution: A Critical Study of the Writer and Communism in the Twentieth Century.* New York: Praeger.

Samuels, Wilfred D. 1990. *Toni Morrison.* Boston: Twayne.

Sartre, Jean-Paul. 1947. *The Age of Reason.* New York: Knopf.

Schatt, Stanley. 1976. *Kurt Vonnegut Jr.* Boston: Twayne.

Scheick, William J., and J. Randolph Cox. 1988. *H. G. Wells: A Reference Guide.* Boston: Hall.

Schneir, Miriam (ed.). 1972. *Feminism: The Essential Historical Writings.* New York: Random House.

Schorer, Mark (ed.). 1962. *Sinclair Lewis: A Collection of Critical Essays.* Englewood Cliffs, NJ: Prentice-Hall.

Schrecker, Ellen. 1994. *The Age of McCarthyism: A Brief History with Documents.* Boston: Bedford Books.

———. 1998. *Many Are the Crimes: McCarthyism in America.* Boston: Little, Brown.

Schreiner, Olive. 1986. *The Story of an African Farm.* New York: Penguin Books.

Schumpeter, Joseph Alois. 1950. *Capitalism, Socialism, and Democracy.* New York: Harper.

Seed, David. 1989. *The Fiction of Joseph Heller.* New York: St. Martin's Press.

Selig, Robert L. 1983. *George Gissing.* Boston: Twayne.

Shabecoff, Philip. 1993. *A Fierce Green Fire.* New York: Hill & Wang.

Shannon, David A. (ed.). 1960. *The Great Depression.* Englewood Cliffs, NJ: Prentice-Hall.

Shaw, George Bernard. 1962. *George Bernard Shaw: Complete Plays with Prefaces.* New York: Dodd, Mead.

———. 1984. *The Fabian Society: Its Early History.* London: The Fabian Society.

Shucard, Alan R. 1984. *Countee Cullen.* Boston: Twayne.

Sinclair, Upton. 1972. *The Jungle.* Cambridge, MA: Bentley.

——— (ed.). 1996. *The Cry for Justice: An Anthology of the Great Social Protest Literature of All Time.* New York: Barricade Books.

Solzhenitsyn, Aleksandr. 1972. *One Day in the Life of Ivan Denisovich.* New York: Praeger.

Spann, Meno. 1976. *Franz Kafka.* Boston: Twayne.

Spivack, Charlotte. 1984. *Ursula K. Le Guin.* Boston: Twayne.

Sprague, Claire, and Virginia Tiger (eds.). 1986. *Critical Essays on Doris Lessing.* Boston: Hall.

Steinbeck, John. 1972. *The Grapes of Wrath.* New York: Bantam Books.

Stowe, Harriet Beecher. 1960. *Uncle Tom's Cabin.* Garden City, NY: Dolphin Books.

Sturges, Henry C. 1968. *Chronologies of the Life and Writings of William Cullen Bryant.* New York: Franklin.

Swados, Harvey (ed.). 1966. *The American Writer and the Great Depression*. Indianapolis: Bobbs-Merrill.

Swift, Jonathan. 1960. *Gulliver's Travels*. New York: Signet Books.

Swinburne, Algernon Charles. 1970. *A Study of Victor Hugo*. Port Washington, NY: Kennikat Press.

Szymanski, Albert. 1983. *Class Structure: A Critical Perspective*. New York: Praeger.

Tabori, Paul. 1972. *The Anatomy of Exile: A Semantic and Historical Study*. London: Harrap.

Thomas, John R. (ed.). 1965. *Slavery Attacked: The Abolitionist Crusade*. Englewood Cliffs, NJ: Prentice-Hall.

Toer, Pramoedya Ananta. 1996. *This Earth of Mankind*. New York: Penguin Books.

Tolstoy, Leo. 1911. *Resurrection*. New York: Crowell.

Toomer, Jean. 1993. *Cane*. New York: Liveright.

Turgenev, Ivan. 1973. *On the Eve*. London: Heinemann.

———. 1983. *Sketches from a Hunter's Album*. New York: Penguin Books.

Turner, Frederick W. (ed.). 1974. *The Portable North American Reader*. New York: Viking Press.

Van Doren, Carl (ed.). 1977. *The Portable Swift*. New York: Penguin Books.

Velie, Alan R. (ed.). 1991. *American Indian Literature: An Anthology*. Norman: University of Oklahoma Press.

Verne, Jules. 1996. *Paris in the Twentieth Century*. Trans. Richard Howard. New York: Random House.

Virtanen, Reino. 1968. *Anatole France*. New York: Twayne.

Vonnegut, Kurt. 1980. *Player Piano*. New York: Laurel Books.

Wade, Michael. 1972. *Peter Abrahams*. London: Evans Brothers.

Wagner-Martin, Linda, and Cathy N. Davidson (eds.). 1995. *The Oxford Book of Women's Writing in the United States*. Oxford: Oxford University Press.

Walker, Alice. 1986. *The Color Purple*. Boston: Hall.

———. 1990. *The Temple of My Familiar*. New York: Pocket Books.

Walter, Jerrold. 1968. *Thomas Hood: His Life and Times*. New York: Haskell House.

Warner, Lucile Schulberg. 1976. *From Slave to Abolitionist: The Life of William Wells Brown*. New York: Dial Press.

Watts, Harold H. 1969. *Aldous Huxley*. New York: Twayne.

Webb, Constance. 1968. *Richard Wright: A Biography*. New York: Putnam's.

Wells, H. G. 1935. *Tono-Bungay*. New York: Modern Library.

Westbrook, Max. 1969. *Walter Van Tilburg Clark*. New York: Twayne.

Wharton, Edith. 1993. *The Age of Innocence*. New York: Collier Books.

Widmer, Kingsley. 1963. *Henry Miller*. New York: Twayne.

———. 1965. *The Literary Rebel*. Carbondale: Southern Illinois University Press.

Williams, Raymond. 1977. *Marxism and Literature*. Oxford: Oxford University Press.

——— (comp.). 1974. *George Orwell: A Collection of Critical Essays*. Englewood Cliffs, NJ: Prentice-Hall.

Winchell, Donna Haisty. 1992. *Alice Walker*. New York: Twayne.

Witt, Shirley, and Stan Steiner (eds.). 1972. *The Way: An Anthology of American Indian Literature*. New York: Vintage Books.

Woodcock, George. 1962. *Anarchism: A History of Libertarian Ideas and Movements*. Cleveland: Meridian Books.

Wortham, Thomas. 1977. *James Russell Lowell's The Biglow Papers*. DeKalb: Northern Illinois University Press.

Wortman, Max S., Jr. 1969. *Critical Issues in Labor*. New York: Macmillan.

Wright, Derek. 1994. *The Novels of Nuruddin Farah*. Bayreuth, Germany: Bayreuth University Press.

Wright, Richard. 1993a. *Native Son*. New York: HarperPerennial.

———. 1993b. *The Outsider*. New York: HarperPerennial.

Wright, William. 1986. *Lillian Hellman: The Image, the Woman*. New York: Simon and Schuster.

Yevtushenko, Yevgeny. 1989. *Early Poems*. Trans. George Reavey. London: Marion Boyars.

Zakin, Susan. 1993. *Coyotes and Town Dogs: Earth First! and the Environmental Movement*. New York: Penguin Books.

Zangwill, Israel. 1895. *Children of the Ghetto: A Study of a Peculiar People*. New York: Macmillan.

Ziolkowski, Theodore. 1965. *The Novels of Hermann Hesse: A Study in Theme and Structure*. Princeton, NJ: Princeton University Press.

INDEX